Figure
Handicapping

Figure Handicapping

A Practical Guide to the
Interpretation and Use of
Speed and Pace Figures

JAMES QUINN

WILLIAM MORROW AND COMPANY, INC.
New York

The author would like to thank the Daily Racing Form, Inc., for granting written permission for its copyrighted material to be reproduced throughout this book.

It is the policy of William Morrow and Company, Inc., and its imprints and affiliates, recognizing the importance of preserving what has been written, to print the books we publish on acid-free paper, and we exert our best efforts to that end.

Library of Congress Cataloging-in-Publication Data

Quinn, James, 1943–
    Figure handicapping : a practical guide to the
interpretation and use of speed and pace figures / by James Quinn.
        p.   cm. — (Winner's circle)
    ISBN 0-688-10582-3
    1. Horse race betting. I. Title. II. Series.
SF331.Q546   1992
    798.401—dc20   92-9899
                                                                                      CIP

Printed in the United States of America

First Edition

1 2 3 4 5 6 7 8 9 10

BOOK DESIGN BY BERNARD SCHLEIFER

Contents

Preface: Reggie's Night   7

Introduction   9
Grand Canyon's 120   12

ONE **Explanations**   19

- Making Figures   19
- Why Make Figures, Anyway?   20
- Par Times   26
- Daily Track Variants   33
- Projected Times   37
- Speed Figures   39
- Pace Figures   49
- Speed or Pace Figures?   53
- Basic Interpretations   59

TWO **Applications**   63

- Claiming Races   63
- Non-Winners Allowances   94
- Stakes Races   107
- Younger Stakes Horses   125
- Kentucky Derby Prospects   132
- Routes to Sprints   135
- Track-to-Track Comparisons   139
- Unreliable Applications   143

THREE **Patterns** 147

- High-Figure Horses 148
- Bounce Patterns 154
- Bounce-Back Patterns 158
- To Bounce or Not to Bounce 160
- The Performance Bounce 164
- All Figures Below Par 167
- When Good Horses Have Bad Figures 170
- When Bad Horses Have Good Figures 174
- Figure Standouts Versus Reality 178
- Wet Figures 181
- Improving Pace Standouts 181
- Identifying Representative Figures 184

FOUR **Realities** 187

- The Basic Education of Ben Bollinger 187
- The Newly Converted 197
- The Unconverted 203

FIVE **Figure Handicapping on the Turf** 207

- A New Approach 207
- How Turf Races Are Different 209
- Why Modern Speed Methods Do Not Apply on Grass 210
- Rating Procedures 213
- Guidelines for Applying the Rating Method 219
- Tricky Situations 229
- The Relative Unimportance of Early Pace 232
- Baptism 234

Appendix 285
Turf Figure Charts 287

Reggie's Night

THE GENTLEMAN [sic] in the multicolored gym suit in the front row, aisle seat, was pointed out, half humorously, half respectfully, as a figure handicapper.

"See that guy? That's our Reggie.

"He's a figure player. Buys the Sheets.

"He's here all the time. Every day. Starts with New York in the morning. Plays southern California in the afternoon. Takes the night action wherever it is. He'll be in that same chair the entire weekend. I guarantee it.

"He's got the figures for all the tracks. No *Racing Form*. Just The Sheets.

"Reggie's a numbers man. And he bets them big. If a horse has a huge figure, Reggie'll bet it just as huge. He's no coward at the windows."

The scene was Las Vegas, Nevada, the race book at the Rio, a gathering spot for local horseplayers a few furlongs below the strip on Flamingo Road. I had arrived with close friend and colleague Tom Brohamer for four days of nonstop handicapping, a ritual in which we indulge three or four times a year. It was late afternoon on a December day and we were settling in for the Thursday program at the Meadowlands.

We took four seats behind Reggie's row and were promptly introduced by a local denizen.

Brohamer and I had spotted a 9-to-1 shot in the first race. So I asked Reggie, impulsively, "Who's got the figure in the first, Reggie?"

The Sheets favored the same 9-to-1 shot. A couple of minutes later the horse had won.

In the second half of the double, my second call was Reggie's first call. Sure enough, by a nose at my expense, Reggie bagged the double. The photo might have been an omen that this would be Reggie's night.

A nicely priced horse upset ours in the fourth. Our host checked Reggie's numbers, as he would race to race, and returned to announce that Reggie again had caught the winner. Reggie then grabbed the fifth and sixth to complete a triple-play, not to mention five of the first six winners.

Reggie's winners had paid $20, $17-and-change, $10-and-change, and a couple of lower-priced mutuels. None of his horses had been betting favorites.

When we won the ninth race together with the same high-figure horse, I felt curious about Reggie's winnings. Portrayed as an aggressive bettor, he had looked the part all evening. It had been a smashing night for figure handicapping.

The tenth and finale soon was upon us, and I could no longer resist a small invasion of privacy. "It's your night, Reggie," I began.

Reggie smiled.

"You must be making a killing. Sure has been a memorable night for the figures.

"So, what's the bottom line for you tonight, Reggie?"

Reggie rocked back slightly in his special chair and exposed himself to the ages.

"It all depends on what happens in the tenth.

"The figure horse is the six.

"If he wins, I'll have had a big night, all right." Taglines:

Speed figures are indispensable to effective handicapping.

The figures are far from everything.

Reggie's six-horse in the tenth race failed miserably.

Introduction

IN A THREE-HOUR 1990 SYMPOSIUM in Las Vegas on the state of figure handicapping in the United States, not one of six prominent panelists mentioned that absolutely the best use of speed figures is to predict whether claiming horses can rise successfully in class.

Considerable and intemperate discussion fastened instead on quantitative adjustments to the basic figures, the complications inherent in track-to-track adjustments, and other esoteric factors and technicalities that might enhance the accuracy of the numbers.

It's been the same since modern figure handicapping—the conversion of actual times into speed and pace figures—began to gain momentum among regular thoroughbred handicappers in 1975. Too much attention to technique, too little attention to interpretation and use.

This book seeks to remedy the imbalance. The need has grown acute. In the past five years the "figures" have been trickling down to the recreational market, to casual handicappers who attend the races irregularly and feel no inclination to make their own figures. The major distributors include Thoro-Graph, Bloodstock Research (data base), The Sheets, and on the widest popular scale with its publication in Spring 1991 until Winter 1992, The Racing Times. Unprecedented competition in the marketplace has aroused debate over who's got the best figures.

But that debate amounts to a waste of time. With advantages and disadvantages that can vary in importance from situation to situation, all of the above merchants, and several others distributing to local markets in weekly newsletters, deal in reasonably accurate figures. It's one thing, though, to access accurate figures, and quite another to know what they mean. It's less important to decide which figures are best than to know when pace figures should supersede speed figures, or when reliance on figures of any kind makes no sense whatsoever.

Leading proponents of figure handicapping have short-changed their customers on exactly these fronts. The early texts on modern speed handicapping concentrated on the making of accurate figures. Interpretive guidelines either were few, and not adequately promulgated, or were missing entirely. As a result, too many figure addicts attempted to beat the races with a blind ambition tied to the numbers. That does not often succeed.

Latter-day seminars have been more attentive to telling prac-titioners what the numbers mean, but have preoccupied them-selves with the numbers alone, discounting the complications that arise when placing the numbers in a context of comprehen-sive handicapping. Certain everyday handicapping situations do not submit readily to figure handicapping, and never have. During Santa Anita 1990 an acquaintance of mine took full credit for tabbing an unlikely winner at 1⅜ miles on the turf. "He had the figure," the guy explained. This was perfect race-track idiom. No conceit at the racetrack today compares with the postrace analysis that alludes declaratively and smugly to the efficacy of one's figures.

My acquaintance had not considered that the winner's "figures" had been earned at middle distances on dirt. These transfer poorly to marathons on grass.

In future grass marathons, middle-distance dirt figures will not apply, but my boastful acquaintance will anticipate that they do. If he repeats the wager a hundred times, he will no longer trust dirt figures on the grass. At what price, success?

"He had the figure." The same throwaway remark is re-peated inappropriately every day at every racetrack in the na-tion. As is painfully true of every independent factor of handicapping, figure horses lose far more frequently than they win, and it's convenient to know the circumstances where high-figure horses have a better chance.

Moreover, as speed figures become more widely distributed, they suffer the ineluctable disadvantage associated in this game with widespread use. Where the fastest horse in the field is plain, all proficient figure handicappers will know it, thereby depressing the odds. It's tougher than ever to beat the races with strict adherence to speed figures.

The noble purpose here is to guide racegoers in the interpretation and use of speed and pace figures.

Part One, Explanations, reviews the art of making figures and presents the rationale for figure handicapping as method. No one should doubt the importance of having accurate figures at the racetrack. Although they are far from everything, the figures are indispensable to continual success. They inform bettors how fast horses have run in the past, as running times do not. No one can expect to beat the races without this basic information. Figures also enhance the recreational aspects of a day at the races. It's greater fun to play well. Key concepts of modern speed handicapping are explained, notably pars and daily track variants. No respectable handicapper on the contemporary scene should be unable to discuss these crucial terms of modern speed handicapping intelligently.

Next we show how speed and pace figures are obtained, and define exactly what the numbers mean. The section ends with a discussion of several basic interpretive guidelines, such as how well the figures can compare horses competing at different distances and at different racetracks.

Part Two focuses on Applications. The relative advantages and disadvantages of figures across the entire menu of major league racing, from claiming races to Grade 1 stakes, are examined carefully. Nuances and subtle variations carry the cause from situation to situation. The figure horse in a $4000 claiming race is hardly interchangeable with the figure horse in the Kentucky Derby, though neither is destined to win. We examine in depth the figure handicapping of three-year-olds, which differs markedly from the figure handicapping of four-year-olds and up. The age groups inhabit two distinct worlds and must be treated distinctly. The section should challenge the previous best efforts of figure handicappers everywhere.

Part Three is Patterns. Combinations of figures frequently offer greater meaning than one figure standing alone, provided handicappers can recognize the patterns the numbers reflect. How to interpret patterns of improving and declining figures? How to recognize the controversial "bounce" patterns? How to handle unusually high or low figures? What to do when the speed figure is high but the pace figure low, or vice versa?

Which patterns of figures have been shown to be highly predictive of success next time, and profitable long-term?

Numerous figure handicappers learn to save their biggest

bets for most-favored patterns. The prime bets trace to windfalls in the past. Winning patterns of figures should always catch the practiced eye, and this book will help casual handicappers spot the best of them.

Realities, Part Four of the book, deals briefly with the real-time experiences of figure handicappers at the races. The basic training of successful figure handicappers follows approximately a two-year curve. We consult Ben Bollinger, a devotee of figure handicapping, who had played the races in southern California for two decades without winning. A subscriber to Thoro-Graph since 1989, Bollinger has become one of the new-born, a consistent winner with speed figures.

In Part Four we also meet a few horseplayers, the Unconverted, who would not use speed figures if guarantees were attached (they represent thousands); and others who never did, but finally have, the Newly Converted. Handicappers will find the conflicting reactions interesting.

The final section, Part Five, delivers what I hope will be a lasting contribution to the game. "Figure Handicapping on the Turf" presents a new approach, and new figures for handicapping grass races. (In the Appendix you'll find figure charts for twenty-eight grass courses.) Conventional figure handicapping does not work well enough on the grass, but this book's methods do. The recommended approach is described in detail, and the results of first tryouts presented. The thousands of figure handicappers who complain they cannot untangle turf races with customary proficiency no longer will have a legitimate excuse for the pratfalls.

It's an especially reassuring way to conclude a comprehensive treatment of figure handicapping today.

Let's get under way with a discussion of perhaps the most provocative moment in figure handicapping during the past decade.

GRAND CANYON'S 120

Two weeks prior to the close of the 1980s, on December 17, 1989, the colt Grand Canyon dispensed the most brilliant two-year-old performance of the decade, and one of the greatest ever. It occurred in the Hollywood Park Futurity (Grade 1), a one-turn mile extending to juveniles a one-million-dollar purse, the money rarely justified by the performance. The 1989 edition stands as an exception to that rule.

Among two-year-olds at the route, only Secretariat has run faster. Not Seattle Slew, not Affirmed or Alydar, and not Spectacular Bid, other speed demons of the 1970s. Had he not succumbed to the deadly laminitis before launching a three-year-old campaign, Grand Canyon might have been one of the ones.

And despite dealing in numbers at the richest echelons of the sport, trainer D. Wayne Lukas has never had a racehorse like him, and might never again.

How do I know this?

The figures told me so.

Competing on a racing surface normal in every respect, and following a six-furlong pace of 1:09.1, Grand Canyon drew off by himself and completed the 1989 Hollywood Futurity in 1:33 flat. The adjusted mile time on a racetrack rated Fast 1 that afternoon was 1:33:1. On a Beyer Speed chart, the corresponding speed figure at Hollywood Park 1989 was 120.

Two-year-olds do not run 120s. To appreciate that, consider that Alysheba, the older handicap champion of 1988, never exceeded a figure of 124 at any distance, anytime.

Grand Canyon's 120 created an almost unprecedented storm of protest and debate among serious figure handicappers.

In the next week's *Los Angeles Times*, correspondent Jay Hovdey quoted leading New York figure handicapper Mark Hopkins, who at the time developed Beyer-style figures for the Bloodstock Research (BRIS) data base.

Hopkins had assigned Grand Canyon a figure of 120 for the Hollywood race, but could not tolerate that estimate of reality. So Hopkins lowered the figure 12 points—approximately six lengths—to 108, arbitrarily. Perhaps intuitively is a more suitable adverb.

In explanation, Hopkins conceded the Hollywood surface had been normal, the daily track variants routine, and the support races leading up to the big event unexceptional in every detail.

His counterpoints weakened his argument, however, and the procedure he had followed.

"If I give Grand Canyon a 120, that means every horse in the field ran the best race of its life . . . and that's just not acceptable . . . it doesn't make sense. . . ."

Why not?

These were two-year-olds entered in the most important juvenile stakes on the American calendar, the Breeders' Cup Juvenile excepted. The race date had followed the Breeders' Cup Juvenile by six weeks, not an unimportant interval in the maturation of an impressively developing racehorse. Grand Canyon had placed in the Breeders' Cup Juvenile won by Rhythm, the figures unexceptional.

Handicappers had every right to expect the top half of the Hollywood Futurity to record the best figures of a juvenile career. Moreover, experienced two-year-olds tend to improve dramatically or decline significantly. In the race of the season, shouldn't the better twos earn their top figures yet? Hopkins's reasoning on the point sounded flawed:

> In fact, runner-up Farma Way was beaten by six lengths, the third finisher Silver Ending by eight lengths. The Beyer speed figures would settle at 107 and 104, respectively, perfectly legitimate numbers for impressively-improving 2-year-old stakes prospects. The others were badly beaten and cannot be rated fairly off the race.

In the aftermath, Farma Way next appeared during Winter 1990 at Santa Anita in front tendon wraps and disappointed. Silver Ending next won the Bay Meadows Derby impressively and later the Grade 1 Arkansas Derby. Later still, the Pegasus (Grade 1) at the Meadowlands. He proved himself no fluke. Farma Way's four-year-old-season, as all know, was recorded on racing's national stage and consistently featured figures above the 4up Grade 1 par.

Hopkins also speculated to the *Los Angeles Times* that the Hollywood maintenance crew might have altered the racing surface between the seventh and eighth races on the futurity card, intimating it happens more frequently when big-ticket stakes events are propositioned.

It did not happen on December 17, 1989, at Hollywood Park. I was there, and paying attention. So were trusted colleagues.

Using Quirin-style speed and pace figures, my numbers for the Hollywood Futurity were hardly less shaking. Grand Canyon got a 116! Quirin sets the $10,000 claiming pars for older horses equal to 100 and improves the figure by a point for every one-fifth second better horses can run. One point equals one length.

The 1989 Hollywood Park stakes par for horses 3up in routes was 113. The mile par for 2YO stakes in December was 107. Grand Canyon recorded a pace figure of 115 and a speed figure of 116. Off the scale! Alysheba's best figure ever, Quirin-style, had been 119. Stakes-winning two-year-olds of December can be expected to earn a 107 or 108. The best of each generation may soar to 110 to 112, approaching the older stakes par.

When confronted by stratospheric figures that might be unreal, figure handicappers distrust the numbers they have created and reexamine the calculations of the daily track variant for the program under study.

I had been similarly provoked at Grand Canyon's 115-116 pace-speed figure, but inclined, even at first, to trust the figures. My daily track variants for the mile that afternoon at Hollywood Park were Slow 1 to the pace call and Fast 2 to the final call. Those numbers not only proved consistent with previous days' variants and symmetrical with the sprints (Fast 2) and routes (Fast 3) on the December 17 program, but also had coincided with the mile variants of other figure handicappers I consulted at the track.

Moreover, on December 17, Hollywood Park had carded three one-turn miles, a reliable source of an accurate variant.

Nonetheless, I hurried to check my December 17 mile variant with Tom Brohamer's, a valued colleague who calculates daily track variants from projected times instead of pars. If I had skipped a beat or two, Brohamer's figures might identify the discrepancy.

To my surprise, Brohamer's mile variant for December 17 was Slow 2 to the pace call, and Fast 1 at the finish. Brohamer's figures for Grand Canyon therefore would exceed mine, as follows:

				Pace	Final
	Brohamer	S2	F1	116	117
Variants					
	Quinn	S1	F2	115	116

Although Grand Canyon's figures had exploded, the figures of runners-up in the Futurity made numerical sense. Farma Way, beaten by six lengths, got a 110, a marvelous 2YO figure,

but not absurd. Silver Ending, beaten eight lengths, earned a
108, one length superior to par. The others were rated below
par by several lengths.

The topper was yet to come. Figure handicappers enjoy insights into racing performances unavailable to all but the most
perceptive handicappers who do not possess the numbers.

For two seasons I had been recording the early-energy requirements of southern California racetracks and the early-
energy expenditures of race winners, a relationship that points
to numerous winners a year. Especially among sprinters stretching out. Needless to say, the data is not widely accessible. The
early-energy par at a mile at Hollywood Park 1989 ranged from
51.80 percent to 52.40 percent. Grand Canyon expended merely
50.78 percent of his energy to the six-furlong call of the Hollywood Futurity, a truly tremendous display. The colt held almost half its energy in reserve. Grand Canyon could have
traveled another furlong, maybe two, at full power that Sunday.
This was a superclassic prospect by any measure.

Almost persuaded Grand Canyon had just delivered one of
the definitive racetrack performances across two decades, I did
have one misgiving. It related to the distance of the Hollywood
Futurity.

Experience has persuaded me that top-rank horses can com-
pile fantastic speed figures in one-turn miles, many of the numbers not repeated around two turns. The most conspicuous
example of 1989 had been New York's Easy Goer, who, as a
3YO, trounced the opposition in Aqueduct's Gotham (Grade 2),
earning a Quirin-style 121—in a one-turn mile. In the Santa
Anita Derby the same season, challenger Sunday Silence had
recorded a speed figure of 115, qualifying as a legitimate contender for the classics, but looking nowhere as sensational as
Easy Goer.

With titles on the line later in Kentucky and New York, Easy
Goer could not reprise the 121, let alone surpass it. Sunday Silence defeated the Phipps standard bearer three times while
never exceeding a figure of 118.

I called upon Andrew Beyer's unmatched experience.
Handicappers have experienced one-turn miles only for five
years at Hollywood Park, I said, and imparted my observation
that truly brilliant horses obtain inflated figures at that special
distance. Did Andy agree?

Beyer did not. Other figure handicappers I've quizzed on the topic do not reinforce me either, though a few looked puzzled enough at the suggestion to convince me I should not abandon the position entirely.

The rationale includes documentation revealing that the energy demands of the one-turn mile fall significantly below that of two-turn middle distances. Powerful racers such as Grand Canyon and Easy Goer can run at full throttle throughout the duration of the one-turn mile. They slow down hardly at all. Pace figures will be routinely sensational, and final figures almost as sensational. Yet the numbers may not look so sensational when the two-turn stakes are contested.

Grand Canyon's 120 connects directly to several salient issues of figure handicapping. A single important race can contain multiple ramifications. How to evaluate:

1. Excessively high figures among several horses in a field
2. A lifetime best figure, inordinately high
3. The accuracy of daily track variants when suspiciously high (or low) figures result
4. The reliability of figures obtained in one-turn miles; how well do they generalize to two-turn routes?

The intense debate in its aftermath reflects the real difficulties for figure handicappers once races like the Hollywood Futurity of 1989 have been dissected. The main problems among contemporary practitioners of figure handicapping no longer involve the techniques of making accurate variants and figures, but the accurate interpretation of the figures and drawing the conclusions these interpretations warrant.

Books, articles, seminars, lectures, and weekly reports are preoccupied with making the figures. From the construction of par-time charts and the projections of expected times, to the calculation of daily track variants and track-to-track adjustments, the techniques of modern figure handicapping have been hammered home for seventeen seasons with clarity and persuasion.

Common complications inherent in the interpretation of speed and pace figures and of figure patterns during the same span have remained largely untangled. When interpretive guidelines are missing, not only do atypical events—such as Grand Canyon's 120—become painfully muddled among practitioners, but repetitive patterns of figure handicapping are not adequately understood. They tend instead to be overlooked or misunderstood.

If this book is successful, handicappers using speed and pace figures will be better equipped to interpret the numbers and the relationships they represent. Perhaps for the first time handicappers will recognize patterns of figures that have become familiar in major league racing. The ambition is lofty, especially in a marketplace that finds more and more recreational handicappers purchasing the figures of professional handicappers for a fee, but without possessing the interpretive knowhow to apply the figures and to make final handicapping decisions.

No one should be misguided in the slightest. Accurate speed and pace figures are indispensable to successful handicapping. Practically to a man and woman, the leading practitioners in this country are disciples of figure handicapping. Among consistent winners, there are virtually no exceptions.

A related perception on the matter is even more convincing. When veteran handicappers who have never practiced the art of figure handicapping finally do, the change of habit invariably moves them up, often dramatically.

To put it differently, no one can beat this game steadily without access to accurate figures.

The reason is practically primal. To evaluate real abilities, handicappers need to know how fast horses have actually run in the past. The figures denote innate speed and pace abilities as nothing else in handicapping does. It's convenient for speed handicappers, and closes the case for figure handicapping, that more races than ever are being won by one-dimensional speed horses. For that reason alone figure handicapping represents a numerical approach to winning at the races that is more important now than ever.

PART ONE

Explanations

MAKING FIGURES

MAKING FIGURES CAN BE deceptively simple. No matter the form of the final numbers, the process involves two fundamental steps: (1) adjusting actual times to reflect track-surface speed on a particular day, and (2) converting the adjusted times to numbers that have been logically arranged on a speed chart.

In the standard lexicon of speed handicapping, numbers found on the speed charts are referred to colloquially as figures. The figures indicate how fast horses have run in relation to some norm, such as the figures earned by the other horses in the field or the typical figures earned by winners of today's kind of race at today's distance. Depending upon specific methods, the value of one point can vary from a half-length to 2½ lengths.

So correct interpretation of the numbers is hinged to (a) the norm, or standard, to which the figure is referenced, and (b) the value of one point. If a horse shows a 96, the figure is weak if horses in today's race typically earn a 98, but strong if the same horses typically earn a 94. If Horse A runs an 82 and Horse B an 81, A's advantage is stronger or weaker depending upon whether a point amounts to one length or 2½ lengths.

Numerous additional interpretations of the figures can guide the handicapping process in concrete, objective ways. Later chapters are intended to deal specifically with virtually all of them.

WHY MAKE FIGURES, ANYWAY?

Examine the six-furlong final times below and determine which of the horses has run faster.

Horse A	1:10.3	Fast 3	
			Track-Surface Speed
Horse B	1:10.3	Slow 3	

Racetrack customers alert to running times see only that two horses have recorded the same final times. Unable to distinguish the pair on speed, they next consider jockeys, post positions, trainers, weight, form, pedigree, trips, distance, running style, and the rest, but already the game has been lost.

Horse B actually can outrun A by six lengths or better, and no combination of other factors can overcompensate for the disadvantage. Horse A competed on a racing surface that was three lengths faster than normal, and Horse B competed on a racing surface that was three lengths slower than normal. The adjusted final times look like this:

Horse A	1:11.1
Horse B	1:10.0

Now which horse do racing's customers prefer? I suspect they would want to wager a bit on B. Those that did would have a splendid chance to cash.

A crucial factor affecting running times is track-surface speed. This varies day to day, usually slightly, sometimes greatly. Track surfaces typically deviate from normal times by one, two, or three lengths, either fast or slow. So a deviation of six lengths between two horses that have recorded exactly the same final times, as in the example, is typical. If handicappers do not adjust speed ratings to control for normal fluctuations in track-surface speeds, the ratings will be unreliable much of the time.

So making figures makes sense to control for differences day-to-day in track-surface speeds. But that's not all, not by a wide margin.

Which of the following horses has run the fastest time?

Horse A	6F	1:11.2
Horse B	7F	1:23.4
Horse C	1¹/₁₆M	1:44.0

Horses in today's race routinely have competed well at different distances. Handicappers must make sensible comparisons or again the game has been lost. Running times at distinct distances are not readily comparable, but speed figures are. That is, a 90 is a 90 is a 90, distance notwithstanding. Here the appropriate interpretive guidelines will be imperative, butthe techniques of modern speed handicapping have eliminated the grossest of errors when comparing horses at different distances.

Now which horse ran the fastest time?

Horse A	6F	1:11.2	96
Horse B	7F	1:23.4	97
Horse C	1¹/₁₆M	1:44.0	102

The fastest horse is C, and by a comfortable margin.

If an improving 3YO stretches out successfully, can it run fast enough to win today?

Can a middle-distance high-priced claiming horse get to the wire in time at 6½ furlongs?

Can a consistent winner at six furlongs do well in long sprints?

Of horses that are versatile, which distance is actually their best?

Fundamental questions about horses' abilities at varying distances pop up daily, and accurate figures guide handicappers to accurate answers. Not always, but often. In contrast, without the figures, racing's customers too often will be betting blind.

Which of the following $10,000 claiming horses has run the faster race?

Horse A	Santa Anita	6F	1:10.3
Horse B	Golden Gate	6F	1:10.0

Shippers dot the racing programs everywhere, and handicappers must learn how to compare horses from different racetracks on speed. Some tracks are fast, some are slow. All tracks will be relatively fast or slow in relation to one another. Speed adjustments track-to-track are not complicated, but they are certainly relevant.

In the example, Horses A and B ran roughly the same time because Golden Gate Fields typically will be three lengths faster at six furlongs than Santa Anita. Anyone who imagines that kind of a Golden Gate shipper will be outclassed at the Great Race Place is seriously mistaken. If A were 5–2 and B 5–1, the bet would belong on B.

Suppose the track surface at Santa Anita had been fast by a length when A last ran, and the surface at Golden Gate had been slow by a length when B last ran. Now which horse should win? It's the shipper, who gets at least a two-length margin on the figures. The adjusted times would be 1:10.4 for A and 1:09.4 for B. Since B ran on a track surface three lengths faster than today's track, its new adjusted time is 1:10.2. If B has been offered at 5–1 against A, because B is a shipper from Golden Gate, and presumably outclassed, that's a terrific bet. But only handicappers in possession of accurate speed figures will know it.

Is that an incentive for making figures? For using figures?

The laundry list continues. Which of the following horses can complete the faster race?

Horse A	6F	45.1	1:10.1
Horse B	6½F	44.4	1:16.2

The example introduces the tricky subject of pace analysis, complicated further by comparing horses at different distances.

Final times can be influenced by numerous factors, but in vital ways by three: (1) relative class, (2) track-surface speed, and (3) pace.

The importance of pace has convinced many contemporary handicappers, including me, to use a combination of speed and pace figures in preference to speed figures alone. If the running times in the example were replaced by figures, can handicappers now find the faster horse?

		Pace	*Speed*	
Horse A	6F	100	102	202
Horse B	6½F	104	103	207

No problem. Horse B has earned both the higher pace figure and the higher final figure. When the pace and speed figures are added, B prevails by five points, a speed-pace advantage of two to three lengths. Notice too that the task of comparing times at distinct distances has been buried in the figures.

Pace figures also permit a number of fascinating comparisons not possible when relying upon speed figures alone. I urge the use of speed and pace figures in combination. The combination of figures not only represents the state-of-the-art in figure handicapping, they provide a new edge at the windows. Not many speed handicappers have advanced to pace figures yet. They miss glorious opportunities that way, but only fellow handicappers in the know can grab the advantage.

That's quite a convincing array of reasons for making figures. To wit:

1. To adjust running times for day to day variations in track-surface speed
2. To compare horses that have competed at different distances
3. To compare horses that have competed at different racetracks
4. To clarify the relationships between final times and fractional times, or speed and pace

Other uses of the figures will appeal variously to handicappers craving every edge. Figures can evaluate horses in the mud. If mud figures have been superior to what has been typical, those horses probably prefer the goo. Numerous horses do, and some pay boxcars. Many horses, in contrast, regress badly in the mud. The figures make plain that tendency too.

The figures also inform handicappers whether horses should run exceptionally well following layoffs. If freshened horses have earned significantly higher figures first time back, handicappers can prefer the horses at fancy odds after a rest.

Looking for patterns of figures that are positive and negative may be the most intriguing and individualistic aspect of figure handicapping, and it's fun. Everybody does it. Favorite patterns distinguish figure handicappers from one another even as successful trainer patterns can distinguish trainer specialists. Favorite figure patterns become so favored because they have proved to be winning patterns. Not as many bettors will share the information. Among those who do, fewer still will choose to bet on it, the razor's edge at the races.

The betting edge represents the real reason why dedicated handicappers have been laboriously making figures for the past seventeen years. Making the figures proceeded from a practical imperative. Despite the several important handicapping purposes the figures have served, the information has not been widely distributed to racing's public.

That changed in April 1991 with publication of *The Racing Times*. Users of the past performances in that newspaper gained instant access to state-of-the-art speed figures. The same figures now appear in *The Daily Racing Form*. In the 1980s too, other national semiprivate speed-figure services, notably Thoro-Graph and The Sheets, expanded into healthy market shares among recreational handicappers. Users astonished by the positive change in their play brought about by the figures became steady clients.

Users of *The Daily Racing Form* previously had been short-changed on the essentials of figure handicapping, and users of the speed ratings and track variants provided by the *Form* had been more than shortchanged, they had been misled. Those speed ratings and track variants consulted widely still by casual handicappers, are tied to a racetrack's best times; the procedure can be seriously flawed, yielding severe distortions in the numbers.

If a minor track features a fast track surface, normal times will approach best times, resulting in relatively high speed ratings. A slower major track will feature better horses but lower speed ratings. The resulting comparisons can be farcical, as when allowance shippers from Turf Paradise appear to have run faster than stakes horses at Santa Anita.

Even less reliable and more troublesome are the track variants of *The Daily Racing Form*, which are calculated as average deviations between the final times of winners on a particular day and a racetrack's best times, for sprints and routes, respectively. On weekdays featuring cheaper, slower horses, the winners' times will be further removed from the track's best times and the resulting variants higher; on weekend days, the opposite, since better, faster horses run closer to best times, providing a lower track variant. The speed of the track surface might not have changed a trace. Worse, the track surface might have been faster than normal during the week, slower than normal on the weekend. The inconsistencies and contradictions wreak havoc with the numbers. Racing's customers cannot possibly cope.

The *Form* variant can be especially insensitive to changing racing conditions in routes. When one route is carded, perhaps two, for cheap horses, the winners' times will be significantly slower than the track's best time at the distance, yielding a ridiculously high track variant. If a track's best time at 1¹⁄₁₆ miles is 1:40.2, and a $5000 claiming winner runs the distance in 1:46.4 in the single route on the card, the day's route variant is 32. The only agreeable reaction to variants of that size is to ignore them. The same anomaly haunts turf races relentlessly, especially where cheaper grass routes are carded.

In a heavily promoted change of procedure a few years ago, *The Daily Racing Form* introduced its speed index. A horse's speed rating and the track variant are added. The sum is compared to 100, the number that would result on a "normal" day. Numbers greater than 100 are assigned a plus and numbers lower than 100 are assigned a minus. But the speed ratings and track variants themselves can be so inaccurate, the speed index qualifies as a meaningless construct. In a scathing *Washington Post* column, Andrew Beyer disparaged the *Form*'s speed index as "garbage in, garbage out." The metaphor is apt.

Assuming the track variant looks normal, not 32, the speed index occasionally can contain its own redeeming virtue. If relatively cheap horses have recorded a plus, mark them up. At least the horses have managed to run faster than the typical winner on that day. Conversely, if relatively classy horses have recorded a minus, mark them down. Good horses pose no adequate defense for running slower than the day's typical winner.

Perhaps the most disconcerting aspect of *The Daily Racing Form*'s speed ratings has been the racing industry's tolerance of an intolerable situation. Racing's customers have deserved better. They have been betting their money on misleading numbers for decades. Why has nobody thought to put a stop to it? The culture of the racetrack promotes conventional wisdom that you can't beat the races. That's untrue, but one reason so few racegoers do beat the races, even occasionally, or even comprehend the seemingly goofy nature of so many race outcomes, is that they have depended forever upon inexcusably inaccurate information about speed. The thoroughbred industry bears a terrible responsibility for that.

Instead of track records or best times, modern handicappers rely on two critical elements to develop accurate speed and pace figures. Figure handicapping may be inherently imprecise, but on the following data items it pays to achieve as much accuracy as possible.

PAR TIMES

Underrated by regular handicappers and overlooked by casual ones, par times play an indispensable role in effective figure handicapping. A racetrack without pars is akin to a golf
course without pars. Nobody would know whether a score on
the twelfth hole was good or bad. In the same way, without
pars it's difficult to say whether the running time of the fifth
race was good or bad.

Pars are averages. A par time indicates how fast a specific
class of horse typically runs a specific distance at a particular
racetrack, such as $20,000 claiming horses running six furlongs
at Santa Anita. Alert handicappers can deliver from memory
the par times of key classes in sprints and routes at their racetracks, including maidens, $10,000 claiming horses 4up, high-
priced older claiming horses, and stakes horses.

A practiced glance at a par-time chart provides handicappers a wealth of information they should not be without. Table
1 presents the 1990 par times for Santa Anita. Pars are calculated from the entirety of the previous season's results charts,
a laborious procedure.

The columns to the left identify the class of the race and a
speed figure that corresponds to the par time for that class at
the regularly run distances. Examine the column of six-furlong
pars.

What do figure handicappers know about Santa Anita?

Well, the track surface is relatively fast. Maidens typically
win in 1:10, and the cheapest stock on the grounds (Mdn-Clm
$32,000) runs only a second slower. On glib surfaces, ordinary
horses more readily can approach the par times of stakes
horses, contributing to an inflation factor among the figures of
overnight horses. The circumstance presses the importance of
obtaining an accurate daily track variant, a topic to be covered
next.

Notice the perfect positive correlation between the classes of
races and their par times. Better horses run faster. The $16,000
claiming horses will run faster than the $12,500 brand, on aver-
age, and stakes horses will run faster than the classified allowance kind, on average. The same patterns are repeated at every
racetrack in the country, large, medium, and small. Studies of
par times have demonstrated beyond dispute the perfect positive correlation between class and speed, ending for all time

Table 1. Santa Anita Par Times

Sprints

Class	Par	Pace (tenths)	6F	6½F	Pace (tenths)	7F
STK	111	43.9	1:08.2	1:14.4	44.2	1:21.2
CLA	109	44.1	1:08.4	1:15.1	44.4	1:21.4
NW3	108	44.2	1:09.0	1:15.2	44.5	1:22.0
NW2	107	44.3	1:09.1	1:15.3	44.6	1:22.1
NW1	105	44.5	1:09.3	1:16.0	44.8	1:22.3
MDN	103	44.7	1:10.0	1:16.2	45.0	1:23.0
M50	100	45.0	1:10.3	1:17.0	45.3	1:23.3
M32	98	45.2	1.11.0	1:17.2	45.5	1:24.0
50	107	44.3	1:09.1	1:15.3	44.6	1:22.1
40	106	44.4	1:09.2	1:15.4	44.7	1:22.2
32	105	44.5	1:09.3	1:16.0	44.8	1:22.3
25	104	44.6	1:09.4	1:16.1	44.9	1:22.4
20	103	44.7	1:10.0	1:16.2	45.0	1:23.0
16	102	44.8	1:10.1	1:16.3	45.1	1:23.1
12,5	101	44.9	1:10.2	1:16.4	45.2	1:23.2
10	100	45.0	1:10.3	1:17.0	45.3	1:23.3

Routes

Class	Par	Pace (tenths)	Pace (tenths)	1¹⁄₁₆	1⅛	Pace (tenths)	6F (tenths)	1 Mile
STK	113	45.4	1:10.1	1:41.2	1:47.4	45.2	1:09.9	1:34.4
CLA	111	45.6	1:10.3	1:41.4	1:48.2	45.4	1:10.1	1:35.1
NW3	109	45.8	1:10.5	1:42.1	1:48.4	45.5	1:10.3	1:35.3
NW2	108	45.9	1:10.6	1:42.2	1:49.0	45.6	1:10.4	1:35.4
NW1	106	46.1	1:10.8	1:42.4	1:49.2	45.8	1:10.6	1:36.1
MDN	104	46.3	1:11.0	1:43.1	1:49.4	46.0	1:10.8	1:36.3
M50	100	46.7	1:11.4	1:44.0	1:50.3	46.3	1:11.1	1:37.1
M32	98	46.9	1:11.6	1:44.2	1:51.0	46.5	1:11.3	1:37.3
50	108	45.9	1:10.6	1:42.2	1:49.0	45.6	1:10.4	1:35.4
40	107	46.0	1:10.7	1:42.3	1:49.1	45.7	1:10.5	1:36.0
32	106	46.1	1:10.8	1:42.4	1:49.2	45.8	1:10.6	1:36.1
25	105	46.2	1:10.9	1:43.0	1:49.3	45.9	1:10.7	1:36.2
20	104	46.3	1:11.0	1:43.1	1:49.4	46.0	1:10.8	1:36.3
16	102	46.5	1:11.2	1:43.3	1:50.1	46.1	1:10.9	1:36.4
12,5	101	46.6	1:11.3	1:43.4	1:50.2	46.2	1:11.0	1:37.0
10	100	46.7	1:11.4	1:44.0	1:50.3	46.3	1:11.1	1:37.1

Adjustments

Females		Three-Year-Olds	
SPR—2L	RTE—4L	SPR—4L	RTE—7L
	RTE—3L (Non-Clm)		

Turf:	Class	Pace	6½F	Pace	1 Mile	Pace	8½F
Non-Clm	108	43.1	1:12.4	1:09.6	133.3	1:09.9	1:46.2
Clm 10	100	43.9	1:14.3	1:10.4	1:35.1	1:10.7	1:48.0

All fractional times recorded in tenths of a second instead of fifths.

fruitless arguments between those embattled camps.

Between classes too, par-time differences are invariably small, one or two lengths. At Santa Anita the lowest level of claiming horse runs seven lengths slower than the highest level of claiming horse. Each claiming class rates one-fifth faster than the preceding level. All tracks are not as perfectly linear, but the general pattern holds. Step-ups in claiming class are not only permissible, they can be easily accomplished. Double jumps can be perfectly acceptable.

The nonclaiming division appears more irregular, also typical of most racetracks. Now the next step-up in class will likely be two lengths faster, instead of one. Double jumps are more difficult under nonclaiming conditions, normally embracing a faster pace and faster final time in combination. In addition, a couple of lengths improvement against a relatively faster clocking is more difficult to achieve than a similar improvement against a relatively slower clocking.

Inspection of a racetrack's par times can advise handicappers at what junctions class rises and drops might be facile or troublesome. Look for a two-length gap in either direction.

At Santa Anita, maidens will be pressed to win the first allowance race. The next stop in the nonclaiming division, to nonwinners twice other than maiden or claiming, will be similarly tough. Winners of two allowance races at Santa Anita normally must improve another four to five lengths before handling stakes conditions. Other major tracks will look similar.

No gaps can be found among the claiming pars. Now an understanding of the claiming-class barriers at local tracks supersedes a knowledge of running times. Claiming drops at Santa Anita prove easiest between the $10,000 and $12,500 levels and between the $25,000 to $32,000 levels. The corresponding class rises there will be difficult, necessitating a consultation with the horses' figures.

Notice the two-length gap at Santa Anita between the only two classes of maiden-claiming races carded there, Mdn-Clm $50,000 and Mdn-Clm $32,000. Dropdowns between those levels win frequently, especially when the pace of the higher-class race has been swifter. The same will be true of maiden-claiming competition everywhere. Look for noticeable gaps of two lengths or more among the par times.

Fractional times on the par chart have been recorded in tenths of a second. Each tenth of a second corresponds to a half-length. Thus a point in the figure column, second from left, equals one length at the final time but a half-length at the fractional time. To put it differently, at the second call two points equals one length.

Notice that the pace at Santa Anita is typically slower at seven furlongs than at six or 6½. This too is rather standard at U.S. racetracks. Despite the longer run down the backside to the turn of a seven-furlong sprint, jockeys typically slow the pace, preferring to conserve their horses' energies at the longer sprint distances. In consequence, numerous sprints at seven furlongs will feature a tantalizingly slow pace, an especially comfortable circumstance for better frontrunners, who regularly steal these races.

A greatly prized virtue of figure handicapping, at any racetrack, is that par times facilitate the tricky comparisons between claiming classes and nonclaiming classes.

At Santa Anita, where should maiden graduates that cannot proceed successfully under nonclaiming conditions be expected to win in the claiming division?

At the $20,000 claiming level.

Why? The par times at the respective class levels are equal. If maiden winners are next entered at $40,000 claiming, they will probably lose. The $40,000 claimers typically run three lengths faster than maiden winners at Santa Anita.

Similarly, horses at Santa Anita that have won one allowance race but cannot win a second allowance race, should be expected to win next at $32,000 claiming. The corresponding pars are 1:09.3. If a winner of one allowance race has been entered at $50,000 claiming, it is probably outclassed. If it is entered instead at $25,000 claiming, the allowance winner probably enjoys a class edge.

At Santa Anita the highest-priced claiming horses are severely outclassed when pitted against stakes horses, in sprints and routes. Par-time differences of a full second amount to a minimum of five lengths. At medium and small tracks, this is usually not the case. The highest-priced claiming horses frequently will record par times equal to the stakes pars.

In addition, at minor tracks maiden graduates that cannot win an allowance race will typically win next at a softer claiming level, perhaps from $12,000 to $8500. The relationships vary subtly from track to track.

In this way par-time charts become helpful guides toward interpreting common rises and drops in class at the various racetracks. Figure handicappers know what to expect.

Studies of par times at the nation's racetracks uncovered another finding veritably monumental in its consequences for figure handicapping. With exceptions, $10,000 claiming horses can be considered pretty much the same everywhere. As on the Santa Anita chart, if the $10,000 claiming pars are set equal to a figure of 100 and that figure is increased or decreased in accord with running times faster or slower than the $10,000 claiming pars, the procedure provides a basis for figure handicapping that facilitates track-to-track comparisons. This fortunate reality has provided the basis for one of the two most popular approaches to figure handicapping in this country.

A broader interpretation of the finding regarding the comparability of $10,000 claiming horses, perfectly acceptable, extends to lower-level claiming horses as a group. Lower-level claiming horses, as from $8500 to $16,000, can ship from smaller tracks to major tracks effectively. Golden Gate Fields can ship $12,500 claiming horses to comparable races at Santa Anita and win regularly. Rockingham Park can send the same lower-level claimers to Belmont Park and win a fair share.

As claiming prices rise, the comparability of claiming horses at major tracks and medium-sized tracks recedes. The $40,000 claiming horses from Golden Gate get hammered at Santa Anita, unless entered for $25,000.

The nonclaiming divisions present figure handicappers with different problems entirely. Maiden graduates and nonwinners allowance winners at medium-sized and minor tracks may ship to major tracks successfully, but far more often they do not. Best bets will be shippers flashing both speed and pace figures superior to par at today's class at the major track. Even so, the intangible qualities of endurance and determination, neither easily quantified, will favor the better-bred nonclaiming horses at major tracks whenever fancy figure horses from smaller tracks appear. Possessing deeper reserves of speed, the major leaguers kick into a faster gear, and win. Not always, but the speed-pace figures must be clearly superior and the price attractive (it frequently is) before the minor league shippers can be bet.

In the nonclaiming division, track class is best evaluated by examining the pars and figures of classified allowance winners. Classified races regularly involve a mixture of high-priced claiming horses, consistent allowance types, and stakes horses. The mix fairly represents the quality of the nonclaiming competition at the respective racetracks.

Classified allowance winners at Santa Anita, for example, regularly will earn speed figures six to seven lengths superior to classified allowance horses at Golden Gate Fields. That's a best estimate as to how many lengths faster Santa Anita nonclaiming horses should be, and a significant difference.

An intriguing aspect of figure handicapping regards nonclaiming horses moving through their nonwinners allowance conditions. A maiden at Santa Anita that earns a 105 while winning would be expected to compete well under nonwinners-once allowances, also a 105 on the Santa Anita chart.

In the same way, allowance figures can often be predictive of a horse's future in the stakes division. Figure handicappers continually keep an eye peeled for younger-developing three-year-olds on the way up the nonclaiming ladder. Accurate figures tell the tale. Excellent figure handicappers probably know more about the stakes potential of younger, improving horses than anyone, including the horses' owners and trainers.

The same figure handicappers gain enviable insights as to the leading Kentucky Derby prospects, the authentic standouts in the local stakes divisions, and the logical favorites for the country's championship races. These special stakes stars typically record well-established speed figures, and those that cannot do not figure to win the big races, regardless of impressive running times or sensational winning margins.

At times the disparity between what figure handicappers comprehend about the local competition and unversed public selectors reach ludicrous dimensions. One of the most overrated, overblown prospects of recent times was Charlie Whittingham's three-year-old colt Excavate. Early in Excavate's juvenile season, in 1990, Whittingham dubbed the colt a Kentucky Derby prospect, and the media swallowed the bait. Before Excavate had won a race, he had been crowned a champion-to-be. In early December of 1990, still a nonstakes winner, Excavate was listed at 5–2 in the Las Vegas Future Books for the 1991 Kentucky Derby.

By winter of 1991, Excavate had not yet recorded a speed figure better than par for nonwinners once other than maiden or claiming. His maiden win had yielded a pitiable Quirin-style figure of 100, below par by three lengths for 3YO maiden winners at Santa Anita. Not a single turf writer in Los Angeles or elsewhere revealed Excavate as the phony he was. No finer argument than Excavate can be delivered in support of the widespread distribution of speed figures. It's convenient for professionals to know what they are talking about.

Par-time charts and the associated speed figures reflect the abilities of older horses. Pars are calculated from the races of older horses, excepting the pars for maidens and the nonwinners allowances. Adjustments are needed to designate the par times of similar races for fillies and mares, for maiden-claiming horses, and for three-year-olds. Fortunately, the adjustments are standard.

Fillies and mares run slower than males by two lengths in sprints and three lengths in routes.

Maiden-claiming horses run slower than horses at the same selling prices by five lengths in sprints and by seven lengths in routes.

Adjustments for three-year-olds vary with the time of the year and apply to claiming races, stakes races, and classified allowance races. They do not apply to maiden races, maiden-claiming races, or nonwinners allowance races. Pars for those races have been calculated utilizing races involving three-year-olds.

In claiming races, three-year-olds typically run slower than older horses by three lengths in sprints, five lengths at a mile, and seven lengths beyond a mile for the first three months of the year; by three lengths in sprints, four lengths at a mile, and five lengths beyond a mile during the second quarter of the year; by two lengths in sprints, three lengths at a mile, and four lengths beyond a mile during the third quarter of the year; by one length in sprints, two lengths at a mile, and three lengths beyond a mile by the final three months of the year. These adjustments estimate reality well enough.

As mentioned, par times are best calculated by poring over results charts for the preceding racing season. Actual times for every class and distance can be listed in columns, correlated, and averaged. Fifteen races to estimate par are recommended, but nine frequently will be enough. Ignore extreme times. Races limited to three-year-olds can be examined separately, a local line that can supersede the standard adjustments.

Figure analysts urge handicappers to pay the price and elaborate personal par charts at least once. The hands-on experience is considered both instructive and informative. Virtually no one complies. Pars instead are purchased locally or nationally, for a fee. This is fair procedure, and saves time and sweat. By whatever means, obtain the pars for local tracks and feeder tracks. The win percentage will improve, as will the average odds on winners and the ultimate return on investment.

Once an accurate, updated par chart has been secured, figure handicappers find the cup half filled. The task shifts to obtaining accurate daily track variants. No one should imagine otherwise. The single most important piece of information in figure handicapping is the daily track variant. The best track variants produce the best figures. Calculating variants can amount to an arty practice. I once imagined there would be as many track variants for a racing day as there were figure handicappers producing them. I have since changed my mind about the diversity, but not about the accuracy.

DAILY TRACK VARIANTS

More than fifteen years since the popularization of modern speed handicapping, in trackside conversations and even formal seminars, quizzical expressions still abound at the mention of the daily track variant.

What is the daily track variant? How is it calculated? Is it useful? How important is it, really? Puzzled faces want to know.

The daily track variant is the measure of track-surface speed on a particular day. It is calculated as the average deviation between expected times, normally pars, and actual times, for sprints and routes, respectively. It is used to adjust actual running times to reflect track-surface speed.

Controversy has stalked the daily track variant since its contemporary incarnation, giving the concept a tortured history. But the basic issues surrounding track variants have been framed poorly. The issue is not whether track variants are important enough to matter, because they irrefutably are, but how to obtain accurate variants given the wild array of running times recorded daily at the nation's racetracks. At times it seems the value of the daily track variant differs in direct accord with the number of handicappers making them.

The constant variation, however, lends the daily variant its ultimate charm. The calculation becomes not a science, but an art. The first lesson to internalize about track variants is that accuracy cannot be obtained mechanically, as by applying arithmetical rules. The problem upsets numerous handicappers, notably those who would prefer to reduce the artistry to computer programming.

To dramatize the problem, below are yesterday's track variants for the nine races at Hollywood Park. It's July 11, 1991.

	Race	Conditions		Actual Times (tenths) (fifths)		Variants	
1st	Clm$10	f 4up	9F	1:11.8	1:52.4	F1	S7
2nd	Clm$25	3YO	8½F	1:11.2	1:44.2	F7	F3
3rd	Mdn-Clm$50	f 3up	6F	45.2	1:12.0	F1	S6
4th	Mdn-Clm$50	2YO	6F	45.8	1:12.2	S3	S6
5th	Alw/Nw2×	f 3up	6F	44.6	1:09.2	O	O
6th	Clm$25	4up	8½F	1:10.4	1:42.4	F7	F3
7th	Clm$50	f 4up	9F/T	1:10.2	1:48.2	F12	F1
8th	Alw/NW2×	3up	8½F	1:10.2	1:42.1	F6	F3
9th	Mdn	f 3up	8½F/T	1:11.2	1:42.3	F4	S1

The card consisted of three sprints, four routes, and two turf routes. Individual race variants at the right indicate the deviations between the actual times (shown) and the par times (not shown) for each race. At the pace calls, fractional times are presented in tenths of a second. Thus at the pace call, one-tenth equals approximately a half length. In the variant column, two points equals one length.

The first race was Fast 1 in relation to par at the pace call (F1), but Slow 7 in relation to par at the finish (S7).

The day provides an interesting array of races and variants, a convenient illustration of the routine complications inherent in obtaining accurate variants. First, sprints and routes are grouped. Turf races are grouped separately. Consider the race variants at the various distances:

	Sprints			Routes			Turf	
3rd	F1	S6	1st	F1	S7	7th	F12	F1
4th	S3	S6	2nd	F7	F3	9th	F4	S1
5th	O	O	6th	F7	F3			
			8th	F6	F3			

The mechanics of calculating variants says to add the race deviations from par and divide the sum by the number of races.

Too frequently it cannot be done that way. Figure handicappers examine individual race variants carefully, looking for atypical and inconsistent deviations.

The first route race looks strangely out of balance with the other three, which were repeatedly three lengths faster than par. The race variant for Race 1 can be judged aberrant and summarily eliminated. The daily track variant for July 11 routes at Hollywood becomes F6 (Fast 6) to the pace call, and F3 (Fast 3) at the final time.

Elimination of the first race makes perfect sense to figure handicappers at Hollywood Park. The $10,000 claiming horses there are bottom-of-the-barrel. Several of the fields are repulsively weak. A race variant of Slow 7 probably reflects a dreadful field, not a slow track surface. The problem arises whenever particular fields consist of inordinately slow horses. Neglecting extremes when calculating daily variants is fair play, especially when they contradict a complementary pattern, as in the example. In statistical compilations concerned with striking averages, extremes are best eliminated. Experience alerts figure handicappers to do the same at a studied glance.

The trio of sprints present a different problem. Two are extra slow, the third at even par. What to do?

In calculating variants, prefer races open to older horses at middle to high-priced claiming levels. Nothing there. Next find the races for maidens 3up and for nonwinners allowance horses. The fifth race was a nonwinners allowance sprint for 3up, an even race. Maiden-claiming races can often be discounted as inordinately slow, but $50,000 maiden-claimers should show something. If the individual variants are averaged, the sprint variant for July 11 is Slow 4.

A slow sprint variant will be incompatible with the day's route variant, but such a phenomenon is not unusual. Figure handicappers best examine the sprint variants at Hollywood Park for the preceding and subsequent days, searching for a pattern that clarifies the July 11 deviations. On each day the sprint variant was Slow 1. Now a judgment that the track surface on July 11 was a couple of lengths slow for sprints is tenable. I sliced each of the maiden-claiming race variants in half, added the resulting sprint variants (S6) and divided by 3. A best estimate of the July 11 sprint variant was S2 (Slow 2). Pace variants can normally be summed and averaged, regardless of inconsistencies or extremes. The July 11 pace variant is estimated at S1 (Slow 1).

The turf course played evenly on July 11 at the finish line, but fast early. Turf variants are Fast 8 (Pace) and even (Final Time). If turf variants are unclear on a specific day, which happens regularly, figure handicappers will cluster the turf variants for a week and strike a five-day average. The weekly average represents the daily track variant on the turf course for each day's races during that week.

With experience, the reasoning and procedure can be accomplished quickly. But computer programs that depend on standard, predictable algorithms will be misguided, as will handicappers proceeding mechanically. Literally hundreds of races and situations will be nonstandard. Only sound judgment formed by extensive and successful experience can control the error factor and arrive at reliable estimates of daily track variants.

Once in hand, daily track variants are used to adjust the actual times. The adjusted times will be converted to speed and pace figures.

When predicated upon an accurate set of par times, daily track variants can be expected to range from three lengths fast to three lengths slow on a majority of racing days. That's a range encompassing seven lengths.

At all tracks, at different times, variants will be extreme. Extreme variants contribute to greater error in figure handicapping, but racegoers without variants will be virtually lost when horses that competed on atypical days return to action. If the track surface has been Fast 8, handicappers obviously need to know that. Not knowing results in imagining winners have run eight lengths faster than they actually have. When those winners are whipped to a frazzle by horses showing apparently slower running times, unaware racegoers scratch their heads. Horsemen then proclaim that final time doesn't mean anything. Turf writers report the actual times with no insight as to what has actually transpired. Excellent figure handicappers smile smugly, while lying in wait for the upcoming betting capers.

Certain complications in the calculations of daily track variants are well-known and have been widely reported. On days when the track surface has been fast early and slow later, or vice versa, figure handicappers split the variant. Sprints might be Fast 3 for races one to five, but Slow 3 for races six to nine. Splitting the variants to reflect track conditions at different points in the racing day can be important and greatly advantageous.

At times the first two races will be unusually fast or slow, and the remaining races typical. The variant again is split.

If an individual race variant proves incompatible with the others, as in the example above, the race is best eliminated from the variant's calculation. To include the awkward race is to distort the calculation.

Probably every figure handicapper comfortably in the black at the races boasts proudly as to the accuracy of his daily track variants. Paradoxically, all of them are right. Making variants is arty stuff, the numbers yielding best estimates of reality, but not reality itself. Human error enters into the equation repeatedly. But if the errors prove systematic, the relationships represented by the resulting figures will be similarly systematic. Shippers will be evaluated poorly in relation to local stock, but figure handicappers can survive their systematic errors—not careless, inconsistent errors—for the duration of a racing season and do better next season.

Few recreational handicappers gain access to useful track variants. *The Daily Racing Form's* track variant is flawed. *The Racing Times* did not publish track variants. The omission by *The Racing Times* was especially rankling to daily handicappers and figure analysts, as the speed handicappers supplying the information were first-rate. Daily track variants supplied by *The Racing Times* would have been state-of-the-art. Instead they were unavailable. That omission continues to plague the new speed figures of *The Daily Racing Form.* As a result, thousands of figure handicappers throughout the country who prefer to make their own figures or to use a style of figures other than those in *The Daily Racing Form* must persevere in calculating daily track variants, a time-consuming task.

Expert figure handicappers regularly ignore par times to calculate daily track variants, and substitute projected times, our next topic.

PROJECTED TIMES

The reliance on accurate pars to estimate daily track variants, although highly recommended, is not the state-of-the-art. Pars are averages. At any class level some races will be faster than average and some races will be slower than average. Thus some winners will exceed par and others will not, not due to fluctuations in track-surface speed, but due to differences in real abilities. Expert speed handicappers refer to the phenomenon as class-within-a-class. They are loath to accept the limitations inherent in the wholesale reliance on par times.

The correction is a reliance on projected times. Whenever a particular field looks significantly stronger or weaker than par, figure handicappers can "project" today's final time, based upon the well-known figures of the specific horses in today.

Consider again the route variants shown on page 34. The first route race (Race 1) reveals a race variant clearly out of balance with the other three routes. On a Fast 3 surface, the first race was Slow 7?

What's up?

Par for older $10,000 fillies and mares at Hollywood Park 1991 at nine furlongs was 1:51.2 seconds, in fifths. The final time of the first race on July 11 was 1:52.4 seconds, or slow by seven-fifths in relation to par. But the race itself was pitiable, consisting of plodders that had never earned a speed figure approaching the $10,000 par. The race itself figured to be run five to seven lengths slower than par, based upon these horses' recent speed figures. A projected time of 1:52.2 to 1:52.4 would have been preferable for calculating the race variant. If a projection were invoked, the race variant would have been Even to Slow 2, far more compatible with the afternoon's other routes.

Projected times will prove far more appropriate than par times whenever races shape up as unusually fast or unusually slow. In contemporary racing, this happens almost daily, notably on the unusually slow side.

The bad news is that only authentic experts in possession of a complete file of speed figures for the horses on a circuit can invoke projected times effectively. Recreational handicappers cannot do it, and should not try. Accurate projections depend upon a number of factors, including prior accurate figures. Making accurate projections qualifies as an artistic endeavor. Beyond a file of speed figures, the projections depend upon a keen sense of relative class, current form, and pace. In other words, excellent handicapping.

Projections can also be misguided. When they are, the resulting variants and speed figures can distort performance evaluation seriously. Even expert figure analysts suffer inaccurate projections; the best of them will correct their mistakes when the horses have run again, but cannot record the projected figures.

In addition, the greater the number of projections on a single card, the more likely one or more of them will be misguided and the resulting figures distorted. Careful figure handicappers project only the few races on a card they clearly understand. Par times serve the same purpose well enough otherwise.

Figure addicts who are apostles of projected times typically extend the concept to its logical conclusion. As well as final times, they project fractional times at each point of call, based upon the evidence provided by several horses in the field. How fast should the first fraction be? The second? The third? Which horses should lead at each point of call? Where will the other contenders be at each call.

Occasionally, a cluster concept is invoked to evaluate final times and develop track variants. Now projections are made for several horses in a field, as many as four and five. The deviations between the projected times and final times of each horse are analyzed, and an average deviation is used as the best estimate of the race variant. The technique is repeated for every race on the card, and the daily track variants are estimated for sprints, routes, and turf races respectively.

Projected times may be esoteric, technical items, but no one should doubt that acrobatic figure handicappers willing to expend the time and energy needed to produce state-of-the-art speed figures rank among the most successful handicappers in the country.

Projected times on the turf are no luxury, but a necessity. The main reason many figure handicappers cannot beat grass races with the numbers is inaccurate variants. After numerous successive trials, many figure handicappers have been known to throw their turf figures in the lake. Conventional speed handicapping techniques and the figures they deliver are often worthless on the grass. The final section of this book explores the subject as never before, and also provides demonstrably effective remedies for the problems.

SPEED FIGURES

Speed figures are numerical representations of adjusted final times. They are derived from speed charts.

The array of numbers on a speed chart reflects the value of a fifth of a second at various distances.

The inimical Andrew Beyer altered the composition of many modern speed charts in 1975 when he proposed that a fifth of a second should have greater value in faster races and shorter distances. Beyer's charts were constructed on the principle of proportional time, the idea that faster horses should be expected to run longer distances proportionately faster than would slower horses.

Prior to Beyer, most speed charts incorporated the principle of parallel time, the illogical notion that all horses should be expected to run an additional furlong in the same time. If Horse A completed six furlongs in 1:10 flat, it should complete seven furlongs in 1:23.1 (in fifths). If Horse B completed six furlongs in 1:11 flat, it should complete seven furlongs in 1:24.1. In this way the slower horse runs the additional furlong in the same 13.1 seconds as the faster horse. Prior to 1975, speed handicapping was bad handicapping.

Examine the speed chart below. Developed as Beyer has suggested, the chart shows the speed figures corresponding to the typical running times at six regularly run distances at Santa Anita. The point of origin for the figures can be arbitrary. The Santa Anita chart has originated at the figure of 80, which corresponds to former $10,000 claiming pars there. Notice that a horse that runs six furlongs at Santa Anita in 1:10 flat, a 94, would be expected to run seven furlongs in 1:23.1 (94), an interval of 13.1 seconds. But a horse that runs six furlongs at Santa Anita in 1:11 flat (80), would be expected to run seven furlongs in 1:24.2 (80), an interval of 13.2 seconds. The slower horse runs the extra furlong one-fifth second slower, a relationship that better mimics reality. A length is not a nose, and is frequently decisive.

At shorter distances, the value of a fifth of a second is greater than at longer distances. At six furlongs on the Santa Anita chart, a fifth of a second is worth 2.8 points. At seven furlongs a fifth is worth 2.3 points. At 1⅛ miles a fifth is worth 1.7 points. The weighting changes from track to track.

Horses earn higher speed figures by running a fifth of a second faster in sprints than by running a fifth of a second faster in routes, another relationship that mimics reality. A sprinter that improves from 1:10 flat to 1:09.4 at six furlongs improves its figure from 94 to 97. A router that improves from 1:52 to 1:51.4 seconds at 1⅛ miles improves its figure from 80 to 82.

Santa Anita Speed-Figure Chart
Based Upon Proportional Times   80 = $10K Clm Pars

6F		6.5F		7F		1M		1¹/₁₆M		1¹/₈M	
1:07.0	136	1:13.0	135	1:20.0	130	1:33.0	140	1:40.0	133	1:47.0	125
1	133	1	132	1	127	1	138	1	131	1	123
2	130	2	130	2	125	2	136	2	129	2	121
3	128	3	127	3	124	3	134	3	127	3	120
4	125	4	125	4	121	4	132	4	126	4	118
1:08.0	122	1:14.0	122	1:21.0	119	1:34.0	130	1:41.0	124	1:48.0	116
1	119	1	120	1	117	1	128	1	122	1	114
2	116	2	117	2	114	2	126	2	120	2	112
3	114	3	115	3	112	3	124	3	118	3	111
4	111	4	112	4	110	4	122	4	116	4	109
1:09.0	108	1:15.0	110	1:22.0	108	1:35.0	120	1:42.0	114	1:49.0	107
1	105	1	107	1	105	1	118	1	112	1	105
2	102	2	105	2	103	2	116	2	110	2	103
3	100	3	102	3	101	3	114	3	108	3	102
4	97	4	100	4	98	4	112	4	107	4	100
1:10.0	94	1:16.0	97	1:23.0	96	1:36.0	110	1:43.0	105	1:50.0	98
1	91	1	95	1	94	1	108	1	103	1	96
2	88	2	92	2	91	2	106	2	101	2	94
3	86	3	90	3	89	3	104	3	99	3	93
4	83	4	87	4	87	4	102	4	97	4	91
1:11.0	80	1:17.0	85	1:24.0	85	1:37.0	100	1:44.0	95	1:51.0	89
1	77	1	82	1	82	1	98	1	93	1	87
2	74	2	80	2	80	2	96	2	91	2	85
3	72	3	77	3	78	3	94	3	89	3	84
4	70	4	75	4	75	4	92	4	88	4	82
1:12.0	66	1:18.0	72	1:25.0	73	1:38.0	90	1:45.0	86	1:52.0	80
1	63	1	70	1	71	1	88	1	84	1	78
2	60	2	67	2	68	2	86	2	82	2	76
3	58	3	65	3	66	3	84	3	80	3	75
4	55	4	62	4	64	4	82	4	78	4	73
1:13.0	52	1:19.0	60	1:26.0	62	1:39.0	80	1:46.0	76	1:53.0	71
1	49	1	57	1	59	1	78	1	74	1	68
2	46	2	55	2	57	2	76	2	72	2	66
3	44	3	52	3	55	3	74	3	70	3	65
4	41	4	50	4	52	4	72	4	69	4	63

Naturally, as the differences in fifths of seconds among race-horses grow larger, the differences in the corresponding speed figures will grow proportionately greater.

The running times on the speed chart should be considered adjusted times, not actual times. As the preceding sections note, the actual times have been adjusted to reflect the track-surface speed on any particular day. If a horse at Santa Anita runs six furlongs in 1:10 unadjusted, the speed figure is 94. But if the track were Fast 3 that day, the adjusted time would be 1:10.3, yielding a speed figure of 86. Quite a difference. Can anyone doubt any longer the importance of daily track variants in modern speed handicapping?

Beyer-style speed charts can also be considered "pure," in the sense that the adjusted times reflect running times that have been modified only by the daily track variant. Other speed charts modeled on the concept of proportional times contain adjusted times that sometimes have been adjusted for a number of factors thought to exert meaningful influence on running times. Some speed handicappers adjust actual times for weight, others for trips, and still others for esoteric elusive factors such as wind velocity.

Here is a crucial point: speed figures do not represent reality, but estimates of reality. The estimates contain error, sometimes small, sometimes gross. At its best, figure handicapping remains an imprecise art. Beyer-style speed figures will be accurate only to the extent the projected times and daily track variants on which the adjusted times have been based have themselves been accurate. When the projected times and track variants are seriously flawed, so will be the resulting speed figures.

Speed figures that have been adjusted for factors in addition to the daily track variant almost invariably will suffer greater degrees of error. That's because every adjustment to actual times introduces an additional source of error. If a point has been added to the basic figure due to a weight shift of four pounds, for example, that figure usually will be more inaccurate than the corresponding figure unadjusted for weight. The same is true of speed figures that have been adjusted to reflect the effects of troubled trips, running paths, jockey handling, or wind velocity. Those adjustments often serve to weaken speed figures, not to strengthen them.

Two established speed-figure services in the United States are Len Ragozzin's The Sheets and Jerry Brown's Thoro-Graph. Both deal in final figures only. Both services provide excellent figures to an increasingly large and grateful clientele.

In both situations, the speed figures are arrayed on a graph that corresponds to a horse's racing career. The graphs and numbers look vastly dissimilar from a Beyer speed chart. The lower the figures, the better. A horse's entire career is reviewed in figures, reading left to right as horses age and bottom to top in the columns representing the months of each racing season. Speed figures are moved slightly to the left to indicate an improved performance and slightly to the right to indicate a declining performance.

Review the graphs of the obscure four-year-old Double Artemis (The Sheets) and champion Lady's Secret (Thoro-Graph) below. Ignore the letters and symbols that appear alongside the numbers.

Double Artemis earned a figure of 23 in its 3YO debut. Following a pattern of unexceptional, inconsistent efforts, the filly finished its 3YO season by recording an impressive 12 and repeated the good race soon enough in its 4YO season, recording a 13 in its last start.

Lady's Secret recorded a 22 in her debut at three. She suddenly improved during spring of her 4YO season, thereafter running numbers between 10 and 6, solid stakes figures. Lady's Secret displayed championship form throughout her 5YO season, in September earning a remarkable 2 and winning the Breeders' Cup Distaff in late October with a 6.

In these charts, division leaders and champions earn figures below 5, solid stakes horses between 6 and 10, good horses between 11 and 15, and the others get lower figures.

Both The Sheets and Thoro-Graph adjust actual running times in undesirable ways. The Sheets can reflect a variety of adjustments and are primarily concerned with capturing "the quality of a horse's effort." By this procedure a horse that has finished second or third can earn a figure superior to the winner. As Ragozzin has explained:

> These figures measure the quality which the horse demonstrated; that is, the physical effort that he put out. If a horse carries more weight than an opponent, or races wider than an opponent, or hesitates at the start while the others get off well, he can run a superior effort while finishing behind a horse who actually ran a race of poorer quality.

Thoro-Graph adjusts for weight shifts and ground lost.

Although excellent, experienced handicappers prepare these figures, their adjustment practices can be riddled with flaws, and regularly will be. In relation to speed figures, trip information is best evaluated analytically and is virtually impossible to quantify accurately. Estimates of physical exertion or total effort

Len Ragozin   **DOUBLE ARTEMIS**   F86

Thoroughbred Da **12 RACES 89** *Sheets*   4 RACES 90

CLAIMED ⟶ 12   w25LR21
THIS DAY

22   AWLR30

⟶ 17"   5OLR16

21"   w2OLR 3
⟶ 19–   TAWLR28

.27   AWLR17
⟶ 20+   18PI 8

30–   AWPI17

F28+   BsAWPH23

34"   AWLR11
26"   AWLR 1
⟶ 23+   w5OPI17

F\M   4YO 15MAR90
13–   wAWLR10

14–   wAWLR20

.15–   wmAWLR26
15   wAWLR16

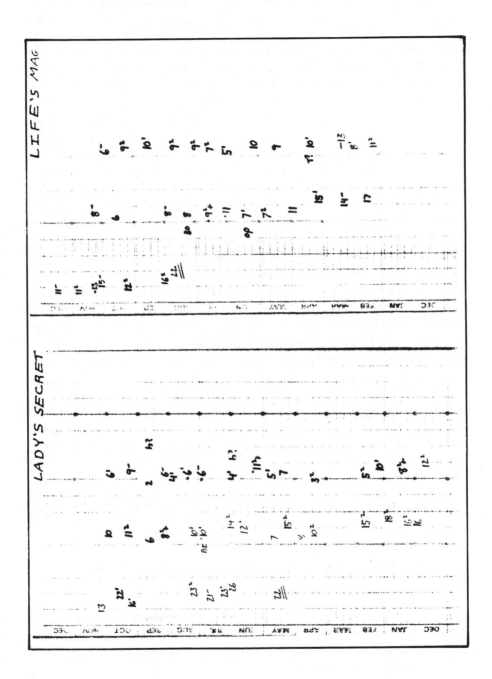

can be highly subjective and are reflected well enough by running times. Energy expenditure may be far more important than ground lost. Ragozzin makes no mention, for example, of horses that have won with speed and power in reserve. If horses behind them that encounter troubled starts or wide swings are awarded pluses, what kind of extra credit is allotted to easy winners possessing obvious reserves?

If Horse A swings four wide on the far turn against a pace of 45.3, while Horse B runs along the rail against a 44.2, both horses finishing in 1:10.4, does A deserve a higher speed figure for the greater exertion in a wide trip? I hope not. Horse B would pickle A virtually every time.

This book holds firmly that speed figures featuring adjustments for trips, weight, and the like will prove far less reliable than figures adjusted solely to reflect track surface. The Sheets and Thoro-Graph prospered in a marketplace characterized by no real competition for years. Almost any figures proved superior to possessing no figures. Users enjoyed a genuine edge at the windows, which they exploited in ways that have been popularly acclaimed by the merchandisers from the beginning.

Now *The Daily Racing Form* publishes Beyer Speed Figures, and local speed services conducted by top professionals supply state-of-the-art figures of one kind or another to just-as-loyal local markets. Neither The Sheets nor Thoro-Graph lays claim to a special edge in figure handicapping any longer.

Another approach to figure handicapping has been less publicized than the others perhaps, but performs equally as well, and in certain situations significantly better. The approach was described in two important books on handicapping by Bill Quirin, a professor of mathematics and computer science at Adelphi University, in Garden City, New York. Along with Beyer, Quirin has exerted a profound influence on the practice of figure handicapping in this country.

While compiling par times at every racetrack in the nation, it was Quirin's discovery that $10,000 older claiming horses were virtually interchangeable in ability. That does not mean that $10,000 claiming horses at Waterford Park can ship into New York and beat $10,000 horses there, but the exceptions are too few and too unimportant to distort the general tendencies, which are very important.

Quirin's methodology sets the $10,000 claiming pars equal to 100. Speed figures improve or decline by a point for each fifth of a second a horse has run faster or slower than the $10,000 claiming pars. Quirin's studies also revealed that pars between classes of horses invariably differ by one-fifth or two-fifths of a second, usually one-fifth. In addition, the adjustments to the older male pars for fillies and mares, three-year-olds, and maiden-claiming horses proved standard from track to track. Thus the numerical relationships between tracks will be highly stable. The Quirin approach to calculating speed figures is especially helpful for evaluating shippers, arguably the figure analyst's biggest headache.

Look a the par-time chart below (Table 2). It was developed for Del Mar, the peculiar but charming resort track near San Diego, California. As before, speed figures corresponding to par times are listed alongside the class levels on the left. As always, $10,000 claiming horses 3up have been assigned a figure 100. Moving up the class ladder, the par figures improve by one or two points, usually one.

Stakes horses at Del Mar record a par of 111 in sprints and 113 in routes. Look again at the par-time chart for Santa Anita. Although actual times differ, stakes horses at Santa Anita also earn a figure of 111 in sprints and 113 in routes. On a Quirin chart, one point equals one length at the final time, irrespective of distance. Variability sacrificed in the speed figures is compensated for nicely by (1) the greater comparability of the figures among various racetracks, and (2) pace figures in relation to speed figures.

This book has concentrated on the figures generated by the two popular approaches to speed handicapping practiced in this country, promoted respectively by Beyer and Quirin, and only nominally on speed figures marketed by The Sheets and by Thoro-Graph. The four approaches can be accepted as comparably effective in well-trained, experienced hands. With strengths and weaknesses attaching to each, the figure handicapper's method of choice depends upon familiarity, convenience, or personal taste.

Only one of the four, however, contributes a style of figure handicapping that controls for the intricate relationships between fractional times and final times, or between speed and pace. Possessing pace figures as a fundamental aspect of comprehensive figure handicapping has emerged as an increasingly significant topic, to which we now turn.

Table 2. Del Mar Par Times

Sprints

Class	Par	Pace (tenths)	6F	6½F	7F
STK	111	44.1	1:08.0	1:14.2	1:20.4
CLA	109	44.3	1:08.2	1:14.4	1:21.0
NW3	108	44.4	1:08.3	1:15.0	1:21.1
NW2	107	44.5	1:08.4	1:15.1	1:21.2
NW1	105	44.7	1:09.1	1:15.3	1:21.4
MDN	103	44.9	1:09.3	1:16.0	1:22.1
MC50	100	45.2	1:10.1	1:16.3	1:22.4
M32	98	45.4	1:10.3	1:17.1	1:23.2
50	107	44.5	1:08.4	1:15.1	1:21.2
40	106	44.6	1:09.0	1:15.2	1:21.3
32	105	44.7	1:09.1	1:15.3	1:21.4
25	104	44.8	1:09.2	1:15.4	1:22.0
20	103	44.9	1:09.3	1:16.0	1:22.1
16	102	45.0	1:09.4	1:16.1	1:22.2
12,5	101	45.1	1:10.0	1:16.2	1:22.3
10	100	45.2	1:10.1	1:16.3	1:22.4

Routes

Class	Par	Pace (tenths)	Pace (tenths)	1¹⁄₁₆	1 Mile	1¹⁄₈
STK	113	45.0	1:09.7	1:40.3	1:34.1	1:47.1
CLA	111	45.2	1:09.9	1:41.0	1:34.3	1:47.3
NW3	110	45.3	1:10.0	1:41.1	1:34.4	1:47.4
NW2	108	45.5	1:10.2	1:41.3	1:35.1	1:48.1
NW1	106	45.7	1:10.4	1:42.0	1:35.3	1:48.3
MDN	104	45.9	1:10.6	1:42.2	1:36.0	1:49.0
M50	100	46.3	1:11.0	1:43.1	1:36.4	1:49.4
MCL	98	46.5	1:11.2	1:43.3	1:37.1	1:50.1
50	108	45.5	1:10.2	1:41.3	1:35.1	1:48.1
40	107	45.6	1:10.3	1:41.4	1:35.2	1:48.2
32	106	45.7	1:10.4	1:42.0	1:35.3	1:48.3
25	105	45.8	1:10.5	1:42.1	1:35.4	1:48.4
20	104	45.9	1:10.6	1:42.2	1:36.0	1:49.0
16	102	46.1	1:10.8	1:42.4	1:36.2	1:49.2
12,5	101	46.2	1:10.9	1:43.0	1:36.3	1:49.3
10	100	46.3	1:11.0	1:43.1	1:36.4	1:49.4

PACE FIGURES

In the era of speed figures, pace figures have remained a relatively scarce commodity at the nation's racetracks. Neither Beyer, nor The Sheets, nor Thoro-Graph traffic in pace figures, and the latter two have argued absurdly that pace does not influence final time. Final-time figures have controlled the marketplace, not because pace does not influence final time, but because for most practitioners no practical alternative to speed figures has existed.

Attention to pace as a fundamental factor in handicapping has experienced a renewal in recent times, as more and more of racing's casual customers gain access to speed figures, thereby driving down the mutuels on "figure" horses.

Although as I write the market remains relatively threadbare, the demand for pace figures has grown. The demand should intensify in the near future.

To put pace figures in proper perspective, three factors exercise a vital influence on final times. They are: (1) relative class, (2) track-surface speed, and (3) pace. Figure services have distributed numbers that have reflected relative class and track-surface speed effectively, but have ignored pace. Beyer Speed Figures are insensitive to pace. Thus, whenever the pace of the race has been unusually fast or unusually slow, the resulting speed figures can be outrageously false.

In a provocative chapter of his *Thoroughbred Handicapping: State of the Art*, Bill Quirin presented indisputable evidence of the importance of pace and described a speed and pace methodology that offers its disciples an enviable edge. Quirin demonstrated that speed and pace figures in combination are commonly symmetrical. Consider the running times below and the corresponding speed and pace figures.

		Adjusted Times		Pace	Speed
Race 1	6F	45.2	1:10.1	98	102
Race 2	6F	45.0	1:11.0	102	98

When the pace figures improve, the speed figures decline. When the pace figures decline, the speed figures improve.

That complementary reality supports a convincing argument for utilizing speed and pace figures in combination. It applies with considerable force to virtually all overnight horses. Low-priced claiming horses are so susceptible to the patterns, their speed and pace figures are frequently as symmetrical as the above illustration. No one who has persisted with Quirin-style figures in combination will refute the assertion.

Nonclaiming horses reveal fascinating variations of the basic symmetry. When maidens graduate to the nonwinners allowance conditions, a decent percentage succeed, but many more fall down. Among the failures, a majority will show speed and pace figures strikingly similar to these:

Maiden race   99   105

where the speed figure of 105 is equal to par for the nonwinners allowance race, but the 99 is three lengths slower than par for the same race.

Almost invariably the pace of allowance sprints will require a pace figure within two lengths of par, if not par or better. Maiden graduates running 99s to the pace call cannot stay in contention and repeat the 105 speed figure. When the pace figure becomes 105 instead of 99, the speed figure usually declines by a few lengths, sometimes by several lengths. An exception is the genuinely talented nonclaiming horse who tolerates the swifter pace and duplicates the rapid final time, or even exceeds its previous best. These are the golden nuggets, en route to stakes opportunities. The impressive improvement, however, is difficult to predict beforehand. The presumption must hold that as the pace intensifies, speed figures will fall.

Familiar figure patterns accompany nonclaiming horses as they progress through the nonwinners allowances and stakes conditions. A soft pace figure intimates the next step might prove to be a giant step. A pace figure more than two lengths slower than par in these races predicts doom.

During the 1991 winter season at Santa Anita, probably the most impressive three-year-old to debut was a son of Relaunch named Split Run. The colt crushed maidens and nonwinners-once allowance horses in its first two starts, recording speed figures in the allowance race that qualified him as a classic prospect. In fact, the Las Vegas Future Books took so much early betting on Split Run, his Kentucky Derby odds plunged in five days from 200–1 to 50–1. The next week at most books he was hammered down below 10–1.

Examine the speed and pace figures recorded by Split Run in his first two races:

		Par	Pace	Speed
Jan 27	Maidens	103	99	106
Feb 18	Alw/NW1×	105	100	111

Split Run overtook the maiden field from behind the pace and scampered wire-to-wire in the allowance race.

Using Quirin-style figures, the stakes par for three-year-olds during winter at Santa Anita is 106. The stakes par for older horses of winter there is 111. Split Run had equaled the older stakes par at Santa Anita, a feat unmatched by Dinard, Best Pal, Apollo, and the rest.

When the graded stakes for three-year-olds arrived, Split Run was sent postward a prohibitive favorite. Numerous figure addicts accepted even-money, and gladly.

But Split Run suffered a serious pace weakness. When forced to compete against stakes-caliber three-year-olds unfurling a pace of 106 for the first six furlongs, Split Run abruptly fell back. He could not dispense a 106 pace figure and duplicate a par speed figure, not to mention the 111 speed figure. Numerous developing horses do the same. Until Split Run collapsed on the swifter pace, no one realized the colt was faking it. Disciples of speed and pace figures in combination could comprehend the colt's collapse.

Pace figures in combination with speed figures present intriguing information usually overlooked by most conventional figure handicappers. For instance, how to predict which sprinters can stretch out effectively, one of the stickiest problems of handicapping? Inspect the speed and pace figures below and select the three-year-old more likely to stretch out successfully:

	Pace	Speed
Horse A	104	96
Horse B	99	103

Horse B shows a lower-to-higher relationship between its pace and speed figures, not severely unbalanced, suggesting he spends his energy in a manner more likely to stretch out effectively. Horse A's prospects are dimmer. Where the pace figure is higher than the speed figure by several lengths, that kind of

unseasoned horse might either spend itself prematurely or resist the kind of handling designed to reserve its limited energies
for a sustained late run. Even if Horse A relaxes during the early
pace of the route, its speed figure might not improve sufficiently
at first-asking to win going long.

And if A is a three-year-old switching today from dirt to turf
for an initial try on grass, it almost assuredly will expire before
reaching the wire.

With pace and speed figures in hand, pace analysis becomes
an informed, refined art. Numerous relationships can be made
clear that would otherwise be obscured.

Users of *The Daily Racing Form* have gained access to Beyer
Speed Figures, but recreational handicappers still are denied
convenient access to pace figures. Inspecting fractional times
remains a practical imperative.

Where speed figures look closely competitive, handicappers
can readily refer to the fractional times alongside. If today's race
is an overnight affair and the probable pace will be faster than
a few of the leading contenders have challenged in the past,
those speed figures might decline. Improving form and emerging class may be counterbalancing factors in the same situation,
complicating the pace analysis, but the relations between speed
and pace prove decisive frequently enough. Do not be too accepting of high-figure horses that have earned best-ever speed
figures against a relatively slow pace. Alternately, if a recent
speed figure looks atypically low, but the fractional time unusually fast, refer to other recent speed figures instead.

Pace figures will be more meaningful in sprints than in
routes. The early pace of the longer races will be sluggish much
of the time. In overnight competition, extra fast pace figures always deserve extra credit, certainly in cheaper races, provided
the associated speed figures have not dropped to alarming
depths. Pace figures will be useless much of the time on the
turf, where so often the early pace varies from an orderly procession to a crawl.

It's true too that speed and pace figures might be variously
more effective, depending on the kinds of races under study.
Yet speed and pace are fundamental factors of handicapping.
Either, therefore, can be decisive under any circumstances.
Making fine distinctions between speed and pace can get mud-
dled, but the topic is fascinating and well worth exploring.

SPEED OR PACE FIGURES?

Arguments debating the desirability of speed figures vis-à-vis pace figures are as fundamentally specious as the arguments a generation ago about speed and class. Both are fundamentally important, and both are frequently interdependent. The relationships among the figures, however, can be as diametrically opposite as the relationships between the concepts are complementary. Whereas speed and class are positively correlated—better horses run faster—speed figures and pace figures can be negatively related.

That is, higher pace figures will frequently result in lower speed figures. Higher speed figures will frequently result from lower pace figures.

Furthermore, although the relationships between speed and pace figures will frequently be symmetrical, notably among ordinary horses, they are not causal. Other factors can play a vital role, especially class and form. In numerous handicapping situations, final decisions regarding the relative importance of speed and pace figures will remain analytical. Handicappers will be challenged to determine which numbers should be most meaningful today.

Nonetheless, several typical situations will be best analyzed by emphasizing pace figures in relation to speed figures, or vice versa. Below are common scenarios and the kinds of figures most likely to impress.

Maiden-Claiming Races—Pace Figures

Maiden-claiming horses remain the cheapest, slowest horses on the grounds. As a glance down the shaded column of the horses' records unmistakably show, their speed figures can be dreadfully low. Many have never recorded a number approaching par for the lowest level of maiden-claiming runners in the barns.

At times, however, one of the horses displays an unusually strong pace figure. That's the horse that figures to win—every time.

Because maiden-claiming horses are so slow and untalented, few of them can mount a stretch charge, even when the pace in front has begun to wither. The animal in control at the second call continues on, perhaps slowing noticeably, and wins. Its unimpressive speed figure is irrelevant. The others have been left behind and cannot catch up.

The classic case is the maiden dropping down to maiden-claiming conditions. Unable to compete effectively with horses graduating to allowance company, maiden dropdowns will regularly exhibit miserable speed figures. But many of them have run well enough for four furlongs against straight maidens. The pace figures shine brightly among today's lackluster bunch. So the maiden dropdowns take the lead early, or wrestle it away during the second fraction, and glide into the stretch in front. They win.

The same pattern occurs less frequently whenever maiden-claiming losers descend from a significantly higher claiming price to today's lower level. A key indicator will be the par times for the respective maiden-claiming classes. If the par times differ by a length, no real advantage exists. But if the higher maiden-claiming level has recorded a par time faster by two lengths or greater, pace pars will be similarly faster, and a definite advantage exists.

Again the pace figure dominates. The maiden-claiming dropdown controls the race sometimes before the second call, protects the lead into the lane, and normally prevails. The cheaper, slower horses do not catch up.

In southern California there are two maiden-claiming classes: $50,000 and $32,000. The par times differ by two to three lengths, currently 1:10.3 at $50,000 Mdn-Clm and 1:11 flat at $32,000 Mdn-Clm. Pace figures of the horses dropping from $50,000 to $32,000 Mdn-Clm often differ by more than two lengths, as between 104 and 96. Speed figures in both cases may be low, such as 86 and 84. The dropdown capable of securing the lead on the faster pace is a solid play, and customarily pays well.

Similar scenarios play themselves out at major tracks and smaller tracks across the country. With so many additional maiden-claiming races cluttering up contemporary cards, this is a figure play worthy of the handicapper's attention.

High-Priced Claiming Races, and
Medium-Priced Claiming Races—Speed Figures

Claiming horses depend upon the only attribute of class most of them possess: speed. Claiming races therefore almost invariably are decided by speed and pace. The fastest horses win. Speed figures tell the tale.

At major tracks, above claiming prices of $20,000 the pace will usually be normal. Classier claiming horses can attend the familiar pace, and the outcome is decided by the horses that can then reach the finish line the fastest. Recent speed figures provide the telltale clues as to the probable winners. Whether claiming horses are moving ahead in class or dropping down in class, handicappers prefer a speed figure at least equal to today's claiming par.

If contenders have finished with a speed figure below today's par, examine the pace. If it was unusually fast, consider the speed figure of the next-to-last start. If that figure is superior to today's par, use it.

Two situations can be problematic in better claiming races.

1. Whenever the pace has been inordinately fast or slow, discount the speed figures. The circumstance is especially pertinent to frontrunners and pace-pressers that have been submitted to an inordinately fast, strongly contested pace, fell back, and earned atypically low speed figures. Try to find a recent speed figure suitable to today's probable pace. Consider that figure representative of what should happen today.
2. Cheaper claiming races are best evaluated by analyzing speed figures and pace figures in combination.

Below $20,000 claiming at major tracks and below $12,500 claiming at minor tracks, few of the horses can deliver par figures at both the pace call and final time. Several of the cheapest races will be abysmally slow. Whenever the pace figure has been abnormally high, the speed figure will be abnormally low, and vice versa. Relatively honest and competitive horses at both the pace call and the final time are the likeliest survivors.

Handicappers can combine the pace figure and the speed figure. The highest compounded rating wins.

3YO Claiming Races/Jan-June—Pace Figures

Three-year-olds entered to be claimed during the first half of the calendar year can be considered washouts, certainly at major tracks. They cannot run fast enough to win an allowance race restricted to horses that have never won an allowance race, and many of them cannot run fast enough to win claiming races either. This is especially true of graduates of maiden-claiming races.

Speed figures exhibited by the cheaper three-year-olds will be volatile and generally poor. Swings of several points will be commonplace.

Discounting speed figures, favor the horses that have competed well enough early to display clearly superior pace figures. If nothing in the field can equal today's par, the top pace-figure contender deserves the nod. As always among untalented horses, the ability to grab the lead into the stretch will frequently be enough. Tiring horses win low-level claiming races all the time.

By July the three-year-old claiming division has begun to achieve a reliable resemblance of form. Trainers have learned to place the youngsters at the claiming levels where they can win, and horses will generally run to their numbers. Speed figures supersede pace figures.

A caution is appropriate here. Whenever three-year-old claiming horses take a significant climb in class, as from $25,000 to $50,000 claiming, and from any claiming race to a nonwinners allowance field, demand the pace figures be competitive. A faster, more severely contested pace typically accompanies a major class rise, and many of the horses cannot withstand the heat.

Shippers/Cheaper Claiming Races—Speed Figures

Among the best disguised of figure plays is the lowbrow claiming shipper from a minor track to a major track. Handicappers instinctively mark the horses down due to track class. If the shipper is accompanied by the higher speed figure, however, it figures.

Studies have revealed clearly that lower-level claiming horses are pretty much interchangeable. Speed and pace figures often dominate in low-level claiming races, and many of the horses at the host tracks will show undeniably dismal figures. Shippers that have earned higher speed figures at a smaller track probably can outrun their hosts. They often do just that at attractive prices. Low-level claiming shippers qualify as reliable figure plays.

Stakes Horses 4up—Speed Figures

The pace of stakes races will usually be honest to fast. Stakes horses get that way by running rapid pace figures before finishing strongly. The best horses sort themselves out at the finish line.

The ultimate extension of the logic embraces Grade 1 horses. Handicappers concern themselves unnecessarily with the probable pace of many Grade 1 races, certainly at classic distances, wondering whether a slightly inferior horse can upset the division leaders as a function of pace. If a potential lone frontrunner of impressive credentials appears in the entries, a long-winded, highly tortured debate ensues as to whether the inferior commodity can steal the race. Far more often than not, the debate amounts to much ado about nothing. Slightly inferior horses do not steal Grade 1 races. The racing game makes more sense than that.

Unless the probable pace of a Grade 1 stakes will be unusually slow or inordinately fast, class laughs at pace in Grade 1 races, a phrase I have employed repetitively and deliberately to emphasize the point. The classiest horses run the fastest times, regardless of running styles, and speed figures supersede pace figures in the highest-class stakes.

Among inexperienced stakes horses, it's another scenario entirely.

3YO Stakes Horses—Pace and Speed Figures

As developing horses, three-year-olds are vastly dissimilar from their older counterparts. As three-year-olds progress from the allowances and minor stakes to listed and graded stakes, they will go as far as natural abilities take them. Three-year-olds that suffer a pace weakness cannot proceed successfully to the graded races at the local track, or to the classics of spring and summer, or to the championship races against older stakes horses during fall.

Nonclaiming three-year-olds can record dazzling final times when the early pace has been soft. Others can crush fields of overnight horses early, posting dazzling pace figures, before cruising to an unexceptional final time. But only the best of any generation can deliver dazzling pace figures and final figures in combination.

The phenomenon resembles the numbers recorded during the winter of 1991 by the good three-year-old Apollo, a southern California stakes sprinter who had supporters wondering whether he might stretch out well enough to beat the leading prospects in the 3YO division. The older stakes par at Santa Anita is 111. Apollo's final sprint and first route at Santa Anita prior to the 1991 classics looked like this:

	Pace	*Speed*	
Sprint	107	111	Won handily
Route	111	107	Lost by a nose

Prior to the route, the Grade 1 San Felipe stakes, local figure handicappers did not know whether Apollo could duplicate his sprint figure of 111 at the longer distance.

As its San Felipe figures indicated, when forced to dispense a pace figure equal to the older stakes par of 111, Apollo recorded a speed figure of 107, roughly par for leading 3YOs of winter.

Interestingly, the final figure of 107 would be strong enough to win a majority of three-year-old stakes races, but not the spring classics and definitely not the championship races for horses 3up in fall. In sprints, however, Apollo might be any kind.

A command of speed and pace figures among the three-year-olds facilitates several of those comparisons season upon season. The handicapping is both rewarding and fun.

Deep Closers—Speed Figures

Pace figures that can be so enlightening when evaluating frontrunners and pace-pressers can be meaningless when evaluating deep closers. Closers remain captives to a running style that places them far behind the early pace. In consequence, their pace figures will be relatively low. The low pace figures reflect running styles, not abilities. A pace analysis will be mandatory to determine whether closers can arrive on time.

Do not penalize closers on pace by confusing their pace figures and running styles.

2YOs in Routes—Pace Figures

Until the juveniles stretch out, figure handicappers know to evaluate them almost exclusively by relying on speed figures. Few handicappers, however, realize that once two-year-olds attempt to route, their pace figures become more meaningful. Few two-year-olds close impressively in routes. Unseasoned at the longer distances, juveniles tend to chase, tire, and fade. Even nonclaiming two-year-old races exhibit that pattern. The horses at the front or pressing the pace wield a huge advantage.

So advantageous is a forward position in two-year-old routes that early speed regularly supersedes early pace. Juveniles on the lead unmolested at the first call repeatedly win. The cheaper the race, even more advantageous the early speed. If early-speed stickouts also possess the dominant pace figures, the case is closed. Those horses figure.

In relatively close situations, in the better two-year-old routes of fall, if one contender displays the highest pace figure, and another the highest speed figure, prefer the horse with the pace advantage. Usually that 2YO will assume command toward the second call, and last. The other juveniles normally tire and, inexperienced at the longer distances, persist only in chasing the leader to the wire.

BASIC INTERPRETATIONS

Speed figures denote how fast horses have actually run in the past. They describe a horse's speed capability, and only its speed. If Horse A has recorded speed figures consistently superior to its competition, it can be considered the fastest in the race. Horse A figures to win to the extent that in this situation speed should be decisive. Where speed should count less, so should speed figures.

Speed figures do not denote a horse's class, its pace preferences, its form cycle, or its ability to run well at longer and shorter distances, although patterns of speed figures can be indicative on these matters.

Speed figures are imprecise. They contain errors, sometimes small, sometimes gross. The figures do not tell handicappers *exactly* how fast horses have run. Horses having the same speed figures not only fail to finish in dead heats, they sometimes finish several lengths apart.

If horses showing comparable speed figures—within a length, perhaps two—engage in a driving stretch duel, the verdict does not necessarily go to the fastest horse, but to the horse able to summon the greatest degrees of speed, endurance, and determination simultaneously.

Horses showing comparable figures may experience vastly dissimilar trips, one perfect, another troubled, and again the fastest horse does not win.

Horses showing comparable figures may arrive at today's race in diametrically opposed stages of their form cycles, one improving, the other declining, such that the horse carrying the slightly advantageous figure loses again.

Horses showing apparently inferior figures may be aided by a surface or post position bias, and once again the high-figure horse is upset.

The point is plain. Although speed figures are damn important, because a thoroughbred's speed is fundamentally important, they are far from everything, because the speed factor is far from everything. Once handicappers have identified the high-figure horses, they normally will have a fair amount of analysis to conduct.

Patterns of speed figures often can indicate whether form cycles are improving or declining, but the patterns themselves can be deceiving. A positive pattern of improving figures may accompany successive class drops, or a series of facile wins against a soft pace, or uncontested romps on the lead. Declining figures may accompany rises in class, or defeats following a too-rapid pace, or a series of troubled trips. Form remains essentially intact.

A sudden high speed figure in an otherwise unexceptional pattern may be attributed to a wire-to-wire romp, or a big win against easy opposition, or a biased track surface, or a wet surface—or it may signify the genuinely rapid improvement of a young developing racehorse, or the rejuvenation of an older gelding following a claim, or the benefits due to first-time Lasix.

A sudden low speed figure following a series of impressive figures may result from an inordinately fast pace, or too steep a step-up in class, or a severely troubled trip, or a negative speed bias on the inside—or it may indicate a genuine deterioration of current form.

In these circumstances, and numerous others, the prescription for success in figure handicapping includes a respectful attention to the other factors of handicapping. As is true of method players generally, the best of figure handicappers will be equally impressive in several facets of the art.

Pace figures denote how fast horses have run to the second call of the race. Pace figures describe ability to the second call in both sprints and routes. Pace figures therefore will be more significant in races where speed and position at the second call matter more. Pace figures will be less meaningful where second-call position matters less, as in stakes races for older runners or on the grass.

Pace figures should not be confused with early speed advantages. Early speed refers to position and beaten lengths at the first call. Early pace refers to fractional time, position, and beaten lengths at the second call.

Pace figures tend to be far more meaningful when the early pace has been contested, especially by horses of comparable class. Horses dictate the pace on the front, and others gain striking position from behind, during the second fraction, notably in sprints. When the second fraction has been contested, faster horses will respond in kind, and cheaper horses fall back quickly. On an uncontested pace, none of the critical give-and-take can occur. The resulting pace figures can be seriously misleading.

Speed figures and pace figures in combination denote the kind of pace horses can set and maintain, or the kind of early pace horses can track and overtake. The combination of figures describes the "race shapes" comfortable for horses, such as fast-fast, average-fast, or fast-slow. Analyzing race shapes becomes a fascinating aspect of figure handicapping for many pace specialists and is not widely practiced.

Perhaps most important of all, speed and pace figures are best interpreted in relation to a standard. Most figure handicappers compare horses with one another, but a more objective comparison is a first priority. The most useful standard is the par time, or par figure, for today's class and distance. A par figure as the objective basis of comparison can be especially helpful when horses attempt to rise in class, as a couple of dozen do every racing day. Either horses have run as fast as par for today's class at today's distance, or they have not. One of the biggest sucker bets in figure handicapping is the top-figure horse in a field where none of the horses have equaled par. That's a race not very susceptible to figure handicapping.

In the absence of par figures as standards of comparison, figure handicappers will confront the proposition of wagering on the high-figure horse in the field. One horse inevitably boasts the high figure. Is it a play?

Maybe; maybe not.

The following sections are intended to provide useful guidelines for making those decisions.

PART TWO

Applications

THE FOLLOWING CONSTITUTES an interesting array of the most common applications in figure handicapping. Dozens more might be included, containing nuances, subtle variations, and seeming contradictions that cannot be considered here. No matter. On those rarefied fronts, experience remains the best teacher.

Certain reliable applications, however, lend themselves splendidly to textbook exposition. The sample races and illustrations to be found here can be found as well every week on every racing circuit in the nation. The examples are intended to eradicate the grossest of errors.

We begin with the figure handicapper's best friends, the claiming races.

CLAIMING RACES

Figure handicappers at major tracks should gaze fondly on claiming races open to older horses with selling prices from $20,000 to $50,000. At smaller tracks similar selling prices customarily range from $10,000 to $25,000, perhaps higher. The handicapping task is elementary. Find the top-figure horse and determine whether it's sharp enough to duplicate the figure. Of the potpourri of races in major league racing, the outcomes that most consistently will depend upon dominant speed figures include the middle- to high-priced claiming races.

The second race at Saratoga on August 1, 1991, presents a

typical challenge for figure handicappers. It was at six furlongs for $50,000 fillies and mares, 3up. Examine the figures of the nine starters. Par is 90, or thereabouts, but nothing lower.

It's instructive to begin by surveying swiftly the past six races (recent consistency) in the record. Find the high and low figures. Consider any obvious patterns of improvement or decline. Try to comprehend as quickly as possible the tale the numbers are telling.

Joy's Jo Jo, for example, has earned her best figures on the turf. The last figure looks awful, to be sure, but is unimportant. It's a waste of time to ponder the impact of woeful figures when horses have been beaten off badly. If the last figure had been 78 instead of 48, a declining pattern would be indicated. But a dreadful figure sticking out in an otherwise sensible pattern is not meaningful and is best discarded. When evaluating figures, do not rely upon badly beaten performances. Figure handicappers prefer to know what horses can do when they have contended for the win.

Joy's Jo Jo recorded a lackluster 81 two back at today's distance but against a clearly superior class. The speed figure, to recall, is generally more meaningful than the company line in claiming races. An 81 falls lengths short of the Beyer Speed par for $50,000 older horses at Saratoga. A glance at the 4YO's other sprint figures reinforces an inference that Joy's Jo Jo cannot defeat $50,000 sprinters at Saratoga.

What about the 93 Joy's Jo Jo recorded on December 31, 1990, at Aqueduct?

Two comments. One, speed figures earned in claiming races limited to three-year-olds do not transfer reliably to similar races open to older ones. The $75,000 claiming price of December 31 is inferior to today's $50,000 caliber.

Do not use claiming races restricted to three-year-olds to predict the figures the same horses should earn against older counterparts.

Two, the further back handicappers search in the record for meaningful figures, the greater the risk those figures will be unrepresentative of today. Among better horses, including better claiming horses, six races can form the standard of recent consistency. It's a flexible, liberal standard. Stick close to it.

HUCKLEBUCKLE
4yo (Apr) filly, gray — **$50,000** CLM. PRICE
Trainer: Philip G Johnson
Owner: Rita Cohen
Sire: **Silver Buck ($7,500)** by Buckpasser
Dam: **Beautiful Prospect** by Mr. Prospector
Bred in FL by Farnsworth Farms
117
Career: 7 1 0 5 — Wet: 0 0 0 0 — Turf: 0 0 0 0 — Dist: 3 1 0 2
1991: 5 1 0 3 $17,230 — 1990: 2 0 0 2 — Sar: 1 0 0 1

10Jly91	5Bel	ft	3+F	Alw27000Nw1x	7f	22.30	45.38	1:11.33	1:24.77	58	3/7	1·	2^{hd}	1^{hd}		$5\frac{3}{4}$	$7^{12\frac{3}{4}}$	MO Vasquez[5]	114 b	11.10	Kryptonic117$^{2\frac{3}{4}}$Ferber's Follies111$\frac{3}{4}$Serape113^{2}	*Dueled outside winner, tired upper stretch*
30Jun91	8Mth	ft	3+F	Alw17000Nw2L	1m	23.03	46.01	1:11.42	1:38.27	66	1/9	1	1^{hd}	1^{1}	$1\frac{1}{2}$	2^{hd}	3^{4}	N Santagata	121 b	3.80	Say Vodka112^{nk}Damie's Sis112$^{3\frac{3}{4}}$Hucklebuckle121$^{2\frac{1}{2}}$	*Broke on top, set pace for 3/4, weakened, gave way late*
15Jun91	4Mth	ft	3+F	MaidenSpWt	6f	22.07	45.49		1:11.90	64	10/12	3	1^{hd}	$1^{1\frac{1}{2}}$		1^{2}	1^{2}	N Santagata	122 b	6.60	Hucklebuckle122^{2}Sportn' Love115^{1}Little Wolf Girl115$\frac{3}{4}$	*Away alertly, set pace throughout, won driving*
23May91	5Bel	ft	3+F	MaidenSpWt	7f	22.58	46.02	1:12.02	1:25.23	65	6/9	1	1^{hd}	$1\frac{1}{2}$		$2^{1\frac{1}{2}}$	3^{8}	JF Chavez	124	4.90	Miss Jazz115^{4}$\frac{1}{2}$Outlastng^{3}$\frac{3}{4}$Hucklbck$\frac{1}{2}$	*Inside speed, tired*
12May91	3Bel	ft	3+F	MaidenSpWt	6f	22.53	46.37	-	1:10.87	65	6/8	5	$1\frac{1}{2}$	1^{hd}		$2\frac{1}{2}$	3^{5}	CA Black	124	2.60	Sister Mac115^{3}$\frac{1}{2}$ListnWll^{1}$\frac{1}{2}$Hucklbck^{3}$\frac{3}{4}$	*Inside speed, tired*
15Aug90	1Sar	ft	3+F	MaidenSpWt	7f	22.47	45.61		1:23.86	64	2/12	3	$1\frac{1}{2}$	1^{hd}			$3^{9\frac{1}{2}}$	CW Antley	117	2.10	Respectability117^{3}$\frac{1}{2}$BunkaBnk^{6}Hucklbck^{2}	*Good spd; tired*
12Jly90	4Bel	ft	3F	MaidenSpWt	6f	21.82	45.08		1:09.84	74	1/10	1	$2\frac{1}{2}$	2^{3}			$3^{9\frac{1}{4}}$	CW Antley	121	5.80	Dream Touch121^{6}$\frac{1}{4}$SistrChrys^{3}Hucklbck^{2}	*Good spd; tired*

Workouts: 26Jly Sar-tr 4f ft 50.87 B — 25Jun Bel-tr 5f ft 1:00.56 B — 31May Bel-tr 5f ft — 20May Bel-tr 3f ft — 2May Bel-tr 6f ft

Winning races and good races in the recent record, and not poor races, provide the telltale clues among the claimers. The 64 of Hucklebuckle's maiden win June 15 cannot approach $50,000 claiming competition. Maidens at major tracks that cannot proceed to the allowances should next win near $25,000 claiming, but this filly probably warrants a steeper descent.

SOUTHERN SOONER
5yo (Apr) mare, bay — **$50,000** CLM. PRICE
Trainer: Robert P Klesaris
Owner: Lazer Two Stable
Sire: **Aloma's Ruler ($3,000)** by Iron Ruler
Dam: **Delta Fleet** by Hawaii
Bred in OK by Grady O. Brewster
119
1989-91: 36 9 7 4 — Wet: 6 3 2 0 — Turf: 2 0 0 1 — Dist: 34 9 7 3
1991: 8 5 1 0 $70,840 — 1990: 19 3 6 3 — Sar: 1 0 0 0

8Jly91	1Bel	ft	4+F	Clm50000	6f	22.62	45.51		1:09.77	95	3/8	1	1^{1}	1^{1}		1^{3}	$1^{5\frac{1}{4}}$	JR Velazquez	113	2.00	Southern Sooner113^{5}$\frac{1}{4}$Company Girl117^{1}$\frac{1}{2}$Sparkling Hannah114$\frac{3}{4}$	*Quickly to front, made pace along rail, drew off thru stretch*
14Jun91	3Bel	ft	4+F	Clm35000	6f	22.57	45.43		1:09.77	91	3/7	1	$1^{1\frac{1}{2}}$	$1^{2\frac{1}{2}}$		1^{3}	$1^{1\frac{1}{4}}$	JR Velazquez	117	0.90	Southern Sooner117^{1}$\frac{1}{4}$Embracing117^{1}$\frac{3}{4}$Kinklets119^{nk}	*Made pace two-wide, drew clear on turn, kept to pressure*
16May91	2Bel	fm	4+F	Clm50000	1m(T)	22.11	44.93	1:10.06	1:35.72	38	1/12	3	1^{hd}	$2\frac{1}{2}$	$7^{8\frac{1}{4}}$	$10^{7\frac{1}{2}}$	$12^{27\frac{3}{4}}$	J Velasquez	113	8.70	Sweet Lassie117^{4}$\frac{3}{4}$Miss Primrose115^{3}Think Double108^{hd}	*Battled lead thru fast fractions, tired early turn*
15Apr91	3Aqu	sy	4+F	Clm50000	6f	22.32	46.20		1:12.30	85	4/7	2	$1\frac{1}{2}$	1^{2}		1^{1}	2^{2}	J Velazquez	115	2.20	Gunner Bay117^{2}SothrnSn^{5}MastrPr^{nk}	*Inside speed, gamely*
8Apr91	1Aqu	ft	4+F	Clm35000	6f	22.80	46.34		1:11.16	90	7/7	1	1^{1}	$1^{1\frac{1}{2}}$		$1^{2\frac{1}{2}}$	1^{2}	J Velazquez	115	2.00	Southern Sooner115^{2}Fogg^{3}$\frac{3}{4}$Nor^{3}	*Out from rail, driving*
27Mar91	8Aqu	gd	4+F	Alw28000Nw2x	6f	22.84	45.95		1:11.29	92	3/6	1	$1\frac{1}{2}$	$1^{1\frac{1}{2}}$		1^{2}	1^{nk}	J Velazquez	117	1.70	Southern Sooner117^{nk}Shenandoh^{5}SwetN'ss^{3}	*Speed, lasted*
7Feb91	1Aqi	wf	4+F	Clm50000	6f	22.44	46.90		1:12.51	59	6/7	1	1^{1}	$1\frac{1}{2}$		4^{5}	$5^{9\frac{3}{4}}$	J Velazquez[5]	108 b	1.20	Cliffie113$\frac{3}{4}$Super Appeal$\frac{3}{4}$SolemnVows^{6}$\frac{1}{2}$	*Dueled, gave way*
10Jan91	3Aqi	ft	4+F	Clm35000	6f	22.59	45.81		1:10.24	97	5/8	2	1^{hd}	1^{2}			$1^{4\frac{1}{4}}$	J Velazquez[5]	108	2.50	Southern Sooner108^{4}$\frac{1}{4}$SixNrr^{nk}WeArAW^{hd}	*Good spd; drew off*
19Dec90	9Aqi	my	3+F	Clm25000	6f	22.77	46.96		1:11.89	97	3/7	2	$1^{1\frac{1}{4}}$	1^{3}			$1^{5\frac{3}{4}}$	J Velazquez	110	2.50	Southern Sooner110^{6}$\frac{3}{4}$Northr^{1}$\frac{1}{2}$WisWmn^{nk}	*Good spd; drew off*

The first authentic contender, with a better-than-par figure of 95 versus today's class, and following a 91 versus $35,000 horses June 14 at Belmont Park.

A dyed-in-the-wool frontrunner, Southern Sooner can be expected to run figures from 90 to 97 at the $25,000 to $50,000 claiming levels. He is clearly vulnerable early against today's caliber, having stopped twice when challenged by $50,000 horses and having lost while recording an 85 at the level April 15.

EMBRACING
4yo (Feb) filly, bay
Trainer: Murray Lankford
Owner: Thomas Flynn Jr
$50,000 CLM. PRICE
Sire: Regal Embrace by Vice Regent
Dam: Topper B. Bold by Bold L. B.
Bred in NY by Empire State Breeding Assoc. & Sam Morrell
117
Career: 22 5 5 3
Wet: 1 0 0 0 | Turf: 2 0 0 0 | Dist: 16 5 4 2
1991: 7 1 2 1 $20.395 | 1990: 14 4 2 2 | Sar: 0 0 0 0

21Jly91	7FL	ft	3+F(S)Stk28250	6f	21.77 44.66	1:09.28	76	4/6	6 615 615 513	414	MJ McCarthy	115 b	8.80	Arctic Queen11511Carr Shaker1191½Princess Sybil1171½	Cupecoys Joy — Trailed 5/8 mile, beat tired rivals
29Jun91	3Bel	ft	4+F Clm75000	7f	22.81 45.34 1:09.33	1:22.20	72	6/7	5 74½ 66¾ 610	511½	MJ McCarthy	115 b	5.40	Sioux Narrows1086Carr Shaker1174Rising Sunflower113¾	Outrun, five-wide turn, did not challenge
14Jun91	2Bel	ft	4+F Clm35000	6f	22.57 45.43	1:09.77	88	4/7	6 76½ 74½ 54¾	21½	MJ McCarthy	117 b	11.90	Southern Sooner1171½Embracing1171½Kinklets119nk	Off slowy, inside, steadied late turn, angled out, strong rally
2Jun91	5FL	ft	3+F(S)Alw14300	5½f	22.14 46.16	1:05.68	74	3/6	6 59 59½ 35	13	MJ McCarthy	116 b	1.80	Embracing1163Bob's Genie1½Viking Mistress½	Driving
21May91	10FL	ft	3+F Alw14300Nw2x	6f	22.40 46.60	1:13.09	64	4/9	9 917 910 510	24½	MJ McCarthy	116	2.10	Crafty's Star1194½Embracng½VikngMst1½	Closed willingly
10May91	9FL	ft	3+F(S)Alw14300	5½f	22.27 46.88	1:06.28	60	7/9	9 915 913 57	33	MJ McCarthy	116	7.10	Elfinity1162½Triangle Lady½Embracingno	Late rally
28Apr91	9FL	ft	3+F(S)Alw14300	6f	21.65 44.80	1:10.62	54	2/9	9 915 917 59½	410¾	MJ McCarthy	116	7.90	Elizabeth Parker1194½Elfnty4½Tringl1¾	No speed, gaining
3Dec90	5Aqu	ft	3F Clm35000	6f	22.83 46.65	1:13.03	70	3/9	8 915 810	31½	MJ McCarthy	116	7.70	Plain Pine116½Appealing Lunch¾Embracingno	Late rally
31Oct90	8FL	ft	3+F Alw12500Nw1x	6f	22.50 46.30	1:12.90	66	6/7	7 713 78¾	1½	MJ McCarthy	115 f	1.30	Embracing115½TokyBnd¾MakmHpp1½	Trailed early, driving
9Oct90	11FL	sy	3+F(S)Alw10900Nw1x	6f	23.30 47.70	1:14.50	72	1/6	5 57½ 43	4¾	MJ McCarthy	118	3.70	Magestic Willowa115½RoseOfIronhdMakemHappynk	No excuse

Workouts: 18Jly Bel 4f ft 49.62 B 12Apr FL 4f ft 50.10 B 6Apr FL 3f ft 37.30 B

Embracing's top figure, three back, is 88, while second that day to Southern Sooner and closing. The pair of figures since and before look uninspiring. One competitive figure in an otherwise uncompetitive pattern is always suspect. Embracing has never matched par at today's class and the 4YO cannot defeat Southern Sooner unless the faster horse stops.

HAPPY DAPPLE
6yo (May) mare, gray
Trainer: Jeff Odintz
Owner: Jewel-E Stables
$45,000 CLM. PRICE
Sire: Lejoli ($1,500) by Cornish Prince
Dam: Dapples by Hunters Creek
Bred in NY by Dutch Acres Enterprises, Inc.
113
1989-91: 42 2 13 8
Wet: 4 0 1 0 | Turf: 5 0 1 1 | Dist: 17 1 7 5
1991: 8 0 3 3 $27,940 | 1990: 14 1 5 1 | Sar: 1 0 0 0

6May91	2Aqu	sy	4+F Clm50000	7f	22.68 45.72 1:10.90	1:24.47	73	3/8	7 53 43 52½	52¼	JF Chavez	117 bf	5.00	Master Print117nkSarabelli113noRising Sunflower113nk	Rail throughout, finished evenly
26Apr91	5Aqu	ft	3+F Alw30000Nw3x	6½f	22.41 45.14 1:10.07	1:16.85	84	4/9	8 83¾ 86¾ 75	23	JF Chavez	119 bf	5.40	Northern Willy1193Happy Dapple119hdHer She Shawklit1192	Outrun half mile, split foes upper stretch, closed well
14Apr91	7Aqu	ft	3+F Alw30000Nw3x	7f	22.75 45.78 1:11.45	1:24.66	80	1/7	7 73¾ 75½ 51½	31½	L Ravelo5	114 bf	8.30	Earthy Gal119nkNorthern Willy1191Happy Dapple1142½	Off slowly, rallied wide into stretch, loomed boldly, hung
10Apr91	1Aqu	ft	4+F Clm50000	1m	23.14 45.89 1:10.90	1:37.68	73	1/6	5 53 53 54½ 37	39½	A Cordero Jr	117 bf	2.10	English Charm1136HotBoots3½HappyDappl5½	Inside, evenly
17Mar91	5Aqu	ft	4+F Clm50000	1m	22.82 45.28 1:09.70	1:36.34	88	7/8	4 86¾ 75½ 54½ 42	21½	A Cordero Jr	115 bf	3.80	Splendid You1131½HappyDpplnkMuffy'sMt1¾	Finished gamely
7Feb91	8Aqu	my	4+F Alw30000Nw3x	6f	22.83 46.34	1:11.71	88	2/7	6 68½ 69½ 67	22½	JF Chavez	117 bf	8.70	Bodust1172½HappyDapplnkSharpImageno	Fast finish outside
20Jan91	8Aqu	ft	3+F(S)Stk86550	170	23.82 47.79 1:12.87	1:42.81	79	1/7	4 41½ 53 610	512	HW McCauley	112 bf	2.50	Proud N' Appeal1175Dusty's Talc110nkLady D'accord116nk	Broadway Handicap — Stumbled; kept under stout restraint
6Jan91	1Aqu	ft	4+F Clm50000	6f	22.92 46.44	1:11.29	81	6/7	6 64½ 58	36	JF Chavez	117 bf	1.10	Solemn Vows1065½Cliffie½HappyDappl1	5-wide: late rlly
2Dec90	8Aqu	ft	3+F(S)Stk87000	6f	23.15 47.31	1:11.74	79	8/8	5 73½ 54	48	A Cordero Jr	114 bf	8.80	Jack Betta Be Rite1194½Twixt Appeal1162½Appropriately1141½	Iroquois Stakes — Raced five-wide; offered a mild rally
16Nov90	6Aqu	ft	3+F Alw33000Nw3x	7f	22.84 45.58	1:24.02	80	4/8	6 77¾ 78½	55¾	R Thibeau Jr	117 bf	3.40	Sparkling Hannah112hdWild Warning1¾Tremolos2¾	Bid, hung

Workouts: 20Jly Aqu 3f ft 36.53 H 8Jly Aqu 3f ft 36.00 H

Sprint figures well beneath par. No redeeming virtues. Out.

SUPERSTAR MISS
6yo (Jun) mare, bay
Trainer: John J Lambert
Owner: Star Track Farms
$50,000 CLM. PRICE
Sire: Triocala ($1,000) by Tri Jet
Dam: Superstar Dust by Dewan
Bred in NY by Flying Zee Stables
117
1989-91: 22 [illegible] 7 3
Wet: 6 2 1 0 | Turf: 0 0 0 0 | Dist: 18 7 6 2
1991: 3 1 2 0 $7.834 | 1990: 10 2 3 3 | Sar: 0 0 0 0

18Jun91	5FL	ft	3+F Alw 7500	6f	22.52 46.43	1:12.20	86	2/6	1 11½ 13 14	13½	D Saul	116 b	1.20	Superstar Miss1163½Magestic Willowa1163Proud Puppy1161	Broke sharply, set pace, led throughout, driving
4Jun91	5FL	ft	3+F Alw 8000	6f	21.89 45.53	1:11.90	80	3/6	2 21 22½ 23	28	D Saul	116 b	4.00	Arctic Queen1168Superstar Miss11612Overbend116½	Good early speed, pressed pace, hard used, no match
14May91	5FL	ft	3+F Alw 8500	6f	22.29 45.64	1:12.15	78	2/5	2 23 22 31½	21½	MJ McCarthy	116 b	0.50	Jack Betta Be Rite1161½SuperstarMiss1163½MusicalTranstn1163	Nicely rated, came on gamely, outfinished
4Nov90	6FL	ft	3+ (S)Stk19150	6f	22.10 45.30	1:10.90	58	2/10	7 75 85¾	814½	A Dentici	112 b	4.00	Rodeo Spurs1152Shine Please1155½Rigid View1152½	

(past performance chart for Superstar Miss — Robert Wade Memorial Stakes, Cupecoy's Joy Stakes, Sonnenberg Handicap, and workouts)

Shippers from minor tracks to major tracks at high-priced claiming classes do not belong unless the speed figures earned at the shipping track are superior to par today. A stricter standard requires the shipper to show figures superior to the other contenders.

Superstar Miss's best figure is her last, at 86, not uncommon for shippers arriving at major tracks. But an 86 earned under allowances at Finger Lakes cannot handle $50,000 experienced claiming runners at Saratoga. The situation differs significantly at lower claiming levels and in the nonwinners allowance series, but against established older racehorses, minor league shippers either display the requisite speed figures or handicappers should shun them.

MOON DRONE

(past performance chart for Moon Drone, 4yo (Apr) filly, gray, $45,000 claiming price, Trainer: Michael Lauer, Owner: Barry Ostrager; Sire: Drone by Sir Gaylord, Dam: Cute Little Moon by Ack Ack, Bred in KY by Woodhaven Farm & H. Pat Wood; 113)

Vastly inferior figures afford this shipper scarcely a chance.

VALID DELTA

(past performance chart for Valid Delta, 5yo (Mar) mare, chestnut, $45,000 claiming price, Trainer: Kenneth A Nesky, Owner: Satch T Bear Farm; Sire: Valid Appeal ($20,000) by In Reality, Dam: Delta Dame by Delta Judge, Bred in FL by Harry T. Mangurian, Jr.; 113)

An interesting situation, quite common. The 5YO Valid Delta exits a wire-to-wire romp with its best-ever figure and sails from $17,500 claiming to $50,000 claiming. Multiple jumps in claiming class following big wins and high figures qualify among the best bets of figure handicapping, but only if the class-climber has equaled or exceeded par at today's level. Valid Delta has not. The mare has fallen shy of the 90s by a couple of lengths.

Moreover, the easy 87 has been recorded in the slop and is not reinforced by another speed figure in the record. A figure out of balance with the full record and incompatible with today's conditions—higher class, fast track—amounts to an unreliable figure. In addition, the pace of Valid Delta's mighty surge in the slop also looks uncommonly fast. The mare customarily runs two to five lengths slower to the pace call. Valid Delta appears no real threat to Southern Sooner today.

COMPANY GIRL

4yo (Mar) filly, bay
Trainer: Robert Barbara
Owner: Big Tarpon Stable

$50,000 CLM. PRICE

Sire: **Cormorant ($10,000)** by His Majesty
Dam: **Talcum Blue** by Talc
Bred in NY by Jerry Fishback

117

Career: [illegible] 34 6 4 3 [illegible]

Wet:	8	1	0	0	
Turf:	2	0	0	0	
Dist:	14	1	1	3	
1991:	5	0	1	0	$7,720
1990:	23	6	3	2	
Sar:	2	0	0	0	

21Jly91	1Bel	ft	4+F	Clm50000	7f	22.75	45.33	1:09.25	1:22.55	**40**	7/7	3	4^{2}	5^{5}	5^{12}	$5^{24\frac{3}{4}}$	JD Bailey	117 b	3.30	Daimon112⁵Ciao Ciao Bambina115²½Sophisticated Sam113¹½	*Early factor four-wide, tired badly*
6Jly91	1Bel	ft	4+F	Clm50000	6f	22.62	45.51		1:09.77	**81**	1/8	6	3^{2}	$4^{1\frac{1}{2}}$	3^{3}	$2^{5\frac{1}{2}}$	JA Krone	117 b	3.80	Southern Sooner113⁵½Company Girl117¹½Sparkling Hannah114¾	*Off a bit slowly, moved up on rail, held place gamely*
29Jun91	3Bel	ft	4+F	Clm75000	7f	22.81	45.34	1:09.33	1:22.20	**73**	4/7	3	6^{3}	$5^{8\frac{1}{2}}$	$4^{9\frac{1}{2}}$	$4^{10\frac{3}{4}}$	JA Krone	113	**3.00**	Sioux Narrows108⁶Carr Shaker117⁴Rising Sunflower113¾	*Rated three-wide backstretch, brief bid 5w midturn, lacked rally*
3Jun91	8Bel	ft	3+F	ⓢStk75000 *Hyde Park Handicap*	7f	22.62	45.46	1:10.28	1:23.60	**85**	1/11	10	$10^{8\frac{3}{4}}$	$9^{5\frac{3}{4}}$	4^{4}	$5^{2\frac{3}{4}}$	WH McCauley	114	11.60	Northern Willy114¹Hello Fanny110¹Lilac's Star112nk	*Rated inside, moved two-wide leaving turn, mild rally*
6May91	2Aqu	sy	4+F	Clm50000	7f	22.68	45.72	1:10.90	1:24.47	**77**	8/8	1	$6^{3\frac{1}{2}}$	$7^{3\frac{3}{4}}$	$3^{1\frac{1}{2}}$	$4^{\frac{1}{2}}$	A Cordero Jr	117	10.70	Master Print117nkSarbilnoRisngSnk	*4-wide bid, hung late*
31Dec90	1Aqu	gd	3F	Clm75000	6f	23.29	46.69		1:11.57	**68**	3/7	6	6^{3}	$6^{7\frac{1}{2}}$		$6^{10\frac{1}{2}}$	A Cordero Jr	114	5.10	Sentimentalize118½Joy's JoJo³MajesticAvenger²¾	*Outrun*
19Dec90	5Aqu	my	3F	Clm100000	6f	23.29	47.54		1:12.32	**75**	7/7	5	$6^{4\frac{1}{2}}$	$6^{4\frac{1}{2}}$		4^{6}	A Cordero Jr	113	5.50	Sarabelli115⁵½ShenandoahnkJoy's Jo Jonk	*Bid, hung*
8Dec90	5Aqu	ft	3F	Clm65000	6f	23.38	47.27		1:12.54	**70**	5/7	7	4^{2}	$3^{2\frac{1}{2}}$		$4^{4\frac{1}{2}}$	JD Bailey	116	4.40	Joy's Jo Jo116nkMajesticAvengr¹¾MineralBath²½	*Bid, hung*
25Nov90	8Aqu	ft	3F	ⓢStk87300 *Schenectady Handicap*	6f	21.88	44.95		1:10.25	**79**	5/8	5	6^{9}	6^{8}		$3^{5\frac{3}{4}}$	JD Bailey	116	4.40	Jack Betta Be Rite118²Proud N' Appeal115³¾Company Girl116nk	*Held in reserve; offered a mild rally*
9Nov90	5Aqu	ft	3F	Clm75000	6f	22.68	46.52		1:12.44	**78**	5/9	9	$9^{4\frac{3}{4}}$	$8^{5\frac{1}{2}}$		$4^{1\frac{1}{2}}$	JD Bailey	112	5.80	Shenandoah112nkByDescnt¹½BumaSlwno	*Late rlly; plcd 3rd*

Workouts: 15Jly Bel 5f ft 1:04.80 B 22Jun Bel 5f ft 1:00.25 H 26May Bel 5f ft 2May Bel-tr 4f ft 19Apr Bel 5f ft

Only two good races by Company Girl in the past six, July 8 and June 3, and neither speed figure can threaten this field. No play.

On figure handicapping alone, Southern Sooner looks best here by open lengths. An intense pace attack might upset the cause, but that eventuality does not appear predictable. The only question left is whether Southern Sooner should be bet.

Knowing that consistent claiming horses 4up represent the most reliable bets of figure handicapping, and relaxed about the early-pace contest here, I can take odds as low as 3–2 on Southern Sooner, and any horses like her.

| ② Sar
Saratoga
August 1, 1991 | | SIX FURLONGS. CLAIMING. Purse $22,000. For Fillies and Mares Three Years Old and Upward. Three Year Olds. 117 lbs. Older, 122 lbs. Non-winners of two races since July 1, allowed 3 lbs. Of a race since then, 5 lbs. Claiming price $50,000; for each $2,500 to $45,000, 2 lbs. [Races when entered to be claimed for $40,000 or less not considered.] | | | | | | | | |

Value of Race: $22,000 Winner: $13,200; 2nd: $4,840; 3rd: $2,640; 4th: $1,320

Last Raced	Horse	A	Wt	M/Eq	Jockey	Odds	PP	St	1/4	1/2	Str	Fin	Comments
8Jul91 1Bel¹	Southern Sooner	5	119		JR Velazquez	1.20	3	1	1¹²	1¹¹²	1²¹²	1ᵘᵏ	Made pace inside, edged clear turn, held on, drifted late
23Jun91 6Bel⁸	Joy's Jo Jo	4	117	b	R Migliore	5.40	1	3	3²	2¹²	2²	2ⁿᵏ	Well placed rail, moved out mid-turn, finished gamely
21Jun91 7FL⁴	Embracing	4	117	b	MJ McCarthy	10.20	4	7	6¹²	6¹¹²	3¹	3³	Off a bit slowly, outrun two-wide, rallied, angled in late
6May91 2Aqu⁵	Happy Dapple	6	113	bl	JF Chavez	9.90	5	8	7²¹²	7¹	7¹¹²	4¹³⁴	Off a bit slowly, outrun, moved in turn, angled out, fin evenly
21Jul91 1Bel⁵	Company Girl	4	117	b	JA Krone	6.70	8	6	5³	5ⁿᵈ	5¹	5ⁿᵈ	Five-wide backstretch, rail turn, lacked rally
12May91 7CD⁴	Moon Drone	4	113	b	CA Black	19.80	7	5	8	8	8	6³	Dropped back early, outrun, swung widest for stretch
10Jul91 5Bel⁷	Hucklebuckle	4	117	b	JA Santos	13.10	2	4	4¹¹²	4²	6¹²	7ⁿᵈ	Four-wide, moved closer mid-turn, tired
18Jun91 5FL¹	Superstar Miss	6	117	b	D Saul	4.80	6	2	2¹	3¹²	4¹²	8	Chased winner from outside, tired upper stretch

Parimutuels	$2	W	P	S	Multiple Wagers	Miscellaneous
3 - Southern Sooner	4.40	2.80	2.80		$2 Exacta (3-1) $26.20	Time: 21.91, 44.67, 1:10.26
1 - Joy's Jo Jo		4.60	4.20		$2 Quinella (1-3) $17.40	Won: Driving
4 - Embracing			4.40		$2 Daily Double (3-3) $31.00	Track: Fast
NY OTB: (C) 4.00, 2.60, 2.60 (A) 4.20, 3.80 (D) 4.00					NY OTB: EX(C-A) 24.60 QU(A-C) 16.20 DD(D-C) 29.00	Off: 1:31pm

Forced to set an uncomfortably fast pace to the second call, Southern Sooner was extended, and tired, but lasted. She repeated her 90-ish figure. The odds did not permit a prime bet to win, as disgruntled figure handicappers hasten to remind us nowadays, but a fairly predictable exacta returned 12–1. The solid figure plays of 1992 pay less than their predecessors of the seventies and eighties, but they still win. Patience, remember, is its own reward.

Double-Advantage Horses

Virtually all purveyors of numerical methods in handicapping have touted the singular merits attaching to double-advantage horses. Each of two numbers are superior to the top rating of anything else in the field. Win probabilities soar and so does the rate of return on investment, even though average odds may dwindle.

Modern speed handicapping has experienced the same phenomenon. The most reliable figure bets support horses that consistently have earned higher figures than the opposition. Until these horses decline, they either win or finish close. Figure handicappers are recommended to stay aboard for the ride.

A particularly attractive application of the double-advantage angle targets the lower-priced claiming horses. Below $20,000 claiming, the majority of horses can be consistently inconsistent, advancing and declining on the figure charts in concert with form cycles, pace, distance switches, or the plain unwillingness of sore, relatively unsound animals.

If contenders in low-priced claiming races show two consecutive speed figures superior to any number earned by the others, that's the desirable brand of double-advantage horses. Superior figures in the last two starts always qualify, and the better the latter's overall consistency, the stronger the advantage. Those horses retain sharp form, perhaps for a series of races.

Examine the speed figures of the main contenders of a $5000 claiming race carded at the Los Alamitos bullring, near Los Angeles. It's a 1¹⁄₁₆ mile race for 3up. The horses have just shipped in from Prescott, Turf Paradise, Caliente, Golden Gate Fields, Solano Fair, Hollywood Park, and Stockton Fair, rendering the contest more of a guessing game for handicappers without figures.

NO MAS SIR VESA

Sire: **Rumbo** ($2,000)
by Ruffinal
Dam: **Princess Alya**
by List
Bred in CA by Fred L. Fredericks

$5,000
CLM. PRICE

5yo (May) horse, chestnut
Trainer: Juan Garcia
Owner: Laurie Cecena

Wet:	1 0 0 0	1991:	8 3 3 1	$8,540
Turf:	0 0 0 0	1990:	6 1 0 1
Dist:	17 3 5 3	LA:	3 0 0 1

117 Jesus G Castanon

SUCH A WAGER

Sire: **Secha Pleasure** ($2,500)
by A Pleasure
Dam: **Front Line Wager**
by Agitate
Bred in CA by Theodore L. Folkerth

$5,000
CLM. PRICE

5yo (Feb) gelding, dk. bay/brown
Trainer: Donna Davis
Owner: H Clark, D Davis & R Wiles

Wet:	3 0 2 0	1991:	8 1 0 1	$5,863
Turf:	2 0 1 0	1990:	0 0 0 0
Dist:	21 6 4 2	LA:	0 0 0 0

118 Alex L Fernandez

Derby Trial Stakes

Workouts: 25Jly Fpx 4f ft 50.10 H 9Jly Fpx 4f ft 51.70 H 3Jly Fpx 5f ft 1:04.10 H 5May Fpx 4f ft 52.50 H 17Mar Fpx 5f ft 1:02.50 H

NOSTALGIC DOLPHIN

Sire: **Nostalgia** ($1,000)
by Silent Screen
Dam: **Golden Dolphin**
by Golden Eagle II
Bred in CA by Caesar Wackeen

$5,000
CLM. PRICE

5yo (Mar) horse, chestnut
Trainer: Robert J Moody Jr
Owner: Pauline Moody

Wet:	2 0 0 0	1991:	8 0 0 2	$1,230
Turf:	0 0 0 0	1990:	0 0 0 0
Dist:	12 1 0 2	LA:	0 0 0 0

117 Marco Rangel

Workouts: 28Jly Fpx 5f ft 1:01.70 H 6Apr Fpx 5f ft 1:01.30 H

But one of the horses qualifies as a double-advantage horse on Beyer Speed Figures. Since the horse did not arrive from Hollywood Park, it shaped up as the best figure bet of the evening.

In its last two races, the 5YO gelding Such A Wager has earned route figures of 78 and 80 a month apart while competing on the northern California fair circuit. The next-best speed figure belonged to No Mas Sir Vesa, a 75 at Caliente, a truly minor oval. Next in line was Nostalgic Dolphin's 67, also recorded at the northern California fairs. None of those figures surpass Such A Wager's lower figure. Listed at 4–1 overnight, a stronger figure play than Such A Wager is not easily found. Make the plays double-advantage, and confidently.

Double-advantage horses qualify at all class levels, but they stand out at the bottom levels where inconsistency rules. Search for similar horses below $10,000 claiming, among claiming races restricted to bottom-of-the-barrel three-year-olds, and among the various maiden-claiming plodders.

Double Jumps and Triple Jumps

Andrew Beyer himself first alerted handicappers to the betting coup with speed figures that is now my favorite. It may represent the best racetrack bet of them all. In a chapter devoted to interpretation problems in his excellent *Picking Winners*, Beyer suggested the best use of speed figures might be to predict which claiming horses can rise successfully in class.

If figure handicappers will extend the basic strategy to claiming horses attempting double jumps and triple jumps following wins where they've recorded a speed figure exceeding today's par, they prepare the traps that will lead to several kills a season.

Look carefully at the past performances for the 6YO Royal Eagle below. While evaluating the Beyer Speed Figures, keep in mind that the claiming par near $20,000 claiming is roughly 85 and near $40,000 claiming roughly 95. At major tracks, claiming races carded as high as $75,000-and-above regularly attract horses fully capable of recording speed figures in the low 100s.

In what races might figure handicappers have hammered Royal Eagle successfully at the windows?

ROYAL EAGLE

6yo (Mar) horse, bay
Trainer: Frank Martin
Owner: Viola Sommer

$50,000
CLM. PRICE

Sire: **Beau's Eagle** ($2,500)
  by Golden Eagle II
Dam: **Growing On Trees**
  by Big Spruce
Bred in CA by Kinderhill Corporation

		1989-91:	22	7	5	3	
Wet:	3	1	2	0	**1991:**	7 3 1 3	$61,520
Turf:	1	0	0	0	**1990:**	6 1 1 0	
Dist:	18	5	5	2	Sar:	0 0 0 0	

117

7Jly91 5Bel wf 4↑	Clm50000	6f	22.28 45.21	1:09.70	1/8	2	2^{hd} 1$\frac{1}{2}$	1^1	2nd	A Cordero Jr	117 b	0.80 On A Roll117ndRoyal Eagle117$\frac{3}{4}$Valid Case117^{nk}
												Dueled rail, put away speed, angled out for str battle, gamely
30Jun91 5Bel ft 4↑	Clm100000	6f	22.55 44.92	1:08.29	2/6	8	8$\frac{1}{2}$ 7$\frac{1}{4}$	5^7	3$^{10}\frac{1}{4}$	CA Black	113 b	1.40*Kid Russell108^{3}DD'parrot116^{nk}Royal Eagle113$\frac{1}{2}$
												Brk in a tangle, off slwly, rail til upr str, angld out, mild bid
12May91 1Bel ft 4↑	Clm75000	6f	22.62 45.66	1:08.91	2/5	1	1$\frac{1}{2}$ 1^{hd}	1$\frac{1}{2}$	1$^1\frac{1}{2}$	CA Black	113 b	3.40 Royal Eagle113^{1}Kid Russell113$\frac{3}{4}$Man It's Cold113^7
												Dueled outside, edged clear turn, repulsed bid, long drive
12Apr91 7SA ft 4↑	Clm50000	7f	22.10 44.70 1:09.70	1:22.10	2/10	9	3$\frac{1}{2}$ 1^{hd}	3$^1\frac{1}{2}$	3$^7\frac{1}{2}$	RA Baze	119 Lb	6.30 Avasaurus115$\frac{3}{4}$Happy In Space116^{1}Royal Eagle119$^1\frac{1}{2}$
Claimed from John W Sadler												*Pressed pace, rail trip, weakened in drive*
13Mar91 5SA sy 4↑	Clm50000	6f	21.70 44.70 56.70	1:09.70	2/10	3	1$\frac{1}{2}$ 1^2	1^2	1^4	J Garcia	115 Lb	4.20 Royal Eagle115^{4}Happy In JustOds1$\frac{1}{2}$ *Good speed, drew off*
24Feb91 2SA ft 4↑	Clm40000	6$\frac{1}{2}$f	21.90 44.30 1:09.30	1:15.70	2/6	3	1^1 1$\frac{1}{2}$	1^1	3$^1\frac{1}{2}$	CJ McCarron	115 Lb	2.70 Abergwaun Lad121^{1}KingOfWit^{nk}RoylEg$^2\frac{1}{2}$ *Good speed, tired*
16Jan91 5SA ft 4↑	Clm20000	6f	21.10 43.70	1:08.30	1/12	2	1^{hd} 1^{hd}	1^2	1$^4\frac{1}{2}$	CJ McCarron	115 Lb	6.60 Royal Eagle115$^4\frac{1}{2}$Overidge^{hd}Sum Dandy^{no} *Good spd; driving*
2Jun90 5Hol ft 4↑	Clm16000	6f	21.90 45.10	1:10.30	2/12	7	2^{hd} 2^{hd}	6$^3\frac{1}{2}$	RA Baze	116 Lb	2.70 Billy Euforico116^{hd}Expldd^{1}Latch$^1\frac{1}{2}$ *Spd to 1/2; weakened*
5May90 5Hol ft 4↑	Clm32000	6f	21.70 44.70	1:09.70	8/11	12			5$^5\frac{1}{2}$	RA Baze	117 Lb	2.90 High Hook119$\frac{1}{2}$RightRddr$^1\frac{3}{4}$SuprbMnn$\frac{1}{2}$
19Apr90 7SA ft 4↑	Clm62500	6$\frac{1}{2}$f	21.90 44.90	1:16.70	7/9	2/7	4	4$^2\frac{1}{2}$	5$^{11}\frac{1}{2}$	K Desormeaux	116 Lb	2.90 MovingIikeawinnerII1^{81}AiYMy^{4}Fish$^2\frac{1}{2}$ *In light, no threat*

Workouts: 20Jly Bel   3f ft 35.21 H   21Jun Bel   4f ft 48.07 B   9Jun Bel   4f ft 50.72 B   26May Bel   4f ft   28Apr Hol   4f ft 48.10 H

First, not visible in the record, prior to April of 1990 Royal Eagle had earned speed figures competitive with $40,000 claiming winners. Jaded due to injury and dropping in class during Spring 1990, Royal Eagle's figures declined in kind, barely competitive by June 2 at the $16,000 claiming level.

When Royal Eagle returned to competition in 1991 (at the same $20,000) claiming level, alert figure handicappers might have expected the horse to repeat his back-class figures. If Royal Eagle did at 6–1, no less, he might easily run away from $20,000 horses. The presence of Chris McCarron in the saddle supported that possibility obviously, and so does something else.

One of the sweetest plays of figure handicapping embraces freshened horses having back class and returning from a lengthy vacation against easy opposition. Expect the horses to duplicate figures comparable to the numbers they boasted prior to the recent decline. At generous odds, the risk makes sense. Long-haul, it's a profitable pattern.

So Royal Eagle does win on a fast course January 16 at 1:08.3 seconds, paying $15.00, and recording a Beyer Speed Figure of 98.

Next the horse is triple-jumped to $40,000 claiming, where its 98 will be competitive, but the odds uninviting. As experienced figure handicappers appreciate, the second start following a long layoff and a winning effort or taxing finish often results in a mild regression. The horses "bounce" from the overexertion first back. Because the comeback performance has been so impressive, the odds next time are invariably lower, yet the horses often disappoint.

The third start is the key. Because the horses have now disappointed in the second comeback race, the odds on the third attempt usually rise again. Rely on the speed figure recorded in the comeback race.

On March 13, Royal Eagle again was raised in class, following an excusable loss, from $40,000 to $50,000. A speed figure of 98, recorded in the $20,000 comeback, fits snugly against $50,000 claiming horses. Royal Eagle's 98 was the highest figure in the lineup by a clear margin. The result was an easy victory and $10.40 payoff.

If claiming horses are double-jumped or triple-jumped in a positive way following a big win in which they have earned a figure better-than-par for today's class, do not be fooled. The horses are not outclassed. Speed counts most in claiming races, and the top-figure horse figures, the class climb notwithstanding.

The ensuing races in Royal Eagle's 1991 record are similarly instructive. On the rise March 13, Royal Eagle recorded a 103, competitive with the highest-priced claiming horses at major tracks.

But the time to bet was not the next start. Following a peaking effort, another regression is predictable. Whenever claiming horses do too much, tapping reserves, they can be expected to fall back, at least temporarily. Claiming horses do not possess deep reserves of speed and stamina, as do many nonclaiming horses.

On April 12, entered at the same $50,000 claiming level, Royal Eagle succumbed badly, running an unimpressive 84. But the setback was predictable by savvy figure analysts.

Next out, May 12 at Belmont Park, following the claim by Frank Martin, Royal Eagle is entered against $75,000 claiming horses.

Can he handle the tougher task? Absolutely. The March 13 figure qualifies Royal Eagle as a contender at the $75,000 level. At 3–1, no great bargain on the board, Royal Eagle continues to impress, this day scoring with a speed figure of 107, a best-ever number.

Notice the next two races reveal a repetitive pattern of a setback followed by a bounce-back. The in-out pattern is almost prototypical of older claiming horses suddenly running speed figures that qualify as best-ever numbers. Big effort, setback, and bounce-back. Figure handicappers who learn how to follow the up-and-down patterns will avoid the setbacks and exploit the bounce-backs.

Looking again at Royal Eagle's repeat start at $50,000 claiming on April 12, examine the past performances of the 5YO gelding below.

AVASAURUS

5yo (Mar) gelding, bay
Trainer: Frank Martin
Owner: Viola Sommer

$70,000
CLM. PRICE

Sire: Avatar ($4,000)
by Graustark
Dam: Spectacular Song
by Sensitive Prince
Bred in KY by Parrish Hill Farm

1989-91: 45 10 10 8

Wet: 13 3 2 2
Turf: 0 0 0 0
Dist: 0 0 0 0

1991: 8 3 0 0 $44,150
1990: 20 5 3 4
Sar: 0 0 0 0

113

Date	Race			Class									Jockey	Wt		Comment
16Jun91	5Bel	ft 4-	Clm75000	7f	22.94	45.49 1:10.20 1:23.09	96	4/6	3	42½	3½	1ʰᵈ 16½	JD Bailey	117 b	1.30	Avasaurus117⁅H⁆Such A Dilemma117⁶½Chopo's Image115¹
																4-w, moved up late turn, dueled outside thru stretch, dh 1st
25May91	1Bel	ft 4-	Clm100000	6f	22.85	46.18	1:10.69 92	7/7	6	5⁵	5⁴	6³½ 4⁴	A Cordero Jr	118 b	1.90	Wonderloaf122²¾Proud And Valid116½D'Parrot112½
																Three-wide, fanned five-wide stretch, lacked solid rally
12Apr91	7SA	ft 4-	Clm50000	7f	22.10	44.70 1:09.70 1:22.10 108	5/10	5	10⁷	9⁴	2½ 16½	GL Stevens	115 Lbb	6.20	Avasaurus115⅛Happy In Space116¹Royal Eagle119¹½
																Trailed into far turn, rail trip, split horses, handily
31Mar91	4SA	ft 4-	Clm25000	1⅟₁₆	22.70	46.10 1:10.70 1:42.10 103	3/8	3	53½	3½	2½ 12½ 1⁹	GL Stevens	115 Lbbf	2.50	Avasaurus115⁹Advocate Training115⁴Gonna Get Rich116¹½
	Claimed from Bill Spawr															*Stalked pace, closed strongly far turn, drew off, handily*
22Mar91	5SA	ft 4-	Clm32000	1m	22.50	45.90 1:10.30 1:35.10 88	10/10	7	85½	86½	5⁵ 52½ 55¼	GL Stevens	115 Lbbf	2.50	Dr. Consequences115ᵐᵏSugr²¾Gac¹½	*Wide early, mild rally*
24Feb91	2SA	ft 4-	Clm40000	6⅟₂f	21.90	44.30 1:09.30 1:15.70 88	11/12	5	83½	117¼	82½ 7⁸	GL Stevens	117 Lbbf	8.60	Abergwaun Lad121ⁿKingOfⁿᵏRoylEp²½	*No factor, no excuse*
18Jan91	3SA	ft 4-	Clm50000	6⅟₂f	21.90	44.30	1:15.10 88	11/11	3	4½	4¹½	53½ 56½	L Pincay Jr	117 Lbbf	4.40	Abergwaun Lad119⁾LamsOⁿᵏJonth³½	*Spd to 1/2; weakened*
1Jan91	9SA	ft 4-	Clm62500	1⅟₁₆	23.10	46.50 1:11.30 1:42.70 88	1/10	6	65½	73½	53½ 6⁸ 69½	RO Meza	115 Lbbf	3.90	J. T.'s Pet116¾HotOperatrⁿSpelVctr½	*Rank; no threat*
20Dec90	3Hol	ft 3-	Clm40000	7f	21.90	44.90	1:21.70 100	5/6	5	44½	4³	42½ 1½	GL Stevens	115 Lbbf	1.00	Avasaurus115½Sun Streak117¹¾One For Nana116²½
	Claimed from Frank Martin															*Held in reserve; driving*
8Dec90	6Hol	ft 3-	Clm40000	7f	22.50	45.10	1:21.50 94	8/8	3	7¹½	53½	2ʰᵈ 2½	GL Stevens	115 Lbbf	5.30	Sensational Star117½Avsrs⁴½Magnt¹	*Mild rlly; 2nd best*

Workouts: 28Jly Sar 5f ft 59.32 B   17Jly Bel 5f ft 1:00.52 H   8Jly Bel 4f ft 49.98 B   28Jun Bel 4f ft 47.05 H   14Jun Bel 4f ft 47.73 H

Avasaurus demolished the $50,000 field April 12 in a classic illustration of the figure horse rampantly on the improve and being triple-jumped in claiming price while carrying a winning figure with him.

While racing routinely and recording nondescript speed figures, suddenly Avasaurus wins by nine and gets a 103 figure when dropped March 31 one level to $25,000 claiming. The 103 surpasses par at the $50,000 claiming level. Avasaurus also shows there assuring back class.

Sure enough, following the big win and the claim, Avasaurus appears twelve days later for a $50,000 tag. As usual, racegoers at Santa Anita could not tolerate the rapid climb in class, especially following the horse's claim from Bill Spawr, a leading claiming trainer on the southern Califonia circuit.

But experienced figure handicappers set themselves for a major bet. The main opposition to Avasaurus April 12 on the numbers was our acquaintance Royal Eagle. Both horses had recorded 103s last out. But as handicappers have seen, Royal Eagle had every reason to regress April 12, and Avasaurus fit the profile of a peaking, rising claiming horse perfectly.

If claiming horses have been racing regularly and suddenly record a monster figure while winning easily, and follow that with a double jump or triple jump in class, string along. The public will shy from the horses, but excellent figure handicappers will be pursuing some of their sweetest bets of the month. At any claiming level the best horses can run approximately five lengths faster than par. Five lengths translate to acrobatic leaps in class for peaking horses, notably those possessing back class comparable to today's.

Following his tremendous effort at 6–1 versus $50,000 horses, Avasaurus also regressed approximately five lengths, earning 92 and 96 in his next two races. Peaking performances soon give way to normal performances.

Improving and Declining Figures

Figure handicappers continually must assess whether horses should repeat their latest figure, improve it, or decline. When sharp enough to win, a majority of experienced racehorses (3up) will record speed figures within five to seven lengths of a few core numbers, up or down. The fluctuations can be assigned to numerous interrelated factors, including the vagaries of thoroughbred form, early pace, trips that vary from perfect to troubled, track biases, and even jockey tactics.

Below, consider a typical array of $20,000 claiming horses showing patterns of improvement and decline that reappear every day. Let's begin with a clear case of improvement.

The 4YO gelding has completed just ten races, the record characterized by almost continuous improvement since the maiden-claiming win of August 10, 1990. That sprint earned Danish To Go a speed figure of 80. While moving ahead in claiming class as a 4YO, Danish To Go's figures have improved from 81 to 84 and 83, then to 88 versus $16,000 horses last out.

What about Danish To Go's 62 of June 15 at Golden Gate Fields? Ignore it. The gelding should not have been stretched from $12,500 state-bred claiming to an allowance try. The poor figure, out of whack with surrounding performances, is characteristic of an overly ambitious class maneuver. Handicappers can ignore disappointing speed figures that obviously qualify as unrepresentative.

What figure might Danish To Go be expected to muster today, versus $20,000 claiming horses at a mile? Should handicappers anticipate another 88, a better figure, or lower?

The class move ahead by one step is perfectly acceptable. Following wins and good races, claiming horses can be accepted at one level higher. Danish To Go won driving last out, so a figure of 88 might represent a maximum. Danish To Go just as readily could fall back to 83 or 84. When claiming horses 4up improve by several lengths while extended against slightly inferior company, they usually will not exceed themselves next time, unless the horses have back class and have won powerfully, and are rampantly on the improve.

A best estimate finds Danish To Go duplicating the 88 against $20,000 company. If the step-up proves troublesome, Danish To Go will probably repeat its more familiar figures of 83 or 84. Should the 88 of July 6 plunge to 83 or 84 today, Danish To Go will probably approach those numbers again when sharp enough to win and realistically spotted. Should the 88 improve to 90, alternately, Danish To Go might simply be a faster racehorse than is now apparent.

Patterns of improvement in claiming races for older horses are customarily incremental, the positive flow sometimes ending at a peaked performance. If the peak performance has been followed by a decline to normal numbers, expect those figures in the future. If the seemingly peak performance is followed instead by additional improvement, anticipate those numbers in the future as well.

The improving horse's opposite number will frequently look like this:

Bold But Valid's figures have declined twice in succession since its impressive allowance score at 85 June 15. At the same or lower class levels, two declining figures in succession amount to bad news. Another class drop, such as Bold But Valid takes to $20,000 today, cannot be expected to reverse the negative pattern. At best, the declining horse might rerun its most recent figure at today's relative class, the 83 two races back for Bold But Valid. The decline more likely will continue.

CHANCYLEIGH
5yo (Mar) gelding, dk. bay/brown — **$20,000** CLM. PRICE
Trainer: David Hofmans
Owner: George Layman Jr
Sire: **Native Uproar** ($1,500) by Raise A Native
Dam: **Oversold** by Barbizon
Bred in KY by J R Bettersworth
1989-91: 34 8 8 4
Wet: 5 2 1 1 | **Turf:** 5 1 0 1 | **Dist:** 8 1 2 2
1991: 9 0 2 1 $17,450 | **1990:** 16 4 4 3 | **Dmr:** 2 0 0 0
116 Julio Garcia

18Jly91 7Hol ft 3+ Clm32000 1⅛ 23.30 46.70 1:11.30 1:43.90 (73) 6/6 4 42 41¼ 31 22 26 DR Flores 116 LBb 5.30 Well Aware1166Chancyleigh1162Idea Que1162
4-wide throughout, bid into stretch, hung final furlong
10Jly91 5Hol ft 4+ Clm40000 1⅛ 23.70 46.50 1:10.30 1:42.70 (83) 2/7 7 77¾ 78½ 66 56 67 DR Flores 116 LBb 12.90 J. L.'s Tribute117½Runaway Dunaway1161Porcupine Ridge1162¾
Trailed for half, rallied inside through far turn, flattened out
19Jun91 7Hol ft 4+ Clm32000 7½f 22.50 45.10 1:09.70 1:28.50 (87) 2/8 8 89¼ 810 34 34¾ E Delahoussy 117 LBb 12.00 Hot Operator1172That's The One1172¾Chancyleigh1172½
Trailed for half, split horses in stretch
19May91 4Hol ft 4+ Clm32000 6½f 22.10 44.10 1:08.30 1:15.10 **83** 4/8 8 88¼ 811 78½ 67 L Pincay Jr 117 LBb 11.80 One For Nana116¾HotOprt½That'sT1¾ *Passed tired horses*
31Mar91 10GG fm 4+ Clm50000 1⅙ Ⓣ24.10 49.90 1:14.50 1:45.10 **72** 3/9 9 98¼ 82¾ 62¼ 63¼ 86¼ RD Hansen 117 LBb **2.30** Rolandthemonarch117½FatdFrF½CannnBr1½ *Moved up, tired*
15Mar91 8GG ft 4+ Clm40000 6f 21.50 43.90 56.30 1:09.10 **83** 6/6 6 617 613 64¼ 43¼ RD Hansen 115 Lb **0.90** Damaskim1121½Blaze Borealis1151½Steel An Emperor115nk
Claimed from Jerry Hollendorfer — *Steadied at start, lost contact with field, mild late rally*
22Feb91 3GG ft 4+ Clm40000 6f 22.10 44.50 56.30 1:08.90 **85** 4/6 5 610 69 34½ 22½ RD Hansen 117 LBb 2.70 Happy Idiot1192½Chancylgnk Damaskm3 *Trailed, mild rally*
3Feb91 8GG my4+ Stk30700 1⅛ 23.50 47.10 1:12.10 1:43.90 **82** 6/6 6 69½ 512 613 43¼ 47 RD Hansen 115 LBbf 2.40 Coax Me Clyde1161Beau's Alliance1123Fairly Affirmed1093
Hallowed Envoy Handicap — *Altered course: couldn't keep up early*
19Jan91 6BM fm 4+ Stk28000 1m Ⓣ25.10 50.10 1:14.50 1:38.90 **79** 5/7 7 76 74¾ 55¼ 58 RD Hansen 115 LBbf 3.60 Neskimo1122½Patchy Groundfog1171Nediym1201½
Old River Ranch Handicap — *Trailed in early going; offered a mild rally*
31Dec90 7BM fm 3+ Stk28000 1m Ⓣ24.10 48.30 1:12.90 1:38.90 **80** 2/8 7 73 84 44½ 32½ B Snyder 115 LBbf 3.60 Chief Terra Cotta117½Beau's Alliance1142Chancyleigh115nk
Fujii Farms Handicap — *Taken up by jockey; checked repeatedly*

Workouts: 3Jly Hol 5f ft 1:02.70 H — 15Jun Hol 5f ft 58.50 H — 15May Hol 4f ft 48.10 H — **30Apr GG 5f ft 1:00.10 H** — **23Apr GG 4f ft 46.50 H**

Chancyleigh offers another glimpse at a declining horse. At the same relative class level, this 5YO's figures have declined twice in succession, the last out a steep drop. Do not anticipate today's class drop to $20,000 will resurrect Chancyleigh's current form, or its speed figures.

When sharp anew, what figures should Chancyleigh be expected to earn? Roughly 83 to 87, but as high as 89.

BOOGIEBOARD BOY
4yo (Apr) gelding, bay — **$20,000** CLM. PRICE
Trainer: Ralph S Crews
Owner: Robert & Marguerite Hathaway
Sire: **Pirate's Bounty** ($10,000) by Hoist The Flag
Dam: **Wicked Fall** by Grenfall
Bred in CA by Martin J. Wygod
Career: 13 1 0 3
Wet: 0 0 0 0 | **Turf:** 0 0 0 0 | **Dist:** 5 0 0 1
1991: 13 1 0 3 $25,975 | **1990:** 0 0 0 0 | **Dmr:** 0 0 0 0
116 Daniel Sorenson

14Jly91 5Hol ft 4+ Clm25000 7f 21.70 44.30 1:10.30 1:23.10 **70** 10/10 2 65¼ 78 86 65½ LE Ortega 116 LB 22.00 Andimo1162Dirty Old Man1161¼Bold But Valid118½
Wide through far turn, no response in stretch
30Jun91 4Hol ft 4+ Clm20000 1⅛ 22.90 46.30 1:10.70 1:43.30 (85) 3/9 2 11 2½ 2hd 22 32¾ LE Ortega 115 LB 35.60 Yourcastleofdreams115¾GoldenSoldier1172BoogieboardBoy1151½
Good speed, pressed pace to deep stretch, weakened late
9Jun91 7Hol ft 3+ Alw35000Nw1x 1⅛ 23.10 45.90 1:10.30 1:43.70 **70** 5/7 6 65½ 68½ 58½ 611 510 RJ Faul 118 Lb 59.10 Expreso Brazil121½King Turk1144½King's Canyon114hd
Outrun throughout, overmatched
27May91 1Hol ft 4+ Clm20000 1⅛ 23.10 46.30 1:10.90 1:45.30 **70** 4/7 6 65 76¼ 56½ 54 43½ RJ Faul 115 Lb 28.20 Spell Victorious1152¾Lyphn¾Goldno *No speed, mild rally*
1May91 9Hol ft 4+ Clm32000 7½f 22.30 45.10 1:10.30 1:29.30 **65** 4/12 10 115¼ 1110 89¼ 814 H Torres5 112 Lb 51.80 Softshoe Sure Shot1174½That'2¾PowrF1¼ *Passed tired ones*
14Apr91 1SA ft 4+ Clm20000 6½f 21.90 45.10 1:10.90 1:17.70 **72** 2/9 6 51¾ 33 41 4¾ H Torres5 110 Lb 43.90 Past Ages117nkGoTThWnnkServcAcnk *Rail trip, outfinished*
28Mar91 5SA ft 4+ ▣Clm12500 6½f 22.10 45.30 1:10.90 1:17.30 **40** 10/10 1 1hd 41¾ 108¾ 1014 JA Santos 115 LB **1.20**eThe Great Tioga1191¾Givots Four113½Estranged1152¾
Claimed from Victor J Nickerson — *Close up wide backside, stopped abruptly*
17Mar91 9SA ft 4+ Clm20000 1⅛ 23.10 46.50 1:10.70 1:43.10 **75** 5/10 8 11 1½ 21 33½ 57 JA Santos 113 LB 15.30 Magnetized1151¼Acrosswrd1¼OrignlTrp1 *Good speed, empty*
10Mar91 2SA ft 4+ Clm16000 6f 21.90 44.90 57.30 1:10.50 **78** 1/9 9 1½ 2hd 3½ 53¼ JA Santos 115 LB 10.50 Run On Home1152HajasalhdCragRnl1 *Hustled early, tired*
17Feb91 1SA ft 4+ ▣Clm16000 6f 21.70 44.70 56.90 1:09.90 **78** 7/9 7 54 75½ 76 35¾ JA Santos 114 LB 4.40 My Lucky Lynnie1154½SeizThChnc1¼BoogibrdBy1 *Late rally*

Workouts: 30Jly Dmr 5f ft 59.90 H — 24Jly Dmr 4f ft 48.10 H — **9Jly Fpx 5f ft 1:01.70 H** — **26Jun Fpx 5f ft 59.90 H** — 20Jun Fpx 5f ft 1:00.50 H

Among claiming horses 4up, whenever an isolated figure sticks out suspiciously, it's probably a fake. Boogieboard Boy's

85 two back surprised and has numerical support neither before the race nor since. Rely today on the horse's core numbers of 70 to 76.

LATEST RELEASE(IRE)

Sire: Kris ($133,000) by Sharpen Up
Dam: Irish Edition by Alleged
Bred in IRE by Moyglare Stud Farm Ltd

1989-91: 27 2 4 6

Wet: 1 0 0 0 | Turf: 14 2 1 2 | Dist: 6 0 1 1

1991: 7 0 0 2 $3.900 | 1990: 7 0 1 2 | Dmr: 2 0 0 2

5yo (Feb) gelding, chestnut — $20,000 CLM. PRICE
Trainer: Julio C Canani
Owner: Segal, Segal & Xitco

116 Frank Alvarado

7Jly91 4Hol ft 3+ StrAlw10000 1 3/16 23.50 46.70 1:11.10 1:55.90 (84) 6/8 7 5⁶ 5⁷ 3³ 2²½ 3⁴¾ GL Stevens 114 LBb 3.20 Realness117¹¾Riflemaker114³Latest Release114²¾ — *Rallied through far turn, bid into upper stretch, outfnshd late*

29Jun91 10Hol ft 4+ Clm10000 1 3/16 23.10 47.30 1:12.10 1:56.30 (81) 8/12 11 12¹¹ 10¹² 6³ 4⁴½ 3³¾ E Delahoussy 116 LBb 4.70 Riflemaker118²½Litigated110¹¼Latest Release116³ — Claimed from Victor J Nickerson — *Trailed briefly, began picking off horses far turn, late rally*

27May91 9GG fm 4+ Clm25000 1½ Ⓣ 49.10 1:14.50 1:40.30 2:31.10 77 1/7 7 7⁹½ 7⁷ 7⁷ 7⁷¼ 6⁷½ R Sibille 116 LBb 3.70 Nice Balloon117ʰᵈMountain Storm119⁴Far Out Bet117² — *Never a factor*

19May91 10Hol fm 3+ StrHcp25000 1¼ Ⓣ 23.90 47.10 1:35.10 2:00.50 82 2/12 12 12¹⁸ 11¹⁴ 11¹⁴ 10⁸ 9⁸¼ JA Santos 114 LBb 35.80 Timdala113²Bet Mehmetʰᵈ FrequentFlyer½ — *Trailed, outrun*

5May91 1Hol ft 4+ Clm25000 1⅛ 23.50 47.30 1:11.70 1:50.30 66 3/8 7 6⁸ 6⁷ 6⁵ 7⁸½ 7¹³¼ RJ Faul 115 LBb 29.00 Runaway Dunaway115¹½Partnr³½WellAⁿᵏ — *Lugged in last half*

20Apr91 3GG fm 4+ Clm40000 1⅛ Ⓣ 25.10 50.10 1:14.90 1:51.90 80 5/7 7 7⁶ 6⁵ 7⁴¼ 7⁵¾ 6⁵½ TM Chapman 115 LBb 14.70 Rolloutthebarrel119ʰᵈIdeaQue²PrivatEnqry½ — *No response*

6Apr91 9SA ft 4+ Clm32000 1 1/16 22.90 46.70 1:11.30 1:42.70 77 6/11 10 11¹¹ 10⁹¼ 9⁵¼ 10⁶ 10¹⁰½ R Faul 115 LBb 32.30 Mount Laguna115ⁿᵏGachAl²IdeaQ½ — *Pinched turn, no rally*

5Jly90 5Hol fm 4+ Clm62500 1¼ Ⓣ 24.10 48.10 1:36.10 2:00.70 75 2/7 6 6⁸¼ 6¹² 5¹⁷ RD Davis 113 Lb 5.60 Putting116⁶½RoylAssgnmʰᵈClearViwBy⁶ — *In hand; lugged in*

16Jun90 9Hol fm 3+ Clm62500 1½ Ⓣ 49.50 2:27.90 (88) 3/8 8 8¹² 6³½ 4⁵¼ C Nakatani 109 Lb 4.30 Novelty113¹½MySonnyBoy³½RoundRivrⁿᵏ — *Off slow; mild rlly*

19May90 9Hol fm 4+ Clm80000 1¼ Ⓣ 48.30 1:36.50 2:00.70 (89) 3/8 8 8¹⁴ 8⁹ 6⁸½ C Nakatani 112 Lb 9.60 Rosen116²My Sonny Boy½Novelty¹¼ — *No speed; no excuse*

Latest Release continues to improve, earning an 84 in the $10,000 starter allowance series last out, a race handicappers can equate to open $20,000 claiming. Figure handicappers might look avidly for Latest Release's top figures during other positive form cycles, but they would be puzzled here. The record shows 88 and 89 speed figures during spring 1990, but those races occurred on the grass. Latest Release might be expected to improve again today, but how much? No one knows. Prefer the latest figure as a best estimate.

PRIME CONCORD

Sire: Super Concorde by Bold Reasoning
Dam: Valinda by Yelapa
Bred in KY by Catherine C Melrose

1989-91: 26 7 5 5

Wet: 0 0 0 0 | Turf: 0 0 0 0 | Dist: 16 4 4 4

1991: 5 2 0 1 $18.775 | 1990: 15 3 3 2 | Dmr: 3 1 1 0

7yo (May) gelding, bay — $20,000 CLM. PRICE
Trainer: Sanford Shulman
Owner: Clear Valley Stable

116 Kent J Desormeaux

13Jly91 2Hol ft 4+ Clm12500 1 1/16 23.70 46.50 1:10.70 1:42.90 (88) 2/8 1 1² 1¹ 1² 1³ 1³½ K Desormeaux118 LBb 1.50 Prime Concord118³½Crack In The Ice115⁶Hero Worker117¹½ — *Clear lead early, bore out backstretch, driving*

6Jly91 1Hol ft 4+ Clm16000 1 1/16 23.10 46.90 1:10.10 1:43.70 83 6/7 5 1ʰᵈ 2ʰᵈ 2ʰᵈ 2½ 3²½ K Desormeaux118 LBb 3.40 Danish To Go116²½Just Jennings115ʰᵈPrime Concord118¹½ — *Broke out of gate prior to start, dueled to stretch, weakened*

23Jun91 1Hol ft 4+ Clm16000 1⅛ 23.50 46.90 1:11.50 1:51.50 83 4/8 1 1½ 1ʰᵈ 1²½ 1² 1ⁿᵒ K Desormeaux115 LBb 2.80 Prime Concord115ⁿᵒJust Jennings115²½Petronack110²¾ — *Broke out of gate at start, bore out throughout, lasted, driving*

16Jun91 1Hol ft 4+ Clm20000 6f 22.10 44.50 57.10 1:09.90 86 5/8 2 2½ 3²½ 4⁶ 5⁹½ K Desormeaux116 LBb 3.30 Black Boots116ʰᵈDr. Hart⁴Smart Too²½ — *Bore out, evenly*

2Jun91 4Hol ft 4+ Clm20000 6f 21.90 44.90 57.30 1:10.30 95 2/10 7 6³½10⁸½ 10¹⁴ 9¹⁴ GL Stevens 116 LBb 12.50 Stan's Boy116⁴½RednckW¹½JetChrʰᵈ — *Took up, placed eighth*

3Oct90 9SA ft 3+ Clm16000 1 1/16 22.90 46.50 1:10.90 1:43.10 73 8/8 1 3² 3¹½ 6⁶ 8¹¹½ P Valenzuela 118 LBb 1.70 Desert Empire116ⁿᵏRaKish¾RoylCmr¹¼ — *Wide trip; weakened*

25Aug90 9Dmr ft 3+ Clm25000 1m 23.10 46.50 1:11.10 1:36.30 (90) 1/7 1 1½ 1½ 2³ P Valenzuela 120 Lb 1.70 Saucy Sam116³PrimCncrdⁿᵏMagnetzd²¾ — *Good spd; outfnshed*

12Aug90 9Dmr ft 3+ Clm25000 1 1/16 23.30 46.50 1:10.70 1:42.70 ([illegible]) 3/7 1 1¹½ 1² 1½ P Valenzuela 116 Lb 2.60 Prime Concord116½BetMehmt²HandsmKⁿᵏ — *Good spd; driving*

5Aug90 9Dmr ft 3+ Clm32000 1 1/16 23.10 45.70 1:10.10 1:42.10 76 4/10 1 1ʰᵈ 2ʰᵈ 8¹⁰½ A Solis 118 Lb 7.60 My Partner117⁴½CancnNtvⁿᵏChessSetⁿᵏ — *Good spd; lugged in*

24Jun90 3Hol ft 4+ Clm40000 1 1/16 46.70 1:11.70 1:44.50 72 2/7 1 2½ 1ʰᵈ 6⁶½ A Solis 116 Lb 3.70 Babyitscoldoutside117ʰᵈOsty²Hol¹¼ — *Spd to 1/2; weakened*

Prime Concord improved by several lengths last out, recording an 88 speed figure while winning handily. The full record suggests that a 90 today would not be surprising. Prime Concord earned that figure last season against today's relative class during an improvement pattern.

When older claiming horses improve, try to find similar patterns in the record. If the patterns appear, expect a repeat.

Speed figures have sorted the lineup above into three declining horses and three improving contenders. Which of the contenders figures best?

Horse	Figure	Pattern
Danish To Go	88	Improve to 90, or rebound to 83, 84
Latest Release	84	Improve to 86, 87
Prime Concord	88	Improve to 90

If the odds on Prime Concord allow a prime bet, it belongs there. Danish To Go requires inviting odds, a potential overlay bet, but no betting support as the favorite or a low-priced contender. Latest Release cannot be supported to win, but qualifies on the undersides of exactas.

The following patterns are typical of high-priced three-year-olds traveling six furlongs. Three-year-olds differ from older horses, and so do the configurations of their speed figures.

First, three-year-old claiming horses run slower than their older counterparts by two to three lengths in sprints, five lengths at a mile, and by six to seven lengths at middle distances. Using Beyer Speed Figures, if the sprint par for older $25,000 claiming horses is approximately 80, the corresponding par for races restricted to 3YOs is approximately 75. At $50,000 claiming, the older par will be roughly 90 and the corresponding 3YO par will be roughly 85. Because the figures have been weighted differently at the distinct distances, the pars hold stable in sprints and routes. Let's review the $50,000 3YO claiming field.

Claiming and nonclaiming, whenever a 3YO shows sudden, dramatic improvement, handicappers can accept the evidence at face value. Cadillac Red certainly fits the profile. Dropped into claiming competition following nondescript allowance races and figures, Cadillac Red won impressively and registered a speed figure of 84.

Once dramatic improvement has occurred, handicappers should expect continual but gradual improvement, and figure handicappers should expect slightly higher figures. In claiming races, prefer 3YOs rising in class following sharp wins and anticipate another two-to-three-length improvement. Cadillac Red passes as a contender against $50,000 three-year-olds. His 84 figure versus $32,000 horses July 29 might improve to 86 to 88 range today.

If Cadillac Red instead regresses against the $50,000 competition, the 84 figure remains the best indicator of its talent, and $32,000 claiming and below represent the desirable class levels. And regardless of how well Cadillac Red performs in high-priced claiming neighborhoods, the gelding does not belong in 3YO allowance company. Its figures have announced that loudly already.

As a general rule, figure handicappers should classify 3YOs according to their best performance in the past 120 days against the most advanced eligibility conditions they've tackled. Ignore the 2YO record.

Unable to beat nonwinners of one allowance race, but competitive at the allowance level while recording solid figures, Got To Fly is practically prototypical of the 3YOs that can be expected to dominate claiming conditions. Not only do speed figures of 88 and 89 surpass the 3YO $50,000 claiming par, they usually have been recorded following the faster, more strongly contested pace dispensed by allowance types.

The dropdown from 3YO allowances to 3YO claiming is tremendous.Even when the allowance figures look marginal, the horses often prevail, and sometimes win big. When the allowance figures look dominant, as does Got To Fly's, the case is closed, unless another 3YO of similar stripes appears in the entries. Claiming horses cannot defeat this kind, even when their figures look competitive. Whenever the price is right, take it.

PIRATE'S OUTLOOK

Sire: Pirate's Bounty ($10,000)
by Hoist The Flag
Dam: Honeyofaprospect
by New Prospect
Bred in CA by Martin J. Wygod

3yo (Apr) gelding, bay **$50,000** CLM. PRICE
Trainer: Clifford Sise Jr
Owner: Deeb, Deeb & Rain

Career:	6	2	1	1		$24,705
Wet:	0 0 0 0	$0	1991:	6 2 1 1	$24,705
Turf:	0 0 0 0	$0	1990:	0 0 0 0	$0
Dist:	6 2 1 1	$24,705	Dmr:	0 0 0 0	$0

115 Laffit Pincay Jr

Workouts: 28July Dmr 5f ft 1:01.90 H   22July Dmr 3f ft 35.50 H   7July Hol 6f ft 1:14.50 H   30Jun Hol 6f ft 1:13.30 H   24Jun Hol 5f ft 1:00.50 H

As do numerous 3YOs, Pirate's Outlook won big against maiden-claiming competition and continued to improve gradually when tested against winners. Today the gelding takes a very logical step-up in class. The figure provides a telltale clue. With the $50,000 par approximately 85, Pirate's Outlook's 82 does not signal success at the higher level. Even if the gradual improvement perseveres, today's figure should be 84 or 85, not quite strong enough.

More likely, Pirate's Outlook will decline in the $50,000 context. When the speed figure does not surpass par on the rise, horses customarily fall back. Not only should today's final time be faster, so should the pace, not to mention the deeper reserves of endurance and determination of the classier horses.

IRON PLEASURE

Sire: Foolish Pleasure ($15,000)
by What A Pleasure
Dam: Exiled
by Iron Ruler
Bred in KY by S. A. LeThenney

3yo (Mar) colt, dk. bay/brown **$50,000** CLM. PRICE
Trainer: Mike Puhich
Owner: Al & Sandee Kirkwood

Career:	10	1	1	2		$42,600
Wet:	3 0 0 1	$13,500	1991:	7 1 0 1	$31,600
Turf:	0 0 0 0	$0	1990:	3 0 1 1	$11,000
Dist:	8 1 1 2	$41,850	Dmr:	0 0 0 0	$0

115 No rider

Workouts: 29July Dmr 4f ft 46.90 H   6July SA 4f ft 48.50 H   30Jun SA 4f ft 48.70 H   17Jun SA 4f ft 47.70 H   7Jun SA 7f ft 1:27.70 H

SLEW'S CROWN

3yo (Mar) gelding, bay
Trainer: Don Collins
Owner: Edward C Allred

$50,000
CLM. PRICE

Sire: **Slew's Royalty ($5.000)**
by Seattle Slew
Dam: **Gairosiere**
by Gairloch
Bred in CA by Central Farm

Career: 4 3 0 0 $36.300

Wet:	0	0	0	0	$0	**1991:**	4 3 0 0		$36.300
Turf:	0	0	0	0	$0	**1990:**	0 0 0 0		$0
Dist:	4	3	0	0	$36.300	**Dmr:**	0 0 0 0		$0

115 Julio Garcia

12Jly91	8Hol	ft 3+	Ⓢ Alw32000Nw1x	6f	21.70	43.90	56.50	1:09.70	81	5/9	1	2^{1}	2^{1}½	2^{2}½	6^{5}	J Garcia	113 LB	4.00	Sligo's Ridge116²Zee Maestro113²¾Pappy Yokum118^no	*Pressured pace, between horses, lugged in late*
29Jun91	3Hol	ft 3	Clm40000	6½f	22.10	44.90	1:09.70	1:16.30	83	1/7	5	1^{hd}	1^{2}	1^{3}	1^{1}¼	J Garcia	116 LB	2.20	Slew's Crown116¹¼Sally's Prince116¹½Fiesta Fair116⁴½	*Rated early, drew clear far turn, lasted through lane*
Claimed from Hector O Palma																				
16Jun91	4Hol	ft 3	Clm32000	6½f	22.10	44.90	1:10.10	1:16.50	83	1/8	7	1^{2}	1^{2}	1^{2}	1½	J Garcia	119 LB	4.30	Slew's Crown119½Sally's Prince116⁴½Publicity's Lad116³½	*Good speed, came out repeatedly through stretch, won driving*
16May91	2Hol	ft 3+	MCl32000	6½f	22.10	44.90	1:09.90	1:16.90	77	9/12	3	1^{2}	1^{2}	1^{3}	1^{5}	J Garcia	115 LB	3.80	Slew's Crown115⁵He'sDomineering¾JamieJon¹¼	*Ridden out*

Workouts: 29Jly Dmr 5f ft 58.90 H **24Jun Hol 4f ft 45.90 H** 9Jun Hol 5f ft 1:01.30 H 1Jun Hol 5f ft 1:01.50 H 24May Hol 4f ft 51.30 H

As suggested, 3YOs are best evaluated by inspecting their best figure against the most advanced competition in the recent record. Iron Pleasure earned an 80 six races back against maidens. That figure cannot defeat $50,000 claiming horses. Iron Pleasure probably will require successive drops in the claiming division before a comfortable level is found.

Slew's Crown earned an 83 against $40,000 claiming competition. The figure was repeated, followed by a small tail-off in a state-bred allowance race. If the allowance race had been open to all comers, Slew's Crown might figure to beat high-priced claiming horses. Some improvement is feasible at the $50,000 level, but not enough. The best figure by Slew's Crown remains an 83. The horse will probably be outrun today.

INTIMATE KID

3yo (Mar) gelding, chestnut
Trainer: William Shoemaker
Owner: Burt Bacharach

$50,000
CLM. PRICE

Sire: **T. V. Commercial**
by T. V. Lark
Dam: **Intimate Girl**
by Medaille D'Or
Bred in WV by Blue Seas Music, Inc.

Career: 8 2 2 0 $51,910

Wet:	3	1	1	0	$8.325	**1991:**	3 0 1 0		$22.625
Turf:	0	0	0	0	$0	**1990:**	5 2 1 0		$29.285
Dist:	6	1	1	0	$46.210	**Dmr:**	0 0 0 0		$0

115 Chris J McCarron

16Jun91	7GG	ft 3+	Alw25000Nw2x	6f	21.50	44.10	56.70	1:09.70	77	9/9	1	2^{1}	2^{1}	4^{2}	6^{2}¾	TM Chapman	113 B	4.50	It's Courting Time119½Ninja Prince122^noDesert Waltz119^nk	*Pressed early pace, tired*
14Mar91	3SA	my3	Alw35000Nw2x	6½f	21.90	45.10	1:10.90	1:17.70	[illegible]	1/4	3	1^{hd}	2½	4^{2}	4^{9}¾	CJ McCarron	115 B	2.70	Jimjen115⁵Unreal Ragout115³Shining Prince115¹¾	*Pressed early pace, empty drive*
18Feb91	8GG	ft 3	Hcp100000	6f	21.10	43.30	55.90	1:09.10	81	2/6	2	2½	2^{1}½	3^{1}	2^{2}½	TM Chapman	117	10.40	Media Plan119²½Intimate Kid117¹½Unreal Ragout117¹½	*Pressured the early pace, useful effort*
28Dec90	8SA	ft 2	Stk79800	6f	21.50	44.30		1:08.70	78	4/5	2	2^{hd}	2^{hd}	3^{5}	4^{9}¼	E Delahoussy	116 B	7.10	Apollo114⁴½Roman Envoy117³½Formal Dinner122¹½	*Challenged for lead outside pacesetter, gave way quarter-pole*
			San Miguel Stakes																	
23Nov90	8Hol	ft 2	Stk107600	7f	21.50	44.30	1:09.10	1:21.90	[illegible]	6/10	1	1^{3}	1½		8^{12}½	L Dettori	115	22.20	Olympio112^hdBarrage115½General Meeting112⁴	*Shot to lead while rank, drifted out on turn, folded top stretch*
			Gr.3 Hollywood Prevue BrCup Stk																	
11Oct90	7SA	ft 2	Alw32000Nw2L	6½f	21.50	44.50	1:09.70	1:16.70	78	6/9	3	1½	1^{hd}	1^{hd}	1½	CJ McCarron	119 B	10.20	Intimate Kid119½RallyRun¹Skyinch¾	*Frcd pace; driving*
11Aug90	1Del	gd 2	MaidenSpWt	5f	22.10	46.10		58.70	—	/7					1^{10}½	SR Jones	118	1.80	Intimate Kid118¹⁰½Count Your Change¹¾Tickle My Ribs¹½	
11Jly90	2Del	sy 2	MaidenSpWt	5f	22.70	46.50		58.90	—	2/7					2^{6}¾	CK Murphy	117	8.60	John Rob John117⁶¾Intimate Kid^nkKeyed To Win⁵½	

Workouts: 1Aug Dmr 3f ft 37.10 H 25Jly Dmr 4f ft 49.70 H **18Jly SA 5f ft 58.50 H** 12Jly SA 5f ft 1:04.50 H 6Jly SA 4f ft 49.90 H

Trained by Bill Shoemaker, to be ridden by Chris McCarron, can Intimate Kid outrun 3YO $50,000 claiming company? Very probably not. Its best figure is 81, recorded in an overnight claiming handicap February 18 at Golden Gate Fields. The Burt Bacharach gelding just appears too slow to survive high-priced claiming conditions.

GREAT SEAL

3yo (Mar) gelding. dk. bay/brown
Trainer: Steve Ippolito
Owner: Carol & Frank Aiacono

$45,000
CLM. PRICE

Sire: **Habitony** ($5,000)
  by Habitat
Dam: **Big Spirit**
  by Big Spruce
Bred in CA by Mr. & Mrs. John C.
  Mabee

Career: 2 2 0 0 $19,800

Wet:	0 0 0 0	$0	1991:	1 1 0 0	$11,000
Turf:	0 0 0 0	$0	1990:	1 1 0 0	$8,800
Dist:	1 1 0 0	$11,000	Dmr:	0 0 0 0	$0

113 **Kent J Desormeaux**

27Jun91 7Hol ft 3 Clm25000 6f 22.50 45.70 58.10 1:10.30 **82** 2/7 6 1ʰᵈ 1¹⁄₂   12¹⁄₂ 13¹⁄₂ CJ McCarron 115 **LB** **1.20** Great Seal115³⁄₄Keep On Turnin118¹Northern Stevens115²⁄₄
Claimed from Gary Jones   *Dueled along inside, drew off, ridden out*
8Jun90 1GG ft 2 MaidenSpWt 5f 21.50 45.30   57.90 **05** 3/6 4 4¹⁄₂   4¹⁄₂ 1³ AL Castanon 118   3.50 Great Seal118⁴Astrological Slew118¹⁄₂River Road Tom1182¹⁄₄
                                                                                Stalked pace, driving

Workouts: 28Jly Dmr 5f ft 1:01.70 H   14Jly SA 5f ft 1:00.50 H   7Jly SA 4f ft 48.90 H   24Jun Hol 4f ft 47.30 H   19Jun Hol 5f ft 1:00.70 H

KLEVEN ELEVEN

3yo (Feb) colt. chestnut
Trainer: P Eurton
Owner: Yap & Yap Daily

$45,000
CLM. PRICE

Sire: **Kleven** ($2,500)
  by Alydar
Dam: **Maui Sands**
  by Against The Snow
Bred in CA by Mr. & Mrs. Joseph S.
  Yap

Career: 5 3 2 0 $9,720

Wet:	0 0 0 0	$0	1991:	5 3 2 0	$9,720
Turf:	0 0 0 0	$0	1990:	0 0 0 0	$0
Dist:	5 3 2 0	$9,720	Dmr:	0 0 0 0	$0

118 **Adalberto C Lopez**

20Jly91 8AC ft 3 Hcp 5000 6f 27.30 44.50 56.30 1:08.90 **84** 3/5 3 2¹ 2ʰᵈ   1ʰᵈ 1ʰᵈ M Hernandez 116   3.90 Kleven Eleven116ʰᵈTorchy Wind110¹⁄₂Baja Prince118⁷
                                                                                Stalked pace, between horses, rallied, gained command, won drvg
22Jun91 8AC ft 3 Hcp 5500 6f 22.50 44.50 56.30 1:08.90 **73** 4/6 2 1ʰᵈ 1¹⁄₂   12¹⁄₂ 1⁴ AC Lopez 120   6.80 Kleven Eleven120⁴Black Robert117ʰᵈPedro Mario109⁶
                                                                                Good speed, set pace, drew off in stretch, won driving
15Jun91 8AC ft 3 Hcp 6000 6f 22.70 44.30 56.30 1:08.90 **76** 1/6 4 3ʰᵈ 2ʰᵈ   2ʰᵈ 2¹⁄₂ RO Larios 116   4.80 Baja Prince118¹⁄₂Kleven Eleven116⁴Jim Campanas115²
                                                                                Saved ground, pressed pace, gamely, finished well
1Jun91 3AC ft 3 MCl 6250 6f 22.10 44.10 55.50 1:09.10 **63** 5/9 4 3¹⁄₂ 2¹   1¹⁄₂ 1² GS Escalona 119   1.10 Kleven Eleven119²Cat Island³California Speed¹¹⁄₂   *Gamely*
18May91 6AC ft 3 MCl 6250 6f 22.70 44.50 56.90 1:09.90 **51** 10/11 7 5³ 65¹⁄₄   4⁵ 2⁴ GS Escalona 119   12.90 Ofanothercolor119⁴KlevenElvn¹⁄₂GingerCm¹⁄₂   *Finished well*

Like Pirate's Outlook and Slew's Crown, Great Seal will be moving ahead in claiming class without a qualifying figure. The needed improvement is always plausible, but unpredictable. Insist on a generous price before taking a chance.

Kleven Eleven has arrived at Del Mar from Caliente with a much-improved figure of 84. The shipper from a minor track may continue to improve but remains a risky bet today. Before accepting minor league shippers, invoke two guidelines. First, the improved speed figure should equal or exceed anything else in today's field. Second, the horse should have earned a qualifying figure at the minor track at least twice. An isolated figure always remains suspect. Kleven Eleven does not measure up on either guideline.

Figure handicappers and class handicappers alike should favor Got To Fly strongly in this spot. A prime bet is warranted at 2–1, and maybe at 3–2. The major threat to Got To Fly should be Cadillac Red, who figures to improve again and surpass par of 85.

The patterns of improvement and decline in the sample races characterize numerous claiming races well enough. They hardly exhaust the possibilities. In the end, the search for favorite patterns, positive and negative, and winning patterns especially, is the fun and challenge of figure handicapping. Before leaving claiming races, a few special topics beg our consideration. The first regards a suspicious kind of improvement pattern. I call it "big improvement, no explanation."

Big Improvement/No Explanation

Inspect the speed figures of the middle-class claiming sprinter Knight's Get Away.

The misleading figure is the 84 recorded in the second race back, the long sprint at Hollywood Park on July 3 for $16,000. Knight's Get Away usually records figures of 70 to 72, or lower. Occasionally, claiming horses will deliver speed figures six to eight lengths faster than normal, but bearing no logical explanation.

A clue to phony figures is their context. If the published record reveals no back class and generally lower numbers, beware. If such a horse previously has earned one comparable number but nothing similar before or since, handicappers can assume the odd figure is unrealistic. It's not likely to be repeated.

Knight's Get Away obtained an 82 May 3 at Hollywood Park, but a 60 before and a 70 after. In like manner, the July 3 figure of 84 was preceded by a 70 and followed by a 72. The 72 of July 13 was predictable by shrewd figure analysts.

The context of concern will frequently include no back class, no comparable speed figure in the published record, or just one similar figure, followed by the lower numbers the horse usually dispenses.

In this lackluster context, if horses like Knight's Get Away are double-jumped in claiming class following a big win and impressive figure, they frequently will disappoint.

As a check, figure handicappers can follow this procedure. Add the impressive figure to the speed figure that preceded it. If the sum excels the combined figures of other contenders, favor the horse. If not, abstain. On July 13, handicappers might have added Knight's Get Away's 84 to its 70 of June 19. The sum of 154 would have amounted to a dubious distinction in the July 13 race. No play.

Below are three additional examples of claiming horses abruptly displaying a high speed figure but offering no real explanation for the performance. Stay on the alert for other false figure horses.

ROUND MESA

4yo (Jun) colt. dk. bay/brown
Trainer: John E Chlomos
Owner: Robert R Negley
$10,000 CLM. PRICE

Sire: **Spinoza**
  by Tom Rolfe
Dam: **Instrumental**
  by Advocator
Bred in CA by Margaret M. Redding

Career:	10	1	2	0
Wet:	0 0 0		1991:	1 0 0 0	$0
Turf:	0 0 0		1990:	9 1 2 0	
Dist:	7 1 1 0		Dmr:	5 1 0 0	

115 Alex Solis

2Aug91	3Dmr	ft 3-	⑤Clm16000	6¼f	22.14	44.82	1:09.53	1:16.00	3b	4/7	5	73¾	78½	7¹⁵	72¹	F Mena	115 LBbf 28.80 Fiesta Del Sol115²Stan's Boy115⁴Devine Force115ⁿᵒ

Close up briefly, climbing early, no factor

19Oct90	10BM	ft 3	Alw19000	1m	22.50	45.10	1:09.50	1:36.10	86	3/7	1	4⁶	4³	5¹¼	B Snyder	117 L	23.40 Port Rainbow117ⁿᵒExclusive Tan117⅜Soltau117½

Unruly during running; came up empty

27Sep90	8Fpx	ft 3	Clm10000	6¼f	22.10	45.70		1:17.30	58	7/10	9	96¾	96¼	8¹⁰¼	A Solis	116 Lb	4.40 Sergeant Jay Tee119½Distant Tear116¾Fireliner116½

Never in serious contention; couldn't offer a challenge

30Aug90	9Dmr	ft 3	Clm16000	6¼f	22.10	45.10		1:16.70	58	6/12	6	64¼	65	68¼	A Solis	117 L	13.10 Haughty's Notion116ⁿᵏValdRm2¼BigBdW¼ Evenly; no threat
16Aug90	3Dmr	ft 3	⑧Clm22000	6¼f	22.10	45.30		1:16.70	60	1/7	7	7⁵	74½	61³	K Desormeaux	117 L	5.50 Wood Spirit116²¼SanFrnnd²¼PowerBs½ No speed; no threat
2Aug90	3Dmr	ft 3	Clm32000	6¼f	22.30	46.10	1:10.70	1:36.90	61	5/7	5	53¼	52	61²¼	K Desormeaux	115 L	2.70 Less Than Zero1151¾He'sllistrs²¼Apprised⁵ Outrun; dull
27Jly90	4Dmr	ft 3-	⑧MCl32000	6¼f	22.70	45.70		1:16.70	70	9/12	5	52¼	52	15¼	K Desormeaux	115 L	3.30 Round Mesa115¼Bravuro ᵐᵏGivots Four1¼ 4-wide; lugged in
24May90	6Hol	ft 3-	⑧MCl50000	6f	21.70	45.10		1:09.70	58	5/10	4	2⁴	3⁴½	51¹½	K Desormeaux	115 Lb	1.40 Royal Alladin1134½HiddnP¾CutBck5½ Spd to 1/2; weakened
3May90	4Hol	ft 3-	⑧MCl32000	7f	22.30	45.10		1:23.50	60	7/12	5	62½	63¾	2⁶½	JM Scott	115	5.90 Intrepidness116²¼Round Mesa115ⁿᵒBeach Hut115²¼

Raced evenly; mustered a late rally

Claimed from James Flaherty

12Apr90	2SA	ft 3	⑧MCl32000	6f	21.90	45.70		1:11.70	68	6/12	5	4⁶		2⁴	JM Scott	118	16.90 Mr. Spark Chief118⁴RoundMs⁴¼Indpndn1¼ Outrun; 2nd best

Workouts: 27Jly SA 4f ft 48.10 H   20Jly SA 4f ft 48.70 H   29Jun SA 4f ft 50.30 H   22Jun SA 3f ft 36.70 H

FESTIN (ARG)

5yo (Aug) horse, chestnut
Trainer: Ronald McAnally
Owner: Haras Sonoita

Sire: **Mat-Boy**
  by Marun
Dam: **Felicidades**
  by Con Brio II
Bred in ARG by Haras Don Yayo

1989-91:	18	7	4	3
Wet:	1 1 0 0		1991:	7 2 2 1	$970,395
Turf:	1½0 0 0		1990:	11 5 2 2	
Dist:	2¹⁰0 1 0		Dmr:	2 1 1 0	

124 Eddie Delahoussaye

20Jly91	11Rkm	ft 3-	Stk500000	1⅛	23.12	47.21	1:11.78	1:49.58	106	4/5	5	51¹	51²¼	5⁸	2³	2³	E Delahoussaye	124 LB	0.50 Marquetry121³Festin1243Silver Survivor1213½

New England Classic — Closer than usual to pace, swung four wide into lane, no threat

8Jun91	7Bel	ft 3-	Stk500000	1⅛	22.19	44.53	1:08.84	1:46.75	121	7/10	9	9¹³	10¹⁷	10¹¹	2¼	1⁷	E Delahoussaye	116 L	5.80 Festin1167Gervazy112ⁿᵏFarma Way123²¼

Gr.2 Nassau County Handicap — Badly during run, mild into gear erly turn, swung 6-wd, powerful rally

11May91	9Pim	ft 4+	Stk750000	1¼	23.55	46.91	1:10.07	1:52.53	113	7/7	5	7¹⁴	7¹⁸	7¹⁷	57¼	45¼	E Delahoussaye	116 L	7.40 Farma Way119⁵Summer Squall120²½Jolie's Halo119ᵐ

Gr.1 Pimlico Special — No early speed, angled out stretch, rallied late

13Apr91	8OP	sy 4+	Stk500000	1⅛	22.91	46.62	1:10.83	1:48.71	108	7/10	7	7¹⁴	7¹²	6³	1¼	E Delahoussaye	115 L	11.10 Festin115¼Primal1152¼Jolie's Halo120¹

Gr.1 Oaklawn Handicap — Unhurried early, raced 4-wide backstreth, rallied inside, drivin

9Mar91	5SA	ft 4+	Stk500000	1¼	23.10	46.10	1:34.90	2:00.30	112	8/10	10	10¹⁰	10⁶	74¼	2²¼	2²¾	E Delahoussaye	115 LB	11.80 Farma Way120²¼Festin115¾Pleasant Tap115½

Gr.1 Santa Anita Handicap — Trailed early, closed five-wide far turn, strong stretch run

17Feb91	8SA	ft 4+	Stk331750	1⅛	23.30	46.90	1:09.90	1:47.30	100	7/9	5	99¼	9¹⁰	91¹	53	33	E Delahoussaye	116 B	9.60 Farma Way118²¼Anshan116¼Lous Cyp111¼Festi116

Gr.2 San Antonio Handicap — Trailed early, moved willingly after six panels, dead heat

18Jan91	8SA	ft 4+	Stk63650	1⅛	23.10	46.50	1:10.30	1:41.70	97	8/9	8	99¼	99¾	85¼	68¼	44¼	E Delahoussaye	121 B	1.10 Stylish Stud115¼Balla Cove114²¼Elegant Bargain114¹¼

Royal Owl Handicap — Never in serious contention; couldn't offer a challenge

16Dec90	7Hol	ft 3-	Hcp60000	1⅛	23.50	46.90	1:10.70	1:41.90	107	2/6	3	3³	52¼	42¼	1ⁿᵈ	1³	E Delahoussaye	122 B	0.80 Festin1223DoubleQck ⁿᵏDach'sFl2 Saved ground, drew off
1Dec90	8Hol	ft 3-	Stk108500	1⅛	23.50	46.90	1:10.70	1:47.50	101	4/7	7	7¹³	7¹⁵	7¹⁰	54¼	41¼	E Delahoussaye	119 B	3.00 Warcraft117ⁿᵒPleasant Tap115ⁿᵏGo And Go115¹¼

Gr.3 Native Diver Handicap — Settled off the pace early, moved inside far turn, closed well

1Nov90	8SA	ft 3-	Stk61700	1m	22.70	45.90	1:10.30	1:35.50	105	4/7	7	7⁷	75¼	75¼	41¼	1¹	E Delahoussaye	118 B	1.30 Festin118¹Earn Your Stripes117¾Double Quick116ⁿᵒ

Most Host Handicap — Raced extremely wide, made a late rally, driving

Workouts: 3Aug Dmr 7f ft 1:25.70 H   29Jly Dmr 4f ft 47.50 B   **14Jly Hol 1m ft 1:37.10** H   10Jly Hol 1m ft 1:42.70 B   4Jly Hol 7f ft 1:27.70 B

D'PARROT

4yo (Apr) gelding, bay
Trainer: Richard Schosberg
Owner: Heatherwood Farm

Sire: **D'Accord ($10,000)**
  by Secretariat
Dam: **Ornately**
  by Val De L'Orne
Bred in NY by Forest Retreat Farms, Incorporated

Career:	19	5	3	3
Wet:	0 0 0		1991:	4 1 1 1	$34,460
Turf:	7 2 1 1		1990:	10 2 1 2	
Dist:	6 3 1 1		Sar:	1 1 0 0	

113

24Jly91	7Sar	ft 3-	Alw41000	6¼f	23.18	44.68	1:08.93	1:16.09	111	7/6	2	11¼	1³	1⁴	15¼	JA Santos	117 bf	11.00 D'parrot1175¼Lord March117¾Mercedes Won117¼

Made pace along rail, drew clear turn, driving

30Jun91	5Bel	ft 4+	Clm100000	6f	22.55	44.92		1:08.29	98	5/8	3	1¹	1¹½	2¹	25¼	ME Smith	116 bf	7.30 Kid Russell1085¼D'parrot116⁵Royal Eagle113¼

Made pace slightly off rail, no match, held on well

25May91	1Bel	ft 4+	Clm100000	6f	22.65	46.18		1:10.69	94	6/7	1	1¹½	1¹½	1¹½	33¼	A Madrid Jr	112 bf	25.40 Wonderloaf122²¼Proud And Valid116¾D'Parrot112½

Quickly sprinted clear, made pace well into stretch, tired

12May91	5Bel	fm 4+	Clm100000	1⅛	23.78	46.58	1:11.26	1:41.69	88	4/10	2	1ⁿᵈ	1ⁿᵈ	1ⁿᵈ	55¼	82⁴	A Madrid Jr	118 b	33.60 Crackedbell118⁵Turning Fr2¼StrngRb⁴¼ Dueled inside, tired
2Nov90	5Med	ft 3	Stk35000	1ⁿᵈ	22.50	45.50	1:11.10	1:41.90	88	3/9	2	32¼	61²	93⁸	HW McCauley	113 Lbf	9.20 Red Pine113³¼Roanoke113¹¼Bob's Brother Chip113⁸¼

Passaic County Stakes — Stopped; eased up

30Sep90	8Bel	ft 3-	⑧Stk93000	7f	22.18	44.83	1:09.79	1:22.61	88	3/11	5	2¹	2½	9¹⁵¼	HW McCauley	113 b	5.40 Zee Best114²¼Diamond Anchor114ⁿᵏHerr Von Kaninchen117ⁿᵏ

Hudson Handicap — Brief speed

3Sep90	8Bel	ft 3	Stk170100	1m	22.64	44.85	1:08.80	1:34.14	92	1/5	5	32¼	36¼	3¹³⁸	HW McCauley	112 b	10.50 Housebuster126¹³Citidancer114³¼D'parrot112²

Gr.1 Jerome Handicap — Speed at rail, couldn't keep up with winner or tired pacesetter

18Aug90	9Mth	ft 3	Stk35000	1⅛	24.30	47.70	1:11.30	1:42.90	88	3/5	2	2ⁿᵏ	1ⁿᵈ	34¼	L Saumell	113 Lb	9.70 Groscar119²¼Super Mario119ⁿᵈD'parrot113²

Ulysses S Grant Stakes — Forced the early pace; useful effor

11Jly90	8Bel	gd 3	Stk96450	1⅛	23.20	46.23	1:09.54	1:41.34	88	1/13	1	3²	4³	13²¼	ME Smith	119 f	35.10 Solar Splendor114¹Divine Warning119²Bismarck Hills114¼

Gr.3 Hill Prince Stakes — Displayed brief speed; eased up

19Jun90	9Mth	ft 3	Stk35000	1⅛	23.50	47.30	1:10.70	1:41.50	86	6/9	5	42¼	42¼	55¼	ME Smith	119 L	4.60 Groscar115ⁿᵏDawn Quixote122²Preppy Pappy119¾

John McSorley Stakes — Saved ground along the inside; lacked a closing rall

Workouts: 12Aug Sar 4f ft 48.60 B   5Aug Sar 4f ft 48.48 B   **18Jly Bel 4f ft 47.30 B**   12Jly Bel 4f ft 47.47 B   27Jun Bel 3f ft 36.20 H

Lower-Priced Claiming Races

Below $20,000 claiming, speed figures hinged to final times can be entirely misleading. As mentioned, Bill Quirin has demonstrated the symmetrical relations between speed and pace figures, such that when pace figures improve, final figures decline, and vice versa. To recall, the symmetry looks like this:

	Pace	*Speed*
Horse A	98	102
Horse B	102	98

Using Quirin speed and pace figures, one point equals a length at the final call, and two points equals a length at the pace call.

The illustration is common. If Horse A runs two lengths faster to the pace call (102), he records a speed figure (98) that has plunged by four lengths. These relationships are especially acute in cheaper races. No one who has used Quirin figures for even a season will dispute the assertion.

The favorite in yesterday's first at Del Mar, a seven-furlong sprint for $10,000 claiming horses 3up (par is 100), had won two of its past three starts at the level, with speed and pace figures that looked like so:

Sparshott Dk. b. or br. g. 6, by Police Car—Avondida, by Stevward
DESORMEAUX K J **$10,000** Br.—Ballymaloe Farms (BC-C)
Own.—Davis-Gilson-Novak Et al Tr.—Baffert Bob **119**

																					Pace	**Speed**
22Jly91-	2Hol	fst	7f	:221	:452	1:233		Clm 10000	3	3	22	21	12½	12	Desormeaux KJ	LBb	116	*1.90	86-13		97	100
7Jly91-	1Hol	fst	6f	:22	:442	1:102		Clm 10000	3	6	76¾	46½	48	45	Desormeaux K J	LB	116	*1.80	83-10			
11May91-	1Hol	fst	6½f	:221	:453	1:163		Clm c-10000	7	4	1hd	11½	15	15	McCarron C J	LBb	116	3.40	89-13		97	104
27Apr91-	1Hol	fst	7f	:224	:463	1:243		Clm 10000	1	3	11	11	2½	22¾	Flores D R	LBb	116	2.50	78-12			
14Mar91-	1SA	my	6½f	:212	:44	1:163		Clm 10000	12	3	52½	35½	410	713	Solis A	LBb	115	5.90	74-19			
3Feb91-	2SA	fm	*6½f Ⓣ	:213	:431	1:132		Clm 70000	7	1	32	69½	610	68	Flores D R	LBb	113	40.40	84-08			
22Dec90-	1Hol	fst	6½f	:214	:443	1:162	3↑	Clm 10000	10	1	2hd	2hd	2hd	1½	Flores D R	LBb	116	*2.80	93-06			
28Nov90-	5Hol	fst	7f	:214	:444	1:221	3↑	Clm 10500	8	4	21	21	32½	32¾	McCarron C J	LBb	115	12.00	91-06			
16Nov90-	1Hol	fst	6f	:221	:451	1:101	3↑	Clm 12500	3	6	85¾	87¾	79	67	Flores D R	LBb	117	*2.40	82-09			
8Oct90-	4SA	fst	7f	:22	:45	1:23	3↑	Clm 12500	12	1	41¾	32½	34	59	Flores D R	LBb	118	3.50	79-17			

Speed Index: Last Race: -1.0 3-Race Avg.: -2.0 9-Race Avg.: -4.4
LATEST WORKOUTS Jun 13 Hol 4f fst :484 H

No other horse in the field showed a speed figure equal to par. Sparshott, however, carried pace figures 1½ lengths below par, in combination with a declining final figure. Two presser types Sparshott would tangle with early showed these pace figures:

	Pace
Eastern Cutlass	103
Gum Swapper	104

Figure analysts might dismiss Sparshott unhesitatingly, unless the horse had boasted past victories at today's level following pace figures of 103–104. Sparshott did not boast the qualifying pace figures, and he lost the Del Mar race to an outsider. When forced to accelerate early to keep abreast, low-priced claiming horses frequently cannot duplicate their recent final figures. They instead fall back. These speed-pace relationships can dominate the dynamics of any claiming race but are especially critical in three situations: (1) low priced claiming races, (2) claiming races restricted to three-year-olds, and (3) all maiden-claiming races.

In cheaper races, figure handicappers can prefer the horses having stronger pace figures, even where the final figures fall slightly below those of other contenders. Yesterday's fourth race at Del Mar presented a classic example. It was a $10,000 claiming route for 3up. Par again is 100. In a tough call, which of the contenders below should figure handicappers prefer?

The best approach first finds the low-priced claiming horse having the fastest pace figure and considers what effect the horse should have on the outcome. Jazz Island's 106 sticks out. He's the probable leader at the second call.

Next, review the other frontrunners and pace-pressers. As a rule, need-to-lead types that cannot attend the pace comfortably to the second call will vanish thereafter.

Our Brand X. is that type of frontrunner. If the 7YO attempts to wrestle the pace away from Jazz Island, his pace figure of 100 must improve dramatically, and his speed figure of 97 will assuredly decline. As events proceeded, Our Brand X. tracked Jazz Island for four furlongs and quit.

El Gran Sid usually wins from just behind the early pace. The same fate awaits this gelding from the outside at a middle distance. If urged to secure position behind Jazz Island, the pace figure will probably improve, but the final figure should also decline. Final-figure handicappers may prefer El Gran Sid here, but the high risk of a declining speed figure forsakes a low price. El Gran Sid ran badly here at 5–2. Unable to get position early, the 5YO dropped back.

Our Brand X. B. g. 7, by Codex—Image of Reality, by In Reality
SOLIS A $10,000 Br.—Hughes L T (Fla)
Own.—Winford M or Doris Tr.—Jory Ian P D **116** | **Pace** 100 | **Speed** 97

20Jly91- 2Hol fst 1 1/16 :464 1:112 1:453 3+Clm 10000 1 3 3nk 3nk 1hd 31¼ Solis A LBb 115 4.20 72-22
4Jly91- 1Hol fst 1 1/16 :46 1:11 1:434 Clm 10000 3 1 1hd 2hd 45 610 Valenzuela P A LBb 116 4.50 72-18
1May91- 4Hol fst 1⅛ :462 1:112 1:514 Clm 12500 1 2 41¾ 42½ 64¼ 66¾ Pincay L Jr LBb 117 4.40 68-25
22Apr91- 9SA fst 1 1/16 :454 1:103 1:443 Clm 12500 1 3 32 33 33½ 63¼ Pincay L Jr LBb 117 *2.00 77-18
3Apr91- 9SA fst 1 1/16 :463 1:11 1:44 Clm 16000 1 3 31½ 42 86 105½ Stevens G L LBb 115 *1.70 77-16
7Mar91- 9SA fst 1 1/16 :47 1:11 1:424 Clm 10000 5 2 2½ 1½ 13 13½ Black C A LBb 115 5.50 89-20
22Feb91- 9SA fst 1¼ :464 1:37 2:033 Clm 10000 7 4 32½ 3nk 31½ 33½ Black C A LBb 115 4.50 72-19
9Feb91- 1SA fst 1 1/16 :464 1:113 1:441 Clm 10000 11 2 1½ 11½ 12½ 34½ Black C A LBb 115 39.00 77-18
17Jan91- 9SA fst 1 1/16 :461 1:104 1:434 Clm 10000 1 1 1hd 31½ 78 813¾ Black C A LBb 115 30.00 70-18
3Jan91- 9SA sly 1 1/16 :464 1:111 1:441 Clm 10000 7 2 21½ 66½ 924 941½ Black C A LBb 115 12.20 40-18
Speed Index: Last Race: -6.0 3-Race Avg.: -7.6 10-Race Avg.: -9.4
LATEST WORKOUTS Jly 15 Hol 5f fst :593 H ●Jun 29 Hol 6f fst 1:121 H Jun 21 Hol 6f fs

Jazz Island ✻ Ch. g. 6, by Island Whirl—Jazz Era, by Olden Times
LOPEZ A D $10,000 Br.—Koley & Lee (Fla)
Own.—Kirkwood A & Sandee Tr.—Puhich Michael **118** | 106 | 94

25Jly91- 9Dmr fst 1 :46 1:111 1:37 3+Clm 10000 9 2 2hd 3½ 54 46¾ Berrio O A LBb 118 4.10 74-22
7Jly91- 4Hol fst 1 3/16 :463 1:11 1:554 3+Alw 10000s 3 3 32½ 32½ 45½ 47½ Berrio O A LBb 114 5.30 101-05
30Jun91- 4Hol fst 1 1/16 :461 1:103 1:431 Clm 10000 2 6 31½ 52¼ 54 65 Berrio O A LBb 113 5.40 80-21
14Jun91- 5Hol fst 1 1/16 :461 1:102 1:424 Clm 12500 4 3 41¼ 34 31½ 1nk Berrio O A Lb 121 7.20 87-13
2Jun91- 1Hol fst 1⅛ :48 1:123 1:503 Clm 16000 5 1 11 1½ 31½ 44½ Berrio O A5 Lb 110 3.40 76-19
18May91- 1Hol fst 1 3/16 :474 1:12 1:563 Clm 12500 3 2 21½ 21½ 1hd 12 Berrio O A5 LBb 113 3.60 105 —
1May91- 4Hol fst 1⅛ :462 1:112 1:514 Clm 12500 2 5 52¼ 32 1hd 1½ Berrio O A5 LBb 110 6.60 75-25
1May91-Bumped, shuffled back 7/8
20Apr91- 2SA fst 1 1/16 :47 1:12 1:443 Clm 10000 5 1 11½ 12 11½ 1¾ Berrio O A LBb 115 5.60 80-18
11Apr91- 9SA fst 1 :461 1:112 1:372 Clm 10000 3 3 21 33 79½ 815¾ Lopez A D LBb 115 6.00 64-22
16Feb91- 9SA fst 1 1/16 :464 1:112 1:423 Clm 10000 6 5 31½ 21½ 49½ 714¼ Boulanger G LBb 113 7.70 76-12
Speed Index: Last Race: -4.0 3-Race Avg.: +1.0 10-Race Avg.: -2.5

Bee Line Ben Dk. b. or br. g. 4, by Sir Ivor—Graceful Dancer, by Northern Dancer
DESORMEAUX K J $10,000 Br.—Hawn W R (Ky)
Own.—Hawn W R Tr.—MacDonald Mark **116** | 95 | 97

26Jly91- 1Dmr fst 1 1/16 :46 1:112 1:434 3+Clm 12500 2 9 95¼ 94¼ 63½ 62¾ Desormeaux KJ LBb 116 10.60 79-17
30Jun91- 4Hol fst 1 1/16 :461 1:103 1:431 Clm 20000 7 9 98¾ 96¾ 86½ 87½ Lovato A J5 LBb 110 13.70 77-21
19May91-10Hol fm 1⅛ Ⓣ:47 1:351 2:002 3+Hcp 25000s 10 5 55¾ 44 66½ 65¼ Martinez F F LBb 111 26.00 85-10
12May91- 4Hol fst 1 1/16 :461 1:104 1:434 Clm 20000 6 6 66¼ 53½ 33 31¾ Martinez F F5 LBb 110 8.10 80-16
12May91-Veered in, bumped break, wide 7/8 turn
20Apr91- 9SA fst 1 1/16 :462 1:103 1:431 Clm 20000 2 5 57½ 57½ 33½ 32½ Martinez F F5 LBb 110 30.40 84-18
24Mar91- 3SA fst 1 :45 1:10 1:362 Clm 25000 2 7 716 713 59½ 58 Hawley S LBb 115 20.10 77-17
10Mar91- 6SA fst 7f :222 :451 1:223 Clm 32000 2 12 1211 1118½ 912 99¾ Hawley S LBb 115 45.40 80-15
27Jan91- 5SA fm 1⅛ Ⓣ:464 1:111 1:482 Alw 35000 5 3 31½ 31½ 64¾ 68¾ Velasquez J LBb 117 12.60 73-18
11Jan91- 7SA gd 1⅛ Ⓣ:474 1:121 1:49 Alw 37000 7 6 66 65 53½ 54¾ Velasquez J LBb 117 20.80 74-16
26Dec90- 5SA fst 1 :464 1:11 1:361 Alw 37000 7 7 78 66 67 55¾ Pincay L Jr LBb 117 24.40 80-13
Speed Index: Last Race: -4.0 3-Race Avg.: -3.3 6-Race Avg.: -3.5
LATEST WORKOUTS Jly 15 SA 7f fst 1:283 H Jun 24 SA 4f fst :501 H Jun 17 SA 4f fst

Hurry And Speedy–Br B. h. 8, by Sporting Yankee—Alna II, by Amiel
VALENZUELA P A $10,000 Br.—Haras Independencia (Brz)
Own.—Cheng-Feng-Sise Jr Tr.—Sise Clifford Jr **116** | 101 | 97

25Jly91- 9Dmr fst 1 :46 1:111 1:37 3+Clm 10000 1 8 87½ 74½ 33 33½ Torres H5 LBb 111 6.20 78-22
12Jly91- 2Hol fst 1⅛ :471 1:12 1:512 Clm 10000 3 4 53 74¾ 83¾ 42¾ Baze R A LBb 115 4.00 74-20
22Jun91-10Hol fst 6½f :214 :443 1:161 Clm 10000 11 8 1111 99¾ 88 47½ Baze R A LBb 116 17.60 83-11
10Aug90- 9Dmr fst 1 :46 1:11 1:361 3+Clm 12500 4 4 53½ 42 31 1hd Baze R A Lb 116 8.30 85-16
19Jly90- 7Hol fst 1 :45 1:101 1:35 Clm 20000 3 1 1hd 2hd 78 815¼ Pincay L Jr Lb 117 4.00 74-11
29Jun90- 5Hol fst 1 :444 1:092 1:344 Clm 32000 1 4 44½ 43½ 53 68¼ Pincay L Jr b 117 8.50 84-16
10Jun90- 7Hol fst 1 1/16 :47 1:113 1:441 Clm 32000 6 1 1½ 2hd 2½ 31¼ Pincay L Jr b 116 4.70 78-20
25May90- 9Hol fst 1 1/16 :46 1:10 1:421 Clm 32000 5 5 55 64¼ 55 42¾ Pincay L Jr b 116 11.50 86-14
3May90- 5Hol fst 1 1/16 :474 1:121 1:434 Clm c-25000 5 8 88¼ 88¼ 89¾ 710¾ Solis A b 115 2.50 70-22
15Apr90- 9SA fst 1 1/16 :47 1:113 1:423 Clm 25000 7 2 2hd 2hd 24 37 McCarron C J b 118 5.60 83-12
Speed Index: Last Race: 0.0 3-Race Avg.: -1.6 9-Race Avg.: -3.8
LATEST WORKOUTS Jly 7 Hol 5f fst 1:023 H Jly 2 Hol 4f fst :524 H Jun 10 Hol 5f f

El Gran Sid ✻ Gr. g. 5, by Halo—Gap Axe, by The Axe II
NAKATANI C S $10,000 Br.—OakCliffThbdBldstkLtd–1985 (Ky)
Own.—Campechiaro-Chemo-FrdmnEtl Tr.—Mitchell Mike **116** | 102 | 98

6Jly91- 1Hol fst 1 1/16 :454 1:10 1:433 Clm c-16000 2 3 33½ 33½ 43½ 54¼ Flores D R LBb 115 3.60 79-14
25May91- 3GG fst 1 1/16 :461 1:104 1:444 Clm 20000 3 2 2hd 2hd 31 49 Valenzuela P A LBb 117 *2.10 65-24
21Apr91-10GG fm 1⅜ Ⓣ:501 1:411 2:203 ⒷHvys Tf Ch H 6 1 11 11 1hd 64 Patterson A LBb 117 *1.00 65-18
21Apr91-Run in divisions
24Mar91- 7GG sly 1⅛ :463 1:112 1:503 Hcp 12500s 3 2 21½ 21 2½ 11½ Patterson A LBb 115 *2.40 72-30
9Mar91-10GG fst 1 :451 1:094 1:352 Clm 12500 2 4 42 1½ 11½ 13 Patterson A LBb 117 4.00 88-12
2Feb91- 9SA fst 1 1/16 :454 1:102 1:431 Clm 32000 4 1 4¾ 99¾ 916 920½ Davis R G LBb 115 8.10 66-11
19Jan91- 3SA fst 1 :454 1:102 1:354 Alw 42000 3 1 2hd 32½ 712 718½ Desormeaux KJ LBb 115 11.00 70-09
30Dec90- 7SA fst 6½f :214 :444 1:15 3+Alw 38000 4 4 43½ 52¾ 57 612¾ Garcia J A LBb 115 24.20 82-12
16Feb90- 7SA fst 1 1/16 :46 1:103 1:431 Alw 42000 3 2 1hd 1hd 3½ 55 Davis R G b 116 22.70 82-19
18Jan90- 8SA gd 1 1/16 :472 1:121 1:434 Alw 42000 4 2 21½ 42 812 821½ Davis R G b 118 9.80 62-32
Speed Index: Last Race: -7.0 3-Race Avg.: -5.3 8-Race Avg.: -8.1
LATEST WORKOUTS Jly 28 Bmr 6f fst 1:132 H Jly 19 Bmr 3f fst :372 H Jly 3 Hol 4f fst

Either Bee Line Ben or Hurry And Speedy might do from behind the pace here, but if Hurry And Speedy chases Jazz Island close up to the pace call, its figure too might decline.

What about Jazz Island? At an impressive 106, the pace figure is three lengths superior to par, but the speed figure is a slow 94, six lengths inferior to par. What to do?

The handicapping best relates Jazz Island's pace figure to other important factors. First, handicappers ascertain whether Jazz Island has previously won with a par figure or better at today's class after setting a pace of 106 or thereabouts. The 6YO has, and repeatedly. Older, consistent bread-and-butter claiming types will often satisfy this standard. In addition, demand the par figure that has occurred this year. Or if few starts this season, last year.

Next, determine whether anything about its trip last out can explain Jazz Island's unusually low speed figure. In its last, Jazz Island broke from the No. 9 post at a mile and was urged while racing wide around the clubhouse turn. The pace figure of 106 was therefore earned the hard way, contributing to the plunging final figure. A more comfortable trip early today could mean a softer pace figure, easily earned, and a stronger finish.

Whether that kind of full-dress handicapping is followed or not, the key to the race analysis remains Jazz Island's dominant pace figure. In lower-priced claiming races, favor horses that can equal or approach par after recording above-par pace figures. This is particularly true when all the speed figures of the leading contenders look unattractive. Do not be fooled by final figures that have followed a weak pace scenario, notably for frontrunners and pace-pressers.

5112 —FOURTH RACE. 1-1/16 mile. 3 year olds & up. Claiming price $10,000. Purse $13,000.

Index	Horse and Jockey	Wt.	PP	ST	¼	½	¾	St.r.	Fin.	To $1
5018	Jazz Island, Lopez	118	5	1	1$^{1/2}$	1$^{1/2}$	1$^{1/2}$	1$^{1/2}$	1$^{1/2}$	·5.20
5019	Bee Line Ben, Desormeaux	116	6	4	5^{hd}	5^1	4$^{1/2}$	2^3	2^2	4.90
5073	Porchetto, Davenport	111	1	7	10	10	8^3	5$^{1/2}$	3$^{3 1/2}$	16.50
5009	Waterzip, Torres	111	7	10	7^{hd}	8^1	7$^{1/2}$	7$^{2 1/2}$	4$^{1/2}$	17.10
4S595	Meadow's Interco,A.Cstnon	116	10	9	8$^{1/2}$	7^{hd}	6^1	6^{hd}	5^2	16.00
5018	Hurry And Speedy,P.Vinzuela	116	8	2	2^{hd}	3$^{1 1/2}$	3^3	3^1	6$^{1 1/4}$	2.70
4462	Baron Of Sonoita, Sorenson	116	2	8	9$^{3 1/2}$	9$^{1 1/2}$	9^4	8^3	7$^{1/2}$	105.0
4595	Our Brand X, Solis	116	4	3	3^2	2$^{1/2}$	2^{hd}	4$^{1 1/2}$	8^4	7.90
4190	Mr. Kleen Kut, Gilligan	117	3	6	6$^{3 1/2}$	4^2	5^{hd}	9^7	9^{13}	20.50
4501	El Gran Sid, Nakatani	116	9	5	4^1	6$^{1 1/2}$	10	10	10	2.90

Scratched—None.

Claimed—El Gran Sid by Mr. & Mrs. M. Bronson (trainer J.Canani) for $10,000.

5—JAZZ ISLAND	12.40	6.40	4.60
6—BEE LINE BEN		6.20	4.20
1—PORCHETTO			6.00

Time—23 1/5, 46 4/5, 1.11 2/5, 1.37 2/5, 1.44. Clear & fast. Winner—Ch g 85 Island Whirl-Jazz Era. Trained by M. Puhich. Mutuel pool—$324,948. Exacta pool—$313,848.

A caution is appropriate. While tuned into pace figures in lower-priced claiming races, figure handicappers cannot ignore speed figures. The relations between the figures carry the cause. Below are three recent races and figures for the 5YO sprinter Sail On Swaps. Today's $16,000 claiming par once again is 100.

Sail On Swaps — **B. m. 5, by Fichte—Swap's Rose Queen, by Kafe Bush**
SOLIS A — **$16,000** **Br.—Buccaneer Cruises (Cal)** — **115**
Own.—Aizenstat A — **Tr.—Machowsky Michael**

24Jly91-	7Dmr	fst	$6\frac{1}{2}$f	:21^{4}	:44^{4}	1:17^{2}	3↑ⒻⓈAlw 35000	10	2	$8^{5\frac{1}{2}}$	$7^{4\frac{1}{2}}$	$7^{6\frac{1}{4}}$	$7^{7\frac{1}{4}}$	Solis A	LB	118	21.60	74-14
3Jly91-	8Hol	fst	6f	:21^{4}	:44^{2}	1:10	3↑ⒻⓈAlw 32000	4	4	3^{3}	$3^{2\frac{1}{2}}$	4^{3}	$4^{5\frac{3}{4}}$	Desormeaux K J	LB	118	5.00	84-11
19Jun91-	3Hol	fst	6f	:22^{2}	:45^{1}	1:10^{4}	3↑ⒻⓈAlw 32000	4	1	3^{1}	$2^{\frac{1}{2}}$	1^{hd}	3^{hd}	Garcia J A	LB	119	2.30	86-15
31May91-	1Hol	fst	6f	:21^{4}	:44^{4}	1:10^{3}	ⒻClm c-16000	7	2	4^{3}	2^{1}	1^{hd}	1^{2}	Garcia J A	LB	116	9.50	87-11
29Jly90-	2Dmr	fst	6f	:22^{1}	:45^{1}	1:09^{3}	3↑ⒻClm 18000	8	3	$7^{4\frac{1}{2}}$	$4^{2\frac{1}{2}}$	3^{2}	2^{1}	Davis R G	L	113	20.60	91-07
26May90-	9Hol	fst	1	:44^{3}	1:10^{1}	1:35^{2}	ⒻClm 25000	5	6	$6^{3\frac{3}{4}}$	$5^{2\frac{1}{2}}$	$6^{6\frac{1}{2}}$	$9^{18\frac{1}{4}}$	Pincay L Jr		117	5.80	69-16
9May90-	3Hol	fst	$1\frac{1}{16}$	:46^{3}	1:11^{2}	1:44^{1}	ⒻClm 25000	7	4	$4^{4\frac{1}{2}}$	$2^{\frac{1}{2}}$	$2^{\frac{1}{2}}$	$3^{\frac{1}{2}}$	Valenzuela P A		116	7.30	78-19
19Apr90-	2SA	fst	6f	:22	:45^{3}	1:11	ⒻClm c-20000	6	8	8^{10}	$8^{8\frac{1}{2}}$	6^{7}	$4^{7\frac{3}{4}}$	Delahoussaye E		116	6.80	73-20
1Apr90-	1SA	fst	$6\frac{1}{2}$f	:22	:45^{2}	1:17^{4}	ⒻClm 20000	5	7	$7^{9\frac{1}{2}}$	5^{7}	4^{2}	$2^{\frac{3}{4}}$	Delahoussaye E		116	5.40	80-17
17Mar90-	1SA	fst	6f	:21^{4}	:45^{1}	1:11	ⒻClm 22500	11	2	$9^{9\frac{1}{4}}$	9^{8}	$6^{5\frac{1}{2}}$	$4^{1\frac{3}{4}}$	Davis R G		114	36.10	79-17

Speed Index: Last Race: −12.0 3–Race Avg.: −5.3 8–Race Avg.: −4.2

Notice the symmetry between the mare's speed and pace figures on May 31 and July 3. On July 3, Sail On Swap's pace figure (105) improved three lengths, but her final figure (94) declined four lengths. This is standard operating procedure, as explained.

But if Sail On Swaps can throttle back to 99 at the pace call today, her speed figure will still be 98, two lengths short of par (100). Figure handicappers who believed the pace figures of July 3 and July 24 gave Sail On Swaps the edge at $16,000 claiming were mistaken. That kind of pace has thwarted Sail On Swaps at the finish. A below-par pace figure has not translated into a par speed figure. Sail On Swaps and her kind will be defeated by horses possessing par figures at the class, notwithstanding faster pace figures.

Pace figures should be much preferred to speed figures in maiden-claiming races, mainly because the final figures of the horses normally will be dismal. Stick close to this guidepost. Anytime a horse dropping in class, from maiden to maiden-claiming, or from a higher-priced maiden-claiming race to a lower-priced maiden-claiming race, holds an advantage greater than a length at the pace call, that horse figures.

At the same time, one of the biggest sucker bets at the races is the maiden-claiming runners-up that last out finished close at today's selling price. Ignore those horses, unless the pace figure is better than par and the speed figure at least approaches par.

A recent winner in a $40,000 maiden-claiming sprint at Del Mar had lost several maiden-claiming contests, but recently had recorded speed and pace figures like this (par is 98).

Midnight Ruler GARCIA J A Own.—Triple Dot Dash Stable Trust	Dk. b. or br. g. 4, by Megaturn—Garden Ruler, by What Luck $40,000 Br.—McMillin Bros & Tackett (Ky) Tr.—Sadler John W				121	Pace	Speed
5Jly91- 9Hol fst 6½f :212 :44 1:16 3↑⑤Md 40000	5 2 3¹ 2ʰᵈ 1½ 3⁴	Santos J A	LBb 121	3.30	88-10	105	98
13Jun91- 6Hol fst 6f :22 :44³ 1:10 3↑ Md 35000	7 2 3³ 22½ 22½ 21¾	Stevens G L	LBb 120	2.60	88-09		
13Jun91-Bumped break, wide 3/8 turn						98	98
29May91- 2Hol fst 6f :214 :44⁴ 1:11 3↑ Md 32000	9 4 22½ 31½ 53½ 45½	Stevens G L	Bb 122	*2.60	79-12	101	93
17Sep90- 9Fpx fst 6f :213 :45¹ 1:11 3↑ Md Sp Wt	5 8 8¹¹ 67½ 44½ 24½	Lopez A D	Bb 114	*2.30	86-10		
1Sep90- 6Dmr fst 6½f :22 :45 1:16 3↑ Md Sp Wt	2 9 — — — —	Black C A	B 118	3.90	— —		
16Aug90- 6Dmr fst 6f :214 :44² 1:09¹ 3↑ Md c-50000	10 3 2½ 2ʰᵈ 1½ 21½	Meza R Q	Bb 116	3.20	92-10		
6Jly90- 6Hol fst 6f :22³ :45² 1:10² 3↑ Md 55000	3 2 1½ 2ʰᵈ 2ʰᵈ 31	Olivares F	b 113	8.00	87-16		
15Jun90- 1Hol fst 6f :214 :45³ 1:10² 3↑ Md 32000	12 1 6⁴ 3ⁿᵏ 2ʰᵈ 2ʰᵈ	Olivares F	116	11.30	88-11		
Speed Index: Last Race: -2.0	3-Race Avg.: -4.6		7-Race Avg.: -2.0				

In its first attempt as a 4YO, Midnight Ruler acted like the majority of maiden-claiming horses. When the pace exceeded par (101), the speed figure was awful (93). The second start, however, represented an even effort (98-98), featuring par figures; not bad, but not quite good enough to support. But in its third try of 1991, Midnight Ruler finished in par (98) following a pace figure (105) 3½ lengths faster than par. Not many maiden-claiming types can do that.

In its next start, Midnight Ruler faced a maiden dropdown that compared interestingly on the numbers:

	Pace	Speed
Midnight Ruler	105	98
Borscht Ryder	103	96

Borscht Ryder is precisely the kind of maiden dropdown that defeats chronic maiden-claiming losers all the time. Two lengths below par (96) at the finish, Borscht Ryder can easily exceed the maiden-claiming par to the pace call (103). Maiden-claiming horses cannot catch up.

Performing almost exactly in step with the figures, Midnight Ruler outran Borscht Ryder by three lengths, after leading by 1½ lengths at the pace call. Borscht Ryder pounded the rest of the field by seven lengths. He lost only because he could not outrun Midnight Ruler to the pace call.

Figure handicappers should understand that if Midnight Ruler had demonstrated merely a superior speed figure (98 to 96), coupled with a pace figure (98) at par, Borscht Ryder would have beaten him. It's crucial to appreciate that. Pace figures supersede speed figures in maiden-claiming affairs and in many other low-priced claiming events.

All Speed Figures Below Par

No sillier mistake is committed so repetitively and unwittingly among figure handicappers than backing the high-figure horse in a field where all the speed figures remain below par. If all horses' speed figures are below par, the race is not very susceptible to figure handicapping, even as handicappers should avoid making distinctions among low-percentage trainers or horses unsuited to the eligibility conditions. It's a fool's play to attempt to select the least slow among a gateful of slow horses. Other handicapping factors deserve precedence.

Consider the ninth race at Saratoga on August 8, 1991, a six-furlong claiming race for $25,000 three-year-olds. Par is approximately 80. Examine the speed figures.

Saratoga

9

SIX FURLONGS. CLAIMING. Purse $18,000. For Fillies Three Years Old, 121 lbs. Non-winners of two races since July 15, allowed 3 lbs. Of such a race since then, 5 lbs. Claiming price $25,000; for each $2,500 to $20,000, 2 lbs. [Races when entered to be claimed for $18,000 or less not considered.]

Coupled: Marquee and Red Tape; Sunny Sara and Tuned Way Up

PRINCIPALLY
3yo (Mar) filly, chestnut
Trainer: Ramon M Hernandez
Owner: Lucille Riccelli
$22,500 CLM. PRICE

Sire: Exclusive Era ($3,500)
by Exclusive Native
Dam: Responsive
by Reviewer
Bred in KY by Harbor View Farm

Career:	18	2	3	2	$42,000		
Wet:	4	0	2	0	$8,160	1991: 11 1 2 1	$21,500
Turf:	0	0	0	0	$0	1990: 4 1 1 1	$20,500
Dist:	12	2	2	2	$35,500	Sar: 0 0 0 0	$0

1095

| 15Jly91 | 1Bel | ft 3F | Clm14000 | 6f | 22.42 45.81 | 1:11.30 71 | 26 4 1hd 1hd | 1hd 2no R Mojica Jr5 | 109 |
2.00 Island's End114noPrincipally1092¾Clark's Gap1072
Dueled outside winner throughout, outgamed in a long drive
| 5Jly91 | 3Bel | my3F | Clm17000 | 7f | 22.87 45.88 1:11.74 1:26.01 59 | 59 1 2½ 23 | 24 45½ RP Romero | 116 |
2.80 Say Jo Jo116PPorcelain Goddess112½Clark's Gap1083
2-wide speed, early leader, chased winner, tired
| 30May91 | 2Bel | ft 3F | Clm17500 | 6f | 22.59 46.12 | 1:11.81 60 | 8/8 5 63½ 2½ | 3½ 43 MO Vasquez5 | 111 |
2.70 Mogambo's Pleasure116¾Lauren Melisa116nkTwo Snaps Up1162
5-wide thruout, circled on turn, challenged midstretch, tired
| Claimed from Jeff Odintz |
| 17May91 | 2Bel | ft 3F | Clm17500 | 6f | 22.69 47.12 | 1:13.06 48 | 7/11 3 62 42 | 32½ 33 MO Vasquez5 | 113 |
7.80 Marisa's Night114½Clark'nkPrincehd   *Rallied, outfinished*
| 25Apr91 | 3Aqu | ft 3F | Clm17500 | 6f | 22.82 47.33 | 1:12.86 58 | 1/5 2 42 2hd | 1hd 1½ MO Vasquez5 | 111 |
1.10 Principally111½Two Snaps Up½Divine Gold9½   *Driving*
| 5Apr91 | 3Aqu | ft 3F | Clm25000 | 1m | 22.48 45.86 1:11.31 1:37.73 65 | 1/8 4 33 32½ 33 | 44 413½ JF Chavez | 114 |
4.70 Catch The Irish1075SpyLdrL1½Nunyjs7½   *Chased pace, wknd*
| 18Mar91 | 5Aqu | sy 3F | Clm25000 | 1m | 23.17 46.64 1:11.87 1:38.96 65 | 3/6 2 21 22 21½ | 23 24½ JF Chavez | 116 |
5.70 Star Testamony1162½Principly1¾ApalachBls nk   *Second best*
| 3Mar91 | 5Aql | wf 3F | Alw27000Nw1x | 6f | 22.30 45.84 | 1:10.89 52 | 4/6 4 42½ 64½ | 64½ 69 JF Chavez | 116 |
12.50 Mezzanotte116½DazzleMeJoPHaiSecreto½   *Wide, nothing.*
| 13Feb91 | 2Aql | ft 3F | Clm35000 | 6f | 22.80 46.33 | 1:12.97 47 | 2/10 6 75 54½ | 814 911 R Migliore | 116 |
2.10 Why Me Susita1091½Express The Blues116½Bella Isabella1121
Moved up inside into stretch, gave way stretch.
| Claimed from Sandra Dimauro |
| 23Jan91 | 5Aql | ft 3F | Clm65000 | 6f | 22.12 45.09 | 1:11.44 61 | 56 1 1hd 2½ | 85 MO Vasquez5 | 107 |
15.00 Baked Alaska107¾DunRmnLdy½Starswhrl nk   *Good spd, tired*

Workouts: 31Jly Sar-tr 4f ft 51.83 B   26Jly Sar-tr 4f ft 54.00 B   29Jun Bel-tr 3f ft 38.02 B   14Mar Aqu 3f ft

---

DIVINE GOLD
3yo (Mar) filly, dk. bay/brown
Trainer: Murray M Garren
Owner: Murray M Garren
$20,000 CLM. PRICE

Sire: Premiership ($7,500)
by Exclusive Native
Dam: Rive Gauche
by Star Envoy
Bred in FL by R. A. Kingwell

Career:	31	3	2	3	$42,740		
Wet:	3	1	0	0	$10,200	1991: 18 2 2 1	$31,100
Turf:	2	0	0	0	$0	1990: 13 1 0 2	$11,640
Dist:	14	1	1	3	$16,740	Sar: 1 0 0 0	$0

1075

| 2Aug91 | 3Sar | hd 3F | Clm35000 | 1⅛ ①22.74 46.77 1:11.69 1:50.30 39 | 3/12 4 84½ 97½1212113112½ MO Vasquez | 116 |
53.50 Spy Leader Lady116¼Red Journey116ACareer Move1161
Three-wide backstretch, could not keep pace
| 24Jly91 | 2Sar | ft 3F | Clm25000 | 1⅛ 23.36 47.30 1:12.60 1:53.12 39 | 6/9 6 53 58½ 913 812 99½ A Cordero Jr | 112 |
8.10 Maryinthemorning1165½Fair Propina116kSpy Leader Lady1164½
Early factor along rail, tired badly
| 12Jly91 | 1Bel | ft 3E | Clm25000 | 1⅛ 23.13 46.62 1:11.39 1:43.96 41 | 8/8 1 11½ 1½ 2½ 22½ 25 MO Vasquez5 | 107 |
15.80 Sunny Barbie116ADivine Gold1075½Turn Right111½
Made pace rail, yielded to winner, wknd final furlong

28Jun91 3Bel ft 3F Clm17500 1½ 22.97 46.87 1:13.26 1:47.57 6¼ 8/9 1 2½ 2½ 1hd 42½ 55½ MO Vasquez⁵ 113   3.10 Two Snaps Up116¼DarbyBls^noShadyDl²½ *Chased, led, tired*
22Jun91 1Bel ft 3F Clm25000 7f 22.77 45.84 1:10.99 1:24.29 5½ 3/8 1 3¹ 3¹½ 88½ 89½ MO Vasquez⁵ 109   10.30 Living In Sin116³Bestrk¹¼Tripi^ns *Chased outside, tired*
10Jun91 6Bel ft 3F Clm25000 6f 23.12 46.87 1:12.35 6½ 7/11 6 5²¼ 42 5½ 6¼½ MO Vasquez⁵ 109   8.00 Rather Be Social112^nsPaulNeet³AppingG²² *Four-wide bid*
5Jun91 2Bel ft 3F Clm17500 1m 22.65 46.07 1:11.93 1:38.70 6½ 6/10 5 1hd 1hd 1hd 11½ MO Vasquez⁵ 113   4.50^sDivine Gold131¼TwoSnps²TeilThT²½ *Dueled outside, drvg*
27May91 2Bel fm 3F Clm35000 1¹⁄₁₆ 23.34 46.19 1:10.77 1:43.24 6½ 1/10 3 43 45 66 75½ 69 MO Vasquez⁵ 111   15.30 Magic Jackie116²CareerMv³HerCntss¹½ *Inside, fell back*
23May91 9Bel ft 3F Clm25000 1m 23.17 47.00 1:12.72 1:39.66 6½ 7/10 3 1² 11½ 52½ 96½ 815½ A Cordero Jr 114   14.10 Quick Glance116³SpitUdg²SunnyBr^no *Inside speed, tired*
6May91 1Aqu sy 3F Clm17500 1m 22.91 46.04 1:11.68 1:38.93 6½ 3/5 3 1¹ 1¹½ 1½ .1² 15 A Cordero Jr 114   3.20 Divine Gold114⁵TotlCnt²RathrB^nk *Inside speed, driving*

Workouts: 9Jly Bel•4f ft 50.24 H   16May Bel•4f ft   12Apr Bel•5f ft

---

HAPPY TAPPER

3yo (Feb) filly, bay	**Sire:** Tap Shoes ($1,500)
Trainer: Donald E Jacobs	by Riva Ridge
Owner: Donald E Jacobs	**Dam:** Revels End
	by Welsh Pageant
$22,500 CLM. PRICE	Bred in NY by Horse Play

Career: 17 5 3 5 $34,222

	Wet:	5 2 0 1	$6,070	1991:	11 4 2 3	$19,110
	Turf:	0 0 0 0	$0	1990:	6 1 1 2	$5,112
	Dist:	15 5 3 3	$23,292	Sar:	0 0 0 0	$0

116

2Aug91 8FL ft 3-F Alw11000 5½f 22.03 46.76 1:06.83 7½ 1/8 4 67½ 45½ 3² 11 MJ McCarthy 115   3.70 Happy Tapper115¹Bedford Seal116²Candalera116³ *Allowed to settle on rail, rallied in stretch, won driving*
21Jly91 6FL ft 3-F Alw11000Nw1x 6f 22.00 45.66 1:12.35 6½ 5/8 4 66½ 67½ 55 3^hd MJ McCarthy 113   13.00 Overpowder115^nkMalwalker³113^dkHappy Tapper113¹½ *Unhurried early, stalked pace gaining late str*
5Jly91 5FL sy 3-F Clm10000Nw3L 5½f 22.84 47.31 1:07.16 6½ 7/7 2 65½ 43 2^hd 13½ MJ McCarthy 115   2.10 Happy Tapper115³Tokyo Bound113¼Sullivan's Carr112^hd *Unhurried early, advanced steadily, gnd cmmd midstr, driving*
25Jun91 5FL ft 3-F Clm10000Nw3L 6f 22.36 46.79 1:13.74 5½ 2/7 5 74½ 75½ 53 2² MJ McCarthy 114   3.80 Dead Ender108³Happy Tapper¹TokyoBound² *Finished well*
12Jun91 4FL ft 3-F Clm10000Nw2L 5½f 22.68 47.54 1:07.78 5½ 1/7 3 2½ 1½ 12 1¹½ MJ McCarthy 115   2.20 Happy Tapper114¹¼A Bout Love²Sweet Lily⁴ *Driving*
31May91 7FL ft 3-F Clm10000Nw2L 6f 22.34 46.56 1:13.89 4½ 1/10 7 42½ 52½ 32 43½ MJ McCarthy 115   2.60 Stark Scarlet112½PeacefulBeat^nkGoldenEmbrac¹½ *No rally*
21May91 9FL ft 3-F Clm10000Nw2L 5½f 22.56 46.70 1:06.60 5½ 6/7 4 44 46½ 46½ 27 MJ McCarthy 114   3.80 Iron Silk Miss116²Happy²StarkS³ *No match for winner*
10May91 7FL ft 3-F Clm10000Nw2L 6f 22.50 46.70 1:13.69 6½ 6/10 4 43 45 25 33 L Hulet 113   15.90 Batus110⁵Sullvn's³Cr^noHappy Tapper² *Lacked late response*
30Apr91 10FL ft 3-F Alw 6700Nw2L 5½f 21.82 46.00 1:05.82 5½ 6/9 7 78 76½ 79½ 614½ MJ McCarthy 115   10.20 Alabama Anne111³Raven³Melanie's Star¹½ *No threat*
14Apr91 5FL ft 3-F Clm10000Nw2L 5f 22.80 47.25 1:00.60 4½ 6/6 5 66 59 44 32½ MJ McCarthy 115   5.30 Rose Garden Lady116¹Vintg W¹¼HappyT⁵½ *Found stride late*

Workouts: 11Apr FL 4f ft 49.50 B   7Apr FL 4f ft 51.10 B   2Apr FL 3f gd 40.30 B

RATHER BE SOCIAL

3yo (Feb) filly, dk. bay/brown	**Sire:** Raised Socially ($4,000)
Trainer: Amos E Bolton	by Raise A Native
Owner: Cyril Austin	**Dam:** Rather Be Dancing
	by Caro
$20,000 CLM. PRICE	Bred in KY by Andrea Pollack Singe

Career: 22 2 3 5 $41,840

	Wet:	4 0 1 1	$4,680	1991:	15 2 3 4	$38,960
	Turf:	2 0 0 0	$0	1990:	7 0 0 1	$2,880
	Dist:	10 2 1 2	$25,200	Sar:	2 0 0 0	$0

116

28Jly91 9Sar ft 3F Clm25000 7f 22.52 45.88 1:10.96 1:24.50 5½ 1/12 11 62½ 75½ 99½ 87½ ME Smith 116 b   13.80 Docent116¹Chief Mistress114^nkSoon To Sin114¹½ *Rail backstretch, turn, moved out stretch, no factor*
17Jly91 9Bel hd 3F Clm50000 1¹⁄₁₆ 22.98 45.71 1:10.64 1:41.89 6½ 12/12 11 97½ 86½ 41½ 58½ 613½ J Cruguet 113 b   36.70 Right Wing Hot116³Cozzinia116^nkDowny Feathers116² *Off a bit slowly, moved up five wide turn, tired final furlong*
10Jun91 6Bel ft 3F Clm25000 6f 23.12 46.87 1:12.35 6½ 10/11 8 72½ 1hd 2hd 1^nk JR Velazquez 112 b   11.40 Rather Be Social112^nkPaul Neeti116³Apping Gal118² *Brushed four-wide late turn, dueled stretch, edged clear, lasted*
27May91 3Bel ft 3F Clm25000 6f 23.10 47.90 1:13.12 6½ 4/8 5 3½ 3½½ MO Vasquez⁵ 116   12.00 Bram Stoker114½Meetmen^noRathrBSc² *6-wide, mild rally*
23May91 9Bel ft 3F Clm25000 1m 23.17 47.00 1:12.72 1:39.66 6½ 5/10 7 66½ 65½ 63½ 74½1017 R Migliore 116   9.30 Quick Glance116¹SpitUdg²SunnyBr^no *Two-wide, fell back*
6May91 1Aqu sy 3F Clm17500 1m 22.91 46.04 1:11.68 1:38.93 6½ 5/5 2 41½ 32½ 32 32½ 37 JF Chavez 116 b   6.70 Divine Gold114⁵Total Control²³Rather Be Social116^nk *Three-wide backstretch, two-wide turn, rail stretch, no rally*
Claimed from Jeff Odintz
17Apr91 5Aqu wf 3F Alw29000Nw1x 1¹⁄₁₆ 24.25 48.52 1:13.10 1:51.60 6½ 6/6 5 65½ 66½ 64½ 512 52½½ JF Chavez 116 b   8.80 Country Strider116¹Brezhr⁴TripiC¹ *Inside, no threat*
13Apr91 5Aqu ft 3F Clm35000 6f 23.20 46.67 1:12.92 6½ 7/9 5 41½ 53½ 53 31½ JF Chavez 116 b   3.30 Peaceful Pioneer113¹MoonOn¹Rathr^nk *Fell back, rallied*
3Apr91 7Aqu ft 3F Alw29000Nw1x 1m 22.85 45.68 1:10.85 1:37.59 7½ 5/6 2 42½ 44½ 43 34½ 29³ JF Chavez 116 b   8.90 Too Fast To Catch116³Rathr^nkBrazi⁵ *Inside, mild rally*
21Mar91 2Aqu ft 3F Clm17500 1m 22.83 46.04 1:12.12 1:40.03 5½ 9/10 4 62 2¹ 2¹ 3½ 3¹ A Graell 116 b   4.30 Mogambo's Pleasure116^nkCatch Thelrish109¾RatherBeSocial116³ *Challenged outside the winner the final 1/2 ...*
Claimed from Michael H Daggett

Figure addicts land immediately on Principally and Happy Tapper, the latter a shipper from Finger Lakes. The two boast 71s last out, speed figures apparently dominant in this lineup. But neither horse has matched par for today's conditions, and both usually record speed figures well in arrears of today's par. No other horse in the race can approach par.

The pratfall here is to support either Principally or Happy Tapper because their most recent speed figures are higher than the others. Comparison handicapping breaks down at many junctures, and this is one of them. This phenomenon—all horses below par—appears most frequently in low-class races, but not exclusively. The horses simply cannot run fast enough to flatter par.

Whenever the predicament appears, figure handicappers must be aware the numbers will be less meaningful than usual. Other factors take on added significance, notably early pace, truly troubled trips, successful trainer patterns, track biases, and improving form.

Excellent figure handicappers everywhere will find glorious opportunities in the claiming races. Devoid of the degrees of endurance and determination that distinguish their classier nonclaiming counterparts, claiming horses run as fast as they can for the six furlongs or middle distances they must. The fastest horses will win much of the time. Figure handicappers in the know wield an enviable advantage.

NON-WINNERS ALLOWANCES

Comes now an emergency call inquiring about the cold-blooded handicapping prospects of a red-hot tip on a horse. It was the third race at Del Mar, August 9, 1991, a six-furlong allowance sprint for Cal-breds 3up which had not won $3000 other than maiden or claiming.

"This is a really strong push from the owners. They say the horse has improved tremendously and is just too good for this mediocre group of state-breds. The name is Sanger Brave.

"How does the horse look on the cold dope?"

I had not visited the race overnight but said I would look quickly. In less than thirty seconds I assured the caller the horse had scarcely a chance and in no way warranted a serious wager.

By coincidence, the race brims with lessons about nonwinners allowance competition, among the toughest of all races to beat consistently, and a source of relentless losses for handicappers overly dependent on speed figures. On Quirin-style figures, par at Del Mar for nonwinners-once allowances is 105. The tip horse shaped up like this:

Sanger Brave
Dk. b. or br. g. 3(Feb), by Chief to Earn—Last Roman, by Stab
DESORMEAUX K J
Br.—Wardell Ranch (Cal)
Own.—Wygant R
Tr.—Hess R B Jr
723¹
114 Pace Speed
26Jly91- 4Dmr fst 6½f :22¹ :45³ 1:16⁴ 3+ⓈMd 32000   8 4 52½ 41½ 2½ 13½ Desormeaux K J LB 116   3.90   84-14   **94** **100**
Speed Index: Last Race: –2.0   1–Race Avg.: –2.0   1–Race Avg.: –2.0
LATEST WORKOUTS   Jly 24 Dmr 3f fst :36⁴ Hg   Jly 19 Dmr 5f fst 1:05 H   Jly 10 Hol 3f fs

Sanger Brave was leaping from bottom-level maiden-claiming conditions to the allowances with a pace figure 5½ lengths below today's par and a speed figure five lengths below. In addition, Sanger Brave's turn time in the maiden-claiming race was 23.1, at least two lengths too slow to survive the second fraction of a major league allowance race.

Even if Sanger Brave had recorded a speed figure equal to par for a nonwinners-once allowance field (105), the horse's pace figure and turn time would have disqualified him without mercy.

Before examining the rest of the field, a few unadulterated assertions about the nonwinners allowance series are in order.

First, speed figures alone cannot beat these races. An over-reliance on final figures probably will throw the worst financial losses of a figure handicapper's season. The reasons should be plain.

As younger, developing horses move from maiden races to nonwinners-once allowances, and from nonwinners-once allowances to nonwinners-twice allowances, their basic abilities, distance preferences, and pace preferences will be changing rapidly. Speed figures recorded at the preceding step can change dramatically, at times improving, but more frequently declining.

The more substantive explanation encompasses both class and pace. Maiden graduates obviously confront a better quality of horse under allowance conditions—faster, sharper, more determined to win. Almost invariably the early pace intensifies. The fractional time will be swifter and the advantage more savagely contested. Horses moving ahead with unimpressive pace figures will be outgunned, regardless of their speed figures.

As will be evident, the pace Sanger Brave faces in the allowance race will be many lengths faster than what he overtook in the maiden-claiming affair. If Sanger Brave attempts to contest that pace nearing the second call, his final figure, not very impressive to begin, will probably plunge.

Moreover, even when maiden graduates can satisfy the pace requirements against allowance horses, the finish will likely be contested in decent time. In other words, the allowance race will be faster and more severely contested at each point of call.

Figure handicappers buy insurance against recurring upsets in the nonwinners allowance series by insisting horses present the proper pace figures and turn times. Where speed figures exceed or equal par, pace figures should be within a length of par at today's class. If pace figures fall two lengths short of par, frontrunners and pace-pressers probably will be outrun.

Turn time qualifies too as a critical factor in the nonwinners allowance series and should not be excused if below par. Turn-time par for allowance sprinters at Del Mar is 23 seconds. Horses that complete the second fraction slower than that and will be moving ahead in allowance class are very unlikely to succeed. Some young horses surprise impressively, but most either fall down badly or suffer a setback due to a lack of seasoning against the faster, more competitive fractions.

Figure handicappers are urged to consider the above standards firm. Regardless of their speed figures, discount horses under nonwinners allowance conditions where pace figures or turn times fail to satisfy par. The strict guidelines serve the practical purpose of eliminating numerous false contenders, thereby alleviating the handicapping burden.

A review of the horses in the allowance field where Sanger Brave was offered as a hot tip reinforces the preceding discussion well. Examine the past performances and the speed and pace figures alongside.

Only two of the horses show higher speed figures than Sanger Brave, but every horse has a significantly faster pace figure and a faster turn time than the good thing.

Oscar Oscar Oscar

Clearly below par of 105 at both the pace call and the finish, and exiting a maiden-claiming race. Out.

Classic Setting

Has missed three times under state-bred nonwinners-once allowances, and the figures indicate why. Too slow early, too slow late. Out.

Baraonet

Out of action eight months and exiting high-priced claiming races restricted to three-year-olds. Most recent figures are best, a positive sign, and the 3YO claiming races occurred in late fall, a more hopeful time than winter, spring, or summer. Claimed third back as well by leading claiming trainer Bill Spawr, to be ridden today by Chris McCarron, and working well. Most recent pace figure is one-half length within par at 104, and speed figure equals today's par. The turn time on Nov 28 is a sensational 22 flat. Contender.

3rd Del Mar

START · 6 FURLONGS · DEL MAR · FINISH

6 FURLONGS. (1.07^3) ALLOWANCE. Purse $34,000. 3-year-olds and upward, bred in California, which are non-winners of $3,000 other than maiden or claiming. Weights, 3-year-olds, 117 lbs. Older, 121 lbs. Non-winners of a race other than claiming allowed, 3 lbs.

LASIX—Oscar Oscar Oscar, Classic Setting, Baraonet, Chime Song, Sanger Brave.

Oscar Oscar Oscar
B. g. 3(Mar), by Jaklin Klugman—Rubies Mildred, by Forceten
STEVENS G L
Br.—Klugman J (Cal)
Own.—El Rancho de Jaklin
Tr.—Olivares Frank T22^4 **114**

Pace 99 Speed 99

																				Pace	Speed
22Jly91- 6Hol	fst	6f	:22^3	:45^2	1:11^1	3↑	[S]Md 50000	2	1	2hd	1½	12½	11½	Stevens G L	LBb	116	2.30	84-13			
3Jly91- 9Hol	fst	6f	:22	:44^3	1:10^1	3↑	Md 32000	7	4	2½	1hd	2hd	2nk	Stevens G L	LBb	117	4.70	89-11			
7Jun91- 9Hol	fst	6f	:21^4	:44^3	1:10^1	3↑	[S]Md 32000	9	2	2½	22½	24	36¾	McCarron C J	LBb	116	*2.00	82-14			
9May91- 3Hol	fst	6f	:22^1	:45^3	1:11^3	3↑	[S]Md 32000	9	3	11½	12	12½	21¼	Stevens G L	LBb	115	*2.10	81-16			
19Apr91- 2SA	fst	6f	:22	:45	1:10^1		[S]Md 32000	8	5	43½	45½	36½	38¼	Meza R Q	B	118	8.50	77-16			

Speed Index: Last Race: –3.0 3–Race Avg.: –2.3 5–Race Avg.: –3.4
LATEST WORKOUTS Aug 4 Dmr 5f fst 1:02^3 H Jly 30 Dmr 4f fst :50^1 H Jly 18 SA 5f f:

Classic Setting
Dk. b. or br. g. 4, by Never Tabled—Classic Pirate, by Pirate's Bounty
VALENZUELA P A
Br.—Wyged M J (Cal)
Own.—Wyged Mr–Mrs M J
Tr.—Nickerson Victor J T23 **121**

																				Pace	Speed
26Jly91- 3Dmr	fst	6½f	:22	:45	1:16^3	3↑	[S]Alw 35000	1	6	2½	2½	32	33¼	Valenzuela P A	LB	121	3.90	82-14		101	98
26Jly91-Off slowly, rank, steadied 1/16																					
15Nov90- 7Hol	fst	6f	:21^3	:44^4	1:10	3↑	[S]Alw 30000	5	2	1hd	41¾	53	53¾	McCarron C J	LB	120	*1.30	86-12		101	100
8Oct90- 7SA	fst	6f	:21^2	:43^3	1:08^4	3↑	[S]Alw 32000	8	4	3½	22	24	45¾	Valenzuela P A	LB	117	*2.10	86-17			
1Sep90- 6Dmr	fst	6½f	:22	:45	1:16	3↑	Md Sp Wt	3	5	1½	11½	14	15½	Valenzuela P A	LB	118	*1.00	88-10			

Speed Index: Last Race: –4.0 3–Race Avg.: –1.0 4–Race Avg.: –1.2
LATEST WORKOUTS ●Jly 22 Hol 6f fst 1:13^2 H Jly 16 Hol 6f fst 1:17^2 H Jly 11 Hol 6f f.

Baraonet
B. g. 4, by Chivalry—Ambica, by Red Fox
MCCARRON C J
Br.—Rigg W C (Cal) T22
Own.—Hogate H
Tr.—Spawr Bill **121**

																				Pace	Speed
28Nov90- 7Hol	fst	6½f	:21^4	:44	1:14^4		Clm 50000	2	6	42	31½	31½	2½	McCarron C J	LB	116	4.30	100-06		104	105
15Nov90- 3Hol	fst	1	:44^2	1:09^2	1:36^2		Clm 32000	3	1	11½	11½	11½	1½	McCarron C J	LB	116	2.60	82-23			
8Sep90- 3Dmr	fst	1	:45^2	1:09^4	1:36		Clm c-40000	3	4	2hd	1hd	3½	46	McCarron C J	LB	115	3.50	80-14			
10Aug90- 3Dmr	fst	1	:45	1:09^3	1:35^4		Clm 62500	5	1	11½	11½	2hd	44¾	Valenzuela P A	L	116	6.90	82-16			
27Jly90- 5Dmr	fm	1$\frac{1}{16}$	Ⓣ:46^3	1:11^3	1:42^4		Clm 80000	1	1	11½	11	2½	89	Valenzuela P A		116	5.00	84-11			
14Jly90- 9Hol	fm	1	Ⓣ:44^3	1:09^1	1:35		Clm 100000	1	1	12½	14	11	23½	Valenzuela P A		116	9.10	85-11			
21Jun90- 7Hol	fst	6f	:22	:45	1:09^2	3↑	[S]Alw 35000	3	7	75½	64¾	56	59	Olivares F T22^4		116	9.80	84-08			
31May90- 8Hol	fm	1⅛	Ⓣ:46^1	1:11	1:49^1		Alw 35000	4	1	14	11½	33	916¾	Valenzuela P A		119	14.50	65-23			
11May90- 7Hol	fst	6½f	:21^2	:44^1	1:15^2	3↑	[S]Alw 31000	2	8	41¾	52	54½	56½	Olivares F T22^4		115	41.50	91-06			
18Feb90- 7SA	sly	1	:46	1:10^3	1:36^1		Alw 37000	5	1	2hd	24	612	625	Flores D R		120	58.40	61-18			

Speed Index: Last Race: +6.0 3–Race Avg.: –1.6 3–Race Avg.: –1.6
LATEST WORKOUTS Aug 7 Dmr 4f fst :47^4 H ●Jly 28 SA 6f fst 1:13^4 H Jly 14 SA 5f fs

Davus
B. g. 3(Mar), by Naevus—Elegant Beauty, by Norcliffe
PINCAY L JR
Br.—Straub Cecilia P (Cal) T22^2
Own.—Straub–Rubens Cecilia P
Tr.—Truman Eddie **114**

																				Pace	Speed
12Jly91- 8Hol	fst	6f	:21^3	:43^4	1:09^3	3↑	[S]Alw 32000	8	3	41½	42½	55	86¾	Flores D R	Bb	113	*1.10	85-10		113	99
15Jun91- 7Hol	fst	6f	:21^3	:44^1	1:09	3↑	[S]Alw 32000	2	4	12½	13	11½	2½	Flores D R T22^8	Bb	114	7.00	94-10		106	107
28Mar91- 8SA	fst	6½f	:21^1	:44	1:16		[S]Zany Tactics	1	2	1½	2hd	64¾	713	Flores D R	Bb	115	21.40	77-16			
14Feb91- 1SA	fst	6f	:21^3	:44^1	1:08^4		Clm 25000	8	1	11½	11½	14	16½	Flores D R	Bb	115	7.80	92-11			
12Jan91- 2SA	fst	6½f	:21^2	:44^2	1:17^3		Clm 50000	8	1	2hd	1hd	53½	810	Delahoussaye E	Bb	116	11.60	72-17			
13Aug90- 10LA	fst	4½f	:21^3	:44^3	:50^3		Saddleback	1	8		32	3nk	35	Flores D R	b	116	*1.20	96-06			
31Jly90- 6LA	fst	4½f	:21^2	:44^2	:50^2		Md 32000	7	1		14	13½	18	Flores D R	b	118	10.50	102-04			

Speed Index: Last Race: –5.0 3–Race Avg.: –2.6 7–Race Avg.: –1.1
LATEST WORKOUTS Aug 5 Dmr 6f fst 1:13 H Jly 24 Dmr 5f fst 1:02 H Jly 8 Hol 5f fst

Chime Song
Dk. b. or br. c. 4, by Captain Nick—Chataquos, by Nantequos
TORRES H
Br.—Valpredo J (Cal)
Own.—Valpredo J
Tr.—Caganich Barbara **113^5**

																				Pace	Speed
1Aug91- 5Dmr	fst	6f	:21^4	:45	1:09^2	3↑	Alw 35000	2	2	12½	32½	69	724½	Torres H^5	LB	116	15.70	67-15		101	xx
7Mar91- 8SA	fst	5½f	:21^4	:44^4	1:03^3		[S]Dimaggio	5	5	42½	44	77	98	Nakatani C S	LB	113	46.90	89-16			
27May90- 5Hol	fst	6f	:22	:45	1:09	3↑	Alw 33000	5	6	41¼	41¼	44	35½	Garcia J A		115	*.90	89-06			
6May90- 7Hol	fst	6½f	:21^2	:43^3	1:14^4		Alw 31000	5	1	1hd	1hd	21½	25	Garcia J A		119	8.20	96-05			
27Apr90- 8Hol	fst	6f	:21^3	:44^3	1:09^3		Alw 31000	3	3	1hd	1½	1½	31¾	Garcia J A		119	10.90	90-11			
8Apr90- 7SA	fst	6f	:21^4	:45^3	1:10		Alw 34000	5	3	3½	21½	56½	519	Desormeaux K J		120	9.90	67-17			
13Sep89- 8Dmr	fst	1	:44^4	1:09^1	1:35^2		Dmr Fut	11	1	11	21½	78	1120¼	Valenzuela P A		117	29.50	69-10			
13Sep89-Grade I																					
1Sep89- 8Dmr	fst	6f	:21^3	:44^2	1:09^2		[S]Graduation	8	3	11½	11½	1½	2½	Toro F		117	9.40	90-11			
18Jun89- 8GG	fst	5½f	:21^1	:44	1:03^1		[S]Quickstep	1	9	98¾	915	916	918	Lambert J		117	*1.50	76-19			
25May89- 4Hol	fst	5f	:22^1	:45^3	:57^3		[S]Md Sp Wt	8	1	12½	12	14	16	Pincay L Jr		117	4.80	98-12			

Speed Index: Last Race: –18.0 3–Race Avg.: –6.0 9–Race Avg.: –2.8
LATEST WORKOUTS Jly 30 Dmr 3f fst :35^2 H Jly 24 Dmr 5f fst 1:00^4 H Jly 17 Hol 4f fs

Davus

The most interesting horse in the field and absolutely the key to the race. Pace figure last out is a sizzling 113 (turn time of 22.2). The gelding could not keep abreast of that pace without losing lengths at the finish, contributing to a typically low speed figure of 99. But two back the pace figure is 106 and the speed figure is 107, both superior to par today. The pace that day was surely more comfortable, a crucial consideration in the nonwinners series. Davus improved abruptly at three, as many horses do, suddenly throttling $25,000 claimers with a pace figure of 106 and a speed figure of 105, allowance quality numbers. The quick move into a sprint stakes was premature, but the 3YO figures well at the preliminary allowance level. Might be the need-to-lead kind of cheap commodity, but more evidence on that is needed at this stage. Can throttle back to a 106 pace figure here, en route to a speed figure of par or better. Contender.

Chime Song

May show early speed but is no match for Davus during the second fraction. Not suited to eligibility conditions. Needs claiming competition.

In the final analysis, the race can be pared to Baraonet and Davus. Baraonet should not be able to defeat the speedy Davus following an eight-month layoff, unless he's just clearly the superior racehorse. A claiming background does not support that case. Sanger Brave does rate an outsider's chance. If Baraonet forces Davus to a pace figure approaching 113, and both collapse, the survivor's speed figure could be as low as 100, which Sanger Brave can deliver. But the upstart's chances depend absolutely on the pace call.

Look again at the speed and pace figures of Davus. A suspicious combination of speed and pace figures under nonwinners-once conditions resembles the 113-99 of Davus's last start. Normally the pace figure will be more realistic. If Davus had recorded a combination of 106-99 instead on July 12, handicappers should abandon the horse. Figure analysts prefer a balance between the pace and speed figures in nonwinners allowance races, with the pace figure no less than a length (two points) below today's par.

A few remarks about Baraonet's turn time of 22 flat are germane. If permitted a 22.3 around the far turn, Baraonet may improve its final figure, all right. That happens regularly. But under allowance conditions, a rapid turn time does not redeem speed and pace figures unambiguously below par.

The turn time (22.4) of Oscar Oscar Oscar fits allowance competition well enough, but neither his pace figure (99) nor speed figure (99) does. Turn time does not carry horses very far in that context. In addition, closers should inevitably reveal a fast turn time, as they maneuver into striking position. A closer's pace figure will often be weak, as a function of running style, but its turn time should impress.

As matters proceeded, Davus grabbed the lead unmolested and nursed it all the way. His pace and speed figures were a familiar 105-107. When Baraonet tired from chasing Davus, Sanger Brave closed well enough to place. But he never threatened the winner.

5129—THIRD RACE. 6 furlongs. 3 year olds & up. Cal Breds. Allowances. Purse $34,000.

Index	Horse and Jockey	Wt.	PP	ST	¼	½		Str.	Fin.	To $1
4545	Davus, Pincay	117	4	3	1½	1½	.	12½	12¾	2.70
(5022)	Sanger Brave, Desormeaux	114	6	1	6	4¹	.	4⁴	2¾	3.80
2151	Baraonet, McCarron	121	3	4	3¹	2²	.	2½	31¾	2.60
5068	Chime Song, Torres	113	5	2	2ʰᵈ	3½	.	3½	45½	16.50
4618	Oscar Oscar Oscar, Stevens	114	1	5	4½	6	.	6	51¼	9.20
5021	Classic Setting, Valenzuela	121	2	6	5ʰᵈ	51½	.	5¹	6	2.50

Scratched—None.

4—DAVUS		7.40	4.00	3.20
6—SANGER BRAVE			4.20	3.20
3—BARAONET				3.40

Time—21 4/5, 44 1/5, 56 1/5, 1.08 4/5. Cloudy & fast. Winner—BG 88 Naevus-Elegant Beauty. Trained by E. Truman. Mutuel pool—$285,598. Exacta pool—$243,336.

$2 EXACTA (4-6) PAID $37.20

Route races can be treated differently. Now the balance of pace and speed supersedes a qualifying pace figure. Ideally, pace figures of routers can fall slightly below their speed figures, assuming the speed figures match par or exceed it. If pace figures exceed par in nonwinners allowance routes, speed figures should too. The latter pattern is especially significant for sprinters stretching out.

A number of horses in the nonwinners allowance route below demonstrate these relationships, and several others that figure handicappers should find interesting. Par at both the pace call and final time is 103.

5th Del Mar

1 1-16 MILES DEL MAR

START ◄   ◄ FINISH

1 ¹⁄₁₆ MILES. (1.40) ALLOWANCE. Purse $37,000. Fillies and mares. 3-year-olds and upward which are non-winners of $3,000 other than maiden, claiming or starter. Weights, 3-year-olds, 117 lbs.; older, 122 lbs. Non-winners of a race other than claiming at one mile or over allowed 3 lbs.

LASIX—Cara Carissima, Ski Bar, Mats Dolly, Steller Story, Verdeuse–Fr, Adorable

Cara Carissima

B. f. 3(Apr), by Caro—Reine Imperiale, by King Emperor

MCCARRON C J
Own.—Evans E P
Br.—Skara Glen Stable (Ky)
Tr.—Lukas D Wayne

114

																Pace	Speed
27Jly91- 7Dmr fm 1	①:48	1:12	1:36³	⑥Alw 38000	4 1	1hd 1hd 1¹ 2¹½	Desormeaux K J	LB	117	12.00	87–10						99	102
6Jly91- 7Hol fm 5½f	①:21²	:43³	1:01	3+⑥Alw 32000	8 6	7¹⁰ 6¹³ 6¹¹ 6¹¹½	McCarron C J	LB	116	4.40	– –							
22Jun91- 7Hol fst 6½f	:21³	:44	1:15⁴	3+⑥Alw 32000	3 4	2¹ 3² 6⁹ 6¹7½	McCarron C J	B	115	2.70	76–11							
18Nov90- 7Hol fst 6f	:22	:45³	1:10²	⑥Alw 36000	1 7	74½ 4² 3² 2²½	Desormeaux K J	B	120	*1.30	85–10							
4Nov90- 6SA fst 6f	:21⁴	:44⁴	1:09²	⑥Md Sp Wt	10 1	2¹ 2hd 2hd 1¹	Desormeaux K J	B	117	*.90	89–12						99	102
60ct90- 3SA fst 6f	:21¹	:44¹	1:09¹	⑥Md Sp Wt	2 6	1¹ 1hd 2¹½ 2²½	Velasquez J	B	117	7.70	87–15							
1Sep90- 4Dmr fst 6f	:21⁴	:44³	1:10	⑥Md Sp Wt	10 7	3² 2² 35½ 36½	Valenzuela P A	B	117	3.30	84–10							

Speed Index: Last Race: (—)   3–Race Avg.: (—)   12–Race Avg.: (—)
LATEST WORKOUTS   Aug 7 Dmr   5f fst 1:00¹ H   Jly 24 Dmr   5f fst 1:00² H   Jly 16 Hol   5f fs

As a rule, turf figures transfer poorly to the main track. Figure handicappers cannot trust the switches, unless both the pace figure and speed figure on the grass have been unusually strong in relation to par. This is rarely the case. Pace figures are particularly suspect on grass, where the early pace can be inordinately slow.

Figure handicappers evaluating Cara Carissima best rely on her maiden figures as best estimates of how well the filly might perform in today's allowance route. Although the race occurred months ago, at six furlongs, it provides dirt figures in a winning effort at a class level once-removed from today's nonwinners field.

The November 4 figures suggest Cara Carissima can win here, to be sure. Not only is the speed figure a competitive 102, the pace figure of 99 complements the speed figure nicely. The figures 99-102 are moving in the proper direction, indicating Cara Carissima can press a near-par pace and still finish strongly. Contender.

Neo Girl

Gr. f. 3(Mar), by Drone—English Girl, by Verbatim

SOLIS A
Own.—Cooke J K
Br.—Elmendorf Farm Inc (Ky)
Tr.—McAnally Ronald

117

													Pace	Speed
27Jly91- 7Dmr fm 1	①:48	1:12	1:36³	⑥Alw 38000	8 3	3½ 31½ 32½ 52½	Solis A	B	120	9.90	86–10			
27Jun91- 5Hol fm 1¹⁄₁₆ ①:47¹	1:11²	1:42¹	⑥Alw 35000	4 2	1hd 2hd 31½ 53½	Valenzuela P A	B	119	9.10	80–13				
12Jun91- 7Hol fm 1¹⁄₁₆ ①:48¹	1:12	1:49	⑥Alw 35000	7 3	31 2½ 1hd 42½	McCarron C J		119	6.80	82–15				
26May91- 4Hol fst 1¹⁄₁₆	:46³	1:11⁴	1:45¹	3+⑥Md Sp Wt	6 2	21½ 21½ 2² 11½	McCarron C J		115	*1.00e	75–2			
27Apr91- 6Hol fst 6f	:22¹	:45²	1:09²	3+⑥Md Sp Wt	6 6	3² 43½ 41¹ 31³½	McCarron C J		115	*.80	79–12			
13Apr91- 6SA fst 6f	:21⁴	:45²	1:11¹	⑥Md Sp Wt	9 7	51½ 21 2¹ 2no	McCarron C J		117	*.70	80–20			

Speed Index: Last Race: –3.0   1–Race Avg.: –3.0   1–Race Avg.: –3.0
LATEST WORKOUTS   Jly 18 Hol   5f fst 1:00³ H   Jly 12 Hol   5f fst 1:00 H   Jun 21 Hol   4f f

Pace: 97   Speed: 100

Skipping Neo Girl's grass efforts, the route figures of the May 26 maiden win are set in the desirable direction, but the filly is not fast enough. Out.

Ski Bar — B. f. 3(Mar), by Baldski—Kobari, by What a Pleasure
NAKATANI C S
Own.—O'Connor P J
Br.—Waldemar Fms Inc–Sams T H (Fla)
Tr.—Shoemaker Bill
114

Pace 99 Speed 100

27Jly91- 7Dmr	fm	1	Ⓣ:48	1:12	1:363	ⒻAlw 30000	2	5	62¼	42	42½	62¾	Delahoussaye E	LB	117	10.80	86-1
12Jly91- 9Hol	fst	1 1/16	:464	1:114	1:434	3↑ⒻMd 32000	3	3	11	13½	17	111	Stevens G L	LB	115	*2.40	82-2
23Jun91- 10Hol	fst	1 1/16	:454	1:11	1:442	3↑ⒻMd 32000	1	3	31½	14	12	2¾	Stevens G L	LB	115	*2.10	7-1
25May91- 9Hol	fst	6f	:221	:45	1:111	3↑ⒻMd 32000	3	8	52¼	41½	31½	32¼	Stevens G L	LB	116	*1.20	81-11
10May91- 6Hol	fst	6f	:213	:444	1:111	3↑ⒻMd 62500	3	11	109¾	911	99	96½	Pincay L Jr	Bb	117	15.40	77-15
10May91-Hopped start, 4-wide stretch																	
11Apr91- 6SA	fst	6½f	:212	:442	1:174	ⒻMd 50000	9	4	33	33	31½	42¼	Delahoussaye E	B	117	7.20	79-18
14Mar91- 4SA	my	6½f	:22	:453	1:182	ⒻMd 50000	3	4	31½	21½	31	35½	Stevens G L	B	117	6.40	72-1
10Feb91- 6SA	fst	6f	:213	:45	1:102	ⒻMd Sp Wt	5	8	64¼	53¾	59	614¼	Stevens G L	B	117	5.40	70-16

Speed Index: Last Race: +2.0 2–Race Avg.: –1.5 2–Race Avg.: –1.5
LATEST WORKOUTS Aug 7 Dmr 4f fst :481 H Jly 3 Hol 4f fst :474 H Jun 17 Hol 5f 1

Ski Bar presents another complication common to figure handicapping. Figures attaching to a big win against maiden-claiming opposition never transfer easily to better company, especially to the allowance races. Only when both the pace figure and speed figure exceed the allowance par do maiden-claiming figures qualify under nonwinners allowance conditions. No exceptions.

Final-figure handicappers are particularly vulnerable on the matter. Possessing only speed figures, they cannot determine whether the fancy maiden-claiming figures exploited a tardy pace, and many do. Six-time maiden-claiming loser Ski Bar is hardly a shining example of the maiden-claiming graduate that succeeds in allowance company.

Steller Story — B. f. 4, by Mehmet—Rosa Soler, by King of Kings
STEVENS G L
Own.—Clear Valley Stables
Br.—Daley R & Jean etal (Ky)
Tr.—Shulman Sanford
119

Pace 95 Speed 102

29Jly91- 3Dmr	fst	1	:461	1:11	1:363	3↑ⒻAlw 30000	6	5	56½	52½	32	2¾	Stevens G L	LBb	119	3.60	82-16
17Jly91- 7Hol	fst	7½f	:223	:452	1:29	ⒻClm c-20000	1	8	75½	87	46	35¼	Delahoussaye E	LBb	116	3.10	– –
26Jun91- 6Hol	fst	6f	:213	:434	1:092	ⒻClm 25000	7	7	88¾	510	38	34½	Delahoussaye E	LBb	116	4.10	88-10
12Jun91- 1Hol	fst	6½f	:222	:45	1:161	ⒻClm 20000	4	7	67½	66½	45	21¾	Delahoussaye E	LBb	116	*2.50	89-09
25May91- 3Hol	fst	7f	:221	:444	1:223	ⒻClm 32000	2	6	53¼	43	46	58¼	Delahoussaye E	LBb	117	3.50	83-11
8May91- 7Hol	fst	6f	:221	:451	1:10	ⒻClm 32000	8	6	53¾	53	3½	31¼	Delahoussaye E	LBb	116	14.00	89-10
2Nov90- 5SA	fst	1	:453	1:102	1:362	ⒻClm 32000	6	7	76¾	44½	33½	33¼	Pincay L Jr	LBb	117	8.90	82-14
12Oct90- 4SA	fst	6½f	:212	:44	1:153	ⒻClm 50000	8	7	86¼	88¼	910	99¼	Pincay L Jr	LB	117	36.10	83-13
9Sep90- 3Dmr	fst	6½f	:214	:442	1:151	ⒻClm 62500	6	2	63¼	63¾	69	614	Pincay L Jr	LB	117	5.50	78-11
13Aug90- 3Dmr	fm	1 1/16	Ⓣ:48	1:122	1:441	ⒻAlw 30000	3	5	65	66	63¾	75¾	Pincay L Jr	B	117	16.90	80-08

Speed Index: Last Race: –2.0 2–Race Avg.: –3.0 2–Race Avg.: –3.0
LATEST WORKOUTS Aug 5 Dmr 4f fst :482 H Jly 26 Dmr 5f fst 1:01 H Jly 13 Hol 4f fs

Another intriguing combination of speed-pace figures. As indicated, off-pace runners cannot be penalized for low pace figures. Steller Story's pace figure of 95, however, remains too low in relation to an allowance par of 103. The figure leaves the horse four lengths in arrears of par at the second call. Two and a half lengths back is far more inspiring, unless the horse has proven itself a powerful one-run type.

As a rule, pace figures of off-pace types in nonclaiming races should be within five points of today's par. Steller Story fails that test by a length and a half. If today's winner exceeds par, Steller Story will be fully extended to finish close. Not many unexceptional closers can catch up in time.

Verdeuse–Fr Ch. f. 4, by Arctic Tern—Toujours Vert, by Northfields
PINCAY L JR Br.—Swettenham Stud (Fra)
Own.—Apple & Milch Tr.—Vienna Darrell 122
15Mar91- 7SA fst 1 1/8 :463 1:111 1:501 (F)Alw 35000 3 3 42 1/2 713 717 725 1/2 Velasquez J LB 121 2.60 53-19
22Feb91- 5SA fst 1 1/16 :464 1:113 1:44 (F)Clm 32000 2 5 54 1hd 11 2no Velasquez J B 114 3.90 83-19 101 103
2Nov90♦2Lingfield(Eng) fst 1 1/4 2:033 Austin Stakes(Mdn) 1nk Rouse B 116 *1.50 – –
2Nov90-Raced on an all-weather racecourse
9Oct90♦6Redcar(Eng) gd 1 1/8 1:50 (T)Fuisborough H 55 Carson W 130 12.00 – –
11Sep90♦7Carlisle(Eng) fm 1 1:384 (T)Barnacle H 53 1/2 Duffield G 134 *5.00 – –
16Jly90♦4Ayr(Scot) gd 7f 1:282 (T)Dumfries H 31 1/2 Hills M 127 8.00 – –
4Jly90♦6Catterick(Eng) gd 7f 1:294 (T)Staindrop Stks(Mdn) 21 1/2 Fortune J 115 4.50 – –
15Jun90♦5Southwell(Eng) fst 7f 1:28 River Plate Stks(Mdn) 31 1/2 Hills M 121 2.75 – –
15Jun90-Raced on all-weather racecourse
30May90♦6Ripon(Eng) gd 1 1:391 (T)ClevelandPotashStk(Mdn) 44 Hills M 116 9.00 – –
22Apr90♦3Carlisle(Eng) gd 1 1:411 (T)(F)EdinburghWoolMillS(Mdn) 54 1/2 Eddery P A 123 5.00 – –
Speed Index: Last Race: –28.0 2–Race Avg.: –13.0 2–Race Avg.: –13.0
LATEST WORKOUTS Aug 6 Dmr 5f fst :594 H Aug 1 Dmr 5f fst 1:02 H Jly 25 Dmr 5f f

In her second race back, Verdeuse recorded precisely the kind of speed and pace figures handicappers prefer in the nonwinners allowance events. The speed figure (103) equals par. The pace figure (101) approaches par. Verdeuse can track a typical allowance pace and still finish well. Contender.

The second line back is preferred for Verdeuse because that's a good race and the last out is awful. Figure handicappers rely on good performances to evaluate horses and they appreciate that the second start following a long layoff and overexertion can cause a temporary setback.

Adorable Vice B. f. 4, by Vice Regent—Love You (Eng), by Linden Tree
VALENZUELA P A Br.—Hunt N B (Ont-C)
Own.—Evergreen Farm Tr.—Whittingham Michael 122
22Jly91- 5Hol fm 1 1/16 (T):47 1:11 1:412 3↑(F)Alw 35000 4 1 1 1/2 2hd 31 1/2 33 1/2 Delahoussaye E LB 121 2.80 84-11
28Jun91- 8Hol fm 1 1/8 (T):482 1:12 1:491 3↑(F)Alw 35000 3 2 2 1/2 33 33 1/2 23 1/2 Delahoussaye E LB 121 5.00 80-15
26May91- 3Hol fst 1 1/16 :47 1:111 1:442 3↑(F)Alw 35000 1 3 31 1/2 31 1/2 22 1/2 21 1/2 Valenzuela P A LB 122 11.10 77-22 101 99
26Apr91- 7Hol fst 1 1/16 :471 1:114 1:433 3↑(F)Alw 35000 3 3 31 1/2 31 1/2 44 1/2 46 1/2 Solis A LB 122 9.50 77-14
28Feb91- 7SA sly 1 :471 1:122 1:382 (F)Alw 35000 8 5 43 1/2 68 617 627 Solis A LB 120 4.20 48-20
9Feb91- 5SA fm 1 1/8 (T):471 1:113 1:49 (F)Alw 35000 9 4 41 1/2 32 1/2 45 1/2 56 Stevens G L LB 120 8.00 73-21
1Jan91- 7SA fst 1 1/16 :463 1:113 1:452 (F)Alw 37000 2 6 64 1/2 44 43 1/2 2no Solis A LB 120 5.20 76-18
6Dec90- 8Hol fm 1 (T):463 1:11 1:351 3↑(F)Alw 32000 3 4 31 1/2 3 1/2 2 1/2 31 Solis A LB 118 8.20 87-11
9Nov90- 8Hol fm 1 1/8 (T):47 1:104 1:482 3↑(F)Alw 32000 5 6 63 1/2 41 1/2 44 33 1/2 McCarron C J LB 118 6.10 82-14
13Oct90- 3SA fst 1 :462 1:113 1:374 3↑(F)Md Sp Wt 9 4 3nk 1 1/2 12 12 1/2 Valenzuela P A LB 117 2.20 78-12
Speed Index: Last Race: –1.0 3–Race Avg.: –14.0 5–Race Avg.: –11.6
LATEST WORKOUTS Jly 18 Hol 3f fst :373 B Jly 13 Hol (T) 5f fm 1:024 H (d) Jly 6 Hol 3f fst

Grass races ignored, three lines back Adorable Vice finished second in a race like today's. Her figures look competitive and move in the desirable direction. But something else bothers handicappers here. Adorable Vice has failed in nine attempts under today's allowance conditions. The 101-102 figures of May 26 are not likely to improve. Younger, lightly raced, improving horses are always preferred in the nonwinners allowance series, the figures notwithstanding. When horses 4up have failed allowance conditions successively, marginal figures should be discounted.

Flying Shadow
MARTINEZ J C
Own.—PetrosianBrosRcngSt

B: f. 3(Feb), by General Assembly—Kiss My Tears, by Topsider
Br.—Galbreath D M (Ky)
Tr.—Scolamieri Sam J

114

29Jly91- 7Dmr fst 6f	:213	:443 1:093	3+ⓕAlw 35000	8 1	53½ 43	34½ 34½	Martinez J C	B 113	11.60	86-16	101	99
15Dec90- 6Hol fst 7f	:214	:444 1:231	ⓕAlw 30000	3 7	66½ 66½	35½ 32½	Martinez J C	B 116	11.90	86-08		
23Nov90- 2Hol fst 6f	:22	:454 1:114	ⓕMd 32000	6 2	32 32½	1hd 12	Martinez J C	B 119	7.70	81-14		

Speed Index: Last Race: (—) 3–Race Avg.: (—) 12–Race Avg.: (—)
LATEST WORKOUTS Jly 20 SLR tr.t 6f fst 1:14 H ● Jly 13 SLR tr.t 4f fst :462 Hg ● Jly 9 SLR tr.t

Flying Shadow represents the proverbial 3YO sprinter stretching out under nonwinners allowance conditions. The speed-pace figures of her comeback effort fall below today's par and are set in the wrong direction. Yet the imbalance is hardly severe and Flying Shadow might improve in a second try following a lengthy layoff. Handicappers best depend upon the below-par figures and probability statistics indicating that the one-sprint stretch-out is a negative pattern. Yet Flying Shadow also looks enticingly like the younger, lightly raced, improving three-year-old that regularly wins this kind of race.

The Sartin pace practitioners cope smartly with situations represented by Flying Shadow. They calculate the horse's energy distribution in its sprints and compare the proportion of energy a horse uses to the pace call to the energy demands at today's racetrack. If a horse's early-energy distribution fits well enough in relation to the early-energy distribution of route winners at the track, the horse is acceptable.

Flying Shadow's early-energy expenditure on July 29 was 52.85 percent, far too high to win Del Mar middle-distance events. Now the sprinter can be tossed away. If Flying Shadow's early-energy expenditure had suited routes at Del Mar, the 3YO would have remained a sticky proposition here.

Because the balance of speed and pace figures counts terrifically in the nonwinners allowances, figure handicappers are encouraged to sum the pair of figures for several contenders and favor the highest-rated horse. Inspect the combined ratings for the horses being evaluated:

	Pace	Speed	Total
Cara Carissima	99	102	201
Neo Girl	97	100	197
Ski Bar	99	100	199
Steller Story	95	102	197
Verdeuse	101	103	204
Adorable Vice	101	102	203
Flying Shadow	101	99	200

The figures award Verdeuse a close nod. Class handicappers would discount runner-up Adorable Vice as unsuited to the conditions. The lightly raced 3YO most likely to improve today is the top filly, Cara Carissima. Flying Shadow remains a possibility, but an attractive price should be mandatory, and is unlikely.

Which brings figure handicappers full circle to an important point of departure. Nonwinners allowance contests are tough to figure, literally. The races are routinely characterized by conflicting evidence, unreliable figures, and a variety of unknowns. Handicappers who trust the figures sufficiently to bet Verdeuse on the bounce-back have no apologies, but the risks are difficult to deny.

5140—FIFTH RACE. 1 1/16 mile. 3 year olds & up. Fillies & mares. Allowance. Purse $37,000.

Index	Horse and Jockey	Wt.	PP	ST	¼	½	¾	Str.	Fin.	To $1
5034	Neo Girl, Solis	117	2	7	7⁴	7³	5½	2½	1¹¼	8.30
5048	Steller Story, Stevens	119	5	8	8	8	7¹	4½	2ⁿᵈ	2.70
5052	Flying Shadow, J.Martinez	114	8	3	1½	1½	1½	1hd	3³	7.70
4451	Adorable Vice, P.Valenzuela	122	7	6	6½	6¹	4½	5³½	4no	6.90
5034	Cara Carissima, McCarron	115	1	1	2½	3³	3½	3¹	5⁷	3.30
3538	Verdeuse, Pincay	122	6	5	5½	5½	6½	6½	6²	7.10
5020	Mats Dolly, A.Castanon	122	4	2	4¹	4¹	8	8	7²½	25.20
5034	Ski Bar, Nakatani	114	3	4	3½	2½	2¹	7²	8	4.80

Scratched—None.

```
2—NEO GIRL ........................... 18.60    8.20    5.00
5—STELLER STORY .............................  4.00    3.00
8—FLYING SHADOW ....................................  4.80
```

Time —22 3/5, 45 3/5, 1.11, 1.37 4/5, 1.44 3/5. Cloudy & fast. Winner—BF 88 Garo Reine-Imperiale. Trained by D. Lukas. Mutuel pool—$508,895. Exacta pool—$546,372. Daily Triple pool—$331,834.

Notice the sprinter's pace set by Flying Shadow. Neo Girl altered her running style radically, winning here from the rear. Her pace-speed figures were 97-101. Closers finished one-two in ordinary time following rapid fractions. If Neo Girl had repeated her accustomed style of pressing the early pace, she would have expired too. But a lightly raced, nicely bred 3YO from a good barn is fully capable of changing running tactics. One more reason the nonwinners allowance series becomes rugged sledding for handicappers.

The same relations are desirable when horses have won a first allowance race and move ahead to nonwinners-twice other than maiden or claiming. A balance of speed and pace figures deserves extra credit. High pace figures can be suspect, unless the corresponding speed figures equal or exceed par.

The importance of pace figures in allowance company can be dramatized by presenting dissimilar styles of figure handicapping for the same horses. These are allowance prospects 3up, nonwinners-twice other than maiden or claiming, going a mile at Del Mar, August 10, 1991. Which do figure handicappers prefer?

	Beyer Speed (Par 90)	*Quirin Speed & Pace* (Par 106)		
For Sure	93	110	109	
Run On The Bank	84	102	98	
Royal Avie	93 (Spr.)	103	103	(%E 52.96)
Balzac's Cope	87	107	99	
Rushmore	97 (Spr.)	100	106	(%E 51.31)
Marlar	90	98	102	
General Meeting	91	107	104	

Final-figure devotees would prefer Rushmore, who recorded his leading 97 in a rugged sprint following a 7½-month lay-away. Rushmore's early-energy distribution (51.31) fits the Del Mar oval splendidly, a plus, but the one-sprint stretch-out after a lengthy layoff is a negative.

Rushmore shows the second-high Quirin speed figure (106), but the corresponding pace figure looks soft. With For Sure and General Meeting in the field, the run to the pace call should require Rushmore to extend himself early. Can he duplicate his speed figure thereafter? Classy horses can and ordinary horses cannot. Figure handicappers are recommended to stick with the percentages.

Royal Avie has a Beyer Speed Figure of 93, but his early energy is unacceptably high at 52.96 (par is 51.76). Royal Avie is not likely to stretch out effectively at first asking.

Quirin speed and pace figures identify For Sure and General Meeting as the strongest contenders, runners-up to Rushmore, and Royal Avie, on Beyer Speed as well. Combining the pairs of figures, For Sure gets 219 and General Meeting 211. Rushmore's combined rating is 206.

For Sure shows the balanced interplay between speed and pace that figure handicappers appreciate in the nonwinners series, and both figures exceed par. Late in its 2YO season and early as a 3YO, General Meeting dispensed four impressive stakes performances. Horses exiting a "good" race in stakes win a disproportionate share of the allowance races they reenter. The Seattle Slew colt also may improve dynamically in its second try following the vacation. For Sure has been improving impressively as well, its figures climbing in each of its last two starts while graduating from maiden ranks to nonwinners-once allowances to today.

If the bettors fancy Rushmore as a result of his impressive sprint, Quirin speed and pace backers might prefer For Sure at an attractive price.

5151—SEVENTH RACE. 1 mile. 3 year olds & up. Allowance. Purse $42,000.

5043 Run On The Bank,Dsrmeaux..116	2	7	8	8	6½	4 1½	1 1¾	12.50
5030 General Meeting, Pincay 117	8	8	4¹	4hd	3hd	1hd	2 1¾	1.60
(4610)For Sure, Stevens...........120	1	'6	5hd	5¹	4½	3hd	3hd	3.10
5030 Rushmore, McCarron 116	6	3	2¹	1½	1¹	2¹	4nk	2.70
4536 Balzac's Cope, Nakatani 116	4	2	3²	3 2½	2hd	5 1½	5 3½	35.20
3792 Malo Malo, Torres 111	5	4	6 1½	6 1½	7 1½	6½	6³	30.90
5070 Marlar, Lopez 116	7	5	7³	7⁴	8	8	7³	26.00
4494 Royal Avie, Delahoussaye 116	3	1	1½	2¹	5 2½	7 1½	8	6.90

Scratched —None.

2—RUN ON THE BANK	....................27.00	7.60	3.20
8—GENERAL MEETING	...........................4.00	2.80	
1—FOR SURE	....		2.80

Time—22, 45 4/5, 1.1 2/5, 1.35 2/5. Cloudy & fast. Winner—DBB C 87 Water Bank-Hand Creme. Trained by D. Lukas. Mutuel pool –$432,462. Exacta pool—$447,896.

$2 EXACTA (2-8) PAID $82.20

General Meeting and For Sure exceeded par here and might have formed a figure player's exacta, except the Del Mar track surface was severely biased in favor of deep closers. Outsider Run On The Bank came from last to first to upset well-laid plans.

In the advanced nonwinners allowances, for nonwinners three times other than maiden or claiming, or for nonwinners four times other than, pace figures are not nearly as distinguishing. That's because the prime contenders in these fields typically possess stakes quality, and virtually all of them can attend a par pace. Speed figurers identify the most probable winners reliably, unless one of the horses qualifies as a division leader and has posted a sensational pace in its preliminary allowance races.

Figure handicapping in the nonwinners allowance series may not be decisive as often as numbers addicts would like, but in knowledgeable hands it's a helpful and frequently decisive tool. Adherents to this book's guidance can grab a vital edge in these difficult races simply by inspecting the pace figures that so often separate the real contenders from the pretenders.

STAKES RACES

When the gutty, determined Best Pal, a Cal-bred gelding, surprised the leading older handicap horses in the country by winning the ten-furlong, $1-million Pacific Classic in August 1991, and paid $11.80, owner John Mabee remarked that if the betting had been left to professional handicappers the horse would have been 15–1.

I should think so. This was a popular upset, the glorious revenge of the underdog, but it's difficult to imagine that figure handicappers of any persuasion could have preferred Best Pal that day. In an informal postrace survey I conducted, no one had favored the horse, and most had considered Best Pal precisely the sort of outsider Mabee described, including me.

Yet the race is brimming with lessons in handicapping, and its outcome underscores one of the least appreciated precepts of figure handicapping when dealing with numbers and mature graded-stakes horses. In particular, Grade 1 horses 4up. Before examining the pertinent figures for the 1991 Pacific Classic, here are a few maxims to adhere to when utilizing figures in stakes races.

1. In stakes races generally, class supersedes speed. The longer the stakes race, the even greater the relative importance of class. The closer the finish, so much more the relative importance of class.

    The implications for figure handicapping follow directly. If an older horse's speed figures have been recorded at today's stakes level or better, accept them. If the figures have been recorded at a lower class level than today's, be skeptical. Horses 4up sometimes improve their stakes status, but not as frequently or dramatically as their younger counterparts.

2. Speed figures earned at middle distances do not transfer reliably to classic distances, notably among Grade 1 horses. When evaluating Grade 1 horses at 1¼ miles, prefer figures in other races at 1¼ miles.

    Abundant evidence has convinced handicappers the same stakes horses that can win powerfully at 1⅛ miles frequently cannot win, at least at first, beyond that distance against the cream of the division.

3. Unless a horse's pace figures look tremendous, and its corresponding speed figure has equaled par, speed figures generally will be more important than pace figures in stakes races open to older horses.

That's because older, established stakes horses by definition will customarily be prepared to set or track a rapid pace before finishing as powerfully as they can. Proven stakes horses ultimately sort themselves out in the drive for the wire. If the finish is close, and many are, the attributes of endurance and determination in combination with late speed will be decisive. The attributes of class are speed, stamina, and determination, and not speed alone. When a horse wins a stakes race by a nose, a head, a neck, a half-length, or a length, speed quotients have normally been reached, and the victory belongs to horses best qualified on the other important attributes.

This is not meant to imply that pace is unimportant in stakes races, only less important much of the time. By all means, if today's pace should be unusually slow or inordinately fast, a pace analysis is very much in order.

4. Excepting the blueblooded champions that appear infrequently, the speed figures of stakes horses will be subject to swings of several lengths, from month to month or from season to season, in concert with improving and declining form cycles.

Division leaders and Grade 1 gems do not run their top figures race after race. They improve, and they decline, usually within a range of speed figures at par and above. A reliable tactic fastens on the stakes horse's top figure in the past six races, regardless of calendar days. The handicapping now is intended to determine how close to that figure the horse can perform today.

Should the horse improve? Should it decline? How close to its best figure might the horse finish today? If all the horses dispense a top performance, which should win? The handicapping is not simple.

5. As a rule among stakes horses, two declining speed figures in succession forms a negative pattern. Do not expect a rebound today to top form.

A dull race following a freshening layoff of four to six weeks is another negative sign. The respite is intended to rejuvenate spirit and limbs. If it does not, form is probably declining and a resurrection to former heights next time should not be expected.

Within that frame of reference, examine the two sets of figures below for the horses entered in the 1991 Pacific Classic. Both Beyer Speed Figures and Quirin speed and pace figures have been listed. Stalwart Charger, an outsider, has been omitted.

Which horse do you prefer, based on the cold dope and related knowledge of handicapping? An in-depth discussion of the race may not uncover the eventual winner, but it can illuminate several propositions relevant to figure handicapping in the stakes division.

Beyer Speed Figures/Quirin Speed & Pace Figures
For Horses in the Inaugural Pacific Classic
August 10, 1991

Horses		Beyer Speed (Par 110)	Quirin Speed & Pace (Par 113)	
Itsallgreektome	Gr. 1 1¼M	113	108	111
Anshan	Gr. 1 1¼M	107	107	108
Farma Way	Gr. 1 1¼M	117	110	114
Twilight Agenda	Gr. 3 1⅛M	113	120	116
Best Pal	Gr. 2 1¼M	109	105	107
Festin	Gr. 1 1¼M	112	104	110
Unbridled	Gr. 1 1¼M	116	xx	109

Notes. Figures represent the last start, excepting Festin and Unbridled. The figures for those horses represent the latest race at 1¼ miles.

Festin's last start occurred at 1⅛ miles against top-grade handicap horses. His Beyer Speed Figure was 108, a decline of 13 points. His Quirin speed and pace figures were 95-103, a decline of 10 points at the final time.

Unbridled's last start occurred at seven furlongs, an allowance prep following a three-month layoff. His Beyer Speed Figure was 113, an improvement of 6 points. His Quirin speed and pace figures were 99-113, another sizable improvement.

It's crucial to evaluate these horses as best you can on performances at 1¼ miles. Only Twilight Agenda had not attempted the distance. Festin and Unbridled showed classic distances within their last six starts, though most recently the distances had been shorter.

Farma Way had negotiated the 1¼ miles the best by far, both

early and late. He also had recorded a 116 in the Santa Anita
Handicap and in the Pimlico Special at 1³/₁₆ miles he earned a
spectacular 122.

Any horses 4up that have not equaled the Grade 1 par, pref-
erably at 1¼ miles, are best eliminated in a situation where several contenders have, unless they possess a significant
redeeming virtue. (Only Anshan falls under that axe.)

Pace figures generally will be unimportant, unless some
horse has dispensed a truly sensational pace figure while finishing above par, which one horse in the Pacific Classic had.

Horse to horse the field proved interesting. Let's skip
through the lineup and try to place the figures in a context of
full-scale handicapping.

Itsallgreektome

The champion grass horse of 1990 is actually easy to dispose of
here. He reveals two strong negatives. Turf form does not easily
switch to the main track and succeed at the Grade 1 level. If a
first effort fails, no second chances.

The pace of the dirt races almost invariably will be swifter
and more hotly debated. Frontrunners and pace-pressers must
make a difficult adaptation. Deep closers possessing a really
powerful finish can get the job done at times, but their prospects improve immeasurably following a weakening pace. Below Grade 1, the transition is more manageable, but a class
edge helps enormously. If the class edge is not there, discount
the figures.

Even more problematic for Itsallgreektome, its speed figures
in 1991 had declined from the heights of 1990. It's a negative
signal figure handicappers should never overlook. When graded
stakes horses' figures have declined from one season to the next,
they figure to lose, at least at familiar levels. If the horses continue to confront the same top company they have become accustomed to, they no longer will beat them. Itsallgreektome would
be one for six in 1991 following the Pacific Classic. He was
intended to return to the turf for the Arlington Million, but
figure handicappers should not expect the 1990 champ to
annex even one more Grade 1 race. Lower-grade races possibly,
but not Grade 1.

Anshan

This 4YO needs a shorter distance in lesser company. The figures do not lie here, and they usually do not once handicap horses have arrived at the midpoint of the four-year-old season. In his last six races, Anshan recorded a pair of 111s, both at nine furlongs in Grade 2 company. That's his best game.

Farma Way

His best race wins it, all right, an assertion the figures document persuasively. Farma Way's last six races on Beyer Speed Figures look like this: 117, 109, 122, 92, 116, and 115. Two of the good ones were earned at 1¼ miles. The 92 occurred in the slop at Oaklawn Park and can be tossed.

The 109 resulted from a suicidal pace duel at Belmont Park in a one-turn 1⅛ miles. The pace figure was a savagely contested 122. Farma Way continued on in an extremely determined performance that day. He next finished in an all-out drive at 1¼ miles in the Hollywood Gold Cup, unable to overtake the good horse Marquetry despite having dead aim.

Farma Way arrived at the Pacific Classic following a freshening forty-two-day vacation. His workouts were steady and fast. But as the low-priced favorite, Farma Way represented an unacceptable risk. Form is questionable, certainly not peaked or improving. At the same time, Farma Way's typical race would be competitive here. A 113 might be strong enough to win, and another 117 would be likely to win.

In the final analysis, Farma Way has questionable form, but every right to win.

Twilight Agenda

The impressive stranger in the field, Twilight Agenda is entering his first Grade 1 race in his first attempt at 10 furlongs. It's a demanding double jump in class and distance that only authentically talented horses can satisfy.

Figure handicappers face a common dilemma here. They inspect Twilight Agenda's rampantly improving numbers in his past two races, wins at Grade 2 and Grade 3, respectively, and they find evidence the horse is genuine:

		Pace	Speed
Del Mar	July 27	120	116
Hollywood Park	July 13	115	114

The kind of older stakes horse able to step up in Grade 1 circumstances possesses a sensational pace figure in combination with a speed figure of par or better. Twilight Agenda passes both tests.

Can he resist Grade 1 horses at ten furlongs? Maybe, and maybe not, but the figures indicate his chances are real. If Twilight Agenda had to improve either figure to prevail here, he should be discounted. But if the numbers tell the tale today, Twilight Agenda can wrestle the lead at the second call and muster enough late energy to hold the advantage. A short price on that possibility may not appeal to handicappers, but a long price would appeal strongly to figure handicappers.

Best Pal

The evidence condemning Best Pal here is solidly stacked. First of all, 3YOs of spring and summer compete at a tremendous disadvantage in stakes races open to older handicap horses. The probabilities are even worse in Grade 1 competition. To defeat mature stakes stars, the 3YOs must be genuinely supreme, which Best Pal is not. At the least, both the pace figure and speed figure should equal par for older stakes horses, and Best Pal has not yet managed that.

In addition, Best Pal has posted truly dismal closing times for a top horse. Two races back, in a Grade 3 stakes limited to 3YOs, Best Pal led comfortably at the stretch call but could not finish the final furlong in 13 seconds and blew.

In Best Pal's favor, the last race has been best, a Beyer Speed Figure of 109, and it occurred at 1¼ miles. He has traveled the classic distance twice in fine company, the second attempt much improved.

Not to be overlooked, leading trainer Gary Jones took control of Best Pal following the loss two back and has prepared the gelding carefully for this occasion. Also, Best Pal won smartly at Del Mar last season, and this peculiar course deserves the references it gets to horses-for-courses.

None of this, however, propels Best Pal to the head of this handicap field. Prior to the race, it's difficult to imagine the 3YO tracking the pace of Farma Way and Twilight Agenda before managing to overtake those cracks or to outfinish the popular closers Festin and Unbridled. At 9–2, the popular homebred looked a definite underlay.

Festin

An easy mark for figure handicappers. A deep closer, Festin's last ten Beyer Speed Figures look like this: 108, 121 (won), 113, 108, 112, 100, 97, 107, 101, and 105. The past seven races occurred in 1991, indicating the horse had definitely improved as a 5YO. Notice the past six figures, a range of 121 to 100, with a tendency toward 108 to 112. The 121 best-ever two races back returned to reality last out (108), and the pattern projects to a 108 or thereabouts again today.

Solid but overrated, Festin's two graded victories in 1991 occurred in the slop and following a suicidal pace. The runner-up finishes in the Santa Anita Handicap and the New England Classic are prototypical of one-run closers in Grade 1 races. If Festin had consistently displayed the high figure here and the pace should be inordinately fast, the horse would make sense. Part one of that scenario is missing.

Unbridled

In 1991 this enigmatic champion 3YO of 1990 has delivered two impressive figures at seven furlongs following layoffs, and two dismal figures in the routes following the seven-furlong explosions. Figure handicappers who applauded the first time Unbridled devastated stakes opposition at seven furlongs with a 116 speed figure, a chorus that included me, were hardly fooled the second time around.

More basically, Unbridled fails a test appropriate to leading stakes horses from one season to the next. If the quality of the performances change for the worse, the figures dropping, the efforts inconsistent, the pattern is unforgivably negative. Leading three-year-olds should duplicate their numbers at four, or exceed them. They should run repeatedly well enough to win. When they do not, something is amiss and handicappers should discount the horses. Eventually the odds will creep up and maybe a bet makes sense under a particular set of circumstances that begs success. Otherwise, assume the horses are not the same, and look elsewhere.

In the final analysis, the 1991 Pacific Classic afforded handicappers lots of lessons about figure handicapping in the stakes, and the probable winners were not difficult to identify. I judged the contest strictly between Farma Way and Twilight Agenda, with Unbridled a wake-up factor. The odds near post time looked like this:

Farma Way	3–2	Festin	not known
Twilight Agenda	6–1	Unbridled	6–1
Best Pal	9–2		

I originally intended to box Farma Way and Twilight Agenda in exactas and play each of those contenders on top of exactas having Unbridled on the undersides. I did that, but also risked a prime bet to win when Twilight Agenda went postward a juicy 6-to-1. I did not expect to lose everything to Best Pal, but the result chart cannot be denied.

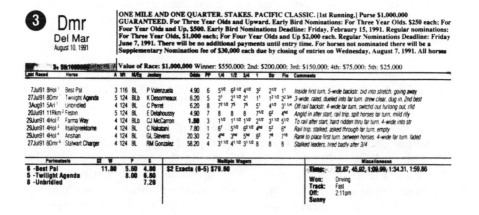

The postscript here is also instructive. Twilight Agenda took a bold lead into the stretch but could not last the extra furlong. Figure handicappers should not be surprised. The majority of stakes winners at middle distances disappoint at first try across the classic distance, their speed figures notwithstanding. Yet they might rebound at ten furlongs later. Seasoning at the distance makes a difference.

Early in 1991 a super-sharp In Excess led handily but tired in his first attempt at ten furlongs and stopped abruptly on the second attempt. He eventually waltzed to an impressive score at ten furlongs in the Suburban Handicap, a mere four months later.

Farma Way ran a dull one. He was well-beaten at a mile, and fell back thereafter. Farma Way immediately fit the gloomy profile of a good horse returning from a freshening layoff with a poor effort. Farma Way is probably declining, and no dramatic improvement next time should be expected.

Festin and Unbridled never did mount a challenge, Festin failing to fire.

Best Pal benefited from a heady ride under Pat Valenzuela, waiting four to five lengths behind the frontrunners, and not trying to press the pace of Farma Way or Twilight Agenda. When the others misfired, Best Pal had one horse to overtake, a newcomer at the distance, who tired in deep stretch. The 3YO ran evenly all the way. His gradual gain in the lane proved good enough.

The improving Best Pal may also have represented the odd kind of good, gutty racehorse who displays an even style and does better at classic distances than at middle distances. If the Pacific Classic had been run over nine furlongs, Twilight Agenda surely would have held. Best Pal would have finished a respectable but unexceptional second. At ten furlongs, however, Best Pal won going away. Figure handicappers get a leg up on the stakes division by affording that happenstance some serious thought.

As the leading handicap horses gathered for the 1991 Pacific Classic at Del Mar, another multiple Grade 1 winner was making noise in New York. A review of the horse's past performances not only reinforces the preceding discussion, but illustrates one of the most intriguing aspects of figure handicapping in the stakes division.

IN EXCESS(IRE)
4yo (Apr) colt, dk. bay/brown
Trainer: Bruce L Jackson
Owner: Jack J Munari

Sire: **Siberian Express** ($15,200)
by Caro
Dam: **Kantado**
by Saulingo
Bred in **IRE** by Ahmed M. Foustok

121

Career: 17 9 1 1
Wet: 1 1 0 0
Turf: 11 5 1 0
Dist: 2 2 0 0
1991: 5 3 0 1 $870,340
1990: 10 5 1 0
Sar: 0 0 0 0

4Jly91	8Bel	ft	3+	Stk500000	1¼	23.91	47.17	1:34.07	1:58.33	[illegible]	3/7	2	1^{hd}	$1^{1\frac12}$	$1^{\frac12}$	1^{1}	1^{1}	GL Stevens	119	**1.00** In Excess119[1]Chief Honcho115[6]Killer Diller113[5]	
				Gr.1 Suburban Handicap																*Rtd spd 2w, drew off far turn, chlngd into str, merely shown whip*	
27May91	8Bel	ft	3+	Stk500000	1m	22.14	44.26	1:09.28	1:35.45	117	5/14	11	$4^{1\frac14}$	$2^{1\frac12}$	$1^{\frac12}$	1^{1}	$1^{2\frac14}$	P Valenzuela	117	4.20 In Excess117$^{2\frac14}$Rubiano111$^{1\frac34}$Gervazy114$^{1\frac12}$	
				Gr.1 Metropolitan Handicap																*Stumbled st, rushed up, took over turn, repulsed bid, edged clear*	
9Mar91	5SA	ft	4+	Stk1000000	1¼	23.10	46.10	1:34.90	2:00.30	[illegible]	2/10	3	3^{2}	$3^{1\frac12}$	$2^{1\frac12}$	4^{5}	4^{9}	JA Santos	118 LB	4.70 Farma Way120$^{2\frac34}$Festin115$^{\frac34}$Pleasant Tap115$^{5\frac12}$	
				Gr.1 Santa Anita Handicap																*Just off leaders backside, moved far turn, hung drive*	
10Feb91	8SA	ft	4	Stk500000	1¼	22.70	46.30	1:34.90	2:00.90	107	2/7	1	1^{1}	1^{1}	1^{nk}	1^{hd}	$3^{1\frac14}$	GL Stevens	121 LB	**0.80** Defensive Play122^{hd}My Boy Adam117$^{1\frac12}$In Excess121$^{4\frac12}$	
				Gr.1 Charles H Strub Stakes																*Weakened in final stages; held in reserve*	
19Jan91	8SA	ft	4	Stk218800	1⅛	22.70	46.50	1:10.30	1:46.70	114	8/9	2		2^{2}	$1^{\frac12}$	1^{3}	1^{4}	GL Stevens	126 LB	11.10 In Excess126[4]Warcraft120$^{2\frac34}$Go And Go123$^{1\frac14}$	
				Gr.2 San Fernando Stakes																*Stalked outside leader, made lead in hand, drew off easily*	
31Dec90	8SA	fm	3+	Stk113100	1⅛	23.30	47.70	1:11.30	1:47.30	104	5/11	2		2^{2}	$1^{\frac12}$	1^{hd}	1^{hd}	GL Stevens	117 LB	**1.90** In Excess117^{hd}Rouvignac113$^{1\frac14}$Kanatiyr115^{nk}	
				Gr.3 San Gabriel Handicap																*Hard held one off rail, stalked, wore down leader*	
11Nov90	8Hol	fm	3	Stk200000	1⅛	Ⓣ23.10	46.90	1:10.30	1:46.70	104	10/12	5		5^{3}	2^{1}		$4^{3\frac34}$	GL Stevens	122 LB	**2.40** Itsallgreektome122^{hd}Septieme Ciel122[2]Anshan122$^{1\frac34}$	
				Gr.1 Hollywood Derby																*Three wide throughout, rallied to lead midstretch, overpowered*	
21Oct90	8SA	fm	3	Stk110300	1⅛	Ⓣ23.30	46.90	1:10.50	1:46.70	101	7/8	1		2^{2}	2^{hd}	1^{1}	$1^{2\frac14}$	GL Stevens	117 LB	2.20 In Excess117$^{2\frac14}$Warcraft118$^{\frac12}$Barton Dene113$^{1\frac14}$	
				Gr.3 Volante Handicap																*Broke out, settle one off rail, made lead on own, hand ride*	
23Sep90	7LaD	fm	3	Stk100000	1$\frac{1}{16}$	Ⓣ23.30	48.70	1:12.70	1:42.10	[illegible]	8/11	6		$2^{1\frac12}$	2^{1}	1^{4}	1^{8}	GL Stevens	115 L	**1.50** In Excess115[8]On The Edge116^{nk}Seti I.115[1]	
				Temperence Hill Handicap																*Won going away*	
19Aug90	8Dmr	fm	3	Stk300000	1⅛	Ⓣ24.70	48.70	1:13.30	1:49.70	87	6/10	9		$4^{2\frac34}$	5^{6}		7^{8}	H Rivera Jr	122 L	5.80 Tight Spot122[3]Itsallgreektome122$^{1\frac34}$Predecessor122$^{\frac34}$	
				Gr.2 Del Mar Invitational Derby																*Rank, squeezed, very rank 1st turn, drifted out, empty*	

Workouts: 28Jly Sar 5f ft 59.98 B **22Jly Bel 6f ft 1:1[illegible] B** 15Jly Bel 4f ft 49.11 B 29Jun Bel 5f ft 1:00.02 B 23Jun Bel 1m ft 1:41.71 B

Typical now of imports, In Excess first attempted to transfer graded-stakes form on the grass to dirt when launching his 4YO season December 31 at Santa Anita. The first try succeeded, a fact handicappers should bear in mind. The very first attempt should succeed, or almost succeed, in good time. A decent placement, as with Itsallgreektome, is not nearly as meaningful.

Shortly after winning on dirt, In Excess qualified as another in a long line of impressive stakes winners at middle distance to unravel late on the first attempt at ten furlongs. On the second attempt at the classic distance, In Excess faltered badly. Notice the speed figure at nine furlongs January 19, a legitimate Grade 1 number, and the lower figures of the next two races at ten furlongs. The pattern is common, speed figures dropping noticeably at the classic distance, even among standouts at middle distances. Thus the recommendation that handicappers evaluate horses at ten furlongs by relying upon previous figures at ten furlongs.

That tactic would have backfired with In Excess four months later, in New York's ten-furlong Suburban Handicap. Not only did In Excess win the stakes, the colt recorded his highest speed figure ever.

The Suburban handicap covers ten furlongs around one turn of gigantic Belmont Park, reintroducing the curious phenomenon whereby so many stakes horses earn their largest figures in one-turn routes.

In theory, ranking stakes horses perhaps possess deep reserves of speed and power more readily tapped around one turn. That is, in the latter phase of those truncated races, top horses just have lots left. Once the extra energy is released, the speed figures can soar uncharacteristically high. Easy Goer's famous Gotham, and Grand Canyon's scintillating Hollywood Futurity, both races at a one-turn mile, are the sensational examples easily cited. The figures leaped off the scale and, in Easy Goer's case at least, were never repeated. In Excess did not jump off the scale in the one-turn Metropolitan Mile perhaps, but the speed figure of 117 represented a best-ever mark after an eighty-day layoff.

The phenomenon arises frequently enough to cause figure handicappers to pause. Until stakes horses duplicate the best-ever figures around two turns at the same distances, rely upon the customary numbers as best estimates of real abilities. When In Excess next appears at ten furlongs around two turns, figure handicappers best anticipate a performance nearer to 114 than to 120.

Below Grade 1 stakes competition, figure handicappers can expect to prosper in the stakes division to the degree they abide by a single, well-known principle. Better horses run faster. Studies of par times at every class of racetrack in the United States have demonstrated a perfect positive correlation between speed and class. That reality finds its fullest expression in the stakes races. The classiest horses will also be the fastest.

Because speed and class are so intertwined as fundamental factors in handicapping, it's no paradox to assert that the best speed handicappers might also be the best class handicappers. Figure analysts who respect the class factor will be best equipped to interpret unusually high or closely matched figures, and absolutely so in the stakes races.

Not only must figure handicappers respect the class factor in stakes races, they must also concede another point not very compatible with their basic thinking. In stakes races, class supersedes speed. To put it differently, the quality of opposition will be more important than the values of speed figures. In any stakes race for horses 3up, the objective is to identify the horses that have recorded the highest figures against the most advanced competition. The point of departure is not the figures, but the quality of the races.

If Horse A has recorded a Beyer Speed Figure of 106 in an open stakes having a purse of $75,000, and Horse B has recorded a 106 in a Grade 2 event, B almost certainly has earned the stronger figure. Moreover, if A holds a slight figure advantage against B, but A exits an open stakes and B exits a listed stakes, figure handicappers should prefer B. The quality of Horse B's competition was almost assuredly greater. Keep in mind that class consists of speed plus endurance plus determination. The last two attributes are not easily quantified, but inexorably must be summoned as the quality of racing improves.

Small figure disadvantages are easily overcome by stakes horses exhibiting comparable speed and possessing definite advantages in stamina and determination. This is the context to indicate anew that speed and pace figures are not reality, but estimates of reality, and those estimates contain error, sometimes small, sometimes gross. That error factor looms larger in better races, where stronger, highly competitive runners can overwhelm horses possessing insignificant advantages on speed and pace.

To pursue the logic, most handicappers have become familiar with the hierarchy of races in the stakes division. Stakes horses compete at six levels of opposition:

Grade 1
Grade 2

Grade 3
Listed

Open
Restricted

If the par figure for stakes horses is 111 to 112, Grade 1 and Grade 2 winners will generally exceed par by three to seven lengths. Grade 3 and listed stakes winners will generally attend par, finishing faster or slower than par by one or two lengths. Open stakes winners will be extended to equal or exceed par, but many will, and restricted stakes winners will customarily finish slower than par.

Figure handicappers would therefore expect Grade 1 and Grade 2 standouts to pickle the Grade 3 and listed types, with few exceptions. Similarly, the Grade 3 and listed winners should enjoy a real advantage against open and restricted stakes winners, with some exceptions. Open and restricted stakes winners can climb higher in the stakes hierarchy at times, usually when razor-sharp and particularly well-suited to today's distance, footing, and probable pace.

At any level of the stakes hierarchy, horses well-matched on the figures are separated best by a fine analysis of the quality of racing against which the figures were earned. The better the race, the more meaningful the figures. A best-case scenario finds the high-figure horse exiting the classiest race. Speed and class in combination will be difficult to deny.

The fatal mistake committed routinely by figure handicappers who eschew class is backing the high-figure horses when they will be outgunned regardless. In graded stakes races especially, high speed figures do not overcompensate for deficiencies on other attributes of thoroughbred class. Figure handicappers should not expect that they will.

Below are presented two stakes races of the kind that appear weekly at racetracks large and small. The first is a restricted stakes at a mile, and easy pickings for figure handicappers, whether they regard the class factor as meaningful or not. The second will not be as elementary, and figure analysts insensitive to the relative importance of class in stakes races can easily become lost.

Review the past performances for the one-mile Windy Sands Stakes at Del Mar, August 15, 1991. Six are entered. Which horse figures best on speed and class combined?

Del Mar

8

ONE MILE. WINDY SANDS STAKES. $60,000 Added. A Handicap for Classified Three Year Olds and Upward which are non-winners of $35,000 at one mile or over in 1991. By subscription of $50 each, which shall accompany the nomination, and $150 to pass the entry box, with $60,000 Added, of which $12,000 to second, $9,000 to third, $4,500 to fourth and $1,500 to fifth. Weights Monday, August 12. Starters to be named through the entry box, by the closing time of entries. *A race with $35,000 to the winner. Nominations closed Saturday, August 10 by 12:00 Noon.

LETTHEBIGHOSSROLL

3yo (May) gelding, gray
Trainer: Bob Baffert
Owner: Michael E Pegram

Sire: **Flying Paster** ($35,000) by Gummo
Dam: **Moonlight Jig** by Jig Time
Bred in CA by Cardiff Stud Farm

Career: 6 4 0 0 $126,190

Wet:	0 0 0 0	$0	**1991:**	6 4 0 0	$126,190
Turf:	0 0 0 0	$0	**1990:**	0 0 0 0	$0
Dist:	1 0 0 0	$0	**Dmr:**	0 0 0 0	$0

111 Corey Nakatani

8Jun91 6Bel ft 3 Stk123400 7f 22.18 45.13 1:10.06 1:23.13 93 9/11 5 9³ 11⁴ 7⁴¼ 5⁶¾ E Delahoussy 119 5.40 Fly So Free122²Formal Dinner122²½Dodge122¹½
Gr.3 Riva Ridge Stakes — *Six-wide dropped back early, moved to rail turn, lacked rally*

27May91 8Bel ft 3+ Stk500000 1m 22.14 44.26 1:09.28 1:35.45 98 14/14 3 5⁴¼ 7⁵½ 7⁵ 10¹¹ 10¹³ J Garcia 107 b 13.20 In Excess117²½Rubiano111¹¾Gervazy114¹½
Gr.1 Metropolitan Handicap — *Gradually angled in late backstretch, dropped back late turn*

24Apr91 8Hol ft 3 Stk71050 7f 21.50 44.10 1:08.70 1:21.30 98 2/3 3 3² 3²½ 1ʰᵈ 1²¾ E Delahoussy 122 Bb 1.70 Letthebighossroll122²¾Media Plan122¹¾Apollo122
Harry Henson Stakes — *Three-wide throughout, circled hot pace, drew off*

11Apr91 8GG ft 3 Ⓢ Stk53700 6f 21.90 45.30 57.50 1:10.30 87 2/6 5 4³½ 2½ 1² 1⁴ C Nakatani 122 Bb **0.40** Letthebighossroll122⁴Caliche'sSecrt117½SewPredictable115¹
Piedmont Stakes — *Broke in tangle, wide move quarter pole, drew off impressively*

28Mar91 8SA ft 3 Ⓢ Stk58000 6½f 21.30 44.10 1:09.70 1:16.10 98 2/8 7 2½ 2ʰᵈ 1¹½ 1ʰᵈ E Delahoussy 117 Bb **1.80** Letthebighossroll117ʰᵈProspectr'sRdg115²SlewTheSurgeon119²½
Zany Tactics — *Dueled early, challenged, held gamely, driving*

23Feb91 6SA ft 3 Ⓢ MaidenSpWt 6½f 21.50 44.30 1:09.70 1:16.30 92 4/11 5 12½ 12 1² 15½ E Delahoussy 118 Bb **1.10** Letthebighossroll118⁵½Prospctr's³½NaevusRans¹ *Drew off*

Workouts: 14Aug Dmr 4f ft 48.70 H **9Aug Dmr 6f ft 1:11.70 H** 4Aug Dmr 7f ft 1:24.10 H 29Jly Dmr 5f ft 1:02.10 H 23Jly Dmr 6f ft 1:11.90 H

FANATIC BOY(ARG)

4yo (Aug) colt, dk. bay/brown
Trainer: Ronald McAnally
Owner: Charles Cella

Sire: **Mat-Boy** by Matun
Dam: **Frau Paula** by Frari
Bred in **ARG** by Haras La Biznaga

Career: 9 4 1 2

Wet:	0 0 0 0	**1991:**	1 0 0 0	$4,125
Turf:	5 1 1 2	**1990:**	8 4 1 2	
Dist:	2 1 0 0	**Dmr:**	0 0 0 0	

117 Eddie Delahoussaye

13Jly91 7Hol fm 4+ Alw55000 1⅛ Ⓣ 24.30 47.70 1:10.90 1:40.10 87 1/6 3 5⁵ 5³¼ 5⁴½ 4³½ 4⁷½ JA Santos 116 B 9.00 Algenib118²½Raj Waki118ⁿᵏVal Des Bois114⁴½
Raced inside, mild rally in stretch, no threat

15Dec90 San Isidro (ARG) a1½ Ⓣ fm LH 3+ Stk 2:22.30 8/22 3⁵ Oscar Conti 119 **3.05** Algenib119²El Duce134³Fanatic Boy119ⁿᵒ
Tr: Gustavo Scarpello
Gr.1 Gran Premio Carlos Pelligrini — *Prominent, shaken up 3 furlongs out with little response*

11Nov90 Hipodromo (ARG) a1½ ft LH 3+ Stk 2:37.90 2/10 1⁷ Jorge Conti 125 2.30 Fanatic Boy125⁷Evaluado125⁶Triunfo Moro125²½
Gr.1 Gran Premio Nacional — *Soon led, went clear after 3 furlongs, won in hand*

7Oct90 San Isidro (ARG) a1¼ Ⓣ sf LH 3 Stk 2:00.90 5/14 2⁵ Jorge Conti 123 **2.70** Algenib123⁵Fanatic Boy123²Tibaldi123²½
Gr.1 Gran Premio Jockey Club — *Led from start, soon clear, ridden 3f out, no match for winner*

15Sep90 Hipodromo (ARG) a1⅛ ft LH 3+ Stk 1:47.46 5/10 1⁶ Oscar Conti 123 **1.25** Fanatic Boy123⁶Lovely One123¹½Festejos123⁷
Gr.2 Premio Coronel M.F. Martinez — *Led virtually throughout, not challenged through final half*

28Jly90 San Isidro (ARG) a1m Ⓣ fm LH 3 Stk 1:35.70 15/16 3³½ D Orcellet 123 4.40 Algenib123¹½Fighter Far123²Fanatic Boy123ⁿᵏ
Gr.1 Argentine 2000 Guineas — *Prominent throughout on outside, finished well*

30Jun90 San Isidro (ARG) a1m Ⓣ fm LH 2 Stk 1:35.10 3/20 1ⁿᵏ Oscar Conti 121 15.60 Fanatic Boy121ⁿᵏLovely One121¹½Lin Yutang121²½
Gr.1 Gran Criterium — *Led after 3 furlongs, clear 2f out, held well late*

10Jun90 Hipodromo (ARG) a1m ft LH 2 MaidenSpWt 1:38.84 3/13 1² Oscar Conti 121 21.65 Fanatic Boy121²Fraliss Toss121ⁿᵏTelen121⁸
Premio La Divertida — *Pressed pace, led 2 furlongs out, willingly*

7May90 Hipodromo (ARG) a7½f ft LH 2 MaidenSpWt 1:31.44 5/10 7⁹½ D Orcellet 122 43.75 Combien122ⁿᵒIn Fraganti122³Fraliss Toss122¹½
Premio Mat Wind — *In touch, ridden halfway, weakened*

Workouts: 14Aug Dmr 4f ft 48.90 H 8Aug Dmr 7f ft 1:26.90 H 27Jly Dmr 5f ft 1:02.50 H 21Jly Hol 3f ft 35.70 H 10Jly Hol 5f ft 1:00.90 H

DEPOSIT TICKET

3yo (Apr) colt, bay
Trainer: D Wayne Lukas
Owner: Overbrook Farm

Sire: **Northern Baby** ($30,000) by Northern Dancer
Dam: **Propositioning** by Mr. Prospector
Bred in **KY** by Leone J. Peters

Career: 9 4 2 1 $375,072

Wet:	2 2 0 0	$259,680	**1991:**	1 0 1 0	$10,000
Turf:	0 0 0 0	$0	**1990:**	8 4 1 1	$365,072
Dist:	1 0 0 0	$0	**Dmr:**	1 0 1 0	$10,000

113 Chris J McCarron — Yearling Price: **$175,000**

2Aug91 8Dmr ft 3+ Alw50000 6f 22.00 44.47 56.27 1:08.54 103 1/6 3 1½ 1ʰᵈ 2ʰᵈ 2ʰᵈ CJ McCarron 114 B 5.30 Bum Annie115ʰᵈDeposit Ticket114⁶Mister Frisky115½
Rail trip, good speed, game inside through stretch, 2nd best

6Oct90 6Bel ft 2 Stk636000 1m 22.48 45.27 1:10.24 1:35.79 92 1/13 6 1¹ 1½ 2ʰᵈ 7⁵¾ 13¹⁸ GL Stevens 122 **1.40** Fly So Free122⁵½Happy Jazz Band122ⁿᵏSubordinated Debt122¹½
Gr.1 Champagne Stakes — *Hard used to get clear, gave way readily when challenged*

15Sep90 7Bel ft 2 Stk115600 7f 23.01 46.06 1:09.97 1:22.53 95 2/4 1 1½ 1½ 2² GL Stevens 122 **0.30** Eastern Echo122²Deposit Ticket122⁴½Groom's Reckoning122²½
Gr.1 Futurity Stakes — *Bk in st, dueled inside, fought gamely*

25Aug90 8Sar my2 Stk232800 6½f 22.01 44.73 1:09.63 1:16.27 98 4/6 3 1¹ 1½ 1⁴½ GL Stevens 122 **1.30** Deposit Ticket122⁴½Hansel122¾Link122ⁿᵏ
Gr.1 Hopeful Stakes — *Sent to front on speed track, made pace away from rail, drew off*

11Aug90 10Mth my2 Stk200000 6f 21.70 44.90 1:11.10 96 5/9 6 4½ 2ʰᵈ 1³¾ GL Stevens 122 2.60 Deposit Ticket122³¾Alaskan Frost122¹½Hansel122ⁿᵒ
Gr.2 Sapling Stakes — *Improved position outside, won duel and gradually drew clear*

21Jly90 8Hol ft 2 Stk101500 6f 21.90 44.50 1:09.10 98 4/8 1 1¹ 1ⁿᵏ 1¹ GL Stevens 117 2.70 Deposit Ticket117¹Avenue Of Flags117¹½Stone God117²½
Gr.2 Hollywood Juv Champ Stk — *Speed to make lead, headed top stretch, fought back on rail*

1Jly90 9CD ft 2 Stk54700 6f 21.70 45.30 57.10 1:10.30 72 5/7 4⁸½ KK Allen 116 3.10 To Freedom121⁵Richman121¹Discover116²½
Bashford Manor Stakes

17Jun90 4Hol ft 2 MaidenSpWt 5½f 22.10 45.50 1:03.10 98 1/8 1 1¹½ 1¹ 1⁴½ GL Stevens 117 **0.90** Deposit Ticket117⁴½Librtng⁶½FarBest²½ *Good spd; driving*

2Jun90 6Hol ft 2 MaidenSpWt 5f 21.90 45.50 57.90 76 2/8 4 1ʰᵈ 1ⁿᵒ 3⁴ P Valenzuela 118 4.10 Sunshine Machine118½Barrag³½Depst³½ *Good spd; weakened*

Workouts: 11Aug Dmr 6f ft 1:13.70 H 29Jly Dmr 6f ft 1:12.90 H 24Jly Dmr 6f ft 1:13.70 H 17Jly Hol 5f ft 1:01.50 H 11Jly Hol 5f ft 1:00.90 H

ANNUAL DATE

5yo (Feb) horse, dk. bay/brown
Trainer: Robert Frankel
Owner: Peter Wall

Sire: **Nostalgia** ($1,000) by Silent Screen
Dam: **Dancing Role** by Droll Role
Bred in CA by Mr. & Mrs. John C. Mabee

1989-91: 21 7 4 2
Wet: 2 2 0 0 | **1991:** 3 2 1 0 $61,000
Turf: 4 0 3 0 | **1990:** 9 1 2 1
Dist: 9 5 0 2 | **Dmr:** 1 0 0 0

116 Laffit Pincay Jr

16Jun91 8Exh my3+ Stk50000 1 1/16 23.10 47.70 1:13.10 1:53.70 4/8 8 87 8 1/2 6 1/2 3 1/2 1nk L Lacoursier 118 bf **1.15** Annual Date118nkCommander Bold115 3/4Charlie Chalmers113 3/4
Gr.3 Lieutenant Governors' — *Rallied inside 1/4 to top stretch, took lead, driving*
20May91 8Exh ft 3+ Stk30000 1 1/16 23.50 47.30 1:12.10 1:44.90 2/6 3 23 23 22 2 1/2 1 3/4 L Lacoursier 116 bf **0.90** Annual Date116 3/4Commander Bold115 3/4Havegotadealforu118 2 3/4
The Victoria Day — *Well placed early, well rated, closed willingly, driving*
27Apr91 8Exh ft 3+ Stk30000 6 1/2f 21.90 45.10 1:10.30 1:16.90 — 5/7 3 44 34 1/2 31 1/2 22 S Krasner 115 bf **1.90** Lucky Baba118 2Annual Date115 1 1/4Martini To Tango115 1 1/4
Province Stakes — *Never far back, closed willingly, no match for winner*
3Nov90 8SA ft 3+ Stk300000 1 1/8 45.10 1:09.10 1:46.10 71 10/14 11 109 1114 1216 1221 1/4 C Nakatani 118 LBb 9.90 My Sonny Boy116 2 1/2Stylish Stud116hdRob An Plunder115 1 1/2
California Cup Classic Hcp — *Four wide first turn, not a factor*
30Sep90 11Fpx ft 3+ Stk150000 1 1/8 47.30 1:12.30 1:48.90 10/10 6 96 43 1/2 55 1/4 C Nakatani 119 Lb **2.60** Elegant Bargain115 1My Sonny Boy117 4Double Quick118nk
Pomona Invitational Handicap — *3-wide entire trip, mild rally far turn, not good enough*
26Aug90 9Lga ft 3+ Stk300200 1m 22.10 45.70 1:10.30 1:35.70 — 4/14 9 89 1/2 87 1/2 56 3/4 GL Stevens 116 LBb **1.90** Snipledo115 4AdventuresomeLove114 2KentGreenCaptainCo116 3/4
Gr.3 Longacres Mile Handicap — *Offered a mild rally; was unable to threaten*
14Jly90 8Hol ft 3+ Stk150000 1m 22.90 45.10 1:08.90 1:34.30 3/7 5 3 3/4 22 31 1/4 C Nakatani 117 Lb 3.70 Prospectors Gamble110 1Music Prospector112nkAnnual Date117hd
Gr.2 Bel Air Handicap — *Stalked outside pacesetter, clear trip, not good enough*
28May90 7Hol gd 4+ Hcp60000 1m 46.10 1:10.30 1:35.70 3/7 5 42 1/4 3nk 13 C Nakatani 114 Lb 8.30 Annual Date114 3MusicMerci1 3/4ExemplryLdrnk *Rated; easily*
28Apr90 9Spt ft 4+ Stk239550 1 1/8 46.90 1:11.50 1:49.70 5/11 4 3 1/2 3hd 47 3/4 C Nakatani 117 b 3.40 Dual Elements118 6Tricky Creek120 1 3/4Blue Buckaroo115hd
Gr.3 National Jockey Club Hcp — *Bore out; raced five-wide*
1Apr90 8SA ft 4+ Stk400000 1 1/8 46.10 1:09.70 1:47.30 2/6 3 24 57 3/4 E Delahoussy 116 Lb 14.90 Ruhlmann123 2Criminal Type119 1 1/2Stylish Winner113 3/4
Gr.2 San Bernardino Handicap — *Stalked leader one off rail, little to offer past quarter pole*

Workouts: **5Aug Dmr 7f ft 1:26.30 H** 24Jly Dmr 6f ft 1:13.50 H 19Jly SA 4f ft 50.70 B

WARCRAFT

4yo (May) colt, bay
Trainer: Charles Whittingham
Owner: Bradley Chandler & C Whittingham

Sire: **Ack Ack** by Battle Joined
Dam: **Became A Lark** by T. V. Lark
Bred in KY by Mary Bradley, Charles Whittingham, et al.

Career: 20 5 8 1
Wet: 2 1 0 0 | **1991:** 5 0 3 0 $94,760
Turf: 5 0 3 0 | **1990:** 15 5 5 1
Dist: 9 4 4 0 | **Dmr:** 1 0 1 0

119 Patrick A Valenzuela

26Jly91 7Dmr fm 3+ Stk62050 1m (T) 24.94 49.47 1:13.11 1:36.34 91 4/6 3 21 1hd 2hd 54 65 1/4 P Valenzuela 120 B 6.80 Blaze O'brien118nkFrenchSeventyfiv115 1 1/2Somethingdifrnt119hd
Wickerr Handicap — *Hard held, slow pace, no excuse, empty in stretch*
19May91 8Hol ft 3+ Stk200600 1 1/16 23.50 46.10 1:09.90 1:40.90 107 2/6 3 1hd 2 1/2 11 1/2 2hd 2 1/2 CJ McCarron 115 **1.20** Louis Cyphre114 1/2Warcraft115 2Anshan116 5 1/2
Gr.1 Mervyn Leroy Handicap — *Dueled early, put away other speed, challenged, gamely, 2nd best*
3May91 8Hol ft 4+ Alw55000 1 1/16 23.30 46.30 1:09.90 1:41.70 107 2/5 2 22 22 22 22 21 1/4 E Delahoussy 117 **1.00** Perforce119 1 1/4Warcraft117 1Morlando119 3
Chased pace, couldn't reach winner, second best
10Feb91 8SA ft 4 Stk500000 1 1/4 22.70 46.30 1:34.90 2:00.90 77 6/7 2 21 21 65 1/2 715 721 1/2 CJ McCarron 117 B 3.50 Defensive Play122hdMy Boy Adam117 1 1/4In Excess121 4 1/2
Gr.1 Charles H Strub Stakes — *Weakened in final stakes; kept near the early pace*
19Jan91 8SA ft 4 Stk218800 1 1/8 22.70 46.50 1:10.30 1:46.70 107 9/9 3 33 31 23 24 CJ McCarron 120 Bf **2.40** In Excess126 4Warcraft120 2 3/4Go And Go123 1 1/4
Gr.2 San Fernando Stakes — *Three wide throughout, no threat to winner*
1Dec90 8Hol ft 3+ Stk108500 1 1/8 23.50 46.90 1:10.70 1:47.50 104 6/7 3 3 1/2 31 2 1/2 1no CJ McCarron 117 f **1.50** Warcraft117noPleasant Tap115nkGo And Go115 1 1/4
Gr.3 Native Diver Handicap — *Three wide forcing pace, challenged entering lane, up late*
10Nov90 7Hol ft 3+ Alw36000 1m 22.50 44.70 1:09.10 1:34.10 4/6 1 2 1/2 2hd 13 1/2 RG Davis 114 f **0.80** Warcraft114 3 1/2Morlando1 1/2On A Roll2 *Stlk pace; easily*
21Oct90 8SA fm 3 Stk110300 1 1/8 (T) 23.30 46.90 1:10.50 1:46.70 2/8 2 32 3/4 41 1/2 32 22 1/4 CJ McCarron 118 Bf **2.00** In Excess117 3/4Warcraft118 1/2Barton Dene113 1 1/4
Gr.3 Volante Handicap — *Saved ground throughout, closed evenly on rail*
7Oct90 7SA ft 3+ Alw40000 1 1/16 23.10 46.70 1:10.50 1:41.50 7/9 1 3 1/2 2no 11 14 1/2 CJ McCarron 114 **1.10** Warcraft114 4 1/2FinalForcsthdGreydar 3/4 *Stlk pace; drew off*
5Sep90 8Dmr ft 3 Stk75000 1 1/16 22.90 45.70 1:10.10 1:41.70 1/7 5 32 1/2 32 2 1/2 CJ McCarron 119 **1.00** Asia115 1/2Warcraft119 1/2Shinko Wine117 3/4
El Cajon Stakes — *Skimmed rail, 3 wide rally far turn, hung through stretch*

Workouts: 12Aug Dmr 5f ft 59.70 H 7Aug Dmr 5f ft 1:00.50 H 2Aug Dmr 3f ft 37.10 B **24Jly Dmr 4f ft 46.50 H** 18Jly Hol (T) 1m fm 1:42.30 H (d)

HABASTAR

4yo (Apr) gelding, bay
Trainer: Pete Eurton
Owner: D & V Enterprises Inc

Sire: **Habitony** ($5,000) by Habitat
Dam: **Laura's Star** by Key To The Kingdom
Bred in CA by Mr. & Mrs. John C. Mabee

Career: [illegible] 3 2 1
Wet: 2 1 1 0 | **1991:** 8 3 1 1 $76,450
Turf: 1 0 0 0 | **1990:** 1 0 1 0
Dist: 6 3 1 0 | **Dmr:** 1 1 0 0

113 Gary L Stevens

28Jly91 7Dmr ft 3+ Alw43000Nw2x 1 1/16 23.29 47.11 1:11.00 1:43.41 4/5 2 42 1/2 31 1/2 12 1/2 12 1/2 11 1/4 P Valenzuela 118 LB 4.50 Habastar118 1 1/4Single Dawn118 5Run On The Bank118nk
3-wide pressed pace, drew clear, held driving
28Jun91 5Hol ft 3+ Alw38000Nw2x 1 1/16 22.50 45.10 1:09.90 1:42.30 4/7 4 44 48 54 1/2 22 42 1/4 L Pincay Jr 117 B 3.10 Prince Colony116hdRun On The Bank116 1 1/4TreatTobeatyafeet116
Loomed boldly into stretch along rail, outfinished for placings
5Jun91 7Hol ft 3+ Alw38000Nw2x 7 1/2f 22.50 45.10 1:09.90 1:28.90 3/7 5 54 65 43 41 L Pincay Jr 117 Bb 3.20 Keep Clear118 3/4Marlar118nkExpress It115hd
In between horses backstretch, carried out through stretch
13Apr91 5SA fm 4+ Alw39000Nw2x 1 1/8 (T) 24.30 47.50 1:11.10 1:47.10 5/8 2 62 1/4 64 1/2 78 1/2 75 1/4 67 DR Flores 120 B 4.80 High Rank115hdBig Warning3 1/2Ornery Guest 1/2 *Dull effort*
27Mar91 7SA gd 4+ Alw35000Nw1x 1 1/16 22.90 46.70 1:11.30 1:43.70 6/6 1 32 31 1/2 1hd 11 1/2 1 3/4 DR Flores 121 B **1.00** Habastar121 3/4King Raj 4Kalabrea 3 1/4 *Wide, driving*
1Mar91 5SA sy 4+ Alw35000 1 1/16 22.70 46.30 1:12.10 1:45.50 3/10 9 68 1/4 69 3/4 32 1/2 21 21 1/4 K Desormeaux121 B **3.10** Reppus Tuolluf118 1 1/4Habestar 5Pappy Yokum 3/4 *Poor start*
9Feb91 4SA ft 4+ MaidenSpWt 1m 23.30 47.50 1:11.90 1:36.50 3/10 1 21 21 2hd 2hd 1 1/2 K Desormeaux119 B **1.20** Habastar119 1/2EasyLeader 5 1/2Pappalard 1/2 *Erratic; stlk pace*
17Jan91 6SA ft 4+ MaidenSpWt 6f 21.70 44.50 1:09.10 6/10 1 2no 21 32 3nk K Desormeaux119 B 3.10 Barron Ribot119hdCatskilhdHabstr3 *Altd crse; came again*
30Dec90 4SA ft 3+ MaidenSpWt 6 1/2f 21.90 44.90 1:16.90 3/8 1 41 1/4 31 1hd 2no K Desormeaux118 B 14.20 Magic Prospect118noHabst2 1/2Barm 3/4 *Svd grnd; just missed*

Workouts: 6Aug Dmr 4f ft 51.10 H 26Jly Dmr 3f ft 37.10 H **21Jly Dmr 5f ft 59.90 H**

Figure handicappers should have noticed the field is restricted to horses 3up which have not won a purse similar to today's at a mile or longer in 1991. The Beyer Speed Figure par for top-grade stakes is approximately 110, but for a restricted stakes, par can be as low as 100. Par figures or better, therefore, should range upwards of 100.

Because horses that have won $35,000 first money at a mile

in 1991 have been barred, stakes winners in sprints will be encouraged to stretch out. If their speed figures qualify and they distribute their energy efficiently, they can be rugged customers.

A quick glance at the field reveals the high-figure horses are Deposit Ticket and Warcraft. The others have not yet surpassed par for a restricted stakes, though Annual Date in previous seasons has, and the 3YO Letthebighossroll approached today's par in a sprint stakes it won last spring.

Warcraft's 107 is not only the top figure in the field, it was earned in Grade 1 company at Hollywood Park. Speed complements class here very well. If Warcraft's 107 had been earned in ungraded company, it would not look nearly as meaningful.

Deposit Ticket's 105 occurred in overnight competition in his first start as a three-year-old. The figure is not easy to interpret because the 2YO record of fall does not transfer well to the 3YO record of summer. A Grade 1 winner as a 2YO, Deposit Ticket's figures should improve at three, and the opening 105 indicates the colt may be too much racehorse for older restricted stakes hopefuls.

On the other hand, Deposit Ticket's 105 in a rapidly closely contested sprint following a lengthy layoff represents a negative pattern. Even good horses that overexert themselves following long layoffs are susceptible to a regression next time, the notorious "bounce" pattern which will be described in detail later.

With the potential exception of Deposit Ticket, Warcraft stands apart on the speed-class dynamic figure handicappers prefer in stakes races. Warcraft had defeated or finished close to classier opposition and has registered higher speed figures in the bargain.

Letthebighossroll might be an upset possibility under restricted stakes conditions if his speed figures were better than par for today's race, but a best-ever 98 does not quite qualify. The presence of Deposit Ticket ensures that Letthebighossroll should not steal the race on the front. The 3YO's step-up in distance and class simultaneously should prove too strict a barrier against the class of Warcraft.

Not to be overlooked, trainer Bob Baffert asked Letthebighossroll to graduate from an unlisted, ungraded sprint stakes limited to 3YOs to the Grade 1 Metropolitan Mile, not only open to older horses, but the most prestigious mile in the country. A foolish, premature trainer maneuver, the resulting setback may endure for many months.

Fanatic Boy satisfies the most important criterion for imports from South America entered in U.S. stakes, namely multiple Grade 1 victories in the homeland. Fanatic Boy annexed a pair of Grade 1 stakes in Argentina, while placing in the most prestigious stakes in the country. But Fanatic Boy recorded a weak overnight figure (87) on the turf first out in the States. A dramatic reversal is possible, but handicappers prefer to wait if a foreigner's debut leaves too much to be desired.

Annual Date's best-ever figures cannot defeat Warcraft, and the recent numbers are hardly competitive.

Habastar boasts only allowance figures against allowance company. He remains badly outclassed in this restricted stakes.

Warcraft and Deposit Ticket were not difficult to isolate in a restricted stakes, but which horse do figure handicappers prefer among the leading contenders in the open sprint stakes below? Par is unknown. The race occurred at the Los Alamitos "bull-ring"—a track with tight turns—near Los Angeles, and contenders have arrived with speed figures earned at various racetracks.

Los Alamitos

9 *6½ furlongs*

SIX AND ONE HALF FURLONGS. CHAPMAN HANDICAP. Purse $50,000 Added. For Fillies and Mares Three Years Old and Upward. By subscription of $10 each to accompany the nomination. $100 to pass the entry box of which $8,500 to second. $6,000 to third, $3,500 to fourth, $2,500 to fifth. $1,000 to sixth, $500 to seventh and eighth. Weights Saturday, August 10, 1991. Starters to be named through the entry box by closing time of entries Wednesday, August 14, 1991. High weights preferred. Nominations close Wednesday, August 7, 1991.

MAHASKA

4yo (Feb) filly, bay
Trainer: Michael Puhich
Owner: Czechmate Stable

Sire: **Just The Time** ($2,000)
  by Advocator
Dam: **Whimsical Aire**
  by Messenger Of Song
Bred in WA by John Konecny & Doris Konecny

Career:	17 5 4 2	
Wet: 1 0 0 1	**1991:** 6 1 1 1	$54,500
Turf: 4 1 2 0	**1990:** 7 3 1 1	
Dist: 10 4 2 0	**LA:** 2 1 0 0	

118   Adalberto C Lopez

29Jly91 9LA ft 3-F	Stk35490	4¼f 21.30 44.10	49.90 **84**	4/7	4 43½		3⁴ 43¾ AC Lopez	119 L	1.90 Excess Energy115¹½Windsong Mana116⁴Mama Simba114ʰᵈ		*Some early foot, had little to offer in lane*
27Apr91 8Hol ft 3-F	Stk107400	7f 21.70 44.30 1:09.30 1:22.10 **79**		2/6	5 32½ 41½		55½ 67½ C Nakatani	116 L	19.50 Survive119ⁿᵏStormy But Valid121¹¼Brought To Mind1173½		*Rail trip, pressed pace, tired*
14Apr91 8SA fm 3-F	Stk211350	1m⊕22.70 45.10 1:08.90 1:33.50 **82**		4/9	1 1¹ 2¹		31½ 85¼ 913½ A Solis	114 LB	10.60 Fire The Groom1153Flower Girl116²Heart Of Joy119½		*Sprinted clear early, hooked, quit in stretch*
23Mar91 8SA fm 4-F	Stk83400	a6¼f⊕21.50 43.70 1:07.30 1:13.30 **90**		6/8	1 1ʰᵈ 1¹½		1½ 2¹ J Velasquez	117 LB	10.50 Flower Girl116¹Mahaska117¹½Survive117¹½		*Good speed, turned back challengers, just missed*
9Mar91 2SA fm 4-F	Stk50000	a6¼f⊕21.10 43.10	1:12.70 **98**	7/8	1 3¼ 3¹		1ʰᵈ 1½ GL Stevens	116 LB	8.40 Mahaska116½Odalea114²Polar Bird114½		*Sat off leaders, three-wide drive, held well stretch, game*
2Feb91 8GG sy 3-F	Stk50000	1m 22.70 46.30 1:10.90 1:38.50 **85**		1/5	1 11½ 1½		11½ 11½ 3² G Boulanger	119 LB	1.10 Vanety Spice116¹½Azusa116½Mahaska119⁵		*Weakened in final stages; showed strong early speed*
30Dec90 8SA ft 3F	Stk110000	7f 22.70 45.50 1:09.50 1:21.70 **80**		6/8	2 1½ 1¹		2³ 79¾ G Boulanger	117 B	8.50 Brought To Mind117¾A Wild Ride119¹¼Mama Simba114½		*Shot to lead, hugged rail, empty midstretch*
2Dec90 7Hol ft 3-F	Alw60000	6f 21.90 44.50	1:08.90 **57**	7/7	4 1ʰᵈ 2½		7¹¹ 7¹⁷ G Boulanger	120 B	4.10 Stormy But Valid119½Class³⁰Papr¹ᵏ		Spd to 1/2; weakened
7Nov90 8Hol fm 3F	⑤Stk60000	1¹⁄₁₆⊕23.30 46.10 1:10.70 1:41.30 **88**		3/8	1 1³ 1¹		2⁵ G Boulanger	117 B	5.20 Annual Reunion117³Mahaska117²Vaguely Charming118½		*Made lead in hand, unable to resist winner, well clear of third*

Las Palmas
Gr.2 A Gleam Handicap
Gr.3 SA Budweiser Breeders' Cup
Las Cienegas Handicap
B Thoughtful
Lafayette BrCup Handicap
Gr.3 La Brea Stakes
Allez France Handicap

Workouts: 23Jly SA   5f ft 1:03.50 B   17Jly SA   4f ft 48.30 H   11Jly SA   4f ft 46.90 B   5Jly SA   3f ft 35.50 H   29Jun SA   3f ft 35.10 H

MAMA SIMBA

4yo (Mar) filly, bay
Trainer: Richard Mandella
Owner: Ralph E & Aury Todd

Sire: **Mamaison** ($3,000)
  by Verbatim
Dam: **Lizzie Rolfe**
  by Tom Rolfe
Bred in KY by Ralph Todd & Aury Todd

Career:	16 3 2 6	
Wet: 0 0 0 0	**1991:** 8 0 1 4	$41,295
Turf: 2 0 0 0	**1990:** 8 3 1 2	
Dist: 11 3 2 5	**LA:** 1 0 0 1	

114   Kent J Desormeaux

29Jly91 9LA ft 3-F	Stk35490	4¼f 21.30 44.10	49.90 **84**	6/7	7 7¹⁰		57½ 33¾ LE Ortega	114 L	2.10 Excess Energy115¹½Windsong Maria116²Mama Simba114ʰᵈ		*Far back early, best stride late, no threat top pair*
7Jly91 3Hol ft 3-F	Alw39000Nw3x	6f 22.10 44.90 57.50 1:09.70 **88**		5/6	1 54½ 52¾		42½ 3½ DR Flores	115 LB	6.50 Magic Sister116½Streamer114ⁿᵏMama Simba115²½		*Lacked room far turn, angled in far turn, swung out str, gaining*
12Jun91 8Hol ft 3-F	Alw39000Nw3x	6¼f 21.90 44.30 1:09.10 1:15.70 **88**		1/6	6 65½ 84¾		4² 42½ E Delahoussaye	116 LB	2.80 Questioning115ʰᵈStreamer115ʰᵈLong Long Trail116²		*Rallied wide into stretch, bid upper stretch, hung*
10May91 8Hol fm 4-F	Alw42000Nw3x	1¹⁄₁₆⊕24.10 48.10 1:11.70 1:41.50 **80**		5/8	6 6⁵ 6⁵ 6⁵		55½ 55½ DR Flores	115 LB	21.30 Gaelic Bird115¹½MySong1ᶠᵉᵏJoilMmr²		*Rail trip, lacked rlly*
23Mar91 8SA fm 4-F	Stk1500	6f 21.50 44.30 56.30 1:08.50 **88**		2/7	6 76¾ 5²		3¹½ 34½ DR Flores	116 LB	5.50 Cascading Gold120⁴Lanikai1141¼Mama Simba1164½		*Split horses turn, late bid middle of track*
8Mar91 3SA ft 4-F	Alw39000	6¼f 22.30 45.10 1:09.10 1:15.50 **98**		6 4 3¹ 3¹		3⁴ 3⁴ DR Flores	115 LB	1.80 Cascading Gold115½France Soir³Mama Simba³			*Wide turn*
15Feb91 8SA ft 4-F	Alw56850	7f 22.30 44.90 1:09.30 1:22.70 **97**		5/8	5 66½ 6⁵		3⁴½ 2¹½ DR Flores	118 LB	3.80 Dominant Dancer114¹½Mama Simba²½Covell1ʰᵈ			*Gaining*
24Jan91 8SA tur 4-F	Alw39000	a6¼f⊕22.50 45.10	1:14.10 **90**	6/8	6 6⁶½ 5³½		4⁴ 43½ DR Flores	114 LB	13.70 Forest Fealty114ʰᵈOdalea⁴GreatStrk½		*Outrun; no threat*
30Dec90 8SA ft 3F	Stk110000	7f 22.70 45.50 1:09.50 1:21.70 **80**		4/8	6 73¾ 73½		54½ 37½ DR Flores	114 LB	9.50 Brought To Mind117¾A Wild Ride119¹½Mama Simba114½		*Three wide early, four wide turn, five wide stretch, evenly*

Las Palmas
Gr.3 La Brea Stakes

Workouts: 12Aug SA   3f ft 37.90 H   18Jly Hol   3f ft 36.90 B   5Jly Hol   3f ft 36.50 B   23Jun Hol   3f ft 34.30 B

HASTY PASTY
6yo (Apr) mare, bay
Trainer: Casey Doyle
Owner: John R Franks

Sire: **Flying Paster** ($35,000) by Gummo
Dam: **Revered** by In Reality
Bred in CA by Cardiff Stud Farm

1989-91: 36 8 5 7
Wet: 4 0 0 3 | **1991:** 8 0 3 2 $45,794
Turf: 7 1 1 2 | **1990:** 15 5 1 0
Dist: 26 7 4 5 | **LA:** 0 0 0 0

117 Jon K Court

31Jly91 11SR ft 3+F Stk33400 6f 21.70 44.50 56.30 1:09.50 88 1/9 8 85½ 75¼ 64½ 22 TT Doocy 118 L 8.50 Wind Shear1192Hasty Pasty1182Big Squaw1151
Elie Destruel Handicap — *Advanced steadily inside to str, angled out, finished well*
18May91 1GG ft 4+F Hcp30000 6f 22.10 44.90 57.10 1:09.90 78 3/5 3 52¼ 52¾ 52¾ 43 R Gonzalez Jr 120 LB 4.40 What Has Been1162Tasteful T. V.1151Lakeland Beauty116hd
Outrun early, lacked needed response
13Apr91 9OP sy 4+F Stk42400 6f 22.01 45.07 1:09.51 88 6/6 5 52½ 43 45½ 36 D Howard 115 L 3.20 Nurse Dopey12331½Spring Flight12121½Hasty Pasty1154
Oaklawn Park — *unhurried, early, late rally*
7Apr91 8OP ft 4+F Alw 3000 6f 21.30 45.10 1:10.20 90 8/8 1 31 3½ 11½ 2 L Snyder 117 L 1.00 Ladyago114Hasty Pasty4½Mane's Whirlnk *Just missed*
16Mar91 9OP ft 4+F Stk50000 1m 23.50 47.10 1:11.90 1:37.10 67 9/9 1 31½ 31 4¾ 67¼ 614 L Snyder 112 L 7.10 Timber Ribbon112nkBeth Believes11431½Nurse Dopey1175
Pippin Stakes — *Well placed, tired*
3Mar91 9OP ft 4+F Stk57500 6f 22.37 46.02 1:10.56 88 5/8 6 62¼ 31 31½ 23 L Snyder 117 L 3.40 Nurse Dopey1183Hasty Pasty117¾Ashley's Avenger1122
Carousel Handicap — *Split horses, rallied late for place*
13Feb91 8SA fm 4+F Stk85625 a6½f ⓣ21.50 43.90 1:07.70 1:13.90 90 4/11 5 44 42¼ 63¼ 84½ J Garcia 115 LB 32.80 Wedding Bouquet1151Linda Card118nkFlower Girl1161
Gr.3 Monrovia Handicap — *Weakened in final stages; showed speed for half-mile*
5Jan91 8SA my4+F Stk105325 6f 21.70 44.90 1:10.30 90 6/6 5 55¾ 54 45½ 35 J Garcia 116 LBf 8.10 Classic Value1162Devil's Orchid1163Hasty Pasty1161
Gr.3 Las Flores BrCup Handicap — *No speed one off rail, no threat rally one off rail*
2Dec90 7Hol ft 3+F Alw60000 6f 21.90 44.50 1:08.90 88 3/7 6 64¾ 53¾ 55½ 55 J Velasquez 119 LBf 11.80 Stormy But Valid119½Classc3PaprPrnk *Outrun; no threat*

Workouts: 25Jly GG 5f ft 1:00.90 H 19Jly GG 3f ft 36.50 H 13Jly GG 3f ft 38.30 H 7May GG 4f ft 48.70 H 1Apr OP 4f ft 48.70 H

SENTIMENTALIZE
4yo (May) filly, dk. bay/brown
Trainer: Steve Wiberg
Owner: Bennett, Domush, Koski, Seefeld & Wilson

Sire: **Maudlin** ($5,000) by Foolish Pleasure
Dam: **Proven Sweet** by Prove Out
Bred in FL by Farnsworth Farms & Skip Taylor

Career: 28 7 6 4
Wet: 2 1 0 1 | **1991:** 4 1 0 1 $12,190
Turf: 2 0 0 0 | **1990:** 18 4 5 3
Dist: 14 3 1 3 | **LA:** 0 0 0 0

114 Ray Sibille

9Jun91 7Bel ft 3+F Alw41000 7f 22.46 45.28 1:10.18 1:23.32 80 4/7 5 64½ 64½ 52 52½ CA Black 117 32.40 Her She Shawklit117¾A Wink And A Nod117¾Sharp Dance117¾
Saved ground throughout, moved closer mid-stretch, tired
18May91 5Pha ft 3+F Alw17135Nw3x 6f 22.98 46.21 1:11.11 90 5/6 3 41½ 31 2½ 11 ME Verge 116 2.50 Sentimentalize1161Jury Charmer1134½Dame's Double1161½
Split foes, driving; strong ride
28Apr91 8Pha ft 3+F Alw16000Nw3x 6½f 22.68 46.10 1:11.33 1:17.91 77 2/8 5 21 21 31 42½ G Jocson5 111 1.10 Stop The Song116¾Jury Charmer1181Dame's Double116¾
Lacked final bid
21Apr91 8GS sy 3+F Stk20000 6f 22.80 46.51 1:11.65 72 3/5 2 2hd 21½ 24 37 CC Lopez 114 3.10 Never My Love1147Tammy's Legs117noSentimentalize1149½
Whaler Stakes — *Challanged winner till stretch weakened*
31Dec90 1Aqu gd 3F Clm75000 6f 23.29 46.69 1:11.57 94 5/7 3 41¾ 33½ 1½ CK Murphy 118 4.90 Sentimentalize118½Joy'sJJ3Majstc2¾ *Late rlly; driving*
12Dec90 8Med ft 3+F Alw16000Nw2x 6f 23.10 46.70 1:11.70 82 4/7 2 43½ 22½ 13 17 J Tejeira 117 2.10 Sentimentalize1177PrincsTwicA3 *Stlk pace; going awy*
2Dec90 5Aqu ft 3F Clm75000 1m 23.64 47.46 1:13.36 1:38.86 74 1/6 6 31½ 31 46 A Madrid Jr 118 2.20 Nordancer11621½ByDescenthdSpeedwll3½ *Svd grnd; bid, hung*
20Nov90 8Pha ft 3+F Alw12500Nw1x 170 22.50 48.10 1:14.50 1:45.10 88 5/9 2 52½ 31 2½ 13½ ME Verge 114 0.70 Sentimentalize11431½Iss'sFnc7CamCntr1 *Boxed in; easily*
24Oct90 6Med ft 3F Clm50000 1m 23.90 46.70 1:12.10 1:37.70 90 7/7 6 56½ 32 11½ 2nk J Tejeira 114 f 2.30 Nordancer114nkSentimentalize6Fatal Romanceno *Missed*

Workouts: 10Aug BM 5f ft 1:00.30 Hgate **2Aug GG 6f ft 1:13.50 H** 25Jly GG 6f ft 1:12.90 H 19Jly GG 5f ft 1:01.50 H 14Jly GG 4f ft 49.30 H

MARGARET'S NATIVE
5yo (Feb) mare, dk. bay/brown
Trainer: Joseph Shufelt
Owner: Frank Gogliano

Sire: **He's Our Native** by Our Native
Dam: **Naggy Maggy** by Norcliffe
Bred in CA by Larry & Sheila Ullmann

1989-91: 23 7 2 7
Wet: 3 0 1 1 | **1991:** 7 0 1 2 $23,100
Turf: 4 0 1 2 | **1990:** 4 3 0 1
Dist: 17 7 1 4 | **LA:** 0 0 0 0

113 Luis E Ortega

19Jly91 8Hol fm 4+F Clm62500 1⅛ ⓣ22.90 45.90 1:09.90 1:41.10 89 4/7 3 12 13 12½ 2½ 23 LE Ortega 116 LB 19.60 Marvelous Wonder1173Margaret's Native116hdMoratempo1191
Clear lead, no match for winner, lasted for plac
3Jly91 7Hol fm 4+F Clm62500 1m ⓣ23.70 46.90 1:11.50 1:35.90 87 6/11 1 11 11½ 11 2hd 31 LE Ortega 116 LB 13.30 Moratempo116½Mittens And Mink116½Margaret's Native1161½
Washed out, lone lead, held stubbornly to wire, held show
9Jun91 3Hol fm 4+F Clm62500 1⅛ ⓣ22.90 45.70 1:10.10 1:41.70 88 5/7 2 2½ 11½ 11 3nk 33 LE Ortega 116 LB 15.30 Grand Award11611½Rachael's Prospect11311½Margaret'sNative1162
Full of run early, outfinished stretch, drifted in stretch
19May91 7Hol fm 4+F Clm62500 1m ⓣ23.10 45.90 1:10.70 1:35.30 84 4/12 3 1½ 1hd 1hd 1hd 63¾ LE Ortega 116 LB 82.50 Sonata Slew11623Cozzyno SongStylshd *Good speed, bore out*
15Mar91 3SA gd 4+F Clm62500 1m 22.70 46.50 1:11.50 1:36.70 72 1/7 5 12 12½ 21 43½ 410½ DR Flores 115 LB 10.30 She Said Maybe117noChalkBx8SontSlw2½ *Good speed, tired*
17Feb91 4SA ft 4+F Clm50000 6½f 21.70 44.50 1:10.10 1:16.50 78 1/8 3 2½ 22 53½ 47½ RD Davis 115 LB 10.10 Lovely Habit1144JBWater1DroAWy3½ *Brief speed, stopped*
13Jan91 8BM ft 4+F Stk28000 6f 22.10 44.90 1:09.50 84 1/7 1 2hd 1hd 42 79½ RM Gonzalez 115 LB 5.10 Wind Shear1162That Knight11321½Bit O' Dip1151½
Duffel Farm Handicap — *Showed strong early speed; stopped*
11Nov90 8BM ft 3+F Stk50000 6f 22.30 44.90 1:09.50 78 6/8 1 2hd 1½ 34 RM Gonzalez 114 L 5.60 Hasty Pasty1183That Knight1111Margaret's Native11431½
Charles H Russell Handicap — *Dueled for lead and gradually weakened in the lane*
26Oct90 8BM ft 3+F Stk25000 6f 22.30 44.90 1:10.10 84 5/5 2 11 11½ 1nk RM Gonzalez 115 LBf 1.90 Margaret's Native115nkOwiseone115hdClassy Vigora1121½
Anderson Ranch Handicap — *Showed strong early speed; all out*

Workouts: 11Aug SA 4f ft 47.50 H 23Jun Hol 4f ft 48.10 H 2Jun Hol 4f ft 47.10 H 14May Hol 5f ft 1:01.70 H 6May Hol 4f ft 47.70 H

Several figures are closely matched. No horse sticks out on speed alone, but one horse enjoys a distinctive edge when speed figures are related to relative class.

Suppose the figures were rearranged as follows:

Horse	*Date*	*Track*	*Conditions*	*Distance*	*Speed Figures*
Mahaska	Apr 27	Hol	Gr. 2/3up	7F	79
	Feb 2	GG	Stk-O/3up	1M	85
Mama Simba	Jul 7	Hol	Alw/NW3X	6F	88
	Mar 8	SA	Clf Alw/4up	6½F	93
Hasty Pasty	Jul 31	SR	Stk-O/3up	6F	88
	Mar 3	OP	Stk-O/4up	6F	92
Sentimentalize	May 18	PHA	Alw/NW3X	6F	90
	Dec 31	AQU	Clm-75/3YO	6F	94
Margaret's Native	Jul 19	Hol	Clm-62,5/Turf	8½F	89
	Oct 26	BM	Stk-O/3up	6F	84

When examining the horses' strongest figures against the most advanced competition they've faced, two contenders deserve the edge. Mama Simba's 93 against classified allowance horses at Santa Anita and Hasty Pasty's 92 in an open stakes at Oaklawn Park are the best of the bunch.

Doesn't the slightly lower figure in the open stakes take precedence? Often it does, but not today. The classified allowance races at Santa Anita regularly involve stakes horses at least comparable to open stakes compeition at Oaklawn Park. Hasty Pasty was defeated by a horse named Nurse Dopey. Mama Simba lost to Cascading Gold.

Additional evidence also favors Mama Simba. On December 30, 1990, Mama Simba finished third in Santa Anita's Grade 3 La Brea Stakes, earning a speed figure of 94, the single strongest figure in today's lineup against the most advanced competition any of these have confronted. The heroine of the La Brea was Brought To Mind and the runner-up was A Wild Ride, two of the finest fillies in the nation.

Moreover, Mama Simba's best figures have been earned in long sprints, similar to today's 6½ furlongs. The July 29 race at Los Alamitos, at 4½ furlongs, no less, was merely a prep at the wrong distance. A rider change from Luis Ortega to Kent Desormeaux reinforces that notion.

In the final analysis, Mama Simba represents the class horse having the best figures and running at her best distance. Even if Mama Simba's speed figures had been slightly lower than her rivals, the class edge would have countered decisively.

Mahaska ran in the La Brea stakes won by Brought To Mind. Mahaska finished seventh of eight, her dullest performance in the published record. Unless Mahaska can upset the Los Alamitos race wire-to-wire from her inside post, she will offer little resistance to a charging Mama Simba.

The top figure of 1991 belongs to Sentimentalize, but no figure analyst worth his numbers would award this filly the nod over Mama Simba. A 90 recorded against nonwinners of three allowance races at Philadelphia Park is not superior to an 88 recorded against nonwinners of three allowance races at Santa Anita. The Santa Anita performance demands outlays of endurance and determination the Philadelphia race cannot begin to match.

In stakes races, to repeat, speed alone is rarely enough. The several attributes of class are summoned simultaneously. Fast horses lacking in comparable measures of endurance and determination will be easily repulsed in the late stages, absolutely so in routes, and usually in long sprints.

Sentimentalize's best-ever figure of 94 occurred in a claiming race of winter limited to 3YOs. Do figure handicappers of New York believe for a moment that kind of 94 at Aqueduct takes precedence over a 93 earned in the Grade 3 La Brea Stakes at Santa Anita? I hope not.

So the essential analysis in a stakes race evaluates speed figures in a class context. The better the race, the more emphasis figure analysts should place on the speed-class dynamics. Lower-level stakes are best analyzed using speed-class as a point of departure but encompassing other vital factors of handicapping, notably pace and form.

A Grade 3 stakes will likely be won by the best horse in sharp form, as long as the speed figures are competitive. A restricted or open stakes having a $50,000 purse (or less) might be won instead by a lone frontrunner, or by the horse benefiting from the early pace, or by the horse rebounding from a troubled trip, or by the horse in an improvement cycle, or by the horse particularly well-suited to today's distance and footing, even though those horses exhibit slightly inferior speed figures.

Figure handicappers who bother to become experts on the class factor will qualify as the best figure analysts of all. Those who take handicapping matters a few steps further, emerging well-versed on all the factors of handicapping, will learn soon enough how to interpret the varieties of speed figures in stakes races. When the high-figure horse does not figure at all, only those figure analysts will understand why and will be fully prepared to do the right thing.

YOUNGER STAKES HORSES

The three-year-olds, as always, are different. As developing horses, they remain unclassified for much of the season. The class-speed relationships that support figure handicapping so well for established horses do not apply.

But something else substitutes just as well.

As high-potential three-year-olds progress through eligibility conditions and into the stakes division, the best of them will be capable of setting, pressing, or tracking a fast pace en route to impressive final figures. To place an opposite spin on the matter, as developing 3YOs graduate to better races, the early pace intensifies and youngsters unable to keep abreast will eventually fall back. Their speed figures will decline. The pattern repeats itself everywhere in the stakes hierarchy, from restricted stakes to Grade 1 events.

The practical imperative demands that figure handicappers evaluate 3YOs in stakes races using speed and pace figures in combination. The recommended procedure is deceptively simple. Add the pace figure and the speed figure. The sum is a pace rating, and the highest-rated horse is best. In sprints, when pace ratings look closely matched, prefer the horses who ran the fastest turn times. The procedure is deceptive because pace analysis supersedes pace figures. The analytical aspect is commonly crucial, but pace handicapping can be a figure analyst's best fun.

Because younger, nonclaiming horses develop as they do, final-time figure disciples can be sadly misled in numerous situations. An ordinary pace allows a decent nonclaiming horse to record a rapid final time. The corresponding speed figures will often impress. But as the pace quickens, only authentically talented horses can keep up and record the same rapid final times, let alone exceed their previous best.

Earlier we recounted the case of Split Run, the 3YO son of Relaunch who dazzled southern California figure handicappers with spectacular final times in his debut and subsequent allowance start. The speed figures were provocative but the pace figures were weak. In his first stakes attempt, at even money, Split Run pressed a seriously rapid pace and promptly faded to the rear when the real running began. He never toppled stakes horses in an abbreviated nonclaiming career.

The situation is rarely as polarized as Split Run's disappearance, but shadings in the pace ratings of nonclaiming 3YOs provide the telltale clues to numerous winners in the sophomore stakes. The co-feature on Travers Day at Saratoga in August 1991 was the Grade 3 seven-furlong King's Bishop Stakes for three-year-olds. The five leading contenders are presented below. The ranking horse on Beyer Speed Figures did not shape up strongly here, due to a dismal pace figure, and neither did the overnight favorite.

Examine the past performances. Review the dual sets of figures provided here:

Horse	Date	Speed Figure	Pace-Speed Figures			
Formal Dinner	7/27	107	100	108	/	208
Apollo	6/30	103	107	110	/	217
Top The Record	7/5	104	111	110	/	221	(slop)
	6/3	93	108	103	/	211
To Freedom	8/2	98	118	104	/	222
Take Me Out	7/31	98	100	110	/	210

Saratoga

7

7 furlongs

SEVEN FURLONGS. KING'S BISHOP. [GRADE III] $100,000 Added. For Three Year Olds. By subscription of $200 each, which should accompany the nomination; $800 to pass the entry box; $800 to start, with $100,000 added. The added money and all fees to be divided 60% to the winner, 22% to second, 12% to third and 6% to fourth. 122 lbs. Non-winners of a race of $50,000 since May 1, allowed 3 lbs.; of such a race since January 1, 5 lbs.; of a race of $35,000 in 1990-91, 7 lbs. Starters to be named at the closing time of entries. Trophies will be presented to the winning owner, trainer and jockey. Nominations Closed Wednesday, July 31.

FORMAL DINNER

3yo (Mar) colt, dk. bay/brown
Trainer: D Wayne Lukas
Owner: Leonard D Mathis

T23

Sire: Well Decorated ($12,500)
  by Raja Baba
Dam: Fantastic Flyer
  by Hoist The Flag
Bred in KY by Dr. W. O. Reed

117

Career: 28 4 4 6 $307,586
Wet:	2 0 0 1	$9,180	1991:	11 2 2 4	$124,081
Turf:	0 0 0 0	$0	1990:	10 2 2 2	$183,317
Dist:	5 0 2 0	$62,974	Sar:	2 2 0 0	$73,260

Yearling Price: $25,000

APOLLO

3yo (Mar) colt, chestnut
Trainer: Gary Jones
Owner: Harold Keith, Keith & Rasmussen

T22³

Sire: Falstaff ($2,000)
  by Lyphard
Dam: Tumble Along
  by Tumble Wind
Bred in CA by Eclipse Investment &
Leon Rasmussen

119

Career: 9 5 2 1 $217,650
Wet:	1 0 1 0	$30,000	1991:	6 2 2 1	$140,250
Turf:	2 1 1 0	$60,250	1990:	3 3 0 0	$77,440
Dist:	2 1 0 0	$25,000	Sar:	0 0 0 0	$0

TOP THE RECORD

3yo (Apr) colt, roan
Trainer: Richard Schosberg
Owner: Heatherwood Farm

T22¹

Sire: Entropy ($2,000)
  by What A Pleasure
Dam: In Record Time
  by Vigors
Bred in FL by Joel W. Sainer

115

Wet:	3 2 0 1	$23,280	1991:	10 5 2 0	$90,120
Turf:	0 0 0 0	$0	1990:	12 3 2 2	$20,457
Dist:	2 0 1 0	$6,856	Sar:	0 0 0 0	$0

TO FREEDOM

TZZ²

3yo (Jan) colt, dk. bay/brown
Trainer: John Tammaro
Owner: Herman Heinlein

Sire: **Blue Ensign** ($10,000)
  by Hoist The Flag
Dam: **Hinda Diplomat**
  by Diplomat Way
Bred in FL by Charles Patton

Wet:	2	2	0	0	$34,846	1991:	8 3 2 1	$157,682
Turf:	0	0	0	0	$0	1990:	4 4 0 0	$115,042
Dist:	3	1	2	0	$90,386	Sar:	2 1 0 1	$67,020

115

Yearling Price: $52,000

Workouts: 13Aug Sar 5f ft 1:03.63 H   8Aug Sar 5f ft 1:00.12 B   28Jly Sar 5f ft 58.25 H   21Jly Sar 5f ft 1:04.00 B

TAKE ME OUT

TZ2

3yo (Apr) colt, bay
Trainer: William I Mott
Owner: Bertram M Firestone

Sire: **Care The Blues** ($20,000)
  by Stop The Music
Dam: **White Feather**
  by Tom Rolfe
Bred in VA by Mr. & Mrs. Bertram R Firestone

Wet:	1	0	1	0	$6,380	1991:	1 1 0 0	$16,200
Turf:	0	0	0	0	$0	1990:	5 1 3 0	$289,220
Dist:	3	2	1	0	$35,880	Sar:	2 1 1 0	$21,480

115

Workouts: 14Aug Sar 5f ft 1:01.15 H   8Aug Sar 4f ft 51.17 B   28Jly Sar 5f ft 59.60 Bgate   13Jly Bel 5f wf 58.37 B   8Jly Bel 4f ft 51.70 B

Figure handicappers in possession of pace figures as well as speed figures can cut to the bone of this Grade 3 sprint immediately. The verdict should be disputed between Apollo and To Freedom. A closer analysis of the two will be necessary, but the others suffer an insurmountable pace weakness. Extended during the second fraction if they intend to stay abreast of To Freedom, they probably will not finish as quickly as before. The speed figures likely will decline. Either To Freedom repulses the early pace and lasts, or Apollo gets a comfortable striking position behind To Freedom and runs the pacesetter down.

Notice how the combined speed and pace figures favor To Freedom and Apollo without debate. On speed figures alone, Apollo ranks third best, To Freedom a throwaway. The differences between the alternative approaches cannot be breached.

It's instructive to examine the horses individually in greater detail.

Formal Dinner

Savvy figure handicappers would not be fooled by this colt's 107 last out. The figure reflects a facile wire-to-wire romp and is not supported by other speed figures in the record, when Formal Dinner did not take an easy lead. In addition, the turn time is 23 flat, a rate of speed during the crucial second fraction that will need to improve. No doubt casual figure handicappers may be attracted to the colt's high speed figure, but that number is less than half the story here.

Apollo

An outstanding sprinter who can set a par pace for 3YO stakes horses and still deliver a speed figure equal to the older stakes par. Recent turf sprints have occurred against excellent older stakes sprinters. Turf sprints transfer to the main track significantly better than do turf routes because the early pace is similarly fast. Apollo has been a multiple stakes winner in earlier sprints having high figures, both at the pace call and final call. Versatile as to running style as well, Apollo is able to sit comfortably behind the early pace and challenge strongly. Turn time outstanding at 22.3!

Top The Record

The big win, big figure last out occurred in the slop, an extenuating circumstance that frequently hypes the figures of horses that prefer the goo. The previous speed figure of 93 is more consistent with the entire record, and figure handicappers should depend upon that number. With a pace figure of 108, Top The Record should be extended early here. If he runs faster than normal, presumably his speed figure will decline. If he runs evenly early, the final figure should not improve. Either way, this 3YO does not figure to win.

To Freedom

The most interesting colt in the lineup, To Freedom last out dispensed a pace figure of 118, five lengths superior to anything else. The pace figure was recorded furthermore in a Grade 3 sprint open to older horses. The turn time that day was a splendid 22.2 seconds. Earlier at Keeneland, To Freedom took the Grade 3, seven-furlong Lafayette Stakes for 3YOs. He's notched four additional sprint stakes, including the Grade 2 Saratoga Special as a juvenile. If To Freedom can throttle back at the second call, he might not be caught here, and that's the reasoning figure handicappers should indulge.

Take Me Out

An interesting 3YO who seventeen days ago pasted a nonwinners-once allowance field in good final time following his second-place finish in last fall's Breeders' Cup Juevnile. This is precisely the kind of 3YO that will be sorely overplayed in this stakes, even by figure handicappers who should know better. The pace Take Me Out pressed on July 31 was extremely slow, translating to a pace figure of 100. The turn time is a blistering 22 flat, but it follows a tardy first quarter of 23 seconds. If Take Me Out attempts to run with To Freedom to the second call, he will have to be a truly top colt to win this race. He must discourage To Freedom and withstand the late challenge of the top sprinter Apollo. Nothing in the record indicates he can accomplish either task.

Because pace figures are not well-distributed and not well-understood in the 3YO stakes context, To Freedom shapes up as an irresistible overlay in this spot. An excellent double play invests a prime bet to win on To Freedom and covers multiple exacta boxes coupling To Freedom and Apollo.

Both bets blew. Take Me Out proved classy enough to press a blistering pace, and win in hand. It happens.

The figure handicapping of two-year-old races is pratically cut and dried. The figures operate best in the juvenile sprints, where the fastest horses figure to win, literally. The two-year-olds run as hard and fast as they can for the six or seven furlongs they must. Pace does not normally apply, but if a talented baby can sit behind the early pace of a short dash and then explode, earning the top speed figure, that's the best kind of 2YO performance. No matter how suicidal the early pace becomes, a relaxed, rated juvenile is unlikely to be killed off.

The picture changes dramatically in the two-year-old routes. Par times do not exist—not enough 2YO routes are programmed to calculate reliable pars—and excepting the Grade 1 standouts, speed figures recorded in sprints will be next to meaningless. The basic problem can be reduced to the juveniles' inexperience at longer distances. Lack of seasoning at the route means the overwhelming majority of two-year-olds will merely chase. Even as jockeys attempt to rate the horses, 2YOs will run similarly as they do in the sprints, as fast as they can for as long as they can.

The priority factor of handicapping is neither final time nor early pace, but early speed. The 2YO in front has a tremendous advantage, many times insurmountable. Handicappers are urged to spend the extra effort to identify which of the juveniles is most likely to grab the lead. Pace figures can be indicative, all right, but gate ability and first-quarter positions plus fractional times can be decisive.

The pattern persists when evaluating the leading two-year-olds. A frontrunning style deserves extra credit, notwithstanding the superior speed figures of other contenders. One of the outstanding distance runners in recent years is the filly Lite Light, a descendant of Majestic Light, whose progeny have accumulated an average winning distance of 7.7-furlongs. As a two-year-old of summer, Lite Light already had proven herself devastating in long sprints. She blew down her foes effortlessly in Del Mar's seven-furlong Sorrento Stakes, a prep for that track's one-mile Debutante. Lite Light's final time, fractional times, and manner of victory in the Sorrento were undeniably powerful, marking her indelibly as the division leader. Quirin speed and pace figures for Lite Light and impressive runner-up Perfectly Proud looked like this:

	Pace	Speed
Lite Light	103	106
Perfectly Proud	107	103

Lite Light had perched two lengths behind Perfectly Proud in the Sorrento until reaching the prestretch call, when she commenced a stunning rally to draw away.

Three weeks later the same group returned for the Grade 2 Debutante, the initial two-turn try for all concerned. Lite Light went odds-on, the bettors undeterred by the longer distance for a daughter of Majestic Light. Perfectly Proud ranked next on the board at 4–1.

Perfectly Proud had displayed higher early speed than Lite Light, and her pace figures suggested a potential two-length lead at the prestretch call. Unseasoned at the route, the brilliant Lite Light might find herself chasing to that point, before tiring around the far turn. Perfectly Proud would tire as well, but could be expected to persevere as best she was able. The pair might finish in the one-two stretch procession so typical of 2YO distance racing, Perfectly Proud hanging on.

It happened in textbook fashion. Perfectly Proud broke quickly and sped to the front around the clubhouse turn. Lite Light chased her in second position. The two proceeded in lockstep down the backside and around the far turn. Approaching the quarter-pole, the jockey urged Lite Light energetically, but the filly could make only mild headway. Perfectly Proud dug in and resisted. The two tiring 2YOs continued evenly thereafter to the wire, Lite Light unable to overtake the length disadvantage.

It happens often.

Once Lite Light had gained experience at the route, learning how to relax early and to measure out her energies efficiently, Perfectly Proud could not finish within five lengths of her. But initially Lite Light lost at a mile, and as the public's odds-on choice.

The lesson can be transported to numerous 2YO routes of fall at every class of racetrack in the nation. Pay extra attention to early speed and early pace. Discount the speed figures recorded in sprints unless the running style should also place the high-figure horses on the lead at the longer distance. The only logical exceptions are the Grade 1 juveniles of fall, who typically do whatever is asked of them and can stretch out to duplicate the figures they earned in sprints.

An additional important guideline suits the figure handicapping of 2YO races. Juveniles can improve dramatically or decline just as obviously. Unlike 3YOs, the 2YOs are not consistently inconsistent. Insist upon improving speed figures. If a 2YO's speed figures decline noticeably, accept the deterioration at face value. Desert the horses. A comeback at three may be entirely possible, but the 2YO campaign is finished, at least so far as winning races is concerned.

KENTUCKY DERBY PROSPECTS

Excellent figure handicappers probably know more about the Kentucky Derby prospects of developing three-year-olds than anybody, including the horses' owners and trainers. By mid-April, in most years, figure handicappers have identified the legitimate contenders and eliminated the imposters with remarkable reliability.

Paradoxically, figure handicappers still do not know which 3YO is likeliest to win. Just which three-year-olds truly belong.

Adherence to a single rule of thumb guides these predictions. Any three-year-old intended to win the Kentucky Derby must record a speed figure equal to or exceeding par for older stakes horses. If the horse is a frontrunner or pace-presser, the corresponding pace figure should be no less than two lengths below the older stakes par.

Occasionally, as in 1991, the Derby winner does not approach the older stakes par in the crucial 3YO preps, but this is unusual. Moreover, speed horses who equal the older stakes par in key Derby preps, but display a dubious pace figure in the process, are unlikely to reach the wire first at Louisville. Some other horse assures a faster pace at Churchill Downs, and the final figures of the contenders who are stretched to keep abreast take a slide.

Using Beyer Speed Figures, 3YO Derby prospects should have recorded a pre-Derby speed figure of 108 to 112. Using Quirin speed and pace figures, the qualifying pre-Derby figures are 107-111. Weeks prior to the 1991 Kentucky Derby, while it was generally agreed the West Coast 3YOs represented a solid slate of Derby prospects, only one of the leading colts had actually posted the qualifying figures. The leading prospects on the East Coast had looked even more dubious. The Derby picture remained despairingly out of focus on speed and pace figures:

Horse	Race	Beyer Speed (Par 110)	Quirin Speed & Pace (Par 111)	
Dinard	Santa Anita Derby	108	107	111
Best Pal	Santa Anita Derby	107	105	110
Sea Cadet	Santa Anita Derby	103	109	108
Fly So Free	Florida Derby	100	108	100
Hansel	Lexington Stakes (Gr. 2)	105	113	105
Strike The Gold	Blue Grass Stakes	103	99	109
Corporate Report	Arkansas Derby	103	106	103
Lost Mountain	Wood Memorial	104	110	108
Cahill Road	Wood Memorial	109	112	111

On the figures, the two colts that did not make the race in 1991 shaped up as the most probable Kentucky Derby winners.

Cahill Road had emerged as the leading contender. Only Cahill Road had recorded a speed and pace figure equal to par for older stakes horses, the desirable numbers.

Had Santa Anita Derby hero Dinard competed, he was an unlikely winner. His pace figures invariably were similar to those he earned in the Santa Anita Derby, and consistently below the older stakes par at least by two lengths. Dinard had been fully extended at the shorter distances. Had Dinard run forwardly in the Kentucky Derby, within a couple of lengths of the leaders, he was not likely to have outfinished Strike The Gold.

Unsatisfactory pre-Derby pace figures are acceptable only for deep closers such as Strike The Gold, whose pace numbers reflect running style, not ability. In the 1991 Kentucky Derby, Strike The Gold recorded a Beyer Speed Figure of 107 and Quirin speed and pace figures of 102-111. The colt improved his final figures by two lengths at ten furlongs. Among the others, only Best Pal ran his race at Churchill Downs.

At 3–1 in the Kentucky Derby, Fly So Free was a dreadfully poor second choice of the bettors. Fly So Free represented a large population of brilliant juveniles and developing 3YOs whose pace figures outstrip their speed figures in the telltale preparations. They rate among the worst of prospects in the Kentucky Derby. Figure handicappers in the future should remain on the alert to spot them.

As the 2–1 favorite in the Derby, Hansel too presented a poor proposition. Recording uninspiring speed figures against the best of his generation, Hansel finally posted a pair of 105s in the Jim Beam Stakes (Grade 2) and the Lexington Stakes (Grade 2). Those figures remained well below the older stakes par. In the Lexington Stakes, at $1\frac{1}{16}$ miles, Hansel suddenly delivered a pace figure of 113. A reasonable pre-Derby analysis saw Hansel scuttling the chances of other pace-pressing types, but unable to finish the job himself. Closers Strike The Gold and Lost Mountain should be most likely to benefit in that scenario. Lost Mountain proved seductive at fantastic Derby odds (76-to-1), but the New York colt blew the clubhouse turn and disappeared early.

Two weeks later in the Preakness Stakes, Hansel at last delivered the quality of figures that frequently can be counted upon to win the Kentucky Derby. He recorded a Beyer Speed Figure of 116, and his Quirin speed and pace figures formed an outstanding combination of 118-118. An inconsistent runner, Hansel nonetheless became the clear choice of figure analysts as the most talented 3YO of 1991.

The paradox of the Kentucky Derby is that the effectiveness of figure handicapping ends where middle distances end. Candidates must display the required numerical credentials, but that is not enough. Often, speed and pace figures that exceed the older stakes pars at middle distances cannot be replicated at the classic distance of ten furlongs. Performance plus pedigree gets the roses. Figure handicappers who have isolated the 3YOs having the qualifying speed figures are recommended to insist they also possess a qualifying dosage index.

Figure handicappers who attend to Kentucky Derby prospects by evaluating their speed and pace figures in the several preliminary stakes collect an enviable windfall. As January flows into February, March, and April, figure analysts inevitably gather numerous insights into the relative abilities of the season's leading three-year-olds. When these horses ship to derbies and stakes races throughout the country, those contests cover distances shorter than ten furlongs. In concert with standard operating procedure in the 3YO division, figure handicappers can merely sum the speed and pace figures they already possess. The horses exhibiting the highest combined ratings figure to win, and several of them will win at inviting prices.

Scouting the three-year-old division months in advance is well worth the time and energy donated. Figure handicappers may not find the winner of the Kentucky Derby, but they should discover several alternative winners in the process.

ROUTES TO SPRINTS

Handicappers in possession of Quirin speed and pace figures have secured the inside track toward solving one of the thorniest problems of handicapping: how to predict which routers can prevail in a sprint.

Probability data have cleared the path to a solution. They have revealed that the horses most likely to switch from routes to sprints successfully show high speed to the first and second calls—four furlongs and six furlongs—of the route races. As predictors of route-to-sprint successes, therefore, speed figures can be poor.

But pace figures can be decisive. And pace figures in relation to certain kinds of speed figures can trigger one of the most intriguing and least understood bets of figure handicapping.

An outstanding illustration occurred at Santa Anita, April 12, 1991, the seventh race. One of the entrants was being triple-jumped in claiming class from $25,000 to $50,000 while simultaneously shortening distance from 1$\frac{1}{16}$ miles to seven furlongs. The eventual winner is an old friend of an earlier section in this book. Review the past performances and the combined speed-pace figures of Avasaurus's route performance of March 31.

Avasaurus — B. g. 5, by Avatar—Spectacular Song, by Sensitive Prince — Lifetime — 1991 5 1 0 0 [illegible]
STEVENS G L — $50,000 — Br.—Parrish Hill Farm (Ky) — 115 — 52 11 10 11 — 1990 20 6 3 4 $100,275
Own.—Summer Viola — Tr.—Martin Frank — $175,395

31Mar91- 4SA	fst	1$\frac{1}{16}$	:46	1:10^{3}	1:42	Clm c-25000	3	5	3^{2}	2^{hd}	1^{4}	1^{9}	Stevens G L	LBb	115	*2.50	93-14	Avasaurus115^{9}AdvocteTrining115^{4}GonnGetRich116^{1½}	Handily	8
22Mar91- 5SA	fst	1	:45^{4}	1:10^{1}	1:35	Clm 32000	10	8	8^{7}	5^{5}	5^{5}	5^{5¼}	Stevens G L	LBb	115	2.50	87-13	Dr.Consquncs115^{nk}SugrRy115^{2¾}GchoAlrt-Ch115^{1½}	Wide early	10
24Feb91- 2SA	fst	6½f	:21^{4}	:44^{1}	1:15^{3}	Clm 40000	11	10	11^{10}	11^{10}	9^{9}	7^{6}	Stevens G L	LBb	117	8.60	86-11	AbergwaunLad121^{1}KingOfWill115^{nk}RoylEgle115^{2¾}	Wide early	12
18Jan91- 9SA	fst	6½f	:21^{4}	:44^{1}	1:15	Clm 50000	11	2	5^{1¾}	5^{1¾}	5^{3½}	5^{6½}	Pincay L Jr	LBb	117	4.40	88-14	AbrgwunLd119^{2}LurnsQust115^{nk}Jonthn'sGold115^{3½}	Wide early	11
1Jan91- 9SA	fst	1$\frac{1}{16}$	:46^{2}	1:11^{1}	1:42^{3}	Clm 62500	1	6	7^{5¼}	5^{3½}	6^{7}	6^{9¼}	Meza R Q	LBb	115	3.90	81-18	J.T.'sPet116^{¾}HotOpertor112^{4}SpellVictorious115^{¾}	Took up 7/8	10
28Dec90- 3Hol	fst	7f	:21^{4}	:44^{4}	1:21^{3}	3↑Clm c-37500	5	4	4^{4}	4^{4}	3^{2½}	1^{½}	Stevens G L	LBb	115	*1.00	97-13	Avasaurus115^{½} Sun Streak117^{1½} One For Nana116^{2½}	Got up	6
8Dec90- 6Hol	fst	7f	:22^{2}	:45	1:21^{2}	3↑Clm 37500	8	4	6^{2¾}	4^{2½}	2^{1}	2^{¾}	Stevens G L	LBb	115	5.30	97-05	SensationalStar117^{¾}Avasurus115^{4½}Mgnetized117^{1}	Wide early	8
17Nov90- 9Hol	fst	1$\frac{1}{16}$	:46^{3}	1:10^{2}	1:42^{3}	3↑Clm 32000	7	4	5^{3}	5^{2¼}	4^{2}	4^{1½}	Velasquez J	LBb	116	8.10	85-15	RecittionSpin119^{½}Sobreslir116^{¾}WellAwre116^{nk}	4-wide stretch	10
4Nov90- 3Aqu	fst	1	:46	1:10^{3}	1:36	3↑Clm 35000	2	2	3^{½}	2^{½}	2^{2}	3^{5½}	Chavez J F	b	117	6.00	76-12	Proud Cat115^{2} Onnagata115^{3½} Avasaurus117^{¾}	Stumbled start	7
22Oct90- 1Bel	fst	1$\frac{1}{16}$	:46^{3}	1:11	1:42^{3}	3↑Clm 35000	4	2	1^{½}	2^{hd}	4^{2}	5^{7¾}	Maple E	b	117	*2.00	81-09	Bolshoi Boy115^{4} Onnagata113^{3½} Earnhardt112^{hd}	Used up	9

Speed Index: Last Race: −3.0 3–Race Avg.: +3.0 4–Race Avg.: +2.7 Overall Avg.: −0.5
LATEST WORKOUTS Mar 17 SA 5f fst 1:01^{4} H Mar 11 SA 4f fst :47^{4} H Feb 23 SA 3f fst :36^{1} H Feb 19 SA 5f fst 1:01 H

	Pace	*Speed*
Santa Anita	113	110
March 31 Route		
Avasaurus	Par 105	

In victory on March 31, Avasaurus had run four lengths faster than par (105) to the pace call (two points equals one length), and five lengths faster than par to the wire.

When horses shorten from routes to sprints, a simple adjustment to Quirin pace figures provides a best estimate of the speed figures horses might record in sprints. Subtract three points from the pace figure.

The adjustment to Avasaurus's March 31 pace figure is equal to 113 minus 3, or 110, coincidentally the same speed figure Avasaurus posted in the $25,000 route. The recommended adjustment is strictly empirical, based upon studies of thousands of races nationwide. This is the procedure found to perform best.

So on April 12 at Santa Anita, Avasaurus was predicted to record a speed figure of 110.

Par at Santa Anita for $50,000 older claiming horses going seven furlongs is 107.

Not only should Avasaurus exceed the local par in the

richer sprint by three lengths, the horse carried another advantage amplifying his chances significantly. In the same $25,000 race where his pace figure was 113, Avasaurus's speed figure reached 110, five lengths superior to par.

Experience with Quirin-style figures indicates that whenever the route-to-sprint pace adjustment remains better than par for today's sprint, and the speed figure of the preceding route has been better than par, the advantage has been strongly reinforced. The higher the above-par speed figure in the route, the better. Avasaurus's 110 speed figure at the route was not merely five lengths above par for $25,000 claiming winners, but also three lengths above par for today's $50,000 claiming group.

Avasaurus was a stickout in the seven-furlong $50,000 sprint, an irresistible figure bet. No other horse could match his converted speed figure, not to mention the greater reserves of stamina a proven router can summon in the stretch run of a shorter race. Here is the result chart.

SEVENTH RACE
Santa Anita
APRIL 12, 1991

7 FURLONGS. (1.20) CLAIMING. Purse $32,000. 4-year-olds and upward. Weight, 121 lbs. Non-winners of two races since February 1, allowed 2 lbs.; of a race since March 1, 4 lbs.; since February 1, 6 lbs. Claiming price $50,000; if for $45,000, allowed 2 lbs. (Maiden or races when entered for $40,000 or less not considered.)

Value of race $32,600; value to winner $17,600; second $6,400; third $4,800; fourth $2,400; fifth $800. Mutuel pool $337,318. Exacta pool $373,194.

Last Raced	Horse	M/Eqt.A.Wt	PP St	¼	½	Str	Fin	Jockey	Cl'g Pr	Odds $1
31Mar91 4SA¹	Avasaurus	LBb 5 115	5 8	10	9¹½	3¹	16½	Stevens G L	50000	6.20
13Mar91 5SA²	Happy In Space	LBb 7 116	8 2	1hd	2²	1hd	2¹	Delhoussye E	50000	13.60
13Mar91 5SA¹	Royal Eagle	LBb 6 119	2 4	3¹½	1hd	2¹½	3¹½	Baze R A	50000	6.30
6Jan91 7SA⁴	Cutter Sam	LBb 6 115	1 10	7hd	3½	4¹½	4¹	Solis A	50000	8.20
30Mar91 7SA⁴	Laurens Quest	LBb 6 115	3 9	6hd	4½	5³	5³	Garcia J A	50000	9.40
17Mar91 3SA²	Future Career	LBb 4 121	6 5	4¹	6hd	6hd	6½	McCarron C J	50000	2.30
27Mar91 3SA¹	My Lucky Lynnie	LB 5 115	9 3	5hd	5½	73½	73½	Nakatani C S	50000	2.80
16Mar91 7SA⁴	Song Of Romance	LBb 4 115	10 6	8³	8¹	9	83½	Patton D B	50000	32.70
17Mar91 3SA⁶	Wave The Flag	B 4 115	7 1	2hd	7½	8hd	9	Flores D R	50000	66.20
13Mar91 5SA³	Just Deeds	LB 5 115	4 7	9¹	10	—	—	Santos J A	50000	29.70

Just Deeds, Lame.

OFF AT 4:13. Start good. Won handily. Time, :22 , :44³, 1:09³, 1:22¹ Track fast.

$2 Mutuel Prices:

5–AVASAURUS	14.40	8.60	6.20
8–HAPPY IN SPACE		10.40	6.60
1–ROYAL EAGLE			5.20

$2 EXACTA 5–8 PAID $367.00.

B. g, by Avatar—Spectacular Song, by Sensitive Prince. Trainer Martin Frank. Bred by Parrish Hill Farm (Ky).

AVASAURUS, devoid of early speed, worked his way through traffic on the far turn while on the move, was never set down in the drive, took command not long after passing the furlong marker, drew away thereafter, was in hand through the final sixteenth and quite probably could have won by a larger margin. HAPPY IN SPACE, wide early,

With par 107, Avasaurus completed the seven-furlong sprint with pace and speed figures of 112-109. The horse trailed by 15 lengths down the backside, but unfurled a tremendous middle move on the inside around the far turn. Avasaurus then angled out into the upper stretch and rallied relentlessly to the finish.

Only the predilection of racegoers to accept routers in sprints of seven furlongs kept the odds on Avasaurus at a respectable 7–1. In a six-furlong sprint, Avasaurus might have been 15–1 or better. He would have won just as impressively.

The route-to-sprint pace-figure adjustment weakens where the estimated speed figure in today's sprint equals or exceeds par, but the speed figure of the preceding route dropped too much below par for that race.

Suppose Avasaurus's speed and pace figures at the $25,000 claiming level on March 31 had looked like this: 113-100.

Instead of five lengths superior to the $25,000 claiming par (105), now the speed figure (100) remains five lengths below par.

The adjustment procedure is followed as usual, but the estimated speed figure will be unsteady in high-priced sprints that should be strongly contested at both the pace call and the wire. In the $50,000 claiming race, Avasaurus unleashed a prolonged middle move during the second fraction. He then persevered just as strongly. If Avasaurus's speed figure March 31 had been 100 instead of 110, the second gear probably would have been unavailable. Instead of finishing strongly, Avasaurus might have finished evenly, his fate dependent upon what had happened in front of him.

Whenever the route-to-sprint adjustment to the Quirin pace figure is bulwarked by a speed figure exceeding par, figure handicappers can support the adjusted figure confidently. When the adjusted pace figure is linked to a speed figure below par, however, a pace analysis supplants a blind allegiance to the numbers.

It's generally true too, as conventional wisdom advises, that longer sprints will be more comfortable to routers shortening distance than will six furlongs. Yet 6½-furlong sprints will be carded much more frequently than seven furlongs. If a router displays the converted figures that qualify to win, it's a potential bet, notably where sprint speed has been tiring.

TRACK-TO-TRACK COMPARISONS

In the printed guidelines to interpreting Beyer Speed Figures which accompanied the publication of The Racing Times, Andrew Beyer wanted to reassure handicappers on the transportability of speed figures from track to track. Beyer responded unequivocally to the following question with a sweeping interpretation.

"Can the figures be used to compare horses who raced at different tracks?"

"This is their greatest strength. A horse who earns a 92 at Delta Downs has run a better race than one who earns a 90 at Santa Anita."

The guideline is entirely disingenuous. Figure analysts who believe horses from Delta Downs showing comparable speed figures can beat their counterparts at Santa Anita have been chasing rainbows with shippers at numerous racetracks across this country.

The preeminent stakes horse on the grounds at Delta Downs who arrived with speed figures in the 110 to 112 range would be an outsider at Santa Anita in a classified allowance race where the top local figures ranged from 106 to 109. In a graded or listed stakes at Santa Anita where the Delta Downs shipper showed a 112 and the local horses nothing above 110, the Delta Downs delegate should be crushed.

At the same time, the Delta Downs shipper carrying an 82 recorded in a $12,500 claiming race and entered in a $16,000 claiming race at Santa Anita where the top local figure is 80, has a superb chance to upset at a generous price. If the 82 shipper in the $16,000 claiming race has arrived from similar claiming races at Golden Gate Fields instead of Delta Downs, it figures to win. But stakes shippers from Golden Gate Fields having slightly advantageous figures in a stakes at Santa Anita typically will be blown away.

The difference is the difference between speed and class. Speed is the hallmark of thoroughbred class, to be sure, but other attributes of class not only exist, they increasingly matter as the quality of the competition stiffens. The attributes of class include speed, endurance, and determination, the three interacting in multitudinous ways. Horses possessing the optimal measures of the combined attributes ultimately distinguish themselves as the classiest racehorses of all. They run not merely fast, but with considerable reserves of endurance and determination.

Speed figures measure speed. They do not assess degrees of endurance and determination, except as these qualities have been expressed in the running times. At Delta Downs, speed figures reflect the horses' speed quotients, all right, but more often than not will reflect only traces of endurance and determination, qualities not in particularly heavy demand at Delta Downs.

How much endurance and determination is required to win at Delta Downs vis-à-vis Santa Anita? What degrees of speed in combination with endurance and determination is typically demanded in better races at Delta Downs vis-à-vis at Santa Anita?

I dare say, usually not nearly as much.

In nonclaiming races, shippers from minor tracks are generally poor propositions at major tracks, not to mention the flagship tracks of New York and southern California, and notwithstanding slightly advantageous speed figures. Can stakes winners at Philadelphia Park with comparable figures ship to the Meadowlands and beat similar stakes horses stabled there? Speed handicappers only wish the game were that easy. Shippers from medium-sized tracks to major tracks upset frequently enough, of course, because either only speed is required to win, or because their superior speed figures do reflect substantial degrees of stamina and determination.

Track-to-track comparisons utilizing speed figures make perfect sense where race outcomes depend almost exclusively on outlays of speed. These tend to be lower-level claiming races, maiden-claiming races, and claiming races limited to three-year-olds. To somewhat less extent, speed figures facilitate comparisons in higher-priced claiming races, many nonwinners allowance races, and some stakes races, where speed remains crucial but may be far from everything.

A revisionist view of the interpretive guidelines for shippers honors the distinction between races where speed is dominant and races where speed is frequently not enough.

Thus a Delta Downs shipper showing a 92 might be expected to beat a $10,000 claiming horse at Santa Anita having a 90, because only speed is required to win a $10,000 claiming race anywhere. The same kind of Delta Downs shipper would be badly outrun at Santa Anita in $32,000 claiming races. At the higher-priced claiming levels, the relationships between speed, pace, and the other attributes of class can become complicated, and speed figures transported from a minor track to a major track begin to disappoint.

A few trusty guidelines encompassing track-to-track comparisons of speed figures might prove beneficial to figure handicappers everywhere.

In claiming races below $20,000, in maiden-claiming races, and in claiming races limited to three-year-olds (all selling prices), speed figures are highly transportable from track to track, regardless of relative track class.

In claiming races for 3up at $25,000 and above, among horses showing comparable speed figures—within a length or two—the advantage generally can be granted to horses from the higher-class track. Shippers from minor tracks having slightly advantageous speed figures—a couple of points—will probably be outrun regardless.

In nonclaiming races, shippers to a higher-class track should show speed figures two to five lengths superior to the local horses. The better the race at the higher-class track, the greater the desirable spread in the figures.

The guidelines are appropriate to the several varieties of speed figures in the marketplace, including Beyer Speed, Quirin speed and pace figures, Thoro-Graph, and The Sheets. Track-to-track comparisons at the lower levels of racing will be generally reliable, but in higher-priced claiming races and in the majority of nonclaiming races, the same comparisons become trickier and less dependable.

As always, there are several exceptions to the general guidelines. Here are a few additional considerations for figure analysts.

At the highest levels of competition, in the graded, listed, and open stakes, figure handicappers are urged to supplement speed figures with careful considerations of the classes of opposition against which the figures were earned. If deeper reserves of speed, endurance, and determination should be required today, perhaps as a result of a faster pace, the preceding speed figures may be a mirage.

A common illustration of the speed-class phenomenon occurs annually in stakes sprints. Most leading sprinters depend on brilliance alone as their trump. Occasional sprinters possess not only the highest order of brilliance, but comparable measures of endurance. The former have scarcely a chance against the latter in the nation's definitive sprints, including Grade 1 sprints and notably the Breeders' Cup Sprint.

In southern California in recent years the premier sprinters have been Olympic Prospect and Sunny Blossom. Neither horse stood a chance in any sprint against On The Line, Precisionist, or Farma Way, however, devastating sprinters so well-endowed of stamina they proceeded to Grade 1 victories at middle distances. Farma Way was a sprinter to begin with, at Santa Anita during Winter 1991. By March of 1991 Farmer Way had won the ten-furlong Santa Anita Handicap, and by spring and summer of the season Farma Way had emerged as a Horse-of-the-Year candidate.

Do figure handicappers believe Olympic Prospect or Sunny Blossom on their most brilliant afternoon could be expected to outrun Farma Way at six furlongs? They could not, regardless of their previous speed figures in stakes sprints.

Olympic Prospect qualifies as a provocative example of the speed-class dynamics exhibited in the better races. Olympic Prospect possessed unmatched speed to the second call of sprints, regularly completing the second fraction in 22 seconds flat. It was no fluke that Olympic Prospect led the charge at the pace call in two consecutive Breeders' Cup Sprints. He prevailed in neither race. In fact, he was badly beaten each time.

After dispensing the swiftest of fractional times, Olympic Prospect would record gigantic speed figures against overnight competition, as well as stakes opposition below Grade 1 stature. But he could not resist the authentic Grade 1 standouts at any sprint distance, his brilliant speed notwithstanding.

Horses such as On The Line, Precisionist, and Farma Way possess significantly greater reserves of speed and endurance. When the exhaustive, competitive running began in the stretch, the stronger horses summoned their deeper reserves of energy and endurance and inexorably pulled away from Olympic Prospect, Sunny Blossom, and other flaming sprinters who traded upon brilliance alone. As indispensable as speed figures can be, they do not capture the intricacies of the most competitive racing in fine detail.

In longer races, the interactions among the several attributes of class will be even more dynamic, rendering the speed figures among horses converging from highly divergent starting points less reliable. The figures will be indicative, to be sure, at least much of the time, but they will not be conclusive.

A regrettable bottom line with speed figures is germane to all varieties of track-to-track comparisons. To the extent the speed-class dynamics of the contending horses trace to highly divergent starting points, as from minor tracks to major tracks, speed figures will not be the single meaningful comparison to embrace. Classier horses run faster, but the converse does not hold. Faster horses are not necessarily classier.

In this context too, a quite common shipping scenario deserves to be emphasized. Whenever the speed-class dynamics between the shipping tracks and receiving tracks can be accepted as essentially interchangeable, speed figures represent a meaningful comparison among shippers indeed!

UNRELIABLE APPLICATIONS

In four situations, figure handicappers are urged to be especially careful, if not downright skeptical, when relying on speed figures.

1. Stakes races at classic distances

To repeat for the emphasis the transition deserves, speed figures earned in stakes races at middle distances do not transport reliably to stakes races at 1¼ miles. A vastly dissimilar population of horses prevail at the longer distance. Speed figures at shorter distances do not apply.

However, speed figures recorded in other stakes races at the classic distances do apply. They are frequently available, especially for horses 4up.

2. Maiden graduates in allowance races

Speed figures obtained in maiden competition usually have resulted following an ordinary or slower pace. In the subsequent allowance race, the pace will often be faster than par, not to mention more savagely contested. Among ordinary horses, which means most, when the pace figures improve, the speed figures decline.

Figure analysts impressed by speed figures recorded among maidens should take extra precautions when the horses meet allowance company. Pay particular attention to the probable pace.

Maiden graduates likeliest to succeed on the first date in the allowances not only will show speed figures matching par for today's conditions, but pace figures that also equal or exceed today's allowance par. Pace figures will be especially important in allowance sprints.

3. Juvenile routes

The speed figures two-year-olds have recorded in sprints do not apply when the youngsters stretch out in fall.

Among the juveniles exhibiting acceptable speed figures, prefer impressive pace figures, in conjunction with early-speed advantages. The cheaper the juvenile routes, even more important the early speed and early pace advantages.

The cream of the two-year-olds can be excepted. These can be expected to duplicate impressive speed figures, or to exceed them. Really top two-year-olds tend to accomplish whatever is asked of them. A frontrunning or pace-pressing style, however, remains very much preferred.

4. Turf races

Figure handicapping on the turf is a rarefied, esoteric art practiced exceptionally well by a handful of dedicated figure handicappers, and abandoned by practically everyone else.

Complications arising from an inordinately tardy pace, or from problems inherent in calculating accurate grass variants, or from the several configurations of turf courses, or from routine maintenance changes—the rails are up, the rails are down, the grass is tall, the grass is short, the horses break from a chute, the horses break along the straightaway—have rendered the conventional figure handicapping of grass races anathema. I have watched a few of the finest figure handicappers in the country toss their grass figures in the lake during the heart of the season.

The small number of expert figure handicappers who use speed figures on grass effectively invariably resort to projected times to calculate daily track variants, not only at the finish line, but at multiple points of call. A handful of handicappers I know swear to projections five and six deep in every grass race. Others project for three or more horses at every point of call.

Anyone willing to offer that sacrifice deserves unlimited success when conducting figure handicapping in turf races.

The rest of the racing world cannot depend on conventional speed figures for analyzing turf races and should not try.

Besides, grass races are truly different. The critical factors of handicapping will regularly be diametrically opposite the factors upon which conventional speed handicapping has been predicated.

In the final sections to come, I shall present the products of three years of study and experimentation with innovative methods of figure handicapping on the grass. The approach has worked impressively at several grass courses, and I submit it with confidence that the ideas, methods, and figure charts can represent a genuine contribution to handicappers everywhere.

PART THREE

Patterns

THE FUN OF FIGURE HANDICAPPING consists of identifying meaning-ful patterns of numbers: winning patterns. All figure handicap-pers do it. They observe an array of numbers and races that have been associated with winning performances in the past. Whether the patterns signify cause-and-effect relationships or not, when the associations are spotted again, serious bets are placed. Patterns that repeat themselves successfully are quickly internalized. Inconsistent patterns are just as quickly deserted.

In that sense, recognizing patterns of figures that represent success becomes a highly individualistic endeavor. Figure handicappers develop a mental file of pattern plays, organized in some sort of personal hierarchy, such that the most success-ful patterns will consistently be translated into prime bets. With experience, the skill of pattern recognition becomes intuitive. Figure handicappers may or may not be able to articulate the sequence of numbers that provide the clues, but they know the patterns when they see them.

In a global sense, certain patterns of figure handicapping have been sufficiently well-documented and detailed to be of widespread use. No one can persevere as a figure handicapper for more than a few days, for example, without hearing about the notorious "bounce" patterns. A horse exhibiting a negative bounce pattern should not be expected to win today, notwith-standing the uncommonly high speed figure it recorded last out.

Other repetitive patterns of figure handicapping deserve at-tention here. They can guide figure analysis in a number of common situations. Nothing could be more routine than evalu-ating the high-figure horses, of which one exists in every horse race, and about which unwarranted confusion abounds.

HIGH-FIGURE HORSES

The sturdiest bets of figure handicapping will be placed on horses 3up that persistently record higher speed figures than today's opposition. At least three consecutive speed figures will be higher than any figure of the other contenders.

Examine the three highest-rated horses in the ninth race at Belmont Park, September 4, 1991. Which do figure handicappers prefer?

Belmont

9

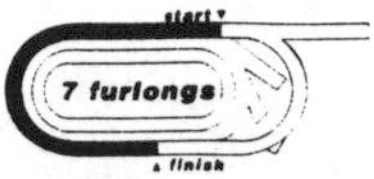

SEVEN FURLONGS. CLAIMING. Purse $18,000. For Three Year Olds and Upward. Three Year Olds, 118 lbs. Older, 122 lbs. Non-winners of two races since August 15 allowed, 3 lbs. Of a race since then, 5 lbs. Claiming Price $25,000; for each $2,500 to $20,000, 2 lbs. [Races when entered to be Claimed for $18,000 or less not considered.]

JUDY PERTY

4yo (Apr) gelding, dk. bay/brown — **$22,500** CLM. PRICE
Trainer: Stanley M Hough
Owner: Triumviri Stable
Sire: **Well Decorated** ($12,500) by Raja Baba
Dam: **Pretty Perty** by Raise A Bid
Bred in **KY** by Dr. William O. Reed
117

Career: 17 3 5 3
Wet: 3 1 1 0 | **1991:** 6 2 0 0 $22,820
Turf: 1 0 0 0 | **1990:** 9 1 5 2
Dist 6 1 2 2 | **Bel:** 2 1 0 0

28Aug91 1Bel ft 3+ Clm25000 6f 22.26 45.37 1:09.79 90 8/8 7 65¾ 62¾ 5¾ 1¾ JD Bailey 115 f 9.20 Judy Perty115¾Man It's Cold117¾I Keep Abreast117¹¾
Rated 4-wide, moved up approaching stretch, angled out, driving
15Aug91 2Sar ft 3+ Clm25000 7f 22.30 44.76 1:10.28 1:23.34 79 3/14 13 1310 1315 145 43¼ JF Chavez 115 f 6.00 Applebred115¹Marching Orders117²Jennifer's Prince117nk
Broke in a tangle, off slow, outrun inside, moved out, rallied
5Aug91 9Sar ft 3+ Clm25000 6f 21.66 44.86 1:11.10 84 4/11 7 76½ 86½ 75 51¾ R Migliore 115 f 5.50 Shine Please117hdSalem's Revenge113¹½Roman Report117no
Bmpd start, outrun inside, mvd closer late tn, finished willingly
19Jly91 9Bel ft 4+ Clm25000 6f 22.29 45.30 1:10.69 69 1/10 4 41¾ 32 44 77¾ JD Bailey 117 bf 5.60 Crafty Mana115¾MarchngOrdrsnoCoastCommnd4 *Rail, tired*
22Feb91 10GP fm 4+ Clm40000 a1⅛ Ⓣ 1:45.90 65 5/10 7 54½ 56 911 911 918½ H Castillo Jr 116 f 12.40 Duckpower114noVortrekker¾Always Runninghd *Outrun*
18Jan91 7GP gd 4+ Alw18000Nw1x 6f 22.30 45.70 1:11.90 79 1/8 5 35 25 24 1nk H Castillo Jr 112 f 3.60 Judy Perty112nkMagicEagl2TimFrThS2½ *Splt rvls; driving*
29Dec90 4CRC ft 3+ MaidenSpWt 7f 22.30 46.10 1:25.90 73 7/9 3 22 21 11 1¾ H Castillo Jr 121 f 0.80 Judy Perty121¾EilsChfStndTerrfcTn3 *Frcd pace; driving*
16Dec90 5CRC ft 3+ MaidenSpWt 6f 22.30 46.30 1:11.90 78 7/8 4 44½ 1½ 13 22 H Castillo Jr 121 f 2.70 Jewel King121²JudyPrty5½MrMereng¾ *Wide trip; 2nd best*
6Aug90 2Wdb ft 3+ MaidenSpWt 6f 22.50 45.70 1:11.90 63 5/6 36½ L Attard 120 0.70 Billy Two Rivers1172½Insistent Beat4Judy Perty2¼
28Jly90 6Wdb ft 3+ MaidenSpWt 6½f 22.30 45.30 1:17.70 72 4/8 31¼ L Attard 120 1.30 Gun Salute117¹¼Trillium DustnoJudy Perty1½

Workouts: 28Jly Sar 4f ft 48.33 B   17Jly Bel 3f ft 35.18 H   **10Jly Bel 5f ft 1:00.11 H**   3Jly Bel 5f sy 1:01.20 B   26Jun Bel 3f ft 37.40 B

LOYKEN

5yo (Mar) gelding, dk. bay/brown — **$22,500** CLM. PRICE
Trainer: Jeff Odintz
Owner: Jewel-E Stables
Sire: **Liloy** by Bold Bidder
Dam: **Kennedy Lass** by Kennedy Road
Bred in **CAN** by Bluegrass Farm Management Corporation
115

1989-91: 40 4 9 9
Wet: 5 0 1 1 | **1991:** 14 3 3 2 $43,280
Turf: 11 0 4 3 | **1990:** 13 0 1 3
Dist 11 1 3 4 | **Bel:** 2 0 2 0

22Aug91 2Sar my 3+ Clm35000 6½f 22.58 45.38 1:10.04 1:16.69 89 2/7 4 21 2hd 2½ 32 R Migliore 114 bf 4.60 Tower Of Treasures119¾Roman Cat113¹¼Loyken1143
Dueled inside, put away speed, tired late
26Jly91 3Sar ft 3+ Clm25000 7f 22.61 45.47 1:09.96 1:22.95 92 8/10 2 21 1hd 1hd 1no R Migliore 115 bf 5.00 Loyken115noRoman Report113⁷Jennifer's Prince117nk
Chased runnerup outside, dueled final half mile
8Jly91 3Bel ft 4+ Clm25000 7f 22.89 46.24 1:10.88 1:23.79 90 1/10 3 11 1hd 2hd 2hd R Migliore 115 bf 7.30 Night Thunder117hdLoyken115noToo True112½
Made the pace along the rail, dueled winner final 3/8's, game
14Jun91 2Bel ft 4+ Clm25000 7f 22.09 44.82 1:09.87 1:22.74 87 11/11 3 33 32 1hd 2nk R Migliore 115 b 4.90 Too True117nkLoykennkWee Stark3 *Wore down speed, game*
1Jun91 2Bel fm 4+ Clm35000 1⅟₁₆ Ⓣ 23.23 46.99 1:11.40 1:41.92 71 2/9 2 2hd 2½ 62¼ 76¾ 69 A Santiago 117 4.90 Skymetz117³½Commnwith[dh]BattleFx4¾ *Chased outside, tired*
29Apr91 1Aqu ft 4+ Clm25000 1⅛ 24.46 49.19 1:14.37 1:54.41 75 6/8 6 85¼ 85¼ 5¼ 32½ 55¾ JF Chavez 115 9.90 Wee Stark117½Crown Land113nkHigh Iron1173¾
Claimed from Amos E Bolton
Off very slow,4-wide bkstr, swept to leader leaving far turn,wknd
6Apr91 2Aqu ft 3+ StrHcp17500 1⅛ 24.25 48.27 1:12.53 1:51.69 77 6/7 4 35 35½ 32½ 45 59 A Madrid Jr 113 7.50 Greek God1211¾WeeStarknkHierrchy7 *Chased 3 wide, tired*
28Mar91 9Aqu ft 4+ Clm25000 1m 22.74 45.30 1:11.05 1:37.62 88 1/8 8 67 66½ 51¾ 41¾ 21 A Madrid Jr 115 7.80 Battle Fox117¹LoykennkCalhounnd *Inside, out, rallied*
20Mar91 4Aqu ft 4+ Clm25000 7f 22.75 45.47 1:10.91 1:23.89 92 8/9 8 65 34½ 31 31½ J Velazquez 113 39.30 Caramel Pie117hdBayoBlrr¹½Loyken2 *Out finished, gamely*
2Mar91 2Aql my 4+ Clm14000 6f 21.84 44.78 1:10.20 59 6/9 5 76½ 710 610 710¾ A Graell 117 b 7.90 Bubba Burn1174½Pauly Saw113¹Frank Lark113½
Claimed from Stanley R Shapoff
Four wide throughout, tired through stretch

Workouts: 17May Aqu 4f ft 47.77 B   17Mar Aqu 4f ft

MAJOR MCCALLUM

6yo (May) horse, chestnut — **$25,000** CLM. PRICE
Trainer: Peter Ferriola
Owner: James Riocio
Sire: **Mehmet** ($5,000) by His Majesty
Dam: **My Dream** by Crowned Prince
Bred in **CAN** by Frank H. Stronach
117

1989-91: 27 6 5 3
Wet: 5 1 2 0 | **1991:** 1 1 0 0 $16,800
Turf: 1 0 0 0 | **1990:** 9 3 1 1
Dist 5 2 2 1 | **Bel:** 14 1 3 1

16Jan91 7Aql sy 4+ Alw28000Nw2x 6f 21.89 44.49 1:10.23 98 1/7 5 45½ 38 35 11¼ D Carr 117 bf 3.70 Major Mccallum117¹¼VictoriouslyBold112³¾HollywoodSuccss117nk
Mustered a late rally; driving
29Nov90 4Aqu ft 3+ Clm35000 6f 22.69 46.25 1:11.28 104 4/8 2 2½ 21 3¾ CC Yang 114 bf 3.00 Dandy Cut117¾Scavenger Hunt117hdMajor Mccallum1143¼
Showed strong early speed; finished gamely
18Nov90 1Aqu ft 3+ Clm35000 6f 22.80 46.75 1:11.82 102 4/7 3 52½ 42½ 1¾ D Carr 115 bf 2.30 Major Mccallum115¾So Private113¾Dandy Cut1193
Mustered a late rally; driving
2Nov90 2Aqu ft 3+ Clm25000 7f 22.09 44.92 1:23.17 98 1/11 2 77¼ 53 11¼ D Carr 115 bf 3.70 Major Mccallum115¹¼RivrPtr¾Damn's3¾ *Late rlly; driving*
5Oct90 9Bel ft 3+ Clm25000 1⅛ 24.13 47.94 1:12.95 1:51.99 84 9/11 3 1hd 2hd 54¼ D Carr 117 bf 4.20 So Private117¹RomanEvent¹¼Distnctlnt¹¼ *Good spd; tired*
27Sep90 2Bel ft 3+ Clm14000 7f 22.88 46.26 1:22.82 90 9/12 3 31½ 3½ 18¼ D Carr 117 bf 9.60 Major Mccallum1178¼CirclMrnkJazzCty1½ *Drew off; roughed*
17Sep90 9Bel ft 3+ Clm14000 6f 22.47 45.35 1:09.41 53 10/12 5 41¼ 53 615¼ RI Rojas 117 bf 6.40 Clear Cataracts1084½TowrngPrsnc7NewHampshrnk *Bid, hung*

Major McCallum consistently has recorded speed figures six to eight points higher than the other two. No figure bet will be more reliable. Because Major McCallum was returning after an eight-month absence, public selectors at Belmont Park preferred Judy Perty or Loyken, placing the high-figure horse third. But if current form has been judged acceptable, Major McCallum literally figures to defeat these opponents. Handicappers should expect that. A peak effort is not required; only a good race and satisfactory odds, as always.

The consistent, high-figure pattern needs no more detail. Horses that invariably earn speed figures higher than the others figure to win, and do. Make the plays, just as consistently.

If Major McCallum were not present here, figure analysts would be forced to choose between Judy Perty and Loyken. The choice should be clear-cut, and represents a subtle variation of the consistent, high-figure pattern.

When horses have been running regularly, observe the pattern of speed figures they display. Which pattern below looks more inviting?

Judy Perty	90	Loyken	89
	79		92
	84		90

Although Judy Perty's latest figure is slightly higher than Loyken's latest, Loyken's pattern of figures look clearly superior. What to do?

Whenever an older horse's (4up) most recent speed figure has been a best-ever number, as Judy Perty's 90 on August 28, handicappers should demand supporting evidence that the performance can be repeated. Add the last figure to the next-to-last. Do the same for the other contenders. If the high-figure horse's combined figures remain tops, accept the horse. If the combined figures do not remain best, beware.

In the example, Judy Perty has earned a combined figure of 169; Loyken gets 181. If the third figure back were added, Judy Perty would be rated 253 and Loyken 271. The accumulated evidence indicates Loyken is the faster horse. Unless Judy Perty's latest figure reflects an improvement pattern that should continue today, prefer the horse having the highest combined speed figures.

Judy Perty's 90 is not part of an improvement cycle, but instead out of context in the entire record. That kind of high-figure horse is less likely to repeat. Figure handicappers best prefer Loyken here, and similar horses in similar situations.

A word of caution. Do not confuse form analysis and figure analysis. If form analysis suggests a decline today, obviously the latest numbers can be misleading. If form should persevere intact, however, adhere to the procedures outlined above.

Another kind of high-figure horse can be difficult to accept at face value. Yet if the figure is valid, the horse should parade to victory today. Only days ago at Del Mar, I botched this kind of figure play. The race was a sprint for $10,000 claiming horses, 3up, that were Cal-breds. The field could be pared quickly to three horses, but the most intriguing contender by far was the apparent figure standout. It's August 30, par is 100. Here are the speed and pace figures for Ama Sharif's last three races.

Ama Sharif	Aug 15	102	104
	Aug 1	97	94
	July 7	100	95

The August 15 speed figure (104) gave Ama Sharif a six-length advantage against a weak $10,000 field of state-breds. But no supporting evidence for the figure could be gathered from the published record. The horse usually recorded figures in the mid-90s, five lengths below the $10,000 par.

Could the August 15 speed and pace figures be accepted as legitimate? Review the past performances:

Before assuming that the atypically high speed figures of older horses are unreal, submit the impressive figures to the following checklist:

- Did the figure result from an unmolested wire-to-wire romp that should not be repeated today?
- Did the figure occur on a wet track surface that has disappeared?
- Was the figure aided by a speed bias or post position bias?
- Did the figure result following a precipitous drop in class?

If none of these circumstances can explain an unusually high figure, as is the case with Ama Sharif, a more positive style of inquiry can be conducted. Do extenuating circumstances exist that indicate the figure might be real and therefore can be repeated or improved today?

A recent claim by a competent claiming trainer qualifies as a positive explanation. Ama Sharif had been claimed five races back by Mike Mitchell, a claiming-race specialist in southern California. Improvement might have been anticipated sooner than the fourth race following the claim, to be sure, but the situation suggests the sudden improvement might be real.

When the checklist and any extenuating circumstances have been exhausted, the final decision of handicappers still may not be an easy call. When ambivalent, handicappers can rely on the odds. If the horse has been overbet by figure addicts, pass. If the odds remain seductive, grab the opportunity. Ama Sharif went postward at 4–1 in the $10,000 claiming race following the impressive 104. The gelding sped to the front and won unchallenged by—would anyone believe it?—six lengths, precisely its numerical spread on the field.

Another variation of the high-figure horse is found among those developing, befuddling three-year-olds. Suddenly one of them records a speed figure significantly superior to anything that has come before. An outstanding illustration is the filly below:

Although its previous figures did not prepare handicappers for Articulation's 84 on August 29, the new speed figure should be accepted at face value. Three-year-olds can improve dramatically, and many do. Whenever a clearly improved speed figure has been earned, expect the horses will repeat the numbers in the near future. Unlike with older horses, do not add the improved figure to the prior figure. Credit three-year-olds instead with their best effort in the past six races.

Paradoxically, three-year-olds often will not repeat the high figure in the very next race. As maturing, developing racehorses, three-year-olds can be consistently inconsistent. But the shiny new number should be duplicated or improved within the next three starts.

Once three-year-olds have recorded a dramatically improved speed figure, they should continue to improve, but at varying rates, depending upon native abilities. Nonclaiming three-year-olds frequently will continue to register dramatic gains, their subsequent speed figures improving again by as many as five lengths (10 points or more). Claiming horses should improve only gradually. Articulation's best in the near future might be 86 or 87, but not 92, 93.

If an improving three-year-old suffers a shellacking while advancing prematurely in class, its speed figure plummeting, handicappers should expect a temporary regression. The numbers may remain flat for a time. Getting whipped to a frazzle while running to exhaustion depletes the energies and dampens the spirits of numerous developing three-year-olds.

The classic case finds impressively improving three-year-olds advanced to graded stakes from the allowances before they are physically and temperamentally set for the more rugged fights. Trainers know they've got a good one, but they move ahead too far too soon. If the horses are smacked down unceremoniously, the resulting speed figures will be unrepresentative of real abilities. So might the next few. When evaluating nonclaiming three-year-olds, figure handicappers should always pay attention to the best figure earned against the most advanced competition challenged.

Where might the youngsters figure to win next? If ready at last to rebound, expect talented three-year-olds will repeat or exceed their previous best.

Sometimes alert handicappers can anticipate a three-year-old's dramatic improvement. The critical clues can be uncovered in the interplay between form and class. Beginning at the May 15 win when favored against maiden-claiming types, look closely at the past performances of Articulation.

Embarrassed at $32,000 claiming against winners, Articulation is lowered next to $16,000 claiming, where it runs well enough for four furlongs and is claimed by a fine young horseman. The subsequent start is again for $16,000 claiming but at the route. Articulation not only carries its speed to the eighth pole August 11, but also the internal fractions look relatively swift. Ignoring daily track variants, the adjusted fractional times of the route convert to projected sprint times of 45.3 and 1:11 flat, hardly unattractive running times versus $16,000 three-year-olds.

If daily variants had been known and applied, Articulation's adjusted times would have been even faster, as Del Mar's track surface was Slow 3 on August 11. Whenever possible, handicappers should adjust actual times to reflect track-surface speed.

The cycle of improvement crested in the sprint of August 29. Articulation led the field wire-to-wire and posted the much-improved speed figure (84), foreshadowed only by a careful in-depth form analysis. With its speed extended, condition sharpened, and stamina strengthened by the route, Articulation was prepared to show its finest when returned to the sprint. Just as importantly, trainer Bob Hess, Jr., did not attempt to raise Articulation in class following the improved route. He kept the horse pegged at a class level where it was ready to win. Claiming $16,000 is exactly one-half maiden-claiming $32,000, the conventional class adjustment.

The only way figure handicappers can expect to predict the big win and big figure by improving three-year-olds is to submit their past performances to an extensive class-form inspection.

Once the sterling figure has been displayed, handicappers should reference it to the pars at the local track. Where should the improving three-year-old be expected to win next? At any class level where the new figure matches par, or exceeds par. Regardless of speed figures, three-year-old claiming horses can rarely move into allowance races and survive. They are beaten off either by an accelerated pace or by a savagely contested stretch run, or by both.

On the other hand, the maneuver from the nonwinners allowances—has beaten half the field or finished within six lengths—to claiming races limited to three-year-olds, regularly results in victories. If the dropdown arrives at the claiming level with today's top figure, that's a speed-class interplay worthy of a prime bet.

BOUNCE PATTERNS

Figure handicappers must take full responsibility for making the "bounce" pattern infamous. The "bounce" is a figure-handicapping concept, to be sure, and handicappers seemingly cannot navigate a nine-race program anymore without confronting one of the horses. That's because racehorses can be susceptible to a number of crazy bounces, rather like an awkwardly bouncing ball.

That is, handicappers must deal effectively with a variety of bounce patterns. Below is the quintessential bounce candidate, the pattern in its purest form:

Belmont

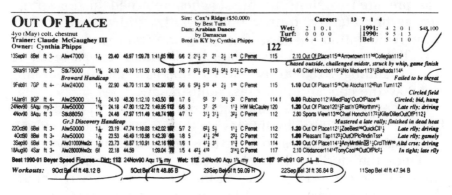

1

1 mile

ONE MILE. ALLOWANCE. Purse $47,000. For Three Year Olds and Upward which have not won two races of $21,650 at one mile or over since January 1. Three Year Olds. 119 lbs. Older. 122 lbs. Non-winners of a race of $21,650 at one mile or over since September 1, allowed 3 lbs. Of such a race since August 1, 5 lbs. Of such a race since July 1, 7 lbs. [Maiden, Claiming, Starter and restricted races not considered.]

Six months and eleven days following its last race, Out Of Place returned to Belmont Park under classified allowance conditions and prevailed in an all-out driving finish. The four-year-old stayed close to a rapid pace at every call before mustering renewed energy for the long stretch battle. While winning on September 13, he recorded an impressive speed figure (106). One of the rare horses able to win more than half of its races,

Out Of Place's comeback triumph improved his lifetime mark to 7 for 13.

Eclipse trainer Shug McGaughey afforded Out Of Place a thirty-day rest and on October 12 entered him next in another classified spot at a flat mile against horses that had not won $21,650 twice at a mile or longer since January 1. On cold dope, McGaughey's horse shaped up as a stickout against the classified foes.

But did Out Of Place figure to bounce? Following the overexertion in the comeback race, should handicappers expect Out Of Place to regress October 12, at least mildly?

The answer is a resounding yes.

Out Of Place satisfies each of four warning signs attending a figure bounce following a lengthy layoff. These are:

1. A layoff of five months or longer
2. An overexertion in the comeback effort, resulting in either a win or a close finish (within a length) in rapid time
3. Following the taxing comeback race, a return to competition within six weeks
4. Low odds in the start following the comeback race

Regarding the premature overexertion, horses that have run close to the pace at every call before winning or finishing all-out in rapid time are especially prone to a bounce. That's a rugged comeback race. It results in muscle soreness and a setback in conditioning, however slight. The negative effects can endure for weeks.

Although numerous bounce situations will appear precarious and handicappers typically experience abundant ambivalence on the matter—will he bounce or won't he, will he win or won't he?—the final warning sign carries the cause. Where a bounce looms as a distinct possibility, low odds should be avoided.

Out Of Place went postward in the October 12 classified race at even-money. Who needs it? If an attractive alternative looks inviting on the tote board, handicappers should take the bait. They will be correct frequently enough to show a healthy profit long-term.

Out Of Place lost the October 12 classified race, finishing second to an overlay that figured nicely.

The second-place finish deserves some notice. Did Out Of Place actually bounce, or was the horse merely beaten? A bounce probably did occur, however slight. The longer the gap between the comeback effort and the subsequent start, the less severe the regression. Horses that return to action in two or three weeks following an overexertion may regress sharply, horses that resume in four to six weeks may regress only mildly, but in each instance a bounce pattern has occurred.

And some horses do win second starts following a layoff and an overexertion regardless. As always, handicappers must manipulate the probabilities intelligently.

Moreover, the bounce tends to occur in the late stages. The horses will normally be competitive until the prestretch call, perhaps until the eighth-pole, before losing momentum. They lack only that final rush to victory. Out Of Place was gaining steadily in the last sixteenth of the Belmont Park classified event, but he took dead aim throughout the stretch and probably would have conquered in sharper form.

More often than not, a solid but unexceptional comeback effort following a lengthy layoff does not precipitate a bounce. The $6250 claimer below returned from a 6½-month layaway and dispensed an impressive race.

Should handicappers anticipate a bounce next time?

Not at all. In fact, a comeback performance that challenges strongly at the second call and finishes within six lengths while beating half the field remains a positive sign of improving form. Ole Marconi should do better still in his second start.

A telltale clue is the speed figure (63). Ole Marconi records speed figures of 73 and 74 in his good races. The 63 of the comeback try suggests the colt remains roughly five lengths below top form. Figure handicappers never expect relatively low speed figures to precipitate a bounce pattern. Unusually high figures scare them away, and so might typically competitive figures in close finishes following a long absence.

Many handicappers would have expected the colt below to have bounced on October 4 when triple-jumped in claiming class, but not figure analysts alerted to the telltale clue.

Away nearly six months, Fair One dominated its comeback race. But the victory was achieved handily, following an ordinary pace and without undue exertion in the stretch, and the speed figure (71) remained clearly beneath the horse's best efforts. A month later, Fair One throttled classier horses even more easily, and figure handicappers should not have predicted a bounce.

Keep in mind that overexertion is part and parcel of the bounce pattern. If that phenomenon is missing, do not expect horses to regress, however sharp the comeback races.

Does the 3YO below figure to bounce? It's October 21.

Numerous handicappers mistake the bounce pattern on its most elementary requirement. Horses away from action for less than three months should never be expected to bounce, at least not from premature overexertion. Supporting had been absent only 53 days before the September 26 win.

Horses bounce from overexertion in part because the lengthy layoff has robbed them of athletic conditioning. Many have been sent out of the racetrack by trainers, to nearby farms or off-track training sites. There they rest, walk, and gallop lightly; then a reconditioning program begins in earnest. Horses inactive just a few months are not usually sent out and do not surrender their athletic trim. The freshening rest contains remarkable recuperative powers. A strong race following the respite advances the horses again to excellent competitive form. No premature bounce occurs, and none should be anticipated.

So when evaluating form cycles following layoffs, figure handicappers best discriminate between short layoffs and long layoffs. A big figure following a long layoff causes concern. A big figure following a short layoff is a highly positive sign.

Other more subtle aspects of the bounce patterns will be upcoming, but first some attention to a complementary pattern much less remarked, but significantly more beneficial to figure handicappers everywhere.

BOUNCE-BACK PATTERNS

Horses that bounce following lengthy layoffs and overexertion in the comeback effort also typically "bounce back" in the third start following the layoff. Too many figure analysts on the lookout for the bounce patterns can be found looking the other way when bounce-back opportunities arise.

The gelding North Stage represents an especially instructive illustration of the bounce-back pattern. Review the past performances, including the speed and pace figures superimposed on the two races following the ten-month absence.

NORTH STAGE 3-N

3yo (Mar) gelding, bay   **$16,000**
Trainer: Robert B Hess Jr   CLM. PRICE
Owner: Hoffman, Kruse & Strugar

Sire: Northrop ($3,500)
  by Northern Dancer
Dam: Cherry Sauce
  by Stage Door Johnny
Bred in CA by Larry Littman

116 Kent J Desormeaux

93 H/1 Career: 7 3 0 1 $32,875

	Wet:	0 0 0 0	$0	1991:	2 1 0 1	$11,050
	Turf:	0 0 0 0	$0	1990:	5 2 0 0	$21,825
	Dist:	6 2 0 1	$26,275	SA:	4 1 0 1	$18,025

110ct91 3SA ft 3   Clm16000   6f 21.64 44.82 57.51 1:10.47 78 3/10 6 6½ 6½   5½ 3² K Desormeaux 118 Llb 2.30 Naevus Rains116ⁿᵏBio Rythem116¹¾North Stage118ⁿᵒ
                                                                               3-w bckstr, far turn, angled out, late rally

4Sep91 3Dmr ft 3   Clm16000   6f 21.98 45.12 57.87 1:10.73 78 1/10 10 4³ 5²   4³ 1¹ K Desormeaux 115 Llb 8.80 North Stage115¹Naevus Rains116¾Sally's Prince117v
                                                                               Lw far turn, angled in stretch, split horses, won driving

1Nov90 5SA ft 2   Clm32000   6f 21.90 45.50   1:11.50 99 3/9 2 2ʰᵏ 1ʰᵏ   5² 6½ O Berrio   115 llb 1.90 Gold Bally115¹¼Meeta Cheetah115¹Showthemyourheels116ʰᵏ
   Claimed from Henry Dominguez   *Saved ground along the inside; challenged for lead, faltered*

18Oct90 5SA ft 2   Clm32000   6f 21.70 45.10   1:11.30 74 2/11 8 1½ 1ʰᵏ   1ʰᵏ 1½ O Berrio   112 b 34.40 North Stage112½DimndbckDᴺᴸL'deeDasc²   *Good spd; gamely*
30Oct90 2SA ft 2   Clm40000   6f 21.50 44.70   1:10.70 Φ 2/12 4 4½ 4¹   4² 4¾ O Berrio   111 llb 69.00 Lazarrito116ᴺᴸL'deeDasc²DimndbckDᴬ   *Wide trip; bore out*
14Sep90 10Fpx ft 2   Stk43180   6½f 21.90 45.90 1:10.90 1:17.30 41 4/9 5 5½ 7½   9¹5½ OL Garrido   114 b 8.90 Palmdale114²¼Frosty Paws114¹¼Chief Sassafras116²
   Beau Brummel Stakes   *Broke well, three-wide first turn, dropped out of it*

11Aug90 6LA ft 2   MdC32000   4½f 21.50   50.50 77 5/10 1 1½   1³¾ OL Garrido   118 b 6.10 North Stage118³⅓FirstWest½Townsthv²¼   *Good spd; driving*

Best 1990-91 Beyer Speed Figures - **Dirt:** 78 4Sep91 Dmr 6f ft   **Dist:** 78 4Sep91 Dmr 6f ft

Workouts: 7OctSA 5f ft 1:01.10 H   1OctSA 3f ft 36.90 H   31Aug Dmr 4f ft 47.90 H   21Aug Dmr 5f ft 1:04.30 H   14Aug Dmr 6f ft 1:18.10 H

The good third-place finish by North Stage following the comeback victory of September 4 actually qualifies as a bounce. Speed figures tell the tale. On Beyer Speed, the gelding declined five points, from 78 to 73. On Quirin speed and pace numbers, North Stage regressed from 103-101 September 4 to 95-98 October 11. The former figures were above par, the latter below par, both at the pace position and final call.

If the pace figure on October 11 had been again above par, à la 103, the final figure that day probably would have plummeted. The race might look pitiful, but the bounce–bounce-back pattern would be just as prevalent.

Importantly, when the pace of the bounce race has been ordinary to slow, the running line will normally not look wretched, and sometimes may be even appealing, as with North Stage's second start after the long recess. Most horses bounce in the late stages, however, unable to gather their depleted energies for a strong finish. The finish may qualify as an acceptable race, or good race, the figures descending only a few lengths. Handicappers should not be fooled. A bounce-back effort remains in the making.

I trust handicappers noticed also that North Stage disappointed in its second start after the layoff as a 2–1 favorite. Absolutely the most rewarding aspect of the bounce, bounce-back phenomenon finds the horses losing as underlays following an impressive performance and recuperating as overlays following the discouraging performance.

Not too many seasons ago the Laz Barrera-trained 3YO Mi Preferido was the outstanding sophomore on the southern California circuit. Between its 2YO and 3YO seasons, the colt had been rested for seven months. The colt returned with a vicious all-out win at seven furlongs, the speed figure quite high.

Next out, in a restricted stakes, the bettors sent Mi Preferido to the post at a ridiculous 2–5. Well placed around the far turn, Mi Preferido bounced outrageously. He did not beat half the field.

In his third start at age three, the bounce-back pattern, Mi Preferido smashed a graded stakes field immeasurably more talented than the restricted group that had left him behind. He paid 9–2 on bounce-back day, when he might have been even-money. That's been my favorite bounce, bounce-back story ever since, no doubt due to the quality of the horse and the generous gift he became on the bounce-back end.

Sweeter odds attending the bounce-back occasion is an integral aspect of this intriguing pattern. Figure handicappers should expect bounce-back candidates to equal or surpass the speed figures recorded in the comeback races. When the odds beckon, make the plays.

Finally, not all horses that win or finish close in rapid time following long layoffs should be expected to bounce in the next. Covering several of the same points, we conclude our discussion of bounce patterns with opposite variations on the theme, perhaps the most confusing, most interesting examples of the bunch.

TO BOUNCE OR NOT TO BOUNCE

Abundant but unnecessary confusion persists among figure handicappers about certain horses' performances following lengthy layoffs and whether they qualify as bounce patterns.

How long a layoff?

Must the first performance following the long layoff result in an all-out victory? What about a close finish in rapid time? What about a second-place finish, or a third-place finish?

How many weeks after the comeback performance must a horse remain inactive so that it might return to the competition comfortably? Three weeks? A month? Six weeks?

Firm adherence to rigid rules does not apply, but flexible guidelines can be set forth to guide decision-making on the trickiest bounce patterns. It's not as complicated as many handicappers have imagined. Which of the two horses below should be expected to bounce next time?

SONNYS RAINBOW

3yo (Mar) gelding, dk. bay/brown **$10,000**
Trainer: Warren Stute   CLM. PRICE
Owner: Mr & Mrs Arthur Fellows

Sire: **Tsunami Slew** ($15,000)
   by Seattle Slew
Dam: **Fast Bird**
   by Hotfoot
Bred in KY by Karen Hartley Soben
& OFPG, Inc.

Career: 16 2 3 1 $40,965

	Wet:	1 0 0 0	$0	1991:	10 1 3 1	$26,665
	Turf:	0 0 0 0	$0	1990:	6 1 0 0	$14,300
	Dist	11 2 3 1	$38,740	Fpx:	3 0 1 0	$5,340

116 David R Flores   Yearling Price: $9,500

19Sep91 10Fpx ft 3	Clm10000	6½f	21.70	45.90 1:11.90 1:18.10	88	4/10 10	8⁴½ 6⁷	3¹	2ⁿᵒ	C Nakatani	114 LB	1.80	Natural Prime116ⁿᵒSonnys Rainbow114◦Borrowed Cash116¹

Off slow, rail early, 4-w bckstr, 5-w far turn, stretch duel

| 20Jun91 1Hol ft 3 | Clm16000 | 6f | 22.10 | 45.10 57.70 1:10.90 | 48 | 1/9 9 | 9⁹ 9¹⁰ | 9¹¹ | 6¹⁰½ | CJ McCarron | 115 LB | 2.80 | Last Of The Blues115ⁿᵒScreen Tale110½Shear Clout115² |
| Claimed from Roger Stein | | | | | | | | | | | | | *Impeded start, in tight soon after start, in tight into far turn* |

| 29May91 4Hol ft 3 | Clm20000 | 7f | 22.10 | 44.90 1:10.50 1:23.50 | 73 | 2/8 8 | 4¹½ 4¹½ | | 2ⁿᵈ | 2¹ | P Valenzuela | 116 LB | 6.40 | Lord Gusto118◦Sonnys Rainbow116½Bifrocate118½ |

Close up early, stalking pace, split horses in lane

| 15May91 1Hol ft 3 | Clm16000 | 6f | 22.10 | 45.10 57.70 1:10.30 | 84 | 2/9 9 | 7³ 5³½ | | 4⁴ | 3⁶½ | P Valenzuela | 116 L | 3.40 | Sally's Prince115◦Special Toy115½Sonnys Rainbow116½ |
| Claimed from J Michael Orman | | | | | | | | | | | | | *Mild rally through lane, no threat* |

3May91 5Hol ft 3	Clm20000	7½f	22.90	45.50 1:11.10 1:30.50	66	3/9 8	8⁴½ 5²½		4³½	6⁶½	E Delahoussy	118 LB	2.90	Knight's Get Away115◦Scm Tⁿᵒ Curr¹½	*Loomed boldly, hung*
21Apr91 1SA ft 3	Clm40000	6½f	21.70	44.50 1:10.30 1:16.90	72	6/9 9	8⁷¼ 9⁸¼		7⁶	6⁵¼	E Delahoussy	116 LB	3.60	Walkonair115¹½Suspense MakerⁿᵒFar Bestⁿᵒ	*Lacked rally*
29Mar91 5SA ft 3	Clm32000	6f	22.10	45.10 57.50 1:10.10	82	5/7 7	7⁶½ 4³		3½	1⁴	E Delahoussy	116 LB	5.10	Sonnys Rainbow116◦Damelo½Big Bang Beauⁿᵈ	*Ridden out*
20Mar91 9SA ft 3	Clm25000	1m	22.70	46.50 1:10.90 1:36.50	74	3/10 9	7⁴½ 8⁹¼		8¹³ 6¹½	4²¼	E Delahoussy	116 LB	6.60	Restless Henry115½Damelo½Dimnd¹½	*No speed, late rally*
3Mar91 5SA gd 3	Alw32000	7f	22.70	46.10 1:11.50 1:24.30	72	5/9 8	9⁹½ 9⁶½		9⁹³ 7⁸½	DR Flores	117 LB	63.10	Stone God120½JamesEsquireⁿᵈLet'sGoFlyingᵈ	*Saved ground*
14Feb91 1SA ft 3	Clm25000	6f	21.70	44.30 56.30 1:08.90	88	2/8 8	8⁷½ 7⁶½		5⁴	E Delahoussy	116 LB	11.40	Davus115⁶½Sonnys Rainbow½Lazarito½	*Mild rally*

Best 1990-91 Beyer Speed Figures - Dirt: 82 29Mar91 SA 6f ft   **Wet:** 72 3Mar91 SA 7f gd   **Dist:** 82 29Mar91 SA 6f ft

Workouts: 16Sep91 SA 5f ft 1:03.90 H   10Sep91 Dmr 7f ft 1:27.70 H   5Sep91 Dmr 6f ft 1:17.70 H   30Aug91 Dmr 5f ft 1:02.30 H   25Aug91 Dmr 5f ft 1:04.30 H

WHAT A SPELL

3yo (Mar) colt, bay
Trainer: Craig A Lewis
Owner: Jim Ford Inc & Lewis

Sire: **What Luck**
   by Bold Ruler
Dam: **Spell Victory**
   by Dance Spell
Bred in CA by Grossmont Equities

Career: 12 4 2 2 $367,225

	Wet:	2 1 0 1	$58,125	1991:	7 3 1 1	$124,475
	Turf:	4 0 2 0	$32,400	1990:	5 1 1 1	$42,750
	Dist	2 0 0 1	$8,250	Fpx:	1 1 0 0	$31,250

117 David R Flores

12Sep91 12Fpx ft 3	Stk53250	6½f	21.90	46.10 1:12.10 1:18.90	98	3/7 2	3½ 2ⁿᵈ	1½	1ⁿᵈ	DR Flores	122 Lb	1.40	What A Spell122ⁿᵈBorder Run1½Pirate's Outlook122½
Foothill Stakes													*Stalked inside, swtchd out, 3-w 1/4, lasted driving*

| 4May91 5Hol fm 3 | Stk109600 | 1m ①23.70 | 47.10 1:10.70 1:34.50 | 89 | 3/10 4 | 1¹ 1½ | 1ⁿᵈ | 6³¼10ⁿᵘ½ | AT Gryder | 116 Lbb | 19.90 | Whadjathink117¹Character112½Soweto117½ |
| *Gr.3 Spotlight BrCup Handicap* | | | | | | | | | | | | | *Good speed, weakened along rail, steadied when beaten* |

| 13Apr91 7SA fm 4+ | Alw50000 | a6½f ①21.70 | 43.70 1:07.70 1:14.10 | 89 | 2/7 1 | 1½ 1½ | 2½ | 2⁵ | DR Flores | 120 Lbb | 1.10 | Gray Sleepy117◦What A Spell120½Bering Gifts120¹½ |
| | | | | | | | | | | | | | *Dueled for the early lead, weakened in stretch* |

| 27Mar91 8SA gd 3 | Stk83625 | 6½f | 21.90 | 44.90 1:09.70 1:16.30 | 97 | 3/7 1 | 1ⁿᵈ 1¹ | 1ⁿᵈ 1ⁿᵈ | DR Flores | 117 Lbb | 3.20 | What A Spell117ⁿᵈBroadway's Top Gun122½Shining Prince114⁶ |
| *Baldwin Stakes* | | | | | | | | | | | | | *Good speed, slowed pace on turn, held gamely* |

| 14Mar91 8SA gd 3 | Stk57600 | 1m ②22.50 | 46.30 1:10.70 1:36.30 | 92 | 2/9 4 | 1½ 1¹ | 1¹½ 2½ | 3³ | DR Flores | 115 Lbb | 2.20 | Mane Minister120½Magnificent Red115ⁿᵏWhat A Spell115½ |
| *Pirate Cove Stakes* | | | | | | | | | | | | | *Clear lead to midstretch, tired last sixteenth* |

18Feb91 8GG ft 3	Hcp100000	6f	21.10	43.20 55.90 1:09.10	94	4/6 3	4²½ 5½½	5³½ 4⁶½	DR Flores	120 Lb	6.90	Media Plan119½Intimate Kd¹½Unreal Rgt½	*No escape, rallied*
7Feb91 7SA ft 3	Alw32000	6½f	21.50	44.10 1:08.30 1:15.10	96	3/7 2	2½ 1½	1⁶	1¹¹	DR Flores	120 Lbb	3.20	What A Spell120¹¹Walk With Ry½Bandix1½	*Drew off; svd grnd*
23Dec90 8Hol fm 2	Stk112800	1m ②23.70	47.50 1:11.30 1:35.30	90	7/11 11	11¹ 9³½	7¹¹½ 2¹¼	DR Flores	114 Lbb	14.90	Satisi115½What A Spell114ⁿᵉEv For Shir114ⁿᵉ
Gr.3 Hoist The Flag Stakes													*Jumped to lead, hugged rail, resisted in str, nailed from outside*

| 6Dec90 5Hol fm 2 | Alw32000 | 1m ②22.70 | 45.70 1:10.30 1:41.10 | 99 | 7/8 4 | 1² 1¹½ 2ⁿᵈ 4⁴ | A Solis | 119 Lbb | 30.00 | Soweto119¹VanBeethovⁿᵏLeFarouche½ | *Good spd; weakened* |
| 17Nov90 4Hol ft 2 | MaidenSpWt | 6f | 21.90 | 45.10 1:10.10 | 86 | 10/10 2 | 2¹ 1² | 1¹ | A Solis | 118 LB | 2.20 | What A Spell119¹Chets'sP4½OldTony¹½ | *Frcd pace; driving* |

Best 1990-91 Beyer Speed Figures - Dirt: 108 7Feb91 SA 6½f ft   **Wet:** 91 27Mar91 SA 6½f gd   **Dist:** 99 14Mar91 SA 1m gd

Workouts: 28Aug91 Dmr 6f ft 1:12.70 H   19Aug91 Dmr 6f ft 1:11.50 H   12Aug91 Dmr 5f ft 59.30 H   7Aug91 Dmr 5f ft 1:03.70 H   1Aug91 Dmr 4f ft 50.50 H

The bounce candidate is What A Spell. Away 4½ months, the colt returned to annex a long stakes sprint in which it pressed the pace early and survived a driving finish. Stick close to these guideposts:

1. Days away is crucial. A minimum of 120 days qualifies, as ninety days does not, and five months or longer is preferable. What A Spell satisfies a minimum standard of days away. Better candidates to bounce would be horses away long enough to have been sent out of the stable to a nearby farm or training center. As rest accumulates, conditioning is lost. An overexertion first race back taxes the muscles and lungs severely, contributing to muscle soreness and a reduction of training effects.

2. Running style is also important. Frontrunners and pace-pressers are more likely to bounce from a too-fast overexertion than closers. The faster horses expend inordinate amounts of energy throughout the running. Energy reserves will be more completely exhausted. Closers run strongly only for a portion of the race. Less energy has been spent, and less conditioning lost.

The horses can rebound strongly, even from a victory following a long layoff.

3. Turf horses that close from mid-pack to the rear are probably least likely to bounce from a driving finish following a long lay-off. Not only do the horses save their energies for one strong, late run, but also the early pace on grass is often slow and comfortable. Mature grass horses that close can win repeatedly following lengthy layoffs, and many of them do, without bouncing.

4. Better horses will be less susceptible to the bounce pattern than will claiming horses, as a rule, but the situation gets complicated. Top horses may bounce as readily as cheap horses, as the case of Mi Preferido demonstrates. A professional who has studied the bounce patterns of every horse on the southern California circuit for years is Frank Romano, an excellent handicapper and high roller. Romano reports simply that among nonclaiming horses, many bounce following a single overexertion, but many others bounce following two overexertions. Local handicappers must know which horses follow which bounce pattern, and treat the horses individually. Consider the case of Bel's Starlet, featured in the box below.

For the majority of handicappers, Romano's advice qualifies as impractical. But it might provoke an intriguing series of local studies among regular handicappers scouting for every edge. I recommend those local studies, absolutely.

Look again at Sonnys Rainbow. Is this a horse that figures to bounce?

Not a bit.

Away ninety days, Sonnys Rainbow has remained in light training throughout, walking, galloping, and working out in a planned training routine. Little conditioning has been sacrificed to time off. Moreover, the gelding is a deep closer, running strongly for merely the final quarter-mile of long sprints. Less chance for an extended exertion following the layoff. Sonnys Rainbow's second-place finish against $10,000 claiming horses September 19 is instead exactly the type of comeback race that foreshadows victory next time. Handicappers should expect that victory, assuming the cold dope pushes the horse across the finish line in time.

5. After an overexertion following a lengthy layoff, horses should be expected to bounce anytime within six weeks. A thirty-day respite is normally not enough. Leading trainer Gary Jones has been quoted as saying experience has taught him virtually all horses need extra time following a long layoff and big race. Handicappers are cautioned to adhere to similar expectations. Most horses that have overextended themselves following long

BEL'S STARLET *H G-N* + *9208*   Sire: **Bel Bolide** ($7.500) *,o7/,o2* *106 A-TC*
4yo (Jan) filly, roan   by **Bold Bidder**   Wet: 1 0 0 0   1991: 3 0 1 2 $23,900
Trainer: Richard Mandella *37 DAYS*   Dam: **Vigor's Star**   Turf: 8 1 2 2   1990: 9 1 2 1
Owner: Golden Eagle Farm   by **Vigors**   Dist: 0 0 0 0   SA□: 2 0 0 2
                                               Bred in CA by Mr. & Mrs. John C. *72/.80* 115 **Kent J Desormeaux**
                                               Mabee

Date	Track	Cond	Dist	Race	Speed	Odds	Finish	Jockey	Wt	Comment
2Sep91	7Dmr	ft 3↑F	Stk56500	6½f	21.95	44.25 1:09.23 1:15.77	66 5 5½ 3³	2ⁿᵈ 2ⁿᵈ K Desormeaux 113 B	12.30	Nice Assay117ⁿᵒBel's Starlet 13ⁿᵒPaper Princess117½
		June Darling Handicap								3-w BCKER, 4-w far turn, bid 3/16-pole, led, outfinished late
20Feb91	7SA	lm 4↑F	Alw43000Nw3x	1m ⊕23.10	46.50 1:10.30 1:34.10	91 5/8 1 43¼ 47	3⁴ 3³ 34½ K Desormeaux 114 B	0.70ᵉHeart Of Joy115ⁿᵒOdalea1154Bel's Starlet1141½		Stalked early, mild rally, fell short
6Feb91	7SA	lm 4↑F	Alw43000	1½ ⊕24.10	47.70 1:11.50 1:47.30	87 26 1 54½ 55½	5³ 2² 35½ K Desormeaux 114 B	4.40	Appealing Missy115ⁿᵒNoble And Nice121½Bel's Starlet1141½ Saved ground along the inside, lagged in
19Dec90	8Hol	lm 3F	Stk62650	1½ ⊕24.10	47.30 1:10.70 1:41.10	96 27 6	63¾ 51½ 2ⁿᵈ 2½ K Desormeaux 114 B	3.20	Dead Heat114½Bel's Starlet114²Somethingmerry1143 Never in serious contention, made bid, hung
		Miesque Stakes								
7Dec90	8Hol	lm 3↑F	Alw36000	1½ ⊕24.70	48.90 1:12.50 1:41.90	98 47 6	73½ 73½ 51½ 5¹ K Desormeaux 112 B	3.80	Lyphard's Melody115ⁿᵉTessieᵃˢTemptᵈᵈ Outrun; no excuse
17Nov90	8Hol	lm 3↑F	Stk82650	1½ ⊕24.70	47.90 1:11.50 1:40.10	98 36 1	2¹ 3¹½ 51½ DR Flores 113 B	10.80	Petaka113ⁿᵒBequest117½Island Jamboree1131½ Rank, restrained inside, dropped back, stayed inside, outkicked
		Gr.2 Dahlia Handicap								
10Sep90	3Dmr	lm 3F	Alw41000	1½ ⊕24.10	47.50 1:11.70 1:41.90	97 6	76½ 5½½ 17½ K Desormeaux 114	1.10	Bel's Starlet 14²½SomthngO4½Cat'tArⁿᵉ Circled; drew off
26Aug90	8Dmr	lm 3F	Stk785400	1½ ⊕24.10	48.10 1:12.70 1:49.90	84 12 12 2	4¹ 2ⁿᵒ 5½½ K Desormeaux 115	2.10	Slew Of Pearls117½Adorable Emilie115¹Annual Reunion117² Stalked one off rail, challenged into the lane, tired
		Gr.3 Del Mar Oaks								
12Aug90	5Dmr	lm 3F	Stk84050	1m ⊕23.90	48.10 1:11.90 1:36.30	96 1/9 1	64½ 6⁸ 2ⁿᵒ CA Black 114	7.80	Lonely Girl116ⁿᵒBel's Starlet114²½Bidder Cream113ⁿᵏ Boxed in, lacked racing room, lost whip
		San Clemente Handicap								
22Jly90	3Hol	ft 3↑F	Alw37000	6f	21.50	44.30	1:09.50	1/6 4 42½ 31½	34½ RG Davis 111	5.00	Devil's Orchid114½PlumPp4½Bel's½ Stlk pace; lugged in

Best 1990-91 Beyer Speed Figures - Turf: 98 10Sep90 Dmr 1½ lm   Dirt: 95 2Sep91 Dmr 6½ft   Wet: 77 17Jan90 SA 1m gd

Workouts: 2Oct SA 5f ft 58.90 H),   26Sep SA 6f ft 1:00.70 H)   18Sep SA 4f ft 49.70 H)   28Aug Dmr 6f ft 1:11.90 H   16Aug SLR 5f ft 1:00.50 H

Despite a long, rugged stretch duel September 2, following a 6½-month layoff, Bel's Starlet did not bounce next time, on October 9 during Oak Tree at Santa Anita. She won big, fooling me and many other figure analysts.

Some horses bounce following long layoffs and two strong performances, not merely one. In general, horses likelier to bounce after two comeback efforts will be:

• Better horses (nonclaiming)
• Horses that do not press the pace at every call
• Horses that remained inactive for thirty days or longer following the comeback race

When in doubt, handicappers best allow the odds to dictate the decision. At low odds, marginal bounce candidates can be passed. At attractive odds, accept the risk.

layoffs will bounce within the next six weeks.

If overextended horses have been left to recuperate for six weeks or longer, the chances of bouncing decline, but they do not disappear. If the odds are low, handicappers should pass.

6. A positive variation of the bounce pattern can be found among leading older (4up) horses. I sometimes refer to the pattern as the "easy-second." Whether the horses have finished second, third, or fourth following a long layoff, the effort will have been far less than extended, prolonged, or competitive. The horses finish vigorously but comfortably. Almost invariably, a bigger stakes objective lies directly ahead on the schedule.

Do not expect these stakes stars to bounce. The comeback race has been used as a prep for the bigger prize. The horses should continue to train sharply following the comeback effort, and can be expected to perform even more strongly next out.

As with other situations relevant to figure handicapping, experience helps enormously. Handicappers confused about bounce patterns can apply these few trusty guidelines and follow their practical experiences carefully.

Another kind of bounce pattern in figure handicapping is related to unusually strong performance, not to premature overexertion following a lengthy layoff. With so many figure handicappers repeatedly referring to horses that should bounce, maybe the widespread confusion is mainly semantics. Many of the following horses do not actually bounce, or regress. They merely return to normal: normal races and normal numbers.

THE PERFORMANCE BOUNCE

Whenever horses suddenly record speed figures significantly superior to an established norm, figure analysts have learned the horses will probably bounce next out. That is, the big figures will decline and often will revert to standard size. Figure handicappers may not understand why the numbers should decline, but it's a bona fide pattern, and customarily they will ignore the horses. The pattern can be referred to as a performance bounce. Too strong a performance last time. Not as strong a performance this time.

As a rule, expectations of lower figures today will be sustained. The filly Quick's Sister provides an outstanding illustration.

In her second race back, Quick's Sister earned a Beyer Speed Figure of 85 and a speed figure of 103 from Quirin, eight to ten lengths faster than the filly had managed to run in a dozen attempts. She won that day by daylight at 7–2.

Next out, September 29, Quick's Sister declined two lengths and failed as the 2–1 favorite. She descended to familiar figures in her next races.

The phenomenon of the high-performance bounce disturbs many figure handicappers, but it need not. The unusually big figure, in my opinion, is typically associated with peak performance, either because current form has peaked or because form remains positive and the circumstances surrounding a particular race tend toward the ideal, such as a lonesome lead, a comfortable pace, a biased surface, a wet surface, or easy opposition. In her three races prior to recording the big figure, Quick's Sister displayed consistently positive form. She probably peaked on September 5, winning off and recording the huge figures.

That kind of peak performance is rarely repeated, at least by unexceptional horses. Horses 4up that have not done so before constitute another group unlikely to repeat a best-ever figure. Figure handicappers can anticipate a decline of two to five lengths. If the best-ever figure horses are overbet while raised in class, handicappers can obviously abstain. The peak performance should have been at least five lengths better than normal, and the horses should not have earned a comparable figure in recent races. Comparable figures might have been registered within the past two years, but not repeatedly.

Whether the rationale is clear or not, a performance bounce is not especially difficult to predict, except for younger, lightly raced horses.

Consider the speed figures for the lightly raced four-year-old Mr. Integrity.

In his second start, at Hollywood Park, Mr. Integrity surprised with a facile win and a speed figure of 99. Younger, lightly raced, potentially impressive horses can do that, especially nonclaiming three-year-olds. The dramatically improved speed figure can be accepted at face value. No performance bounce should be expected.

Stretched out to a mile under nonwinners-once allowance conditions, Mr. Integrity next blasted the field apart and returned with a speed figure of 112. Although an improved figure might have been expected, the 112 compares well to older stakes horses. Is Mr. Integrity that powerful?

It's too soon to know.

But the speed figure was so dramatically improved, some decline was probable, notably since Mr. Integrity had sped wire-to-wire unmolested. At odds-on, Mr. Integrity represented a poor bet in his next race, on August 24 at Del Mar.

The October 2 race represents a critical test for understanding Mr. Integrity. Within two or three races of a dramatically improved speed figure, authentically talented horses will duplicate the number, or approach it. Ordinary horses will run toward their previous best. On October 2, Mr. Integrity should earn either a figure near 112 or a figure near 99. Which would it be?

At odds-on again, while awaiting the results, figure handicappers should not be betting.

As matters proceeded, Mr. Integrity proved to be the genuine article. He registered a 109 on October 2, bouncing back toward the enormous 112. The four-year-old remains essentially unclassified, but the pair of speed figures suggest he will be competitive under any allowance conditions and against numerous stakes horses.

If younger, lightly raced horses suddenly record super figures, figure handicappers should expect some drop-off temporarily, but the genuine articles will bounce back soon enough. Ordinary horses will not. Especially untrustworthy are maiden-claiming graduates and three-year-old claiming types that abruptly dispense a huge figure. The large majority will decline just as abruptly. Gradual gains in the figures of ordinary horses can be accepted, but not acrobatic leaps.

Figure handicappers must learn to deal effectively and confidently with inordinately large speed figures that appear out of context with the full record. Big, bold, but isolated figures stick out in numerous past-performance records. The subtle variations can be deceiving. Practice makes a positive difference. As with skill training generally, pattern recognition improves with repetition.

ALL FIGURES BELOW PAR

A nasty trap of figure handicapping springs itself upon un-
wary handicappers whenever the contenders in untalented
fields have been rated below par. It happens often in maiden-
claiming races.

At the nub of the problem is the tendency of figure handicappers to become comparison handicappers in the extreme.
That is, they compare horses on the figures, but ignore other
relevant circumstances that can be meaningful.

At a Las Vegas race book a few seasons ago a newcomer to
the figures, but an otherwise savvy handicapper of numerous
years, engaged me in an extended debate about the appropriate
bet in a maiden-claiming sprint for two-year-old fillies. The discussion lasted upwards of fifteen minutes, until post time im-
posed a natural end of the line.

My associate had spotted a figure horse at a nice price and
he didn't want to let go.

Examine the past performances of the five contenders form-
ing the guts of the race. Par for $50,000 maiden-claiming two-
year-old fillies at Hollywood Park in Nov-Dec 1990 was 97.
Here are the speed and pace figures for the five contenders:

	Pace	Speed
Uptown Gal	97	93
Gun Trial	100	96
Shine So Brightly	94	95
Real Bubbly	—not known—	
Doll Collection	102	90

The debate began innocently enough, my friend noting that
either Gun Trial or Shine So Brightly figured on the figures. As
Gun Trial was 7–5 and Shine So Brightly 8–1, the question
posed was whether the higher-priced contender should be
backed at the odds versus the slightly faster filly.

When I responded that neither filly figured to win on the
cold dope, the discussion quickly enlivened. My inquisitor insisted that Shine So Brightly shaped up as a reasonable bet on
the numbers—and why not?

First, each contender has finished slower than today's par
(97) on speed, always a red flag in figure handicapping. It's silly

6th Hollywood

START
6 FURLONGS
HOLLYWOOD PARK
FINISH

6 FURLONGS. (1.08) MAIDEN CLAIMING. Purse $19,000. Fillies. 2-year-olds. Weight, 119 lbs. Claiming Price $50,000; if for $45,000 allowed 2 lbs.

Uptown Gal
B. f. 2(May), by Marfa—Overwhelme, by Stalwart
MCCARRON C J   **119**   Br.—Lucas D W (Ky)   1990 2 M 1 0 $3,600
Own.—Lukas D W   Tr.—Lukas D Wayne $50,000
     Lifetime 2 0 1 0 $3,600

5Oct90-1SA 6f .214 .453 1:114ft 12 B 117 1¹ 12½ 1½ 2² VlnzulPA⁴ ⓕM32000 75-19 CloudRcer,UptownGl,PulRevere 12
     5Oct90—Veered in start
7Sep90-4Dmr 6f .214 .45¹ 1:111ft 13 B 117 9⁷½10¹²10²⁰10²⁹½ Solis A⁹ ⓕM32000 54-12 LghtnngWtr,CostmKt,ActonAnn 11
     7Sep90—Wide early

Speed Index: Last Race: -6.0   2-Race Avg.: -20.0   2-Race Avg.: -20.0   Overall Avg.: -20.0
Nov 25 SA 6f ft 1:13² H   Nov 19 SA 4f ft :51⁴ H   Nov 12 SA 4f ft :48¹ H   Nov 5 SA 5f ft 1:00² H

Gun Trial
Dk. b. or br. f. 2(Feb), by Court Trial—Gunite, by Crozier
SOLIS A   **119**   Br.—Lucas F W (Fla)   1990 3 M 2 1 $14,800
Own.—Emerald Meadows Ranch   Tr.—Mayberry Brian A $50,000
     Lifetime 3 0 2 1 $14,800

5Oct90-3SA 6f .21¹ .44¹ 1:091ft 3½ B 117 2¹ 31½ 35½ 36 Garcia J A³ ⓕMdn 84-09 MobilePhone,CrCrissim,GunTril 12
     5Oct90—Bumped start
12Aug90-6Dmr 6f .214 .45 1:102ft 10 B 117 1hd 11½ 11 2nk Hansen R D³ ⓕMdn 88-09 ImprtnntLdy,GnTrl,I'mRllDncng 12
     12Aug90—Bumped at 1/2
19Jly90-4Hol 5½f .214 .45² 1.044ft *8-5 118 2hd 3¹ 31½ 2¾ PdrozMA⁶ ⓕM50000 93-12 Hat Girl, Gun Trial, LorettaWolf 12
     19Jly90—Lugged out drive

Speed Index: Last Race: -7.0   3-Race Avg.: -1.6   3-Race Avg.: -1.6   Overall Avg.: -1.6
Nov 23 SA 4f ft :47¹ H   Nov 9 SA 3f ft :36⁴ H

Shine So Brightly
Dk. b. or br. f. 2(Feb), by Slew's Royalty—Washington's Star, by Mr Washington
VELASQUEZ J   **117**   Br.—Hoover & Mazzone (Cal)   1990 2 M 0 1 $4,290
Own.—Tomassian J   Tr.—Marikian Charles M $45,000
     Lifetime 2 0 0 1 $4,290

12Nov90-4Hol 6f .222 .453 1.11 ft 8 LB 119 11½ 1½ 1½ 3² VelsquezJ¹ ⓕSMdn 83-11 FnTlk,SymphonyAtS,ShnSBrntly 9
17Oct90-6SA 6f .212 .44² 1.092ft 5½ B 117 2²½ 2³ 49 10¹⁷¾ OlivaresF¹¹ ⓢMdn 71-11 LBzcch,Cynd'sPrspct,MssWt,fro 12
     17Oct90—Lugged out trip

Speed Index: Last Race: -6.0   2-Race Avg.: -12.0   2-Race Avg.: -12.0   Overall Avg.: -12.0
●Nov 28 SA 3f ft :34¹ H   Oct 29 SA 4f ft :47² H

Real Bubbly
B. f. 2(Feb), by In Reality—Champagne Lover, by Champagne Charlie
DESORMEAUX K J   **119**   Br.—Lin-Drake Farm (Fla)   1990 4 M 0 0 $310
Own.—Oak Tree Farm & Timm   Tr.—Cleveland Gene $50,000
     Lifetime 4 0 0 0 $310

27Sep90-7Fpx 6f .221 .463 1:124ft 9 LB 116 3² 2½ 9⁸½ 99¾ Olivares F³ ⓕMdn 72-10 ClPolyTime,Mrf'sLdy,Wilm'sQuil 10
     27Sep90—Bumped start
1Sep90-4Dmr 6f .214 .44³ 1:10 ft 34 L 117 2¹½ 7¹⁰12²6¹2²⁹½ Meza R Q¹¹ ⓕMdn 60-10 IslandChoice,Quimper,CrCrissim 12
12Aug90-6Dmr 6f .214 .45 1:102ft 35 117 4² 53½ 79 914¾ Black C A² ⓕMdn 73-09 ImprtnntLdy,GnTrl,I'mRllDncng 12
28Jly90-6Dmr 5½f .212 .44⁴ 1:04 ft 91 117 9⁷¾10¹³10²⁰10¹⁴½ Meza R Q¹¹ ⓕMdn 79-09 Shorouk,TitiBought,D'OrRuckus 12
     28Jly90—Wide trip

Speed Index: Last Race: -18.0   3-Race Avg.: -22.0   4-Race Avg.: -19.5   Overall Avg.: -19.5
Nov 24 SA 5f ft :59¹ H   Nov 18 SA 5f R 1:00 H   Nov 12 SA 5f ft 1:00² H   Nov 9 SA 7f ft 1:28³ H

Doll Collection
B. f. 2(Feb), by Lines of Power—Doon's Doll, by Matsadoon
SANTOS J A   **119**   Br.—Drakes C (Ky)   1990 1 M 0 0
Own.—Whitham C & Liz   Tr.—McAnally Ronald $50,000
     Lifetime 1 0 0 0

7Nov90-4Hol 6f .213 .44⁴ 1:094ft 7½ B 119 3½ 2hd 33 68½ Solis A⁸ ⓕM62500 82-07 PulRever,Avis'Sont,PrfctExchng 10

Speed Index: Last Race: -11.0   1-Race Avg.: -11.0   1-Race Avg.: -11.0   Overall Avg.: -11.0
Nov 23 Hol 5f ft 1:00 H   Nov 17 Hol 4f ft :48 H   ●Nov 5 Hol 3f ft :34⁴ H   Oct 31 Hol 6f ft 1:17² H

to attempt to identify the least slow among a field of slow race-horses, however exact the figures. In-depth handicapping replaces figure handicapping at this unhappy junction.

Moreover, on figure handicapping alone, both Gun Trial and Shine So Brightly suffered a fatal shortcoming regularly overlooked among cheaper horses, and Shine So Brightly's case looked rather desperate.

Neither horse having the fastest speed figures figured to control the pace at the second call. At 94 on pace, Shine So Brightly figures four lengths in arrears of Doll Collection at the pace call. If Shine So Brightly runs faster early, improving the 94 to 102, she will almost assuredly run more slowly late, dropping the 95 to 91. Studies of speed and pace figures in combination proved the point beyond dispute. Among frontrunners and pace-presers, when pace figures increase, final figures decrease; particularly among claiming horses.

If Doll Collection were absent here, Gun Trial would figure strongly, having run to the pace call (100) approximately two lengths faster than par (97). But facing a faster pace, and having a final figure below par, Gun Trial at 7–5 should be dismissed.

Trained by the outstanding Brian Mayberry and dropping from maiden to maiden-claiming conditions, Gun Trial certainly remains seductive here, even on comprehensive handicapping, as my persistent neighbor pointed out, but at 7–5 cannot be tolerated. In cheaper competition, pace figures matter mightily. Again, if slower horses are forced to speed up during the early stages, most of them will decelerate in the late stages.

With a pace advantage of a length (102), Doll Collection deserved a longer look here, but her final figure (90) dropped off too steeply to qualify. If allowed a slower pace, Doll Collection should improve her final figure, all right, but not by seven lengths. At 6–1 the filly can be disregarded.

The eventual winner was Real Bubbly, a contender featuring the dropdown from maiden to maiden-claiming ranks. The jockey switch to Kent Desormeaux, four workouts in fifteen days, and improved early speed last out provided extra added attractions. So did the fantastic odds.

Hollywood **6 FURLONGS. (1.08) MAIDEN CLAIMING. Purse $19,000. Fillies. 2-year-olds. Weight, 119 lbs. Claiming Price $50,000; if for $45,000 allowed 2 lbs.**
NOVEMBER 30, 1990
Value of race $19,000; value to winner $10,450; second $3,800; third $2,850; fourth $1,425; fifth $475. Mutuel pool $240,283. Exacta pool $261,833.

Last Raced	Horse	M/Eqt.A.Wt	PP	St	¼	½	Str	Fin	Jockey	Cl'g Pr	Odds $1
27Sep90 7Fpx9	Real Bubbly	Lb 2 119	7	4	41½	2hd	11½	11¾	DesormuxKJ	50000	59.30
7Nov90 4Hol6	Doll Collection	LB 2 119	8	2	21	1½	23	2¾	Santos J A	50000	6.40
	Junior Queen	B 2 119	11	5	73½	62	3½	33½	Stevens G L	50000	2.40
5Oct90 1SA2	Uptown Gal	LB 2 119	1	12	52½	4hd	4½	4¾	McCarron CJ	50000	15.70
8Nov90 2Hol2	Premier Affair	LB 2 117	2	8	8½	84	71½	5hd	Meza R Q	45000	15.70
6Oct90 3SA3	Gun Trial	B 2 119	6	3	1½	31½	51½	61¼	Solis A	50000	1.40
29Aug90 2Dmr7	Huck's Appeal	B 2 112	4	10	111½	91	91½	7¾	DvenportCL5	45000	244.60
5Sep90 6Dmr10	Soha'star	LB 2 119	3	6	6hd	71½	81	8½	Nakatani C S	50000	44.60
12Nov90 4Hol3	Shine So Brightly	LBb 2 117	12	1	3½	51½	61	9nk	Velasquez J	45000	8.60
	Bec's Turn	B 2 117	9	7	12	11½	101½	102½	Ortega L E	45000	233.80
18Oct90 5Bel5	Gold Bijoux	LB 2 119	5	9	101	10hd	116	117	Garcia J A	50000	13.80
4Nov90 6SA6	La Bandida	b 2 119	10	11	91½	12	12	12	Black C A	50000	102.00

OFF AT 3:23. Start good. Won driving. Time, :21⅗, :45, :57⅖, 1:10⅗ Track fast.

$2 Mutuel Prices:			
7–REAL BUBBLY	120.60	44.60	12.00
8–DOLL COLLECTION		10.20	5.40
11–JUNIOR QUEEN			4.20

$2 EXACTA 7–8 PAID $1.125.00.

B. f, (Feb), by In Reality—Champagne Lover, by Champagne Charlie. Trainer Cleveland Gene. Bred by Lin-Drake. Farm (Fla).

REAL BUBBLY, in contention early, vied for the lead on the far turn while along the inner rail, drew clear in the upper stretch and went on to prove best. DOLL COLLECTION, a pace factor from the start, was brushed by GUN TRAIL turning into the stretch and kept to her task enough through the stretch to prove second best. JUNIOR QUEEN, outrun early and wide down the backstretch, entered the stretch five wide, came on in the drive but could not get up. UPTOWN GAL broke slowly, advanced quickly along the inside early to get into contention before going a quarter of a mile, was boxed in turning into the stretch and weakened in the drive. PREMIER AFFAIR lugged out down the backstretch.GUN TRAIL, a pace factor to the stretch, became a bit difficult to handle turning into the stretch when lugging out a bit to brush with DOLL COLLECTION and weakened in the stretch. HUCK'S APPEAL raced greenly early. SOHA' STAR broke a bit awkwardly. SHINE SO BRIGHTLY, close up early and wide down the backstretch, gave way. BEC'S TURN raced greenly early and was wide down the backstretch. GOLD BIJOUX was four wide into the stretch. LA BANDIDA, wide down the backstretch after breaking slowly, was five wide into the stretch.

Owners— 1, Oak Tree Farm & Timm; 2, Whitham C & Liz; 3, Cooke J K; 4, Lukas D W; 5, Allen R; 6, Emerald Meadows Ranch; 7, Fisher & Manzi; 8, Clearman & Idriss; 9, Tomassian J; 10, Hitbound Stable; 11, Sommer Viola; 12, Silver Creek Ranch Inc.

Trainers— 1, Cleveland Gene; 2, McAnally Ronald; 3, Robbins Jay M; 4, Lukas D Wayne; 5, Stein Roger; 6, Mayberry Brian A; 7, Manzi Dominick; 8, Mulhall Richard W; 9, Marikian Charles M; 10, Meairs John M; 11, Martin Frank; 12, Ferraro Stephen.

Unable to secure the lead at the pace call, Gun Trial and Shine So Brightly promptly expired. Figure handicappers might have anticipated that.

On reflection at the finish, my associate noted that winning trainer Gene Cleveland had not won a race "in two seasons." Again the assertion, while valid, was fundamentally insignificant. Low-percentage trainers are far more likely to tally in maiden-claiming races. When other factors look appealing—jockey switch, solid workouts, improved early speed—do not dismiss maiden-claiming contenders on the trainer factor.

If the horses shape up as tolerable, so must be their trainers.

WHEN GOOD HORSES HAVE BAD FIGURES

Among the stickiest problems of figure handicapping is the consistent hard-knocking claiming horse that suddenly reveals declining numbers. The last line clearly represents a disappointing performance, following a small decline the race before.

Today's race will be at the same class level as last out, or maybe a minor drop, but not a precipitous drop.

The instinct is to toss the horse, citing the declining figures as evidence of deteriorating form. Yet a deeper instinct arouses the handicapper's hesitation. The last line looks peculiarly unrepresentative, the second race back a familiarly solid performance.

Will the consistent hard-knocker rebound to former heights, or continue the dive?

Another figure horse I strongly preferred on opening day of the Hollywood Park fall meeting, 1990, lined up against precisely this kind of figure phenomenon at the $32,000 claiming level, the contest at seven furlongs for 3up. The four-year-old I liked revealed an intriguing figure situation, a pace-distance twist that might render the colt a juicy overlay today.

Examine the pair of contenders below.

On recent evidence, Babyitscoldoutside shaped up as a seductive figure play here. Referring to Thoro-Graph figures alone, last out only, Babyitscoldoutside gets a 12^1 and High Hook a 16, the latter number presumptively an extension of a decline that began September 6 at Del Mar.

Moreover, the Quirin pace figure for Babyitscoldoutside's middle-distance race last out at Santa Anita is a strong 112. To convert Quirin pace figures of routes to sprint figures (final), subtract 3. I estimated Babyitscoldoutside might run a 109 at seven furlongs at Hollywood Park, then lowered the estimate by two points (107) to reflect the track-to-track par differences at $1^1/_{16}$ miles between Santa Anita and Hollywood Park. The Hollywood seven-furlong par for older $32,000 claiming horses is 105.

The Quirin-style speed figures earned by High Hook in its winning sprints at Del Mar were 107 (August 6) and 106 (July 13).

I felt Babyitscoldoutside would whip a sliding High Hook this day, and almost salivated when the odds on the four-year-old steadied at 9–2. Actually, I gave High Hook little recognition here.

But wait a minute! My Thoro-Graph consultant Ben Bollinger insisted High Hook would run back to its best figures today, a trio of 9s. He alluded to the horse's pattern as 0-2-X, a shorthand I dare not attempt to explain.

But the logic was far from unpersuasive. Consider again the pattern of High Hook's latest five Thoro-Graph figures:

Oct 4	16
Sept 6	11
Aug 22	9
Aug 6	9
July 13	9

High Hook consistently dispenses a figure of 9. He tailed off to 11 at Del Mar on September 6, a $6^1/_2$-furlong sprint versus $50,000 claiming horses, the toughest group High Hook had ever challenged. Examine that line again. Notice that High Hook tracked a dizzying 44 flat pace to the quarter-pole, before expiring by a half-length in a furious final time (1:14.4).

This is the key race in High Hook's pattern. As Bollinger stated it, High Hook had overextended himself trying to defeat rugged horses in a rapid race at every call. The overextension resulted in a 2-point decline in the figures (9 to 11).

When this happens to good horses, the next figure should be a further and more significant decline. In fact, the steeper the decline, the better. Bollinger noted he would prefer High Hook even more if the last figure had been a 26, not just 16. The unusually poor effort reflects the overextension the race before.

Following the dismal performance, the genuine article resurfaces, and the consistent hard-knockers rebound to prior high figures.

High Hook followed the script absolutely. From mid-pack, the eight-year-old gelding moved up powerfully entering the stretch. He then chased, collared, and gamely defeated a second eight-year-old gelding named Bright And Right, also a hard-knocker who ran a big one this day.

Babyitscoldoutside was hardly disgraced. He finished a game third, beaten scarcely two lengths, despite being used between horses early on the pace and never getting a breather. But High Hook won, and impressively, and I doubt Babyitscoldoutside could have handled him under the best circumstances.

Below is the result chart. High Hook's figure, Quirin style, was a familiar 106.

SEVENTH RACE
Hollywood
NOVEMBER 7, 1990

7 FURLONGS. (1.20%) CLAIMING. Purse $19,000. 3-year-olds and upward. Weights, 3-year-olds, 120 lbs.; older, 122 lbs. Non-winners of two races since September 26 allowed 3 lbs.; a race since then, 5 lbs. Claiming price $32,000; for each $2,000 to $28,000, allowed 2 lbs. (Races when entered for $25,000 or less not considered.)

Value of race $19,000; value to winner $10,450; second $3,800; third $2,850; fourth $1,425; fifth $475. Mutuel pool $190,531. Exacta pool $156,962.

Last Raced	Horse	M/Eqt.A.Wt	PP St	¼	½	Str	Fin	Jockey	Cl'g Pr	Odds $1
4Oct90 5SA⁸	High Hook	LB 8 117	7 2	6ʰᵈ	4¹	42½	1ⁿᵏ	Solis A	32000	*2.10
17Oct90 4SA²	Bright And Right	LB 8 113	5 3	52½	32	11	22	Pedroza M A	28000	4.30
7Oct90 4SA⁴	Babyitscoldoutside	LBb 4 118	3 5	2½	2¹	2½	31½	Pincay L Jr	32000	4.60
20Oct90 5SA⁶	King Of Bazaar	LBb 6 113	6 7	7	7	55	41¼	Velasquez J	28000	23.50
27Oct90 9SA³	Right Rudder	LBb 6 117	4 1	1½	1ʰᵈ	31	56	McCarron CJ	32000	2.10
24Mar90 3SA⁶	No Story	LB 4 113	2 4	4ʰᵈ	6ʰᵈ	6ʰᵈ	6⁹	Davis R G	28000	27.50
20Oct90 5SA⁴	Cancun Native-Mx	LB 5 113	1 6	31½	51½	7	7	Santos J A	28000	8.60

*—Actual Betting Favorite.

OFF AT 3:48. Start good. Won driving. Time, :22, :45, 1:09½, 1:21½ Track fast.

$2 Mutuel Prices:	7-HIGH HOOK	6.20	3.80	2.60
	5-BRIGHT AND RIGHT		4.20	2.80
	3-BABYITSCOLDOUTSIDE			3.00

$2 EXACTA 7-5 PAID $19.00.

B. g, by Exceller—Eehook, by Francis S. Trainer Spawr Bill. Bred by Hudson E J Sr (Ky).

HIGH HOOK, allowed to drop back early after an alert start, raced wide down the backstretch while not far back, came on steadily in the drive and got up. BRIGHT AND RIGHT, in contention early and wide down the backstretch, engaged for the lead approaching the quarter pole while three wide, battled for command the rest of the way and could not quite outfinish HIGH HOOK. BABYITSCOLDOUTSIDE vied for the early lead and weakened late. KING OF BAZAAR, devoid of early speed, entered the stretch four wide and could not gain the needed ground in the stretch. RIGHT RUDDER vied for the lead until coming to the furlong marker and weakened. NO STORY had no visible mishap. CANCUN NATIVE-MX had early speed and faltered badly.

Owners— 1, Sell C R; 2, Gleason Melissa; 3, Siegel M-Jan-Samantha; 4, Ridgewood Racing Stable Inc; 5, Richmond J Jr; 6, Murphy-Sasselli-Sigband Mmes; 7, Belmonte-Friedman-Stephen .

Trainers— 1, Spawr Bill; 2, Canani Julio C; 3, Mayberry Brian A; 4, Hronec Philip; 5, Marshall Robert W; 6, Murphy Marcus J; 7, Mitchell Mike.

Overweight: Babyitscoldoutside 1 pound.

Right Rudder was claimed by Charles R; trainer, Shulman Sanford.

Postscript

The main ingredients of the pattern are a telltale three:

1. A consistent runner, especially claiming horses; that is, horses that regularly earn the same impressive kind of figures
2. A slightly declining figure (two points), following an unusually demanding effort, often against classier horses
3. A decidedly poor performance following the small decline, the figure dropping by as many as 10 to 20 points

The dismal performance amounts to an aberration, a temporary setback due to overexertion. Forgive the abysmal figure. Expect a rebound to the horse's best figures today. Especially if the consistent winner is being lowered slightly in class.

WHEN BAD HORSES HAVE GOOD FIGURES

Not long into the Santa Anita winter season of 1991, in mid-card of December 31, I was startled to hear from my Thoro-Graph informant that the figure horse in the ninth race was the contemptible gelding Time For Sakarto.

"He's a strong play today," insisted Ben Bollinger. "He's clearly best on the numbers. Plus he's dropping into a dead field and gets a switch to [Gary] Stevens . . ."

This is the kind of convoluted thinking for which figure addicts might be publicly punished, if not by flogging, at least by exposure.

It was a $12,500 claiming event at a mile for 3up Cal-breds. Time For Sakarto's record looked like this:

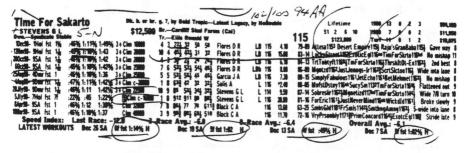

The seven-year-old was 2 for 51 lifetime, 0 for 20 in the past two years. A chronic nonwinner, a truly desperate racehorse!

What matters today, of course, to figure devotees, is that Time For Sakarto sports a superior figure.

But does he?

Below are the Quirin-style speed and pace figures for the gelding's last three races. Par today is 101—no adjustment downward for claiming Cal-breds, which usually match the pars of open claiming races in southern California.

	Pace	*Speed*
Dec 1	100	94
Nov 12	102	103
Oct 28	102	98

Excusing the December 1 flop, a forgiving concession, the bet today is predicated on the November 12 final figure, a $20,000 performance, and two lengths superior to today's par. The pace figure for that day beats today's par too, but this extra ammunition is superfluous to Thoro-Graph users.

The drop to $12,500 claiming, jockey switch to Stevens, and the restriction to Cal-bred competition, bulwark Bollinger's support for the high-figure horse.

But something far more fundamental destroys the case entirely, and here Thoro-Graph users, privy as they are to a complete history of a horse's figures—51 races describing Time For Sakarto—cannot be lightly excused.

Horses like Time For Sakarto—2 for 51 lifetime, with many more seconds and thirds than wins—when they do run well, inevitably finish close to the winner, not in front, and regardless of the winner's figure.

If the winner November 12 at $20,000 claiming had run a 100, Time For Sakarto would not have won by earning its 102, but would have been beaten a length or two anyhow, earning a 99 or 98. If the winner instead earns a 105, Time For Sakarto runs close enough to lose, earning a misleading 103. When Time For Sakarto drops to lower levels, instead of supplying the 103 figure handicappers expect, the horse now dispenses a 98, or a 94 even, as Time For Sakarto did at 4–1 versus $16,000 claimers December 1.

The point is plain. When older chronic nonwinners earn high figures, discount the figures. If the horses typically run close while losing, or run not at all, do not be lulled into a figure bet that represents a mirage.

When horses like Time For Sakarto do win, the feat is accomplished by one of two contrivances. One, the horses unexpectedly draw clear in the upper stretch, and gallop evenly to the wire. No stretch contest emerges, which would allow the animals to lose, as they prefer. Two, a rapid, hotly contested pace collapses in mid-stretch. The chronic nonwinner ambles along evenly and picks up the exhausted horses nearing the finish.

Neither circumstance is amenable to figure handicapping.

The logical figure horse in the $12,500 claiming race where Bollinger preferred Time For Sakarto was not altogether evident at face value. It looked like this:

The speed and pace figure for Gibson's Choice's last three races:

	Pace	Speed
Dec 15	102	83
Nov 18	108	100
Nov 5	95	103

Par today, to recall, is 101.

The last line can be tossed, although its effects cannot. After claiming the consistent four-year-old gelding for $12,500 October 24, low-percentage trainer Jude Feld wins with it for $16,000 twelve days later, and thirteen days after that gets an impressive second in a $12,500 starter handicap at Bay Meadows. The starter handicap at $12,500 translates to open claiming competition of $25,000, at least, and may include horses valued as high as $50,000. In fact, the winner, Traveled In Search, is a hard-hitting good one in northern California. Gibson's Choice blazed a sizzling pace that day (108), not its customary running style, and held second, almost winning.

On December 15, at Hollywood Park, trainer Feld demonstrated why he has not yet been nominated for anyone's Hall of Fame by sticking Gibson's Choice, at the peak of its form, in an allowance route his horse can scarcely survive. Under Chris

Davenport, the low-level gelding is plastered unmercifully, after attempting to contest the pace.

On figures, either the November 18 or November 5 race beats today's field clearly. Thoro-Graph clients would disagree, unaware of, and unimpressed by, the November 18 pace figure. But among frontrunners and pace-pressers, final figures and pace figures can be added, should be added, the technique flattering Gibson's Choice on November 18. The appropriate figures to rely upon, however, occurred November 5, a sluggish pace at today's relative class, perhaps a notch better.

If the allowance debacle has not thrown Gibson's Choice out of kilter, he figures to rebound successfully. On that point, the sharp workout at six furlongs on the training track December 24 (1:14.1) has been reassuring.

If Gibson's Choice reverts to his accustomed running style, positioned a few lengths behind the pace, and responds as he did November 5, he should earn a figure above par (101), and prevail against today's opposition, including Time For Sakarto's recent 103. The bettors backed Gibson's Choice as their 2–1 fa-

NINTH RACE **Santa Anita** DECEMBER 31, 1990	1 MILE. (1.33⅖) CLAIMING. Purse $15,000. 3–year–olds and upward bred in California. Weights, 3–year–olds 118 lbs.; older 121 lbs. Non–winners of two races at one mile or over since October 2 allowed 2 lbs.; of such a race since November 6 allowed 4 lbs.; since October 2 allowed 6 lbs. Claiming price $12,500; if for $10,500 allowed 2 lbs. (Maiden or races when entered for $10,000 or less not considered)

Value of race $15,000; value to winner $8,250; second $3,000; third $2,250; fourth $1,125; fifth $375. Mutuel pool $305,760. Exacta pool $486,857.

Last Raced	Horse	M/Eqt.A.Wt	PP St	¼	½	¾	Str	Fin	Jockey	Cl'g Pr	Odds $1
15Dec90 9Hol8	Gibson's Choice	LB 4 117	8 1	2¹½	2³	1ʰᵈ	1¹	1¹½	Flores D R	12500	2.20
28Nov90 5Hol9	Fearless Days	LB 5 116	7 7	6½	4½	4¹½	2½	2²½	DelhoussyeE	12500	16.90
21Dec90 9Hol4	No Story	LB 4 115	1 3	1ʰᵈ	1½	2¹½	3²	3³	Davis R G	12500	10.40
14Dec90 5Hol10	Flying Revenge	LBb 4 115	3 2	3¹½	3½	3ʰᵈ	4¹	4¹½	Pedroza M A	12500	36.00
1Dec90 1Hol5	Time For Sakarto	LB 7 115	10 5	5¹	7½	7¹½	6¹½	5²½	Stevens G L	12500	5.70
8Dec90 5Hol7	Papa Stan	LB 4 116	2 6	7¹	10	10	9²½	6ʰᵈ	Santos J A	12500	15.80
12Dec90 5Hol1	Simply Fabulous	LB 4 119	4 10	9½	8ʰᵈ	5¹½	5½	7½	Solis A	12500	2.90
16Dec90 2Hol1	Rising Cari	LBb 6 115	5 4	4½	5¹	6¹	7½	8¹½	Boulanger G	12500	8.00
12Dec90 5Hol3	Remar	LBb 6 115	6 8	8²½	6¹½	8ʰᵈ	8½	9⁴	Baze R A	12500	7.20
21Dec90 9Hol6	Interbend	LB 4 115	9 9	10	9¹	9ʰᵈ	10	10	Meza R Q	12500	66.90

OFF AT 4:48. Start good for all but SIMPLY FABULOUS. Won driving. Time, :23⅖, :47, 1:11⅖, 1:23⅖, 1:36⅖ Track fast.

$2 Mutuel Prices:	8–GIBSON'S CHOICE	6.40	4.40	3.80
	7–FEARLESS DAYS		12.20	6.60
	1–NO STORY			5.80
	$2 EXACTA 8–7 PAID $113.20.			

Dk. b. or br. g, by Just Right Mike—Forward Move, by Fleet Discovery. Trainer Feld Jude T. Bred by Rupert Nancy L (Cal).

GIBSON'S CHOICE, a pace factor from the outset, had the lead at the furlong marker and kept to his task to remain in front the rest of the way. FEARLESS DAYS, outrun early, rallied to threaten at the quarter pole, forced the issue through the final furlong but could not get by GIBSON'S CHOICE in the last furlong. NO STORY, a pace factor to the furlong marker, weakened a bit. FLYING REVENGE, close up early, entered the stretch four wide and weakened in the drive. TIME FOR SAKARTO was wide down the backstretch. SIMPLY FABULOUS lost his best chance when he broke poorly to get away quite well behind the field, made a move to get closer on the far turn but expeded so much energy in doing so that he gave way in the drive as a result. RISING CARI was outrun. REMAR was wide down the backstretch. INTERBEND, wide down the backstretch after being four wide into the clubhouse turn, was five wide into the stretch.

vorite, offering Time For Sakarto at 5–1, justifications for avoiding both horses today.

As events proceeded, Gibson's Choice not only reverted to winning form, but was pushed to his best figure in months (105) by a seemingly out-of-form recent shipper from Exhibition Park.

Time For Sakarto, alas, did not run well enough to lose even by a few deceiving lengths. He did not get a call. Beaten eight lengths, Time For Sakarto's final figure was a more typical 97, three lengths slower than par for older $10,000 claiming males.

FIGURE STANDOUTS VERSUS REALITY

The Alydar colt below towered above an overnight handicap field on the figures. He showed the high speed figure, high pace figure, and had looked especially terrifying at today's distance, a one-turn mile, at the same track just thirteen days ago.

The main competition on local figures is also presented, and the disparity on the numbers should be plain.

[Handwritten annotations: 108/106 108 AA; C-107/108 107 AF]

Greydar 6++
STEVENS G L   120
Own.—Calumet Farm Inc

Ro. c. 3(Mar), by Alydar—Majestic Gold, by Hatchet Man
Br.—Calumet Farm (Ky)
Tr.—Lukas D Wayne
Lifetime 10 3 4 1 $94,210

1990 7 2 3 1 $79,375
1989 3 1 1 0 $14,835

12Nov90-7Hol	1 :44² 1:09 1:34 ft	*2	B 114	2½ 2½ 11½ 14½	StevensGL ⑥Aw34000 94-14	Greydr,BoldCurrent,FutureCreer 11
21Oct90-9SA	7f :22 :44² 1:21 ft	3½	B 114	4² 2nd 2½ 2½	StevensGL 1 Aw36000 92-13	Timebank,Greydar,Mr.DndyDncer 9
21Oct90—Broke slowly						
7Oct90-7SA	1½ :46³ 1:10² 1:41²ft	8-5	B 116	1hd 1hd 2¹ 34½	VlenzulPA ! Aw40000 91-12	Warcraft, Final Forecast,Greydar 9
7Oct90—Stumbled start						
29Sep90-11Fpx a1¼ :47¹ 1:11³ 1:48²ft	*9-5	B 122	4² 3¹ 3² 2nk	Flores DR ⑥Pom Dby104 —	Dchi'sFolly,Greydr,RocketGibrltr 9
29Sep90—Stumbled start						
2Sep90-7Dmr	1½ :46¹ 1:09⁴ 1:40²ft	*7-5	B 116	1¹ 11½ 1½ 2hd	VlenzulPA ! Aw41000 99-07	Shaynoor,Greydr,AdvocteTrining 7
13Aug90-7Dmr	1 :45² 1:09² 1:35³ft	*2	B 114	3½ 1² 1³ 1½	StevensGL¹ Aw36000 88-14	Greydar, Oh Wow, Insert 7
6Aug90-7Dmr	6f :21³ :44 1:07⁴ft	4	116	53½ 55½ 45½ 410½	StevensGL² Aw33000 91-08	Coe'sTizzy,CandymanBee,Mcheth 7
6Aug90—Broke slowly						
16Dec89-10Lrl	7f :23 :45² 1:24¹ft	3½	113	5⁴ 46½ 48½ 517½	Pino M G² Bimelech 75-19	Smelly,WoodenInjun,AggieSocial 5
22Oct89-5Lrl	6½f :22⁴ :47 1:19²ft	*4-5	120	44½ 21½ 11½ 1³	DesormeuxKJ⁹ Mdn 82-16	Greydar,Bardland,SaratogSmrts 14
7Oct89-7Pim	6f :23⁴ :47⁴ 1:12³ft	8½	120	52½ 2² 2³ 24½	Rivera H Jr¹¹ Mdn 78-26	Jon'sHoney,Greydr,TemperTime 12

Speed Index: Last Race: +8.0   3–Race Avg.: +5.0   5–Race Avg.: +4.6   Overall Avg.: +2.3
Nov 20 SA 5f gd 1:02² H   Nov 6 SA 5f ft :59³ H   Oct 29 SA 5f ft 1:01 H   Oct 16 SA 5f ft 1:00³ H

[Handwritten annotations: 111/104 104 AS]

Due To The King
DELAHOUSSAYE E   114
Own.—Seltzer Bonnie J

Dk. b. or br. c. 3(Apr), by King Concorde—De Declare, by Peter Vadnais
Br.—Seltzer Bonnie J (Cal)
Tr.—Dotson James W
Lifetime 19 5 2 3 $203,813

1990 13 4 2 1 $137,025
1989 6 1 0 2 $65,788
Turf 4 0 1 0 $13,750

3Nov90-4SA	6f :21 :43¹ 1:08²ft	6½	LB115	7⁶ 66½ 66½ 53½	NtCS⁵ ⑤Ca CpSptH 91-11	VlintPete,SenstionlStr,AnswerDo 9
3Nov90—Wide stretch						
29Sep90-11Fpx a1¼ :47¹ 1:11³ 1:48²ft	3	L 114	3² 4² 5⁴ 75½	Garcia JA⁴ Pom Dby 99 —	Dchi'sFolly,Greydr,RocketGibrltr 9
7Sep90-12Fpx	6½f :21¹ :44² 1:16¹ft	*6-5	LB122	52½ 21½ 21½ 1hd	Garcia J A¹ Foothill 96-10	DueToThKing,CndymnB,CovWy 10
29Aug90-8Dmr	7f :22 :44¹ 1:20⁴ft	19	LB115	54½ 54½ 4³ 54½	BazeRA⁷ P O' Brn H 93-12	SnstonlStr,FrostFr,ErnYourStps 9
29Aug90—4-wide stretch						

The two rated one-two in the wagering, Hollywood Park bettors supporting Greydar at even money.

Greydar would break from the rail, and Hollywood Park had experienced a negative rail bias since opening day, three weeks ago. Examine the past performances, the figures, and the data presented below the horses' records.

WINNING POST POSITIONS

HOLLYWOOD PARK
(November 7 to November 18, Inclusive)

	(Main Track)							(Turf Track)					
	....SPRINTS.....			.....ROUTES......				....SPRINTS.....			.....ROUTES......		
	(Under One Mile)			(One Mile & Over)				(Under One Mile)			(One Mile & Over)		
P.P.	STS	WINS	PCT.	STS	WINS	PCT.	P.P.	STS	WINS	PCT.	STS	WINS	PCT.
1	46	2	.04	30	2	.07	1	2	1	.50	21	3	.14
2	46	1	.02	30	3	.10	2	2	0	.00	21	4	.19
3	46	1	.02	30	6	.20	3	2	1	.50	21	3	.14
4	46	10	.22	30	4	.13	4	2	0	.00	21	3	.14
5	46	5	.11	30	0	.00	5	2	0	.00	21	1	.05
6	46	7	.15	29	2	.07	6	2	0	.00	19	6	.32
7	43	6	.14	25	5	.20	7	2	0	.00	17	0	.00
8	32	3	.00	21	1	.05	8	2	0	.00	13	0	.00
9	29	0	.00	18	2	.11	9	1	0	.00	8	1	.13
10	25	5	.20	16	2	.13	10	0	0	.00	8	0	.00
11	21	4	.19	12	3	.25	11	0	0	.00	4	0	.00
12 & UP	13	2	.15	9	0	.00	12 & UP	0	0	.00	3	0	.00

Can an even-money shot with a four-length advantage on the figures, capable of setting a faster pace, and the class of the field, overcome a negative post position bias?

It depends on the intensity of the bias.

The one-post at Hollywood Park had been 2 for 46 in sprints, the two-post 1 for 46. With win percentages below those of other posts by greater than 50 percent, the inside posts were clearly performing at a real disadvantage.

At 2 for 30 attempts in routes, the inside in routes is not quite as hapless. Or is it? One-turn miles are routinely grouped with two-turn routes in the *Form's* post position compilations. In fact, no horse had yet won from the one-post in one-turn miles.

The figures aside, a serious wager on Greydar appeared preposterous. Par here was 109. It wasn't as though Greydar had recorded a 112 or 113 at the distance and might cruise around regardless. Where par figures exist against a strong negative bias, the bias supersedes the figures.

Figure handicappers might have anticipated that, and prepared to scour the field for logical alternatives. Shippers from the Meadowlands, Louisiana Downs, and Bay Meadows studded this field, with figures available for none of them. Greydar looked best on cold dope, all right, but one of the shippers looked like this:

Figures always work best in expert hands, and especially well for expertise that encompasses know-how extending beyond the cold numbers. Figure handicappers who did not know that the Gator Handicap is a listed stakes open to older horses, or that the Rare Earth Derby attaches to a purse of $100,000, or that the Balmoral Derby is also a listed stakes, purse of $50,000, operated at a disadvantage. They could not recognize Bedeviled as the well-backed listed stakes winner and classy hombre that he definitely was.

Situated outside, owned by John Franks, trained by Jack Van Berg, to be mounted by Kent Desormeaux, at 6–1 Bedeviled represented an attractive alternative to a frontrunner running at even money against a vicious negative rail bias. The retreat from older listed stakes horses to overnight three-year-olds constituted a noticeable dropdown, notwithstanding the trip from Louisiana to southern California. In eight races lifetime, Bedeviled had already shipped to six racetracks, and had won at three of them.

If Greydar disappeared fighting the bias, this was the likeliest benefactor. At the odds, the wager makes perfect sense, even for figure handicappers fastened to the figures. With the exacta offered as well, figure handicappers can protect their heresy in a combination bet featuring Greydar top and bottom.

The running testified as to how troublesome the negative rail bias can be. Greydar did not get a smell.

The moral should be obvious. Whenever other handicapping

factors might logically predominate, figure standouts only look unbeatable. The numbers are intended to represent reality, not substitute for it.

WET FIGURES

Is it too obvious to declare that several horses record by a wide margin their most impressive speed figures on wet tracks? Here is an undeniable illustration.

PENNY'S BUCK

3yo (Mar) colt. dk. bay/brown $75,000
Trainer: Robert P Lake CLM. PRICE
Owner: Ping W Tam

Sire: **Buckaroo** ($10,000)
  by Buckpasser
Dam: **Penny's Chelly**
  by Rixdal
Bred in FL by Harriet Heubeck &
  Elmer Heubeck Jr.   **113**

Career:	15	3	2	2	$61,120	
Wet:	3	2	1	0	$32,720	**1991:** 11 2 2 2 $51,020
Turf:	1	0	0	0	$0	**1990:** 4 1 0 0 $10,200
Dist:	0	0	0	0	$0	**Sar:** 1 0 0 1 $3,120

Penny's Buck moves up boldly in the goo. Figure handicappers like that. Many of them might cut and paste Penny's Buck, such that the 3YO becomes an entry in a file of horses that prefer mud and slop. On the next muddy occasion, the telltale races might be missing from the published record.

Yet something is amiss in the Penny's Buck scenario. What's wrong with this picture?

It's Penny's Buck's paltry odds. Figure handicappers dig for mudders that not only improve dramatically, but also pay high odds in the process. In other words, the mud intimates a form reversal that might return a generous overlay to the winner's circle.

When horses have won big in the mud with abnormally high figures and pay high odds in the upset, those are the prized specimens in the figure handicapper's mud and slop file.

IMPROVING PACE STANDOUTS

In low-level claiming races, claiming races limited to 3YOs, and especially maiden-claiming races, speed figures are often so abysmally bad as to be meaningless. Figure handicappers should hunt eagerly for stickout pace figures, which under a variety of circumstances will be decisive and at attractive prices.

Below are the speed figures for a lineup of $32,000 maiden-claiming horses (bottom of the barrel) traveling 6½ furlongs at Fairplex Park on September 13, 1991, a Friday, no less. Which do figure handicappers prefer?

Turn To Pass	39	Derby Creek	47
Christian's Hope	49	New Mexico	43
Bobbery	32	Siku	67
Animal Talk	59	Yucaipian	22
Karl Nijinsky	54	Sabre Fare	35
Tank's Ruler	51	Custom Work	53

Not surprisingly, the favorite was Siku, ostensibly the figure horse at 67.

Now consider the past performances for Siku and the eventual winner by the length of the stretch.

Now examine the pace figures for Bobbery and Siku in their last two starts:

		Pace	Speed
Bobbery	Aug 23	104	84
	Aug 19	107	70
Siku	Sept 4	95	96
	Aug 8	91	90

Bobbery should command the lead from Siku here by five to eight lengths at the second call. In cheap races, that's conclusive whenever surrounding circumstances suggest additional improvement today.

Review Bobbery's past performances again. Obviously the colt has been blasted to the rear in the late stages of its races, five times in succession.

Yet the most recent race shows marked improvement at the stretch call. Today the horse is dropping a peg on the maiden-claiming ladder. Today also represents the third start following a lengthy layoff. Third and fourth races following long layoffs normally deliver best efforts. The trainer is D. Wayne Lukas, a horseman in possession of few outright plugs. A leading bull-ring jockey stays aboard for today's dropdown.

In any context of incremental improvement, standout pace figures in cheap races can be expected to dominate. The awful speed figures and humiliating finishes do not apply. Handicappers want to know what horses can do when they run their race, not when they've stopped. A despairingly bad finish in a context of rapid pace figure supersedes below-par speed figures when horses have persevered but faltered.

Bobbery won the Fairplex Park race by no fewer than 16 lengths and paid $8.00. Pace analysts might have considered the mutuel a handout.

Probably the biggest sucker bet of figure handicapping lands on cheap claiming horses whose speed figures top the woeful field they face, but nonetheless settle significantly below par for today's class and distance. The Quirin-style par for the Fairplex maiden-claiming sprint was 98. When both the speed figure and pace figure undercut par, the horses should be tossed. When all the horses in the field possess speed figures below par, the race is not very susceptible to figure handicapping.

But it may be highly conducive to pace analysis.

Other than a superior pace figure, handicappers should require only some additional traces of improvement. Bobbery showed improving form, a drop in class, and the third start following a lengthy layoff for a prominent stable. That's more than enough, and often tantamount to success. If the odds beckon, by all means make the plays.

IDENTIFYING REPRESENTATIVE FIGURES

A pattern unmentioned by Thoro-Graph, The Sheets, or by most other figure analysts qualifies as perhaps the best figure play of them all. The pattern consists of a couple of poor-performance figures preceded by a winning figure that applies absolutely today. The pattern can be recognized only by alert, well-tooled handicappers.

One of the shrewdest, most persuasive figure analysts in the country is New York's Mark Hopkins, a contributing writer for *The Racing Times* and now *Daily Racing Form*. In September of 1991, Hopkins presented a bettable pattern of speed figures that defy improvement as an illustration of the topic. Unable to locate a better example, I shall instead paraphrase his. First examine the past performances of Hopkins's discovery and entertain his introduction to the betting opportunity.

"At first glance, Notable Tsar's form is less than inspiring. Badly beaten in each of his last two races, he's the type of horse easily overlooked. Those handicappers who dug a little deeper into Notable Tsar's past performances, however, discovered a wonderful betting opportunity."

On September 14, 1991, at Belmont Park, exactly a month following his wretched race of August 14, Notable Tsar was lowered into a $25,000 claiming race at 1 1/16 miles by his new trainer, and won smartly. He paid $19.20. As Hopkins tells, horses like this may be few and far between, but the mutuels make the waits worthwhile.

To begin, whenever one or two dismal speed figures have been preceded by an impressively sharp speed figure, handicappers should instinctively pause to consider whether the woeful figures can be excused. In his third race back, Notable Tsar had recorded a Beyer figure of 90, and not for the first time.

Since then, Notable Tsar showed speed figures of 71 July 1 at Belmont Park and 72 August 14 at Saratoga. A clue the 72 might be excusable can be found in the trip line of the past performances: "Wrestled back, rated two-wide, swung out, did not threaten." Notable Tsar usually raced forwardly, or at least comfortably behind the early pace. When taken back out of the gate due to mishap, numerous horses lose interest, and so do numerous jockeys. The August 14 figure can surely be excused.

On July 1, Notable Tsar had attempted to duplicate his excellent form of June 19 on the turf, a footing on which the gelding had finished out of the money in five previous attempts, also shown in the past performances. The July 1 figure is also forgivable.

The third race back remains the most recent representative line in Notable Tsar's record. That performance resulted in a Speed figure of 90. If Notable Tsar could duplicate the 90 against $25,000 claiming horses, he might readily win.

Hopkins also provided the latest Beyer figure and betting odds for each of the horses entered in Notable Tsar's $25,000 claiming race of September 14.

Horse	Last Beyer Figure	Odds
Onnagata	89	6-to-1
Space Above	86	9-to-2
Hawking S.W.	85	2-to-1
Gin And Bitters	83	11-to-1
Pocket Streaker	82	9-to-5e
Bowdoin Street	78	16-to-1
Sayaret	73	9-to-5e
Notable Tsar	72	8-to-1
Uncle Ale	62	29-to-1

Other circumstances present on September 14 convincingly supported the case for a strong rebound.

The Belmont track surface was wet that day. Handicappers should notice Notable Tsar's best-ever speed figure of 90 on June 19 was recorded at Belmont Park on a wet track surface. The horse won at 8–1 by three handy lengths, after pressing the pace throughout.

The past performances also reveal Notable Tsar's best-ever speed figures for three distinct categories: dirt, wet tracks, and at a distance within a sixteenth of a mile of today's distance. Notable Tsar's 90 occurred at Belmont Park on the dirt at 1⅛ miles on a wet surface. Hopkins notes that rarely will handicappers see that a single race provides a horse's best-ever figure in the three separate categories.

The final, conclusive piece of the puzzle surrounded the new trainer. It was Dave Monaci, a fresh Big Apple face particularly adept at winning with recent claims. Monaci did not claim Notable Tsar, but obtained the horse privately—information supplied on race day by *The Racing Times*'s excellent New York public selector, Kurt Paseka. The September 14 race at $25,000 claiming would be Notable Tsar's first for Monaci.

Trips, track surface, trainer pattern, high speed figure preceding a pair of poor but excusable figures—everything fell in place and could be tied together like a pack of dynamite.

The specifics will vary interestingly, but whenever speed figures too obviously poor have been preceded by good speed figures, handicappers are urged to discover whether an exploitable pattern exists. When the details of the pattern can be stitched together in a way similar to the Notable Tsar situation, and the odds beckon, make the plays. Because the overlays have been identified as a function of painstaking, fundamentally correct handicapping, many of the horses will win. Profits will run high.

Of the several bettable patterns of figure handicapping, poor-but-excusable recent performances will be most transparent to the best of handicappers everywhere. The pattern therefore approaches the ideal.

PART FOUR

Realities

THE BASIC EDUCATION OF BEN BOLLINGER

OVER A WEDNESDAY LUNCH in the Santa Anita Turf Club during winter of 1991, not two years since he had become a dedicated figure handicapper, Ben Bollinger looked, sounded, and was deadpan serious when he told me, "I honestly believe I have more winners than anyone."

We had just compared notes on the afternoon's program. The consultation had been a habit of roughly two years, or ever since Bollinger had begun buying, at thirty dollars a day, the speed figures developed and marketed by Thoro-Graph. To borrow Bollinger's guess-timate, we liked the same horses "about 75 percent of the time."

Our speed figures, vastly dissimilar in kind and origin, proved compatible in the majority of races. No surprise, really, as professional speed figures might be expected to exhibit a strong degree of compatibility, yet Bollinger had frequently complimented me on achieving the same insights as to the probable outcomes as he himself possessed. The compliments were genuine, even heartfelt, and customarily delivered with a touch of irony. Outside of Thoro-Graph's clientele, I doubt that Ben had ever met another figure handicapper.

Ben's salute qualified as reminiscent too of the male bonding that evolved among a few thousand figure handicappers across the nation in the years since Andrew Beyer in 1975 had annointed speed handicapping as "the way, the truth, and the light." Implicit in the salutations was the message that figure handicappers stood among the chosen few; the only people capable of beating the races. The assertion was no more valid then than it is now, as there can be several ways to skin the races. What was true in the late 1970s that no longer applies, however, is that expert figure handicappers then enjoyed a tremendous edge on the game. As more and more horseplayers turned to speed figures as the method of choice, à la Ben Bollinger, inexorably the precious edge receded. Expert figure handicappers still beat the races, only not as easily and not as profitably.

Frankly, I had initiated the comparisons we both came to appreciate. "What's Thoro-Graph's best bet of the day?" I would challenge Ben. "Who's got the top figure in the next race?"

My interest traced to curiosity regarding the accuracy of the Thoro-Graph numbers. I had been applying speed figures of varying vintages for upwards of a decade, but had not experienced Thoro-Graph's numbers. They proved to be professional and excellent, to be sure, as Bollinger had assured me at first inquiry.

Perhaps the overarching endorsement of figure handicapping is that I have never met anyone whose game the figures did not improve. Thoro-Graph's figures had moved Bollinger up immediately, and he is not the type to let anyone deny it.

At the lunch, as usual, Bollinger and I agreed on several of the day's most probable winners, but we differed sharply about the first. Sure enough, as if on cue following Bollinger's assertion about having more winners than anyone else, his horse won. The payoff was generous too. In the next several minutes, Ben jabbed me lightly regarding the daily parade of winners he was fully capable of finding.

Figure handicappers can be unabashedly cocky about their numbers. It practically goes with the territory. As opposed to a shallow display of vanity, however, the cockiness is more commonly a stylized expression of confidence and enthusiasm, exhibited not only in the boxes and corridors, but also at the windows, where confidence truly counts.

Sitting across from Ben at the lunch, experiencing a man near the top of his form, bursting with expertise, confidence, and a competitive eagerness for the races to begin, I wandered back to another time, not long ago, when the experience of Ben Bollinger at the races had resembled another character altogether.

I would regularly encounter Ben among a circle of insiders at Santa Anita near the replay monitors behind the private boxes occupied by owners, horsemen, bloodstock agents, and assorted handicappers. Ben was then the quintessential insider. He had direct access to the inside information that passes as currency among racetrack denizens throughout a day at the races.

Bollinger boasted firm connections to the stables of Darrel Vienna and Mel Stute, successful journeyman trainers on the southern California circuit for years. Both stables were relatively large. Each featured a glossary of horses that would appear virtually every day in the fancier claiming races, allowances, and stakes. Hardly a week would elapse without one of them sending forth a first-time starter in a maiden special weight. In a glorious tradition that will never end, the horses were typically touted as absolutely good things.

Even in those days, Bollinger would join me for a rundown on the afternoon's betting prospects. Now it was Ben who would launch the conversation. It went something like this:

> This one's the best bet of the day. Right here [pointing], in the seventh. Don't worry about the long layoff. He's ready. They're betting big. They don't care about losing him [to a claim]. They get the claim, the purse, and the bet.
>
> You know me. I don't usually talk like this. I don't like to tout. I don't trade in inside information unless it's special. But this is a special situation. The horse is going to win. I wouldn't say this to many people. I know you like to handicap. You know what you're doing. I wouldn't tout you if it wasn't absolutely a good thing, you know that!
>
> Do you like anything special today? Got any best bets yourself?

With apologies to Ben, day after day, week after week, for several seasons, literally, it was always the same sad speech. The barns liked their horses today. And they've got another one coming up on Saturday. "I do not normally trade in inside dope, but this information is special. Anyone should be pleased to know about it."

Even as he passed the worthless information along, Bollinger would deny he was doing it. An urbane professional man, a conductor, musician, and educator, beyond fifty years of maturity, Bollinger sometimes sounded as if he actually resented the flimsy opinions he nonetheless carried to the betting windows.

As if Ben knew the inside information were bogus and the horses were likely to lose. But what were the alternatives? Like so many, Bollinger was otherwise unarmed. A veteran of two decades at racetracks, he was not yet a handicapper.

Indeed, the tipped horses almost always disappointed. On numerous occasions too, the negative outcomes would be followed by loud, angry outbursts cast toward the stupid jockeys, luckless trips, and ungodly fates.

In retrospect, the new Ben Bollinger can explain the old Ben Bollinger succinctly and clearly.

> I had no firm opinion of my own. I did not know how to handicap. I liked early speed and loved Lone-F horses [lonesome frontrunners], but I held no strong opinions.
>
> I had played the races for twenty years, and for twenty years—without exception—I had been a loser doing it my way. I played inside information because I believed horsemen and other insiders knew more than I did.
>
> Now I know better. Speed figures have changed my life at the racetrack. Now I know what I'm doing. I don't need any inside information. Even if I get it, I won't use it if the figures contradict whatever I've been told.
>
> It's still nice to know a successful stable is trying to win with a horse, but that information has become meaningless to me unless the figures say the horse is genuinely capable of winning.

Ben Bollinger backed five winners on the afternoon we met for lunch. He grabbed two exactas and a Pick 3 besides, and he missed a modest Pick 6 by one race. It became a soaring day for figure handicapping.

Later Ben conceded that the Santa Anita meeting had been proceeding below expectation. The figures had been inconsistent, and Santa Anita did not shape up as a swimmingly successful meeting. Ben was winning, but barely.

The suddenly hesitant, restrained tone of Bollinger's comments resurrected a curious phenomenon applicable to his recent life at the races: the education of a figure handicapper. I suggested the learning curve extends approximately two years. Ben agreed, and immediately began to describe his own basic training.

"The first phase amounts to blind ambition. I just bet the

top-figure horses. I had more winners than ever. I bet more and won more. Enough horses won to reinforce the pattern. Bet the best figures. It looked like the secret of beating the races.

"That phase lasts about six months . . ."

Phase 1 of a figure handicapper's education, Bollinger's blind ambition, is marked by a dramatic increase in handicapping proficiency, at least for most users. It's convenient to know at last how fast horses have actually run in the past. The information helps to predict how fast the same horses might be expected to run in the future.

But in the large majority of situations, like Bollinger's, the improved proficiency has erupted from a base near zero. The improvement is impressive, all right, but it is not sufficient. What looks at first like the secret of beating the races is merely an effective method of handicapping. Whether betting the high-figure horses blindly leads to profits or losses, the bottom line in either direction will not be especially significant.

After six months of winning more frequently, but not enough to accumulate meaningful profits, novice figure addicts begin to realize the top-figure horses may not be everything, after all. Still to be mastered are the trickier applications associated with intelligent interpretation and use.

What do the numbers mean?

How do speed figures relate to the other fundamental factors of handicapping?

How do the figures apply under the circumstances of today's race?

When are speed figures less meaningful, or not meaningful at all?

The problems associated with effective interpretation and use introduce the second and crucial phase of a figure handicapper's education. Unfortunately, it's here, at Phase 2, that almost everyone wanders astray. Bollinger committed the crucial mistake. As he tells it:

> I began studying patterns. From the early Thoro-Graph seminars, I knew the basic patterns of improvement and decline. Also the common bounce patterns, and when horses should run their top numbers, and when they almost certainly should regress. But there were so many variations in the numbers, and I wanted to find the more sophisticated patterns that fewer handicappers would identify.

The trick was to find patterns of figures that were well-disguised and would uncover the kinds of overlays that would translate into real profits. Outstanding figure horses that could key exactas and triples, and maybe be singled in Pick 6s.

I put a lot of effort into studying patterns for another six months. It's a continuous thing which I still enjoy doing, and I've learned how to recognize certain patterns that have paid off for me repeatedly. I play them confidently whenever I find them. . . ."

A favorite figure pattern of Bollinger's I had been unaware of, but since have exploited profitably, has been recorded in the "Patterns" section of this book. In the esoteric lexicon of figure handicapping, Bollinger refers to the pattern as 0-2-X, a shorthand that lends the procedure a kind of arty charm, if not grace.

Pattern recognition may be popularly accepted as the second phase of a figure handicapper's education, but the technique has been badly misplaced. Pattern recognition best arrives later, after the more fundamental matters of interpretation and use have cleared the way.

Understanding how speed figures should be related to class, form, pace, trainer, track bias, trips, and the rest is fundamentally more important than recognizing patterns that suggest a certain figure may improve or decline. Knowing how speed figures apply variously in claiming races, the allowances, the stakes, and even maiden-claiming races, gets figure handicappers far more nourishment from their numbers than abject reliance on a sequence of numbers that represents pattern 0-2-X.

Phase 2 of a figure handicapper's education can be characterized broadly as effective interpretation and use. It's a catchall phase whereby figure handicappers are encouraged to broaden their knowledge and skill in handicapping. The trick to becoming an expert figure handicapper is akin to becoming an expert class handicapper, pace analyst, trip handicapper, trainer specialist, and so on. Learn to relate the figures to everything else there is to know.

That kind of understanding not only supports effective figure analysis as nothing else can, but also it guides successful pattern recognition. The critical question is not whether a sequence of numbers represents a pattern called 0-2-X, but whether the figure pattern should be meaningful or decisive today.

Figure patterns exist in a context. They are best interpreted and used in context. It's one thing to recognize that a $40,000 claiming horse bounced last season following the kind of figure he recorded last out, and quite another to appreciate that this season the horse has a better trainer, won with reserves of speed and power last out, and in general has been running as if he enjoys a new lease on life. That kind of newborn claiming horse is very unlikely to bounce, the figure patterns notwithstanding.

Following interpretation and use, Phase 3 concerns itself with pattern recognition. Now the patterns, once recognized, might also be interpreted. Bollinger admits to the recommended sequence.

> Now I just try to relate the figures to everything else I know about the game. That's the ultimate challenge and fascination. It's a continuing kind of education. I realize that now.
>
> Getting comfortable with the role of the figures in the overall scheme of handicapping is a key phase. Learning what the figures mean, and recognizing the familiar patterns that are positive and negative, but not expecting the figures to do too much.
>
> It takes about two years. I think that's about right. I'm just about there now. I'm very comfortable with speed figures. What they can do for me. And what they can't do.

Transposing phases 2 and 3 inadvertently, Bollinger nonetheless has completed the two-year education of a figure handicapper, and, I might add, having graduated with distinction:

Phase 1. Mechanical Play (top-figure horses)   6 Months
Phase 2. Interpretation and Use   1 Year
Phase 3. Pattern Recognition   6 Months

The phases overlap incessantly, with emphases shifting by phase, and the education remains continuous, alongside other basic applications in full-dress handicapping.

Bollinger's continuous education with speed figures has included a disconcerting circumstance he has learned to dislike. It reared its ugly head only weeks ago, when I bumped into Ben en route to wagering on the first race and daily double.

Ben had already bet his figure horse in the first. He asked whether I had the same horse.

"No. The pace figure is well below par. I prefer the six horse. The early pace here figures to be quick, and your guy should not be able to keep up and repeat the final figure."

Ben said nothing, but his expression soured and his demeanor no longer reflected its customary confidence.

The first was a sprint for older $10,000 claiming horses. At lower claiming levels, pace figures routinely supersede speed figures, a circumstance Bollinger had come to appreciate but with which he felt defenseless. Thoro-Graph speed figures are insensitive to early pace, as are most final figures. Where early pace matters, speed figures will be less reliable than normal and can be regularly misleading.

This time my horse won. Ben's figure horse, possessing a pace weakness, collapsed shortly after the second call (which was faster than par) and finished well-beaten.

Ben walked by the box shortly following the finish.

"I hate it when you tell me one of my horses has a pace weakness. There's not much I can do about it. But I've learned to take it seriously. I've seen too many of them lose. . . ."

I suggested lightly to Ben that he pay attention to pace analysis, at least in the cheaper races—and in the nonwinners allowances too.

He shook his head affirmatively.

I lost track of Ben for months after Santa Anita closed in late April. I heard he had made a score when In Excess shipped from southern California to New York and devastated the field in the Metropolitan Mile. That was a smart play which transcended a strict reliance on speed figures, and precisely the kind of action for which I had long since become a Bollinger admirer.

In Excess had recorded excellent speed figures on dirt—the colt had switched from stakes races on grass—at Santa Anita, but had failed to repeat the numbers against Grade 1 opposition and had trailed off badly in the Santa Anita Handicap. When In Excess emerged a few months later in New York, it was important to know the colt responded positively to layoffs and that a mile around one turn constituted a perfect distance.

Under those conditions, In Excess not only might duplicate his best dirt form, but might exceed himself. In Excess did exceed himself in the Metropolitan Mile, at 4–1, and Bollinger reaped the spoils. It was good handicapping, not just figures.

Not until late summer at Del Mar did I encounter Ben again. The 1991 summer season at Del Mar had been painstakingly difficult for handicappers, with form reversals running rampant throughout the meeting, less than 25 percent of the favorites winning for ghastly stretches, and speed and pace figures dying a slow, slow death.

Anticipating an opportunity for commiseration between the two of us, I inquired of Ben how he was making out at old Del Mar.

"I'm ahead $19,000," he replied succinctly.

I was astonished. "How did you do it? With the figures?"

"Yes."

"Not to win, I'll bet . . ."

"No. In the exotics. I've been hot the past three weeks. I'm keying high-figure horses in exactas and triples, and I've linked enough of them to long-shot winners and seconds.

"I haven't done anything in the win hole, pretty much like everybody else. . . ."

I walked away aware without doubt that Bollinger was blithely on his way to a third consecutive winning year, another testimony to the power of professional speed figures.

To complete the cycle, at Santa Anita during Oak Tree in October, Bollinger advised me that Thoro-Graph had assigned its biggest figure ever (no kidding) to In Excess's performance in New York's Woodward Stakes.

"The figure is a minus two. Unheard of . . ."

"The best-ever figs before this were a minus three-quarters. Two horses. Sunday Silence and something else. I forget just now . . ."

The idea was for me to bet a bundle on In Excess in the Breeders' Cup Classic.

"Don't forget, Ben," I cautioned my friend, not for the first time, "speed figures earned at nine furlongs do not transfer reliably to ten furlongs."

Ben nodded agreeably, but no way had he changed his mind.

I remembered an incident a few years back, while Ben was trapped in his maniacal phase with speed figures. A sprinter stretching out to 1⅜ miles on the turf went wire-to-wire and paid handsomely for the upset. I had risked a prime amount on

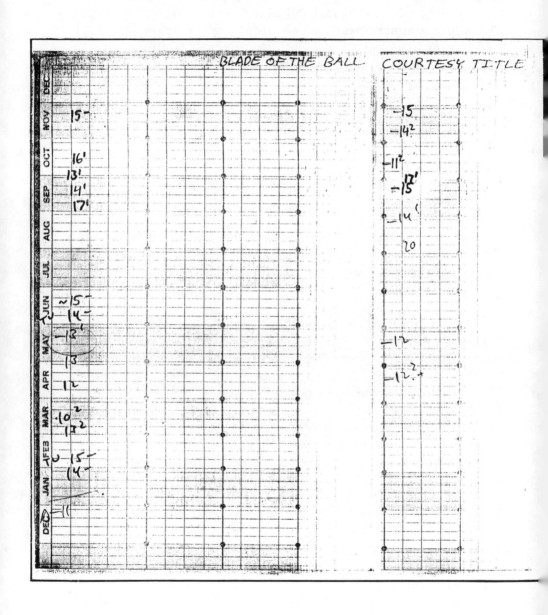

another horse that ran terribly. I encountered Ben at the replay monitor.

"I had the winner," he announced.

"Really, how?"

"He had the figure."

On hearing Bollinger prepared to honor In Excess's nine-furlong figure at ten furlongs in the Breeders' Cup Classic, I wondered whether he might ever again support a sprint figure on dirt at a marathon distance on grass.

I hope not.

Because in the education of a figure handicapper, on the matters of interpretation and use, not to mention pattern recognition, the ultimate teacher is experience, notably painful experience.

Ben Bollinger agrees, very definitely.

THE NEWLY CONVERTED

Albert Fisher, the very same Albert Fisher who would not be caught carrying a file of speed figures a year before, plopped down between me and Tom Brohamer for the afternoon's action at the Frontier Race Book in Las Vegas, Sunday, December 8, 1991. He revealed a stack of The Sheets for Bay Meadows. He did not have a *Racing Form*.

The fourth race was soon approaching, and Albert announced he had a figure horse that would upend the even-money favorite. The race was a $25,000 claimer, for 3up, at $1^{1}/_{16}$ miles on the turf. He presented The Sheets for the favorite and the upset candidate. Review them now.

Paraphrasing Albert, Blade of the Ball could do no better than a 15. Courtesy Title had just run an 11 and had recorded another 11 three races back. Because each of the 11s had followed a pair of slower numbers, some concern was expressed that Courtesy Title might bounce back to a 15. Even so, he should beat the favorite at a decent price.

I concurred. Brohamer concurred. Beyer Speed Figures in *The Racing Times* also gave Courtesy Title the edge, but less decisively, a one-point advantage. Albert preferred the bigger edge accorded Courtesy Title by his own numbers, which he had been buying, on weekends primarily, for Bay Meadows exclusively ("because the odds there are generally better"), for a few months.

As usual, the figures had moved Albert up; improved his game significantly. He testified he had been winning more consistently, and getting good value besides. He talked animatedly at length about a 12-to-1 shot that had won handily and stood apart on the numbers.

Courtesy Title won smartly on the Bay Meadows turf, but a gnawing detail spoiled the plot. Blade of the Ball had been scratched by the vets en route to the gate. The payoff was $6.40 or thereabouts.

I asked Albert about the next race, a six-furlong sprint for $12,500 maiden-claiming Cal-breds, 3up. My pick was a shipper from Stampede Park, in Canada, named Nat's Pearlybird, to be ridden by jockey leader Ron Hansen.

Flipping through The Sheets, Albert rejected horse after horse for the awful credentials they presented. He vacillated among these four:

California Angel	Motel Game	Run Roger Run	Squire Hoedown
23	21	23^2	22^1
22	25^1	20^2	20
20^2	26^2		28^2

"California Angel is going the wrong way. Even if it repeats its best number, not quite good enough.

"Motel Games's 21 last out looks like a winner here, but the horse should bounce back to its typical figures of 25, 26. The 21 is too much improvement for this kind of horse.

"Run Roger Run shows the same pattern as California Angel. Even its best number is no good.

"Squire Hoedown shows just three races and is much improved. His last two figures in tandem probably look best here. It's a bad bunch, but I would go with Squire Hoedown."

Albert did not mention Nat's Pearlybird. In fact, he found no sheet for the shipper. When I mentioned I liked Nat's Pearlybird a lot, Albert fumbled through The Sheets once more, looking for the horse's figures. But The Sheets do not cover Stampede Park. "Ah," said Brohamer, "the case of the missing figures."

I showed Albert the shipper's past performances. He was exiting a dreadful effort under nonwinners allowance conditions but had placed twice in open claiming competition at

Stampede Park. Nat's Pearlybird was getting blinkers today and was dropping into a maiden-claiming field devoid of early foot.

Brohamer and I supported the horse. Albert was tempted, but resisted. Nat's Pearlybird won.

"Ah," Brohamer rubbed it in. "The case of the missing figures."

"Don't despair," I teased Albert, "there's a figure standout in the next race."

"I know," he replied. "It's my best bet of the day. I've already sent in a prime bet on the horse."

It was a $16,000 six-furlong sprint for two-year-old fillies. On Beyer Speed the figure horse looked even more inviting than he did on Albert's Sheets. Examine the top pair:

	Mevue	Homing Port
Beyer Speed	61	53
The Sheets	21^2	21
	28	24^1
	25^1	21
	28^1	29

After reviewing The Sheets myself, I inquired of Albert why Mevue qualified as a standout, considering the pair of 21s dispensed by Homing Port.

"Homing Port always bounces following a good effort. Look at the last 21. It bounced back to 24, and the horse has done the same thing before."

Yet Albert did not expect Mevue to bounce back to its previous 28 following its 21 last out. "That's just an improved performance."

Mevue, with an off-pace style, shot out of the pack entering the stretch and collared the frontrunners near the sixteenth-pole. One of the speed horses resisted. In a stiff drive, Mevue put her head in front about fifty yards out and appeared to edge clear.

But Mevue was running on the wrong lead, and after gaining a small advantage, she flattened. The speed horse continued to dig in, and exactly at the wire pushed its nose back in front of Mevue.

Albert was crestfallen. He had won the race apparently, but lost it again in the final agonizing stride. It was his best bet of the day and it stung.

By now Brohamer and I had conspired to enjoy watching

Albert living and dying with his much-prized figures. Albert's analyses of the day's program consisted entirely of interpreting the figure patterns he found on The Sheets, without consultation of *The Daily Racing Form*'s past performances or the Beyer figures in *The Racing Times*.

In the next race Brohamer preferred a three-year-old named Eager N' Quick on Quirin-style speed figures, but Albert disagreed sharply. He showed Brohamer the horse's sheet. "His last race was a bad decline," said Albert.

When Brohamer's horse won, Albert revisited his figure pattern and could only shake his head in bewilderment.

"Didn't you say the rail at Bay Meadows was not the place to be?" Brohamer asked Albert gently.

"Yes. It's not the place to be."

"Well, Eager N' Quick ran on the rail out of the one-hole in his last. That figure could be discounted."

Without the past performances, Albert had not realized that.

Albert's figures caught the eighth race favorite and blew the ninth, which brought us to the tenth and final race of the day. This was another six-furlong sprint for $6250 horses 3up. The leading figure horses were exiting the same race, another $6250 race run on November 27, which had been won by Majestic Caper. Albert preferred Believe A Promise because, he insisted, the horse had the top figure.

Examine the past performances, paying careful attention to the Beyer Speed Figures and The Sheets figures printed below. See anything peculiar? I certainly do. Albert didn't see it, because he did not have the past performances.

MAJESTIC CAPER

5yo (May) gelding, bay
Trainer: Bryan Webb
Owner: Mt High Stable

$6,250
CLM. PRICE

Sire: **Magesterial** ($5,000)
by Northern Dancer
Dam: **Maui Caper**
by No Robbery
Bred in **KY** by Gen. W. R. Buster & D. L. Martin

122 **Ron J Warren Jr**

1989-91: 26 3 2 2

Wet:	0	0	0	0	
Turf:	9	0	1	1	
Dist:	16	3	1	1	
1991:	11	2	1	1	$10,625
1990:	6	0	0	1	
BM:	7	2	1	1	

27Nov91	4BM	ft	3+	Clm6250	6f	22.50	45.70	58.10	1:11.10	[redacted]	9/9	1	2^{1}	2½	2½	1^{1}	RJ Warren Jr	119	Lb	4.20	Majestic Caper119^{1} Marta's Boy119^{1} Believe A Promise119^{1}	*Broke out, stalked pace, challenged 1/4 pl, dueled, clear late*
9Nov91	7BM	ft	3+	Clm6250	6f	22.70	45.90	58.30	1:11.10	[redacted]	9/10	1	2^{hd}	2^{hd}	2½	$1^{1½}$	RJ Warren Jr	117	Lb	7.60	Majestic Caper117^{1½} Lot's Curiosity117^{nk} Rindo Try117^{1}	*Broke sharply, dueled 3w backstr, turn, drew clear deep stretch*
27Oct91	10BM	ft	3+	Clm6250	6f	22.70	46.50	57.90	1:10.90	[redacted]	9/9	1	$5^{3¾}$	3^{4}	3^{4}	3^{1}	RD Hansen	117	Lb	4.10	Hot Trip117^{no} L'brave117^{1} Majestic Caper117^{2}	*Manuevered to rail backstretch, late rally*
13Oct91	7BM	ft	3+	Clm6250	6f	22.70	45.10	57.10	1:09.70	[redacted]	4/8	8	$5^{4½}$	$6^{8½}$	5^{8}	$6^{2½}$	JK Court	117	Lb	10.80	Bracoy117^{1¾} Nature Boy½ Wild Lookout^{no}	*Late rally*
6Oct91	9Fno	ft	3+	Clm8000Nw2m	6f	21.70	45.50	58.90	1:09.90	[redacted]	9/10	4	3^{nk}	$5^{2¾}$	9^{8}	8^{8}	P Atkinson	116	Lbf	3.60	Jim Campenas116½ Herty's^{hd} WickrBe^{2}	*Dueled 4-wide, quit*
2Sep91	8Sac	ft	3+	Clm8000Cnd	5½f	21.90	44.50		1:02.30	[redacted]	11/11	8	$9^{4½}$	$8^{4¼}$	$7^{6½}$	$7^{5½}$	DM Davis	116	Lb	4.80	Toe River116½ You Had It^{1½} Classy Dan^{1}	*Lacked rally*
24Aug91	7BM	ft	3+	Clm6250	6f	22.50	45.10	57.30	1:10.30	[redacted]	1/8	5	3^{1}	$4^{2¾}$	$2^{2½}$	2^{3}	R Sibille	117	Lbf	7.30	Lori's Wonder119^{3} Majestic Caper117½ Baltistan117^{nk}	*Rushed up inside, taken back turn, kept to task, mild rally*
Claimed from Steve Miyadi																						
11Aug91	10BMF	ft	3+	Clm10000	5½f	21.70	44.70		1:03.10	[redacted]	6/8	7	$8^{4¾}$	$8^{5¼}$	$8^{7½}$	$6^{9¾}$	BC Campbell	117	Lbf	5.70	Smiley Bo117^{1½} ModrnCmfrt^{3½} DancDrctr^{3}	*Passed tired ones*
28Jly91	10SR	ft	3+	Clm12500	6f	21.50	44.10	56.30	1:08.80	[redacted]	7/10	3	5^{5}	6^{7}	$6^{5½}$	$5^{2½}$	BC Campbell	117	Lf	6.80	Ono Gummo117^{nk} Major Buper^{nk} Smiley Bo^{1}	*Closed well*
23Feb91	5SA	fm	4+	Alw36000Nw2x	6½f ⓣ	21.90	44.70	1:08.10	1:14.30	[redacted]	10/11	2	2^{hd}	2^{hd}	11^{15}	11^{19}	R Faul	115	LBf	64.30	Now Listen114½ EghtLttrMn^{3} Raketmnsch^{1}	*Speed half mile*

Best 1990-91 Beyer Speed Figures - Dirt(ft): [redacted] 24Feb90 SA 6f ft **Dist:** [redacted] 24Feb90 SA 6f ft

Workouts: 23Nov BM 5f ft 1:03.70 H — 17Nov BM 5f gd 1:01.50 H(d) — 3Nov BM 4f ft 49.30 H — 15Sep BM 5f ft 1:01.10 H — 1Sep BM 5f ft 59.30 H

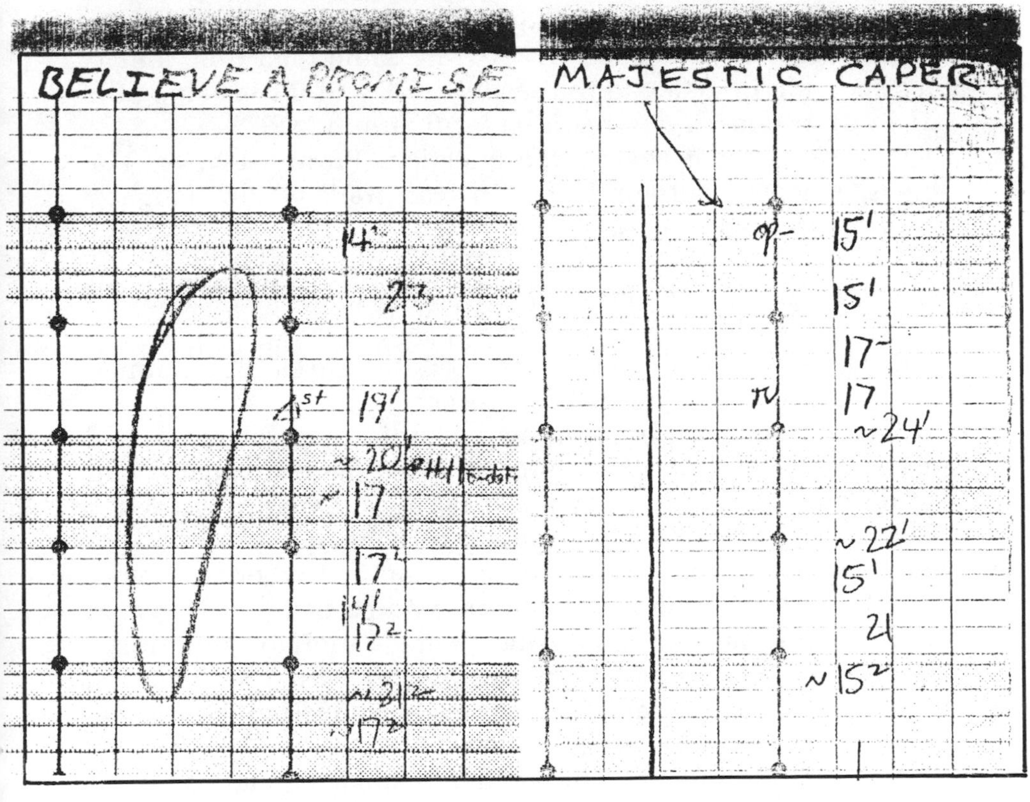

In the race won by Majestic Caper in which Believe A Promise finished third, beaten two lengths, The Sheets assigned Believe A Promise a higher figure than the winner. Majestic Caper gets 15^1 but Believe A Promise 14^2. Beyer Speed has awarded Majestic Caper a 79 and Believe A Promise a 74.

How to explain the anomaly?

Albert was stumped.

The Sheets gives extra credit for "effort," or perseverance in the face of adversity, and they discount a perfect trip, however fast. Notice the trip line in the past performances for Believe A Promise on November 27. The gelding was "forced six-wide [on the far] turn . . ." He then closed willingly. The "effort" expended as a result of the troubled trip, coupled with a vigorous finish, earns a losing horse a bigger figure than the winner, who simply stalked the pace, took the lead, and held.

This amounts to dangerous procedure. It confuses horses' trips and their abilities, at least much of the time.

As Len Ragozin was asked at the Third National Conference on Thoroughbred Handicapping at the Mirage in Las Vegas in March 1990, "If two horses record the same final time, but A goes six-wide in a 45.4 to the second call, and B runs along the rail in 44.2, does A deserve a better figure than B?"

Ragozin did not answer the question. Presumably, on The Sheets, A would outrank B, but in real life B would slaughter A. Pace supersedes trips.

Albert pondered the matter, but was not dissuaded. He remained loyal to his figures and supported Believe A Promise. I thought Majestic Caper would win again.

It was much ado about nothing. Both horses disappointed their backers. We adjourned for dinner.

Albert Fisher has been an avid handicapper for years, and for years he had proceeded without speed figures, playing well enough to win a little or lose a little in any year. A tendency to confuse the relative importance of a horse's class and its trainer, speed and post position, pace and jockey, or the fundamental and the incidental, as it has with so many journeyman handicappers, has prevented Albert's graduation to better times.

Maybe that is about to change. Armed with speed figures, Albert has joined the ranks of the Newly Converted. He has become a figure man. As of December 1991 he was locked in the Blind Ambition phase of a figure handicapper's education, a capitulation to mechanical play. A guy formerly buried in the past performances but without a clue about the horses' true speed finds himself now buried in The Sheets but without even looking at the past performances.

The Newly Converted cling to speed figures as if they represented the wellspring of life itself. In a matter of weeks they would be lost without the figures. The reason is understandable, and most agreeable. The figures have moved them up. But if speed figures are indispensable, they are not everything, not by far—a repetitive theme of this book. Understanding that takes the Newly Converted roughly six months.

I predict that before this book has been published, Albert Fisher will have abandoned mechanical play, proceeded to engage the complicated processes of interpretation and use with the keen intelligence he possesses, and graduated to a new style of pattern recognition.

Instead of noting that a horse usually runs a few 24s or 25s before recording an 18 but then bounces back to the mid-20s and occasionally can surprise with best-ever 18s and 19s, but never anything better than that, Albert will note instead whether the horse is outgunned on relative class to begin with, or that the probable pace today will be too fast to permit the horse to repeat its latest figures, or that a low figure resulted from a negative inside speed bias, or that a best-ever figure represented peaking form and should return to normal for that reason alone.

There is a difference. It's the difference between figure handicapping and comprehensive handicapping.

THE UNCONVERTED

A paradox of the racetrack juxtaposes its denizens unabashedly committed to thoroughbred handicapping but equally uncommitted to speed and pace figures.

For years I have prodded novelist William Murray to embrace the charms provided by the figures. He has remained steadfastly uninterested. Bill is a rabid handicapper. He savors the mental challenge. He relishes the intrigue. He revels in the problem solving. He agonizes in defeat and exults in victory. Bill wears a bad day at the races in pained expressions on his face. It's precisely when he's losing that acquaintances cannot fail to observe how desperately Bill Murray wants to win at the races.

Moreover, Murray betrays an abiding respect for excellence in handicapping. An aspect of the Shifty Lou Anderson mysteries I especially admire is Murray's remarkably respectful portrayal of professional handicapper Jay Fox. Fox is not merely a horseplayer, he's a carefully sketched handicapper who not only engages the races in a deliberate, rational style, but also manages to win. The hangers-on at the boxes in Murray's novels may be the drifters, dreamers, and lowbrows that have reinforced the Runyonesque character of the racetrack for too long a time, but Jay Fox emerges as a man applying his craft and enjoying his game, and fully in possession of his life. Fox steers the hapless horseplayers around him, including Shifty, on to a straight course at the racetrack.

Murray understands that skillful players do prosper at the racetrack, and that they even supply valuable guidance to friends and acquaintances. Jay Fox may stand as a solitary figure carrying forth that cause in racetrack fiction.

How can a guy who so thoroughly comprehends the fundamental importance of knowing how fast horses actually have run betray an aversion to the very evidence that documents that speed? Even Jay Fox uses speed figures.

In truth, as long as I have enjoyed an acquaintance with Bill Murray at the races, I realize, surprisingly, right now, as I write, that I have achieved virtually no insight as to Bill's handicapping methods. He speaks frequently of trainers and trainer maneuvers. He can be unsparing of jockey mistakes. He attends as best as his schedule permits to trips and form cycles. And as must be so of serious handicappers unarmed with speed and pace figures, Bill judges the relative class of the main contention. He likes to develop a sense of which horses are actually best.

When last I played alongside Bill, at the Del Mar satellite pavilion, during Hollywood Park, fall of 1991, he was cooking hot, playing as well and as confidently as I can remember. On the whole, he plays well, coping, or winning and losing tolerable amounts. He has beaten Del Mar several times, no piece of cake. Speed figures would move Bill up, and as is regularly the case, probably dramatically. Still he resists.

Sensing a shift in attitude, in spring of 1990, a few months in advance of Del Mar, Bill's favorite time, I volunteered, "If you like, Bill, I'll send you the speed and pace figures each week during Del Mar, including the figures for Hollywood and Santa Anita.

"You can see whether they make a significant difference in your bottom line. You might even like using them."

Bill declined.

"I'm just not into the figures. For one thing, I don't have the time. It's an effort to use the figures. I just like to open the *Form* and begin to handicap from the printed page."

Fair enough.

Bill's observation about the extra time and effort required to use speed figures intelligently is essentially correct, and those requirements have traditionally been prohibitive for most race-goers if the daily tasks include the making of the figures. As far as I can determine, the Unconverted fall into two broad categories:

1. Time and effort savers
2. Class handicappers

Of the second group, I can point to a close friend who eschews figure handicapping, proceeds in his handicapping with class evaluation at its heart, and practices a fast and successful game wherever he plays. Expert class handicappers can do just as well as any other battalion of method players, including speed handicappers, thank you, and they can discover an array of wagering opportunities weekly to quench any appetite.

On the other hand, class handicapping has receded in importance in recent times, as more and more races are devoured by the cheaper speed horses. Low-level claiming races, maiden-claiming races, and claiming races limited to three-year-olds, now dominate even the major league cards, and these races remain the province of speed and pace handicapping. Class handicappers have more incentive than ever to become acquainted with the figures.

Of the tremendously larger category—handicappers averse to the time and effort demands of figure handicapping—a new kid on the block rushed to the rescue. *The Racing Times* published Beyer Speed Figures, as *The Daily Racing Form* now does, informing the casual audience, for the first time in the history of the sport, as to how fast the horses have actually run in the past.

The Unconverted now can purchase *The Daily Racing Form* and gain instant access to professional speed figures. They unhesitatingly are urged to do so.

Once the Beyer figures have been engaged, the problems do not go away, but shift from access to interpretation and use. Beyer Speed Figures can be characterized by wide variation in the numbers, even for the same horses. Casual handicappers will experience that variation as confusing and overbearing. Many will entertain the figures for a couple of weeks, before throwing in the towel once again.

Those who persevere can begin the bumpy road toward the education of a figure handicapper. They can start with mechanical play, proceed to a lengthy involvement with the complications of interpretation and use, and emerge with the customary high regard for pattern recognition. Bill Murray has begun his figure-handicapping journey at last.

The education is clean, stimulating fun.

And in the end, the graduates will testify, almost to a man and woman, that they have become better handicappers than they had ever imagined they could be.

Figure Handicapping on the Turf

A NEW APPROACH

SEVERAL SEASONS AGO, midway in the Santa Anita winter season, my friend and colleague Dick Mitchell astonished me with the observation that sixteen consecutive grass selections of mine had finished first or second. As turf races are carded intermittently, one or two an afternoon, sometimes none, I had been unaware of the streak.

Since the beginnings of my racetrack adventures, however, certainly following the first five years, I had been keenly aware of a personal regard for turf races. The explanation is agreeable. My handicapping from the start had been nicely suited to grass racing. I prospered on the turf, and still do.

There was also the convenient contrasting circumstance. A plain majority of regular handicappers did not find turf races hospitable. Many complained loudly about grass, notably about the course at Hollywood Park, which in the 1970s stood as a graveyard for frontrunners.

Not as flagrantly perhaps, these circumstances persist today. Few daily handicappers prefer turf races. The reason, openly stated, is the relative lack of success handicappers experience on the grass.

The absence of success traces absolutely to faulty methods. In particular, the procedures of modern speed handicapping can be poorly suited to grass racing. Pace methodology can be similarly flawed, notably where undue emphasis is placed on second-call fractional time, as on dirt. Much of the time, conventional figure-handicapping procedure just does not apply to turf racing.

Evidence of the assertion has been widely dispersed at the nation's leading racetracks. High-figure grass horses disappoint their backers again and again.

I have watched a sampling of this country's shrewdest figure handicappers toss their grass numbers in the lake during the core of the season. The figures were not working satisfactorily. Excellent figure handicappers were repeatedly stumped. They reluctantly switched to alternative methods, or abstained altogether.

The figures (numbers) that handicappers like so much might be used to unravel turf races, all right, but not traditional figures, not conventional speed and pace figures, not the kind of figures that work so well so much of the time on the dirt.

What was needed were new figures, based upon new thinking and new factors. Figures derived from a clear understanding of how turf races are run, and which factors will be ultimately decisive.

"Figure Handicapping on the Turf" is the result of more than three years of thinking, experimenting, and testing of rating methods in grass races. It presents a new and significantly better means of evaluating grass horses numerically. It permits comparisons at different distances, and among horses coming together from different racetracks. High-rated horses will be strong contenders today, and many of them will win at generous prices.

The Appendix following this section presents charts of turf figures for each of 28 racetracks. All major and most medium-sized tracks have been included. A few minor tracks are represented too. The charts need to be updated occasionally, but not annually. When new turf courses are constructed, or new surfaces are laid, as at Santa Anita in 1989, new charts obviously will be required. Recommendations for other revisions should be clear.

I hope handicappers will find the turf-figure charts helpful, not only for evaluating grass runners at the local tracks, but for evaluating shippers and when traveling to new and unfamiliar surroundings. The charts should prove valuable assists for disentangling turf simulcasts and for excursions to the race books of Las Vegas.

The rationale for the charts, and procedures for utilizing

them effectively, are hardly complicated. These explanations follow immediately. Handicappers open-minded about the possibility of having new and better tools on the grass are encouraged to begin applying the rating methods today.

HOW TURF RACES ARE DIFFERENT

Few practiced handicappers would quarrel with the proposition that grass races are distinct.

The courses are different. Horses exit on straightaways or out of chutes. The rails are up, the rails are down. The grass is long, the grass is cut short. The turns are sharper, the stretch run is shorter.

The horses are different too. Conformation favors shorter, more angular pasterns and dishlike feet. The turf stride is straight, gliding over the ground in a forward paddling motion, with less up and down curling movement of the front legs. Bloodlines count heavily, horses bred for grass outperforming the others on the surface by a wide margin.

The pace is different. It's slower by as many as five lengths during the first quarter-mile, by six to ten lengths during the first six furlongs. Jockeys typically take hold out of the gate, conserving horses' energies on the turf from the outset. The finish is then fast and furious, the margin of victory typically narrow. Tiring horses rarely survive on the grass, as they regularly do on dirt.

So why, in the face of obvious differences, do handicappers expect the same rating methods that work well on the dirt to work equally well on the turf? Why do figure handicappers, in particular, expect their methods will be perfectly transportable to the turf?

Of course, the methods are not very transportable at all. Of the brands of figures that have significantly impacted the practice of speed handicapping in this country—Beyer Speed, Quirin Speed & Pace, Thoro-Graph, Ragozin's Sheets—none even approaches on grass the effectiveness they can achieve on dirt. More often than not the figures perform poorly on the turf. Even leading figure handicappers cannot be confident of making a profit from grass figures, and several ended the quest long ago.

The explanation is hardly complicated. Whereas a great majority of dirt races are won by speed horses, whether the edge belongs to early speed, rate of speed (pace), or final-time speed, the great majority of turf races are not. The aspect of brilliance (speed) that counts on the turf is late speed, the ability to finish fast. In fact, three factors predominate on the turf: late speed, endurance, and competitive spirit (class). Among inexperienced grass runners, pedigree counts heaviest.

The purpose here is to present a method of figure handicapping that reflects the factors that are most decisive on grass, notably late speed and relative class. The proposed method embraces a few familiar concepts of modern speed handicapping, notably pars and transportable figures, but the logic, calculations, and figure charts are dissimilar. The method applies to route races featuring experienced turf horses. Comparisons among distances and racetracks will be tenable, such that a classified event of 1¹⁄₁₆ miles at Garden State can be compared to a stakes race at 1¹⁄₈ miles at Bay Meadows.

Needless to say, effective figure handicapping on the turf represents a leap forward in the general practice. The cadres of figure handicappers and others who formerly have sworn themselves to abstinence on the turf can resurrect a vital aspect of their game. The new methods will equip them to identify contenders, winners, and generous mutuels previously not within their grasp.

WHY MODERN SPEED METHODS
DO NOT APPLY ON GRASS

Of the fundamentals of handicapping—speed, class, pace, and form—the factor that most dramatically distinguishes grass racing is pace. On grass, with the softer footing demanding deeper reserves of endurance, jockeys conserve horses' energies as best they can for a final furious run to the finish. Horses that tire, or merely run too low on energy reserves, are likely to lose.

On dirt, as stated earlier, speed horses wrestle from the start for the lead or for favorable position. Early fractions tend to be swift. Horses not within striking position at the prestretch call finish at a tremendous disadvantage. Frontrunners and pace-pressers win significantly more than their fair share of dirt races. Off-pace types and deep closers win less than half the rightful share of the races.

On grass, the real racing begins approaching the prestretch call and intensifies thereafter. Late speed, or finishing power, counts far more than early speed or early pace. In combination with late speed, stamina and determination are often decisive.

The circumstance is documented irrefutably by studies of how winners distribute their energy at the various distances. Sprinters and routers on dirt use significantly more energy than do turf horses to the pace call. At Santa Anita 1990, January 25 to April 1, the percentages of early energy expended by winners of sprints, dirt routes, and turf routes, respectively, looked like this:

Sprints	52.72%	Early Energy
Dirt Routes	51.72%	Early Energy
Turf Routes	50.60%	Early Energy

In fifty days of racing, only one turf winner had expended 51 percent of its energy at the pace call. On average, the early-energy distribution of turf winners amounts to a savings of energy equal to 11 to 12 lengths. On no less than eight of those racing days the early-energy output of turf winners was less than 50 percent, a phenomenon I have not yet experienced on the dirt. And Santa Anita's new grass surface rates among the most glib in the nation.

Final times and fractional times of dirt races become relatively predictable for specific classes of horses, the clockings hovering about par, plus or minus the predictable two to three lengths, unless the track surface has become biased, or a stickout horse runs away.

The pace and final times of grass races are relatively unstable, far more various, depending upon running styles, course configurations, and jockey tactics. Fractional times fluctuate wildly, and so can the resulting final times.

But the prevailing circumstance is a relatively slow pace, followed by a furious all-out finish.

Speed-handicapping methods sensitive to normal predictable patterns and relations among pace and final times do not encounter those patterns and relations as routinely on the turf. Fluctuating final times and a slow pace are instead the norm. What is routine on grass is the fast furious finish in the late stages.

Methods of figure handicapping on the turf might better be concerned with fast finishes than fast final-fractional times.

There is too the overwhelming technical problem inherent to speed handicapping on the turf. How to calculate accurate daily track variants on grass?

Indispensable to effective speed handicapping, accurate variants are readily calculated for dirt races. Normal fluctuations about par for multiple sprints and routes on a card are standard fare, such that extreme deviations can be logically explained or inexplicably discarded. Puzzling programs do occur, but these are exceptions. Leading speed handicappers come to distinguish themselves and their numbers by the unique quality of their variants.

Obtaining accurate daily track variants on the turf is frequently an elusive, lost art, even for dedicated speed handicappers.

Only one grass route is carded, or two; the first at a mile on the straightaway, the second at 1$\frac{1}{16}$ miles out of a chute. The rails are up, the rails are down. The rails are out, the rails are in. The pace is unusually slow, the pace is faster than par. The grass is long, the grass is short.

When it rains, the grass is soft or yielding, affecting running times tremendously; or the grass is good, affecting running times hardly at all.

Speed handicappers compensate as best they can by clustering grass variants weekly, looking for rational patterns that might reflect track-surface speed. Careful professionals rely on projected times, now making sophisticated projections of the expected times at the various points of call as well as at the finish, based upon the particular composition of each field.

None of the adaptations works especially well or consistently well. In consequence, grass figures contain too much error too much of the time. The error is reflexively assigned to technique; regrettably, of course.

An alternative explanation is that grass racing and the procedures of conventional speed handicapping are essentially incompatible. To the extent this explanation rings true, new procedures and new figures are the only reliable antidote.

RATING PROCEDURES

As the outcomes of turf races depend ultimately on expressions of late speed and relative class, so must any rating method designed to cope with them successfully.

As its point of departure, the method presented here invokes the grass pars of classified allowance horses as the key indicators of the late-speed standard at a specific racetrack. That is, the closing times of classified horses represent the late-speed pars for the regularly run distances at the track.

Consider the grass pars and closing times of classified horses at two dissimilar tracks at opposite ends of the country.

Hollywood Park

	1M	1¹/₁₆M	1¹/₈M
Clf Alw Pars	1:10.1—1:35.2	1:10.2—1:41.2	1:11.0—1:48.1
Late-Speed Pars	25.1	31.0	37./1

Laurel

	1M	1¹/₁₆M	1¹/₈M
Clf Alw Pars	1:11.4—1:36.3	1:11.4—1:43.0	1:11.4—1:49.3
Late-Speed Pars	24.4	31.4	37.4

At a mile on the grass, the late-speed par at Hollywood Park is 25.1, the late-speed par at Laurel is 24.4. If each of these pars is assigned a figure of 100, equating classified turf runners at Hollywood Park and Laurel, a basis of intertrack comparisons is set.

The rating method, in fact, sets the late-speed pars of classified horses on grass at all racetracks equal to 100.

The choice of classified horses as the basis of comparison is crucial, and not arbitrary. Bill Quirin has shown that in the nonclaiming division relative track class is best determined by references to each track's maidens and classified allowance horses. Once track-surface speed has been held constant, the better maidens and classified types will earn higher figures.

In major league racing, turf races typically involve better

horses. Classified races typically bring together high-priced claiming horses, established classified allowance runners, and a variety of stakes horses. The classified allowance pars reflect a wide spectrum of the local track's classier horses.

In calculating classified allowance pars on grass, both the fractional time at the second call (six furlongs) and final time are required. The late-speed par is the difference between the two. Late-speed figures will be calculated as the difference between a race's final time and fractional time, modified by a horse's lengths gained, or lengths lost.

In sum, figure handicapping on the turf begins with these four steps:

1. Calculate the classified allowance pars on grass at the track's regularly run distances.
2. Calculate the classified allowance pace pars—at the second call or after six furlongs at middle distances—at the same distances.
3. Calculate the late-speed pars for classified horses at each regularly run distance. Late speed refers to the difference between the final pars and pace pars.
4. Assign a figure value of 100 to the late-speed pars at each of the regularly run distances.

By this design, a turf figure greater than 100 means horses have finished as fast or faster than classified horses typically finish at the track. A turf figure below 100 means horses have finished slower than classified horses typically finish at the track. Thus stakes horses would be expected to earn figures significantly above 100, and lower claiming horses would be expected to earn figures below 100.

Standard Weightings

The importance of the finish in grass races and the close calls so characteristic of turf races holds out the crucial consideration of figure handicapping on the turf. How should one length be weighted?

One point cannot equal one length. A fast-closing length should clearly be set equal to more than one point on a figure chart. In addition, a length should probably have greater value as the distance of the finishing time increases. That is, the ability to finish fast for three-eighths of a mile deserves greater value than the ability to finish fast for a quarter-mile or for five-sixteenths of a mile.

Here the concept of proportional time promoted by Andrew Beyer in the construction of modern speed-handicapping charts is perfectly compatible with the present purpose, but with an intriguing twist.

To recall, Beyer argued that one-fifth of a second should be valued proportionately, depending on speed and distance. A fifth of a second, or one length, possesses greater value in shorter races and faster races. As distances lengthened, or races slowed, the value of a fifth of a second would decline. Using the pars of selected classes of claiming horses, Beyer urged speed handicappers to obtain the value of a fifth of a second at each of the regularly run distances, and construct speed-figure charts from those starting blocks.

When considering late speed on the grass, the value of a fifth of a second can be obtained for each finishing time, such as the final quarter-mile or the final three-eighths. Except now the value of a fifth of a second increases as the distance increases. Finishing faster for longer counts greater. In addition, as the value of a fifth of a second at a distance as short as a quarter-mile will be small, it might be weighted arbitrarily by doubling the value. By this strategy, a fifth of a second, weighted by a factor of two, would represent approximately two lengths. On the figure chart, one point would represent roughly one-half length. The logic, and calculations, would be highly compatible with the close, furious finishes of most grass races.

To implement the strategy, several weightings and rating procedures were tested. A breakthrough occurred when the basic unit of analysis was set as a quarter-mile of 25 seconds, which corresponds well with the classified late-speed par at a mile of most major tracks.

The value of a fifth of a second at a quarter-mile of 25 seconds (1/125) is .008. Instead of multiplying by 1000 to reflect the value of one-fifth in an entire race, I multiplied by 100, to reflect the value of one-fifth during a portion of the race.

A weighting of 8 would have been untenable anyway, as an increase or decrease of one-fifth second would have meant a corresponding figure increase-decrease of 8, far too wide a gap.

But a weighting of 0.8 (.008 × 100) is remarkably suitable, especially when doubled according to the basic strategy. Thus the weighting of one-fifth of a second at a quarter-mile was set equal to 1.6.

The next step occurred logically, although not immediately. Three-eighths of a mile is half again as far as a quarter-mile. Thus the value of one-fifth at three-eighths of a mile might be half again as great as 1.6, or 2.4.

The value of one-fifth at five-sixteenths of a mile—the late-speed interval at $1\frac{1}{16}$ miles—merely splits the difference between 1.6 and 2.4. It became 2.0.

Using these values for one-fifth of a second at the standard finishing intervals, in combination with the classified pars, a turf-figure chart can be constructed for any racetrack. (See the turf-figure chart for Hollywood Park in Appendix.)

Instantly, or so it seemed, these figures generated improved results. The comparisons and evaluations they facilitated were sound and reliable. They picked winners routinely. Knowing the basic directions were now clear, I busily constructed turf-figure charts for several racetracks.

The next steps involved the kind of experimentation and trial-and-error testing that might evolve into a coherent methodology. A few trusty adjustments would be necessary, and so would a number of guidelines for rating horses, selecting races to be rated, comparing distances, and making final evaluations.

Before proceeding to those matters, let's continue to set down the stepwise procedure for figure handicapping on the turf:

5. Obtain the value of a fifth of a second at a quarter-mile of 25 seconds, an approximate estimate of the late-speed par at a mile of classified horses at many racetracks. That value is equal to .008.
6. To convert the value of a fifth of a second at a quarter-mile to a weighted integer for making figures, multiply .008 by 100, to reflect a portion of a race, and double the product. The product of .008 × 100 is 0.8. Weighted by a factor of 2, 0.8 × 2 is 1.6.
7. As opposed to making figures on the dirt, as turf distances increase, the value of one-fifth of a second of late speed becomes correspondingly greater. Use the following weightings:

$\frac{1}{4}$M	$\frac{1}{5}$th =	1.6
$\frac{5}{16}$M	$\frac{1}{5}$th =	2.0
$\frac{3}{8}$M	$\frac{1}{5}$th =	2.4

8. Use the values above and the classified allowance pars (late-speed pars equal 100) to construct a turf-figure chart for each racetrack of interest.

Adjustments

Experience with the method suggests no necessary adjustments for age or sex. The standard adjustments to the final-time pars for age/sex are not sufficiently large, so that when the corresponding adjustments to the pace pars are set, the late-speed pars will be virtually the same.

For the same reason, happily, the method is not sensitive to *normal fluctuations* in running times resulting from the application of the daily track variant. Up to ±3, the variant is not meaningful in these calculations. At Fast 3, the pace variant is Fast 2, such that final time/fractional time differences will hardly change.

Extreme variants of a full second or greater, however, will arouse the familiar headaches. To illustrate, consider Hollywood Park, where the classified pars at a mile are 1:10.1—1:35.2, yielding a late-speed par of 25.1. If the turf variant for the mile at Hollywood is Fast 5, the adjusted pars are 1:10.4—1:36.2, now yielding a late-speed par of 25.3.

On the Hollywood Park turf-figure chart, 25.1 gets 100, and 25.3 gets 97, a 3-point swing, or approximately 1½ lengths.

So while normal track variants can be ignored, extreme variations from par cannot. Where daily track variants are known, and are considered large, apply the variants to the actual running times before calculating a horse's late speed. Leave beaten lengths at the pace and finish alone. Otherwise, ignore daily track variants. In new and unfamiliar surroundings also, track variants might be assumed to be normal, and ignored.

The adjustment not to be ignored concerns the probable effects of the six-furlong pace on the energy distribution of the horses. Although early pace is not a complicating factor in the majority of turf races and can be discounted, sometimes the six-furlong pace will be unusually slow or unusually fast, causing unwanted effects on the numbers.

First, when the early pace is normal, no adjustments apply. We establish a par zone equal to the pace par minus a full second as "normal" for turf races. At Hollywood Park, the pace par at a mile is 1:10.1. Thus the par zone will be 1:10.1 to 1:11.1. If a race's six-furlong pace falls within that zone, no adjustment. Par zones have been erected to define the normal early pace of turf races at each regularly run distance at every racetrack. Refer to the Hollywood Park chart.

If the early pace has been "unusually slow," defined as six lengths or slower than a track's pace par for the distance, a simple adjustment is required. To the horse's late-speed figure, add 100 and divide by 2. If a Hollywood miler earns a 104 following an early pace of 1:11.3, the adjusted figure is 102 (104 + 100/2).

An unusually slow pace allows horses to conserve inordinate degrees of energy, and subsequently finish faster than normal. The correction brings the abnormally high turf figure back toward the classified par (100). The recommended procedure urges handicappers to calculate the turf figure as usual and then adjust if the pace of the race were unusually slow.

Conversely, an adjustment is appropriate when the early pace has been faster than par. The adjustment applies only to frontrunners and pace-pressers (within one length of the leader), not to off-pace types and deep closers.

For each one-fifth of a second frontrunners and pace-pressers have exceeded par at the pace call, add 2 points to their late-speed figures. If a Hollywood miler gets a 98 after setting a pace of 1:09.3, handicappers would add 6 points to the rating, awarding the horse a 104.

That horse would be rated superior to the horse that finished faster following the unusually slow 1:11.3, 104 to 102, by a length.

A pace faster than par depletes the energy reserves of unexceptional frontrunners and pace-pressers on the grass. The correction awards the rating that might be earned where early pace equals par or proceeds slower than par.

The recommended adjustment associated with "off" tracks is simple, but requires a judgment call by the handicapper. Turf courses might be labeled "good," "soft," or "yielding," but the empirical question is whether the weather conditions proved sufficiently severe to slow final times by two seconds or more.

If it has, calculate a horse's late speed and subtract a full second. Use that adjusted time to find the appropriate turf figure.

No additional numerical adjustments are recommended.

The rating procedures will be quickly comprehended by interested handicappers, but these occur in a context, as do all rating procedures, of full-dress handicapping. How to identify genuine contenders to begin, and select the ratable races? How to interpret the figures, notably figures in combination, or in a pattern?

And what about class evaluations? If a pair of classified allowance contenders earn similar figures, but one is a Laurel horse and the other from Hollywood Park, does the higher-class track deserve the nod? What if the Laurel horse has been competing in open stakes and the Hollywood horse in overnight races? What if several contenders have come together from open ungraded stakes at several tracks, a common scenario?

The following sections provide useful guidelines for answering those questions, and others. The guidelines are based on the author's experience with the rating method.

Before proceeding, here are three additional steps in the development of the rating method:

9. To determine a horse's turf figure, calculate its late speed at the distance—same or closely related—as the difference between the race's final time and fractional time, modified by the horse's lengths gained or lengths lost, and find the corresponding figure on the appropriate racetrack chart.
10. Adjust for an "unusually slow" or "faster than par" early pace by lowering or increasing the basic figure, using the calculations recommended.
11. Adjust for an "off" track surface as handicappers determine, by calculating a horse's late speed and subtracting a full second. Use the adjusted late speed to find the appropriate figure on the track's chart (see Appendix).

GUIDELINES FOR APPLYING THE RATING METHOD

Rating methods and the numbers they yield are wonderful tools that can greatly enhance, but cannot substitute for, comprehensive and fundamentally sound handicapping. The best method players, the best figure handicappers, ultimately will be those handicappers amassing the broadest array of knowledge and skill.

In expert hands, accurate figures will be more powerful than ever.

It's important in figure handicapping to identify the real contenders and select the ratable races; that is, races that best represent the horses' current form and class and also reflect customary running styles.

On the grass, these tasks can be guided by a few trusty, if peculiar, guidelines.

Regarding contenders, prepare to rate any horse that has dispensed a good race—finish in the money or within three lengths—against today's class or better in its last six races. The last six races is the standard of recent consistency among better horses.

Among the qualifiers, discount any that reveal clearly declining form in each of its last two starts, unless the last running line occurred sixty days ago, or longer, and the horse shows an impressive series of freshening workouts leading up to today's return. Declining form rarely survives on the turf.

If form is merely questionable, and the horse is dropping in class today, accept it. Class dominates in the late stages on the grass.

If claiming horses below $25,000 will be moving up in class by two levels or more today, consider any showing an impressive stretch gain or stretch run in either of the last two starts. This is especially desirable of claiming horses shipping from a higher-class track to a lower-class track. If these kind have no turf experience, but are bred for turf, accept them gleefully and assume they will finish equally as well or better on turf as on dirt.

Discount rising claiming horses that run on the lead or press the pace but ordinarily tire in the late stages.

Regarding three-year-olds, discount any, regardless of prior dirt performances, that can be expected to set a fast pace, or press that kind of pace, even if they are bred for turf. Brilliant three-year-olds regularly disappoint, many at miserly odds, when first they transfer their speed to the grass. Inexperienced on the softer footing, they simply squander too much energy too soon.

Prefer three-year-olds that can relax and come from behind, especially if they are bred for turf.

Regarding the ratable races, mark any of the most recent six that are good, and prefer races at today's exact distance, or if these are missing, prefer races at closely related distances, or within one-sixteenth of a mile of today's distance.

Be cautious when tempted to compare races at a mile with races at a longer middle distance, especially at 1⅛ miles. Check the pace pars at the varying distances. If the mile pace is customarily faster by several lengths, the comparison will be unreliable. If the pace pars at the mile and at middle distances are similar, the comparisons will be tenable.

Using the classified pars presented earlier for Hollywood Park and Laurel, the mile pace at Hollywood is 1:10.1, but the 1⅛-mile pace is 1:11.0. Handicappers at Hollywood Park should hesitate to compare milers and nine-furlong horses, notably when the early pace of the two races has been radically different. Yet the pace par at Hollywood Park at 1¹/₁₆ miles is 1:10.2, comparable to the mile pace. These comparisons make more sense.

At Laurel, the pace par is 1:11.4 at a mile, 1¹/₁₆ miles, and 1⅛ miles. Comparing races at the varying distances introduces no peculiar pace problems at Laurel.

Know your racetrack, an old axiom, applies here too.

In addition, prefer good performances, not poor performances. Numerous grass horses that come from behind will show stretch gains of several lengths perhaps, while finishing in the rear half of the field and never threatening at the prestretch or stretch calls. That kind of stretch gain is entirely misleading. It reflects the pace of the race or the ability of other horses, and not necessarily the ability of the horse to be rated. Handicappers want to know how well a horse has performed when it has run well.

At times the past performances will reveal no recent turf races at today's distance, but a few at a closely related distance, or a race at a closely related distance will appear unratable due to an unusually slow or fast pace. In these circumstances, handicappers can adjust closely related final times up or down to project a horse's final time at today's distance.

Review the Hollywood Park chart again. At the top, far right, notice the adjustments column and the numbers 6–6. These numbers reflect the differences in fifths of a second among the track's classified pars at a mile and 1¹/₁₆ miles, and at 1¹/₁₆ miles and 1⅛ miles. Thus a horse at Hollywood Park that has run 1¹/₁₆ miles in 1:42.0 would be projected to complete the mile in 1:36.0 (1:42–6). A horse that runs 1⅛ miles in 1:47.2 should go 1¹/₁₆ miles in 1:41.2.

By this procedure handicappers can project horses' final times at today's exact distance before calculating the late speed and finding the figures that apply.

If handicappers obtain multiple figures for a succession of

good performances in the recent record, use the top figure, unless it looks desperately out of line with the others. The procedure will be safer where two or more high figures are similar. Where multiple figures conflict in inexplicable patterns, use the most recent figure, unless the distance or early pace appear unreliable. In that circumstance, prefer the most recent figure that represents today satisfactorily.

Only yesterday (I swear), the feature at Hollywood Park was a classified allowance mile on the turf for older fillies and mares. It illustrates the above discussion impressively, notably since the winner was the high-rated horse I could not have selected otherwise.

Examine the past performances and use the turf-figure chart for Hollywood Park to rate the horses.

8th Hollywood

29Mar89-7SA 1 :451 1:10 1:37 ft 4½ 120 45 32½ 31½ 11 VlnzlPA1 ⒻAw36000 83-17 FormdblLdy,BgCtyMss,RlctntGst 8
Speed Index: Last Race: -2.0 3-Race Avg.: -1.6 8-Race Avg.: -0.2 Overall Avg.: -0.7
●Jly 9 Hol 3f ft :35² H ●Jly 2 Hol 1 R 1:39² H ●Jun 26 Hol 7f R 1:28² H Jun 20 Hol 6f R 1:13 H

Hickory Crest
PINCAY L JR 114
Own.—Gann E A
Ch. m. 5, by Caro—Patience Worth, by Mr Prospector
Br.—Rosenthal & Levy (Ky)
Tr.—Frankel Robert
Lifetime 23 4 4 3 $123,386
1990 6 2 4 0 $75,350
1989 10 1 0 3 $36,475
Turf 10 3 3 0 $79,321

6Jun90-8Hol 1 ⓣ:4541:10 1:35 fm 3½ 117 11½ 11½ 12½ 12 PincyLJr5 ⒻAw38000 89-11 HickoryCrest,Bldomro,ExcllntLdy 7
5Apr90-8SA 1 ⓣ:4531:10 1:35³fm 4½ 1105 11½ 11½ 12½ 21½ CstnnJL2 ⒻAw47000 83-15 Kiwi, Hickory Crest, Remedios 7
17Mar90-5SA a6½f ⓣ:21³ :4331:13⁴fm *3 1125 32 11½ 13 12 CstnnJL2 ⒻAw38000 92-08 HckrCrst,ElgncInDsgn,DrmngBl 10
22Feb90-5SA a6½f ⓣ:21 :4311:13²fm *3 1115 32½ 32 3½ 21½ CstnnJL1 ⒻAw42000 92-06 Sedulous, Hickory Crest, Dreamt 8
22Feb90—Troubled trip
24Jan90-3SA a6½f ⓣ:21² :4331:131fm 5½ 1125 32 2hd 2½ 21½ CstnnJL8 ⒻAw38000 94-05 Sexy Slew, Hickory Crest, Trin 10
11Jan90-7SA 6½f :22 :444 1:16²ft *6-5 1125 2½ 21½ 22½ 23 CstnnJL6 ⒻAw38000 85-16 InvrnssLdy,HckoryCrst,CmdyCrt 7
26Jly89-7Dmr 6f :21⁴ :443 1:09³ft 3½ 118 44 54 86¼ 86¼ DlhssyE6 ⒻAw33000 84-16 Racer'sFolly,SingingPirte,Jo'sJoy 8
3Jly89-3Hol 6½f :21² :433 1:15¹ft 3½ 122 44½ 35½ 32½ 36½ PdrzMA4 ⒻAw31000 92-10 Bistra, My Treat, Hickory Crest 6
17Jun89-4Hol 1 :45 1:09⁴ 1:35³ft 2½ 120 32 22 22 35½ PdrzMA6 ⒻAw33000 80-15 StickyWl,SugrplumGl,HckoryCrst 6
17Jun89—Wide into stretch
19May89-7Hol 6f :22 :444 1:09¹ft 6 119 4nk 1hd 13½ 16 PdrzMA2 ⒻAw27000 95-08 Hickory Crest, Sabatini, I'mEarly 7
Speed Index: Last Race: 0.0 2-Race Avg.: -1.0 2-Race Avg.: -1.0 Overall Avg.: -0.4
Jly 7 Hol 6f R 1:13⁴ H Jun 26 Hol 4f R :50 H Jun 20 Hol 5f R 1:01³ B Jun 14 Hol 3f ft :36¹ B

Light Ice
STEVENS G L 114
Own.—Wimborne Farm
B. f. 4, by Arctic Tern—Lady Winborne, by Secretariat
Br.—Winborne Farm Inc (Ky)
Tr.—Whittingham Charles
Lifetime 16 4 1 4 $114,875
1990 5 1 0 1 $38,725
1989 11 3 1 3 $75,150
Turf 11 2 1 4 $80,175

30May90-8Hol 1⅛ ⓣ:4841:12⁴1:43³fm 8 118 21 21½ 33 34½ StvnsGL3 ⒻAw60000 73-26 Nikishk,TropiclStephnie,LightIce 6
30May90—Rank 7/8 turn
19Apr90-8SA 1 ⓣ:4521:08²1:34 fm 8 119 44½ 44 55½ 56¾ McCrrCJ1 ⒻAw54000 86-07 LfAtThTop,BrghtAsst,Agrlfromrs 5
24Mar90-8SA a6½f ⓣ:21¹ :43 1:13 fm 13 115 66½ 67½ 68½ 610 DsrKJ3 ⒻLs CngasH 86-04 StylshStr,‡StormyBtVld,HotNovl 6
24Mar90—Bumped hard start
1Feb90-7SA 1⅛ ⓣ:4631:12¹1:49³gd 6 119 53½ 52½ 2hd 12 McCrrCJ6 ⒻAw47000 82-18 LightIce,Sherard,Dncingintheprk 7
1Feb90—Bumped start
5Jan90-8SA 1 ⓣ:4541:09¹1:33⁴fm 5½ 120 75½ 76 56 45½ McCrrCJ3 ⒻAw47000 89-07 Agrlfromrs,CollctvJoy,SngSwtSyl 8
5Jan90—Wide into stretch
22Dec89-8Hol 1⅛ ⓣ:4821:12³1:43 fm*6-5 115 42 41½ 4½ 1½ McCrrCJ4 ⒻAw38000 79-18 LightIce,MroonBuck,ChrmedOne 7
22Dec89—Lacked room 1/2

***Jabalina Brown**
ALMEIDA G 116
Own.—Haras Rosa do Sol
B. m. 5, by Dark Brown—Destination, by Logical
Br.—Haras Rosa del Sur (Arg)
Tr.—McAnally Ronald
Lifetime 20 5 4 1 $144,424
1990 5 0 1 1 $38,280
1989 7 2 1 0 $77,380
Turf 16 3 4 1 $93,417

15Jun90-8Hol 1⅛ ⓣ:4741:12 1:41²fm 7½ 116 52½ 31½ 22½ 23½ AlmeidG6 ⒻAw60000 84-11 T.V.OfCrystl,JblnBrwn,SwtRbrtII 6
12May90-8GG 1⅜ ⓣ:4831:38²2:15³fm 12 111 55¾ 53½ 45½ 45½ AldG2 ⒻYrba Bna H 88-09 Petitelle,DoubleWedge,BrownBss 5
31Mar90-8GG 1⅛ ⓣ:4621:10²1:42³fm 17 114 716 711 57½ 34½ AldG6 ⒻGldn Ppy H 94-05 SrosBrig,FormidblLdy,JblnBrown 7
31Mar90—Grade III
18Mar90-8GG 1⅛ :46³ 1:10 1:42 ft 18 114 811 79½ 810 85¾ AldG6 ⒻMs AmrcaH 82-19 FantsticLook,AmyLouise,Dwnelo 9
25Feb90-8SA 1 ⓣ:4541:09⁴1:34¹fm 58 114 1012109¾ 97½ 85½ AldG2 ⒻBna Vsta H 87-08 Saros Brig,RoyalTouch,Nikishka 10
25Feb90—Grade III
17Dec89-8BM 1⅛ :46 1:10 1:42¹ft 4 115 59 55 23 1¾ AlmdG6 ⒻChl Hsp H 86-18 JblinBrown,AmyLouis,HllownBby 9
17Nov89-5Hol 1 ⓣ:4631:10¹1:34²fm 8 115 32½ 52½ 53½ 53 BolngrG2 ⒻAw45000 89-09 InvitedGuest,RintrRngd,Dvi'sLmb 6
17Nov89—Wide into drive
7Oct89-10LaD 1⅜ ⓣ:4931:40²2:15⁴gd 4 112 1½ 32 34 42¾ MRQ7 ⒻGold Hrv H 84-16 GailyGaily,MariJesse,GenerlChrge 8
7Oct89—Grade II
17Sep89-8BM 1⅛ :47 1:11² 1:46³m 2½ 114 38 37½ 2hd 15 CpTM2 ⒻTznBdCpH 59-40 JblinBrown,AmyLouise,ClenLines 4
17Aug89-7Dmr 1 ⓣ:4741:12 1:36²fm 2¾ 116 34 43½ 43 43½ VlnzlPA1 ⒻAw42000 85-16 YoungFlyr,GoldFrcrckr,SgrplmGl 8
17Aug89—Rank 7/8 turn
Speed Index: Last Race: -5.0 3-Race Avg.: -3.0 7-Race Avg.: -2.1 Overall Avg.: -1.1
Jun 30 Hol 5f ft 1:00³ H Jun 24 Hol 4f ft :48 H Jun 9 Hol 6f ft 1:16² H Jun 4 Hol 5f ft 1:02³ H

Warning Zone
MEZA R Q 114
Own.—Covella & Hernandez
B. m. 5, by Inverness Drive—Passionate Baby, by Full Pocket
Br.—Sugar Hill Farm No 1 (Fla)
Tr.—McAnally Ronald
Lifetime 22 8 3 4 $274,450
1990 6 1 1 2 $66,550
1989 7 4 0 1 $146,375
Turf 9 2 2 1 $114,425

2Jun90-8GG 6f :21 :43¹ 1:08³ft *3-5 120 32 31 2½ 1nk MezaRQ1 ⒻOrnda H 95-10 WrningZone,PlumePoppy,GrnNot 5
28Apr90-8SA a6½f ⓣ:21 :4311:12⁴fm 5½ 119 11½ 13½ 13 2½ MzRQ1 ⒻMt Wlsn 96-03 PprPrncss,WrnngZon,TrpclStphn 8
24Mar90-8SA a6½f ⓣ:21¹ :43 1:13 fm 4½ 116 11½ 11½ 2hd 43 SlsA1 ⒻLs Cngas H 93-04 StylshStr,‡StormyBtVld,HotNovl 6
24Mar90—Placed third through disqualification; Bumped start
4Mar90-7SA a6½f ⓣ:21 :44 1:14 fm 5½ 117 21½ 21½ 31 52½ PncLJr4 ⒻB Thtfl 88-09 HotNovel,LindaCard,VarietyBby 13
14Feb90-8SA a6½f ⓣ:20⁴ :43 1:13 fm 4½ 118 22 2½ 1½ 84¾ MRQ9 ⒻMnrva H 91-04 Down Again, Sexy Slew,HotNovel 9
14Feb90—Grade III
6Jan90-8SA 6f :21¹ :43⁴ 1:08¹ft *9-5 119 2hd 1½ 1hd 32½ MzRQ7 ⒻLs Flrs H 92-08 StormyButVlid,Surviv,WrningZon 7

7513 —EIGHTH RACE. 1 mile (turf). 4 year olds & up. Fillies & mares. Allowance. Purse $60,000.

Index	Horse and Jockey	Wt.	PP	ST	¼	½	¾	Str.	Fin.	To $1
7351	Jabalina Brown, Almeida	116	4	5	5	3^1	2^1	$2^{1/2}$	1no	5.70
6782	Warning Zone, Meza	114	5	1	1^4	1^3	$1^{1/2}$	$1^{1/2}$	$2^{1/2}$	2.20
7242	Light Ice, Stevens	114	3	3	3^{hd}	5	5	5	3^{nk}	4.90
6755	Formidable Lady, P.Vinzla	116	2	2	2^1	2^{hd}	3^{hd}	4^{hd}	4^{hd}	2.20
7351	Down Again, C.Black	114	1	4	4^1	4^{hd}	4^1	$3^{1 1/2}$	5	2.90

Scratched—Hickory Crest.

4—JABALINA BROWN	13.40	6.40	2.80
5—WARNING ZONE		4.00	2.40
3—LIGHT ICE			3.00

Time—24 1/5, 47 3/5, 1.11 3/5, 1.35 3/5. Clear & firm. Winner—b.m.85 Dark Brown—Destination. Trained by Ronald McAnally. Mutuel pool—$198,187. Exacta pool—$210,764.

$2 EXACTA (4-5) PAID $48.20

JABALINA BROWN trailed early, moved up gradually on the backstretch, pressed the issue on the far turn, kept to her task with determination in the drive and was able to just get up in the final jump to nip WARNING ZONE. The latter went to the front at once, moved over to the inner rail before going a quarter, drew well clear in the opening quarter, held on gamely through the drive but was nosed out by the winner at the finish.

Down Again

Not an easy horse to rate. Only two miles in the last six races, neither good, but both acceptable (within six lengths of the winner in a higher-class race). Its finishing time Feb 25 was 24.3, a figure of 105. On Nov 5, finishing time is 24.4, a figure of 103. Down Again gets a 105.

Formidable Lady

Two good races in last six, one at 1¹⁄₁₆ miles at Golden Gate, the other at a mile at Santa Anita. Finishing time at GG is 31.3, which projects to 25 flat at a mile, for a figure at GG of 103. Finishing time at Santa Anita is 24 flat, figure of 100. Formidable Lady earns a 103.

Hickory Crest

The last running line is ratable, to be sure. Late speed is 25 flat at Hollywood Park, for a figure of 102.

Light Ice

Using the last running line, distance at 1¹⁄₁₆ miles, late speed is 31.2, for a figure of 106, but the pace of the race was "unusually slow" at Hollywood Park. The adjusted figure is 103. The poor race at a mile April 19 is not rated.

Jabalina Brown

Using the last running line, at 1¹/₁₆ miles, Jabalina Brown finished following a slow pace at 29.4, which gets a figure of 112. The adjusted figure is 106. In situations of this kind, additional evidence is strongly recommended. At a mile at Hollywood Park on Nov 17 (seven races back), Jabalina Brown finished in 24.2, beaten three lengths, earning another 106.

Warning Zone

A sprinter, Warning Zone last attempted a mile at Santa Anita Nov 5 (seven races back). Finishing time was 25.2, a figure of 89, but the frontrunner set an early pace five lengths faster than the pace par at Santa Anita. The adjusted figure is 99.

Jabalina Brown earned the top figure by 1½ lengths and won the race by a thrilling nose as the highest-priced choice in the field.

Handicappers should not fail to notice the tardy pace set by Warning Zone, or that Jabalina Brown ran last at the first call. The winner circled the field on the turn and wore down Warning Zone throughout the stretch, barely winning. I especially like that a turf figure earned at 1¹/₁₆ miles applied successfully to a mile race.

Key Race

Moments of discovery or serendipity come so beautifully wrapped in the peaking sensations we rarely feel. I knew I had grabbed onto something useful without a doubt after handicapping the Grade 2 Bay Meadows Handicap during fall 1989. It was December 16, to be precise. I had just completed what I had hoped would be a few final adjustments in the rating procedures, and I considered the race a test case. The horses in the field came together from Bay Meadows, Gulfstream Park, Arlington Park, Hollywood Park, Laurel, and Santa Anita.

By conventional handicapping, it was a difficult race. Let's review the nine-furlong race, purse of a quarter-million, using the figure charts from the various tracks to rate the contenders.

Fair Judgment

On a "good" surface, last out, finishing time at 1⅛M at Hollywood is 35.4, figure of 117. No adjustment for an "off" track, in my opinion.

Simply Majestic

Another "off" track last out. Finishing time at a mile at Gulfstream is 26.1, for a figure of 86. The adjusted time, 25.1, Gulfstream Park, gets a 94. An unacceptably low figure for an outstanding stakes horse. I next rated the April 29 race at Golden Gate, same circuit, at 1¹/₁₆ miles. Late speed now is 30.3, the figure a splendid 114. A difficult choice, the recent 94 or distant 114. Anytime handicappers dig beyond the recent record, certainly the last six races, the risk of committing an egregious error arises.

Delegant

The second line back, at Bay Meadows, another "off" track, the adjusted late speed is 35.4, for a figure of 105.

Nediym

No complications here. Last line, at Hollywood Park, late speed at nine furlongs is 36.1, a figure of 112.

Ten Keys

Second race back, a state-bred stakes on a "yielding" surface at Laurel, late speed, unadjusted, is 35.2, for a figure of 125.

River Master

The last running line is ratable. Finishing time is 36.1, for a figure of 112.

Colway Rally

The English-bred import has a good race at Gulfstream. Finishing time is 29 flat at 1¹/₁₆ miles—no adjustment for a deep closer against a fast pace—for a figure of 118.

7th BayMeadows

BAY MEADOWS

1⅛ MI. TURF

ABOUT 1⅛ MILES. (Turf). (1.46) 57th Running of THE BAY MEADOWS HANDICAP (Grade II). Purse $250,000 guaranteed. 3-year-olds and upward. By subscription of $200 each to accompany the nomination, $2,000 to pass the entry box and $3,000 additional to start, with $250,000 guaranteed, of which $137,500 guaranteed to the winner, $50,000 to second, $37,500 to third, $18,750 to fourth and $6,250 to fifth. Weights, Saturday, December 9, 1989. Starters to be named through the entry box by the closing time of entries. A trophy will be presented to the owner of the winner. Highweights preferred. Closed Wednesday, December 6, 1989 with 23 nominations.

Coupled—Nediym and Colway Rally.

Fair Judgment

BLACK C A T117 **117** — **B. h. 5, by Alleged—Mystical Mood, by Roberto**
Br.—Farish—Hudson—Hudson Jr (Ky) — 1989 5 2 2 0 $110,050
Tr.—Mettee Richard C F35⁴ — 1988 7 1 2 0 $90,609
Own.—Tsurumaki T — **Lifetime** 16 5 4 0 $269,298 — **Turf** 16 5 4 0 $269,298

26Nov89-8Hol 1⅛Ⓣ:49 1:132 1:50 gd 4¼ 117 67 43½ 2½ 1¾ DlhossyE 2 Citatn H 78-22 FirJudgmnt,QuitBoy,SkipOutFront 6
26Nov89—Grade II; Wide far turn

22Oct89-11Lrl 1¼Ⓣ:50 1:42 2:073sf 38 126 109 88½ 69½ 810¼ StevnsGL 9 Bud Intl 49-38 Cltech,YnkeAffir,MistrWondrfulII 11
22Oct89—Grade I

7Sep89-8Dmr 1 1/16Ⓣ:493 1:132 1:431fm *1 120 64 63¾ 51¾ 21½ Stevens G L 5 ⓇHcp0 82-19 In Extremis,FairJudgment BonVent 6
7Sep89—Bumped start

24Aug89-8Dmr 1 Ⓣ:463 1:103 1:35 fm *2 115 78½ 73½ 44½ 2nk Stevens G L 1 Aw50000 96-09 Payant, Fair Judgment, Zelphi 8
24Aug89—Wide into stretch

24May89-8Hol 1 1/16Ⓣ:48 1:113 1:41 fm 2¾ 114 64½ 63 2½ 1½ Stevens G L 4 Aw45000 89-11 FairJudgment,Pasakos,LoyalDouble 6

5Nov88♦5StCloud(Fra) a1 1:424yl 5 128 Ⓣ 42¾ Reid J Prix Perth(Gr3) FrenchStress,Somorumujo,Mlspin 14

23Oct88♦4Longchamp(Fra) a7f 1:24 sf *4-5 138 Ⓣ 55½ Reid J Px d lFrt(Gr1) Salse, Gabina, Big Shuffle 13

30Sep88♦3Goodwood(Eng) 7f 1:293gd *9-5 124 Ⓣ 11½ Reid J Supreme(Gr3) FairJudgment, Alquoz, Luzum 8

4Sep88♦4PhoenixPk(Ire) 1¼ 2:062gd 16 132 Ⓣ 65¼ Reid J Phnx Champ (Gr1) IndinSkimmer,ShdyHights,Triptych 9

14Jun88♦1Ascot(Eng) 1 1:47 fm 20 131 Ⓣ 43¼ Reid J QueenAnne(Gr2) Waajib, Soviet Star, Then Agein 5

Speed Index: Last Race: 0.0 3-Race Avg.: -4.0 5-Race Avg.: -1.4 Overall Avg.: -1.4

Dec 11 Hol 6f ft 1:143 H Dec 6 Hol 4f ft :482 H Nov 22 Hol 5f ft 1:004 H ●Nov 16 Hol Ⓣ 7f fm 1:274 H (d)

Simply Majestic

CORDERO A JR T94 **122** — **Dk. b. or br. h. 5, by Majestic Light—Beaming Bride, by King Emperor**
Br.—Keswick Stbs & Augustus (Va) — 1989 13 8 0 3 $723,718
Tr.—Parisella John F26¹/25¹ — 1988 12 5 2 2 $667,455
Own.—Sabarese T M — **Lifetime** 43 18 4 7 $1,661,463 — **Turf** 14 5 1 4 $553,275

4Nov89-7GP 1 Ⓣ:472 1:112 1:37 gd 4¾ 126 11 12 11 51½ CordrAJr 3 Br Cp Mile 86-13 Steinlen, Sabona, Most Welcome 11
4Nov89—Grade I

21Oct89-10Crc a1⅛Ⓣ 1:483fm *1-2 117 19 19 14 11 CstllHJr 8 Miami Bud 75-22 Simply Majestic, Maceo,BoldCircle 8
21Oct89—Grade III

27Aug89-9Lga 1 :451 1:091 1:341ft *4-5 122 2hd 1hd 11 11 HnsenRD 5 Lga Ml H 98-18 SimplyMjstc,CrystlRun,HrmonyCrk 9
27Aug89—Grade II

19Aug89-9Tdn 1⅛ :453 1:093 1:49 ft *1-5 122 23½ 22 22 1½ HnsenRD 5 Bd Br Cp H 92-11 SimplyMjstic,StopthStg,RosnWrror 8

19Jly89-8Atl 1 3/16Ⓣ:471 1:103 1:531gd *9-5 119 14 12½ 2½ 36¼ CrdrAJr 5 U Nations H 91-06 YnkeeAffir,SlemDrive,SimplyMjstic 5
19Jly89—Grade I

24Jun89-10Suf 1⅛ :47 1:11 1:492ft 2½ 120 11 1½ 2½ 32¼ Velasquez J 2 Mass H 89-16 PrivteTerms,Grncus,SimplyMjestic 8

18Jun89-10Rkm 1 1/16Ⓣ:473 1:112 1:423fm *2-5 126 2hd 1hd 2hd 12 SnttN 2 Bud Brd Cp H 104-06 SimplyMjestic,Achenr,MkeThMost 6

7May89-8GG 1⅛ :453 1:084 1:472ft *1-2 128 14 13 13 13½ Hansen RD 1 Knsgtn H 88-14 SimplyMjstic,RcttonSpn,Bosphorus 4

29Apr89-8GG 1 1/16Ⓣ:474 1:114 1:422fm *1-2 121 14 1½ 1½ 1no HnsnRD 6 All Amer H 90-12 SmplyMjstc,OngngMstr,AstrntPrnc 6
29Apr89—Grade III — F30³ = T118

16Apr89-8GG 1 1/16 :453 1:084 1:394ft *1-3 124 11 13 14 17 CordrAJr 5 Bd Brds Cp 100-13 SimplyMjestic,NoMrker,PerfecTrvl 7

Speed Index: Last Race: -1.0 3-Race Avg.: -2.3 5-Race Avg.: +1.0 Overall Avg.: +4.4

●Dec 10 Aqu ⊡ 5f ft 1:012 H Dec 3 Bel tr.t 7f ft 1:282 B

Delegant

CHAPMAN T M T105 **114** — **Gr. h. 5, by Grey Dawn II—Dahlia, by Vaguely Noble**
Br.—Hunt N B (Ky) — 1989 11 3 0 3 $173,797
Tr.—Whittingham Michael F36⁴/35⁴ — 1988 8 3 1 0 $66,525
Own.—Evergreen Farm — **Lifetime** 24 6 1 5 $247,331 — **Turf** 22 5 1 5 $230,831

13Nov89-8SA 1¼Ⓣ:462 1:344 1:58 fm 5½e 115 33 53 66 811¾ BlackCA 3 C F Brk H 94 — Alwuhush,FrnklyPerfect,Speedrtic 10
13Nov89—Grade I; Jostled start

21Oct89-8BM a1⅛Ⓣ:49 1:132 1:51 yl 3½ 116 77 64¼ 63¼ 4¾ ChpnTM 1 Tanforan H 74-25 BigChill,VarietyRoad,HardRockHnk 9
21Oct89—Grade III

23Sep89-9AP 1½Ⓣ:49 2:042 2:29 fm 2½ 119 32½ 32 33 35 Fires E 3 L Armour H 89-10 GreenBarb,BroadwyTommy,Delegnt 7
23Sep89—Grade II

4Sep89-9AP 1½Ⓣ:504 2:073 2:322fm 3½ 118 43½ 21½ 2½ 1no Fires E 7 Hcp0 77-23 Delegant,BroadwayTommy Djedar 10
4Sep89—Four Wide.

12Aug89-9AP 1¼Ⓣ:52 1:442 2:111sf 24 113 53½ 52½ 44 34¾ Fires E 3 Arlgtn H 33-62 UnknwnQnttyII,FrstyThSnmn,Dlgnt 5
12Aug89—Grade I

22Jly89-9AP 1⅛Ⓣ:484 1:141 1:523sf 4½ 120 77 74½ 66¼ 47½ Fires E 1 Swns Son 66-26 FrstyThSnmn,HstyEmpr,EclsvPrtnr 7
22Jly89—Grade III

***Nediym** T112
B. c. 4, by Shareef Dancer—Nilmeen, by Right Royal V
VELASQUEZ J 113
Br.—H H Aga Kahn (Ire) 1989 7 2 1 0 $118,228
Tr.—Drysdale Neil F36' 1988 8 1 2 2 $44,011
Own.—Clover Racing St Et al
Lifetime 18 4 4 2 $180,093 Turf 18 4 4 2 $180,093
2Dec89-7Hol 1⅛Ⓣ:4621:0941:462fm*8-5 117 54½ 52½ 1½ 12 Pincay L Jr5 Aw45000 96-14 Nediym, Charlatan III, Trokhos 8
2Dec89—Lugged in final 3/8
8Oct89-8Bel 1½Ⓣ:4742:0212:271gd 16 126 21½ 3½ 58 712½ Samyn J L4 Trf Clsic 75-16 Yankee Affair, El Senor, MyBigBoy 7
8Oct89—Grade I
23Sep89-8Bel 1⅜T:5111:43 2:204sf 14 126 11 11 32 48½ SmynJL8 Man O' Wr 44-47 Yankee Affair,MyBigBoy,Alwuhush 8
23Sep89—Grade I
3Sep89-8Bel 1¼T:4921:3642:00 hd*7-5 113 31 3½ 62 89 VsquzJ4 Manhattan H 85-13 Milesius, Salem Drive, My Big Boy 8
3Sep89—Grade I; Rank
29Jly89-8Bel 1½Ⓣ:4942:0342:27 hd 7½ 113 36 1½ 12 2½ VsquzJ7 Swrd Dncr H 88-06 El Senor, Nediym, My Big Boy 7
29Jly89—Grade II

Ten Keys T125
Dk. b. or br. h. 5, by Sir Ivor Again—Mabs a Babs, by Exceedingly
DESORMEAUX K J 118
Br.—Bendit R (Md) 1989 14 5 4 1 $310,795
Tr.—Pino Michael V F35² 1988 11 3 1 1 $120,914
Own.—Linhoss C T
Lifetime 43 15 8 3 $633,068 Turf 29 13 5 3 $583,812
12Nov89-10Lrl 1½Ⓣ:173 2:344yl 3 121 55 33 3½ 12½ DsrmKJ7 Turf Cup H — — TenKeys,Coosaragg,PoliticlProfit 13
12Nov89—Grade III
5Nov89-10Lrl 1⅛Ⓣ:4921:14 1:51 yl *4-5 120 66 67½ 31½ 11½ DsormuxKJ2 SFind H 78-22 Ten Keys, Rebuff, Timely Warning 9
22Oct89-11Lrl 1¼Ⓣ:50 1:42 2:073sf 15 126 1111 911 811 57 DsormxKJ2 Bud Intl 52-38 Cltech,YnkeAffir,MistrWondrfulII 11
22Oct89—Grade I
30Sep89-9Med 1⅛T:47 1:1111:421yl 2½ 114 66½ 64½ 21½ 1¾ DsrmxKJ2 Cliff Hng H 91-14 Ten Keys, Wanderkin, Soviet Lad 7
30Sep89—Grade III
7Sep89-9Pim 1⅛Ⓣ:4721:1121:421fm *2½ 119 88 87½ 54½ 2hd Pino M G2 Aw40000 92-08 Band Leader, Ten Keys, Rebuff 8
19Aug89-9Mth 1⅛Ⓣ:4931:1331:504yl 6½ 114 108½ 87½ 76½ 65½ PinoMG6 Lngfelow H 88-18 DoubleBooked,YnkAffir,VlidFund 10
19Aug89—Grade II
16Jly89-10Rkma1⅛Ⓣ 1:474fm 5½ 115 1012 94½ 54 21½ PnMG6 New Hamp H 101-06 Closing Bid, Ten Keys, Achenar 11
16Jly89—Grade III
3Jly89-11Lrl 1 Ⓣ:4641:1121:343fm*3-2 119 106½106 79½ 38½ PnMG4 Frt Mchnry H 89-08 HighlndSprings,BndLeder,TenKys 11
17Jun89-10Pim 1⅛Ⓣ:5011:1631:51 yl 9-5 116 109 66 2½ 14 Pino MG2 Chieftain H 48-45 TnKys,HghlndSprngs,Ktchnr'sRrd 10
3Jun89-10GS 1⅛Ⓣ:4841:1221:482fm 3½ 117 56½ 55½ 44 23½ Pino M G2 Camden H 96-11 GreenBrb,TenKeys,Arlene'sVlentine 5
Speed Index: Last Race: 0.0 3–Race Avg.: –1.6 9–Race Avg.: +0.5 Overall Avg.: +0.5
Dec 7 Bow 4f ft :51 B Dec 3 Bow 5f ft 1:03 B Nov 28 Bow 7f ft 1:274 H Nov 22 Bow 4f ft :493 B

River Master T112
B. c. 3(Mar), by His Majesty—Rieshamme, by Riverman
MCCARRON C J 114
Br.—Cardiff Stud Farm (Cal) 1989 7 4 1 1 $221,450
Tr.—Whittingham Charles F36' 1988 2 M 1 0 $5,200
Own.—CrdfStdFm–RdBrnsBn–Tmst
Lifetime 9 4 2 1 $226,650 Turf 6 3 1 1 $207,150
19Nov89-8Hol 1⅛Ⓣ:47 1:1011:47 fm *2½ 122 43½ 42½ 3½ 3nk McCrrCJ3 Hol Dby 93-09 LiveTheDrem,ChrlieBrly,RivrMstr 13
19Nov89—Grade I; Checked, wide
29Oct89-8SA 1⅛Ⓣ:4541:0931:454fm *1 123 33½ 32 74½ 85 DlhossyE7 Volante H 98 — Seven Rivers, Bruho, RaiseAStanza 9
29Oct89—Grade II; Lugged out lane
23Sep89-8BM 1⅛Ⓣ:46 1:1021:443fm*4-5 121 59½ 47½ 35½ 1¾ McCrrCJ8 Ascot H 80-18 River Master,SummerSale,ArtWork 9
23Sep89—Grade III; Rough journey
20Aug89-8Dmr 1⅛Ⓣ:4731:1121:48 fm*8-5e119 32½ 32½ 23½ 25½ McCrrCJ8 Dmr Dby H 87-09 Hawkster, River Master, Lode 9
20Aug89—Grade II
6Aug89-8Dmr 1⅛Ⓣ:4731:1031:423fm*3-2 115 32½ 32½ 21 11¾ McCrrnCJ8 La Jlla H 87-13 River Master, Tokatee, Art Work 8
6Aug89—Grade III

***Colway Rally** T118
Ch. h. 5, by Final Straw—Beswellia, by Frankincense
DELAHOUSSAYE E 113
Br.—LondonThoroghbrdSrvcsLtd (Eng) 1989 10 2 1 2 $58,221
Tr.—Canani Julie C 1988 3 0 2 1 $11,684
Own.—Clover Rcng Stb (Lese) Inc F29
Lifetime 25 6 6 7 $130,771 Turf 25 6 6 7 $130,771
3Nov89-9GP 1⅛Ⓣ:47 1:1031:403fm 33 116 119½117½ 64½ 22½ DlhssyE5 Theatrical H 94-08 IronCourage,ColwayRlly,Wnderkin 13
19Aug89♦3Curragh(Ire) 1 1:341gd 4½ 129 Ⓣ 33 McKnD Desmond (Gr3) LlynGwynnt,UpwrdTrend,ColwyRlly 7
30Jly89♦7Cologne(Ger) a1 1:38 sf 6½ 126 Ⓣ 32 Ives T Osterm Pkal(Gr3) Alkalde, Annabelle, Colway Rally 11
11Jly89♦4Newmarket(Eng) 7f 1:244gd 6 128 Ⓣ 42½ Ives T Bunbury Cup H Baldomero,Pinctd,KnightofMercy 18
21Jun89♦4Ascot(Eng) 1 1:404fm 10 140 Ⓣ 72½ Ives T Royal Hunt Cp H TruePnche,WoodDncer,CuveChrli 27
10Jun89♦6Haydock(Eng) 1⅛ 1:431gd *4 140 Ⓣ 1½ Nichols D Willows H ColwyRlly,DncngMnrch,GldPrspct 14
26May89♦4Haydock(Eng) 1⅛ 1:42 gd *4 136 Ⓣ 11½ Ives T Daresbury H ColwayRlly,Andx,NorthernPrinter 11
Speed Index: Last Race: +2.0 1–Race Avg.: +2.0 1–Race Avg.: +2.0 Overall Avg.: +2.0
Dec 13 Hol 4f ft :494 H Dec 7 Hol Ⓣ 6f fm 1:14 H (d) ●Nov 30 Hol Ⓣ 7f fm 1:263 H (d) Nov 24 Hol Ⓣ 6f fm 1:133 H (d)

SEVENTH RACE BayMeadows DECEMBER 16, 1989

ABOUT 1 ⅛ MILES.(Turf). (1.46) 57th Running of THE BAY MEADOWS HANDICAP (Grade II). Purse $250,000 guaranteed. 3-year-olds and upward. By subscription of $200 each to accompany the nomination, $2,000 to pass the entry box and $3,000 additional to start, with $250,000 guaranteed, of which $137,500 guaranteed to the winner, $50,000 to second, $37,500 to third, $18,750 to fourth and $6,250 to fifth. Weights, Saturday, December 9, 1989. Starters to be named through the entry box by the closing time of entries. A trophy will be presented to the owner of the winner. Highweights preferred. Closed Wednesday, December 6, 1989 with 23 nominations.
Value of race $250,000; value to winner $137,500; second $50,000; third $37,500; fourth $18,750; fifth $6,250. Mutuel pool $247,561. Exacta pool $274,953.

Last Raced	Horse	Eqt.A.Wt	PP	St	¼	½	¾	Str	Fin	Jockey	Odds $1
12Nov89 ^{10}Lrl^{1}	Ten Keys	b 5 118	5	6	$9^{1/2}$	8^{hd}	4^{1}	3^{2}	1^{3}	Desormeaux K J	8.10
3Nov89 ^{9}GP^{2}	Colway Rally	5 116	9	11	11^{5}	11^{6}	8^{2}	4^{2}	$2^{1/2}$	Delahoussaye E	a-3.40
2Dec89 ^{7}Hol^{1}	Nediym	4 113	4	4	2^{hd}	$2^{1/2}$	2^{1}	2^{hd}	3^{nk}	Velasquez J	a-3.40
13Nov89 ^{8}SA^{8}	Delegant	5 114	3	5	$6^{1/2}$	$5^{1/2}$	5^{hd}	$5^{1\frac{1}{2}}$	4^{hd}	Chapman T M	45.90
4Nov89 ^{7}GP^{5}	Simply Majestic	b 5 122	2	1	1^{3}	1^{3}	1^{3}	1^{1}	5^{3}	Cordero A Jr	1.60
26Nov89 ^{8}Hol^{1}	Fair Judgment	b 5 117	1	12	12	12	12	$6^{1/2}$	$6^{2\frac{1}{2}}$	Black C A	21.00
21Sep89 ^{4}Fra^{7}	Sweet Chesne	4 115	10	9	$8^{1/2}$	9^{1}	$6^{1/2}$	8^{2}	7no	Dettori L F	92.90
19Nov89 ^{8}Hol^{3}	River Master	3 114	6	2	3^{1}	3^{2}	3^{1}	7^{1}	$8^{1/2}$	McCarron C J	3.60
18Nov89 ^{8}BM^{2}	Big Chill	6 114	11	8	7^{2}	$7^{1/2}$	$10^{1/2}$	9^{1}	$9^{1\frac{1}{2}}$	Judice J C	33.30
23Nov89 ^{8}Hol^{6}	Variety Road	b 6 114	8	7	5^{hd}	$6^{1\frac{1}{2}}$	9^{hd}	10^{1}	$10^{1/2}$	Hansen R D	23.40
2Dec89 ^{7}BM^{2}	Polar Boy	3 111	7	3	$4^{1\frac{1}{2}}$	$4^{1\frac{1}{2}}$	7^{1}	11^{2}	11^{5}	Davis R G	18.30
26Nov89 ^{8}Hol^{3}	Skip Out Front	7 115	12	10	10^{2}	10^{hd}	11^{2}	12	12	Toro F	15.50

a-Coupled: Colway Rally and Nediym.

OFF AT 4:20 Start good. Won driving. Time, :23⅗, :47⅕, 1:11⅕, 1:36⅖, 1:46⅗ Course firm.

$2 Mutuel Prices:

5-TEN KEYS	18.20	6.80	8.00
1-COLWAY RALLY (a-entry)		4.40	4.80
1-NEDIYM (a-entry)		4.40	4.80

$2 EXACTA 5-1 PAID $77.80.

In a smorgasbord of stakes shippers at nine furlongs, the rating method indicated Ten Keys should win it comfortably, by roughly three lengths over Colway Rally 125 to 118. The result chart stands as eloquent testimony to the efficacy of that prediction.

Winning by exactly three lengths, according to Hoyle, as it were, Ten Keys paid a delicious $18.20. The $2 exacta returned $77.80, or 37.9–1. In moments like these, far apart, to be sure, thoroughbred handicapping qualifies as the greatest game of all.

TRICKY SITUATIONS

All rating methods are susceptible to the intricacies embedded in the past performances of so many horses. The author Mark Cramer refers to the "dialectics" of handicapping, or the subtle variations of the past performances that render almost every race analysis unique. I have always liked the term, despite its academic tone, because it captures the reality so well. The subtle variations of similar, but distinct, handicapping situations can be amazingly numerous.

Handicappers will confront a wide array of problem situations when implementing the rating method promoted here. Below I discuss several of the most interesting I have encountered while experimenting with the procedures. The first will be a nagging source of confusion to many practitioners, because it reflects how different turf races can be from races on dirt.

Odd Distances

The peculiar configurations of grass layouts contribute inevitably to the carding of races at unusual distances. The rating method controls for the worst of the problems.

Several racetracks program grass races repeatedly at 7½ furlongs, around two turns, normally out of a chute that winds into the clubhouse turn quickly. Del Mar, in southern California, featured the races for decades, as lately have Canterbury Downs, Bay Meadows, Golden Gate Fields, Hawthorne, and Louisiana Downs.

The adjustment to the turf-figure charts parallels the regularly run route distances symmetrically. Extrapolating from the value of one-fifth of a second at a quarter-mile, five-sixteenths, and three-eighths, a one-fifth second at the final three-sixteenths of the 7½ furlongs is valued at 1.2.

As usual, the par figure for late speed at 7½ furlongs will be 100, and for each one-fifth second of late speed faster than par, the figure is increased by 1.2 points. A horse that finishes a full second faster than par at 7½ furlongs earns a 106.

Where chutes, rails, and "about" distances are carded regularly, handicappers encounter races at a mile and 70 yards. Now the adjustment attaches to the actual times of the races. To the final time of the horse to be rated at a mile and 70 yards, add 2⅖ seconds. The adjustment corresponds to the difference in par between turf races at a mile and 70 yards and at 1¹⁄₁₆ miles. These differences tend to be standard. Review the grass pars at Canterbury Downs as an illustration.

Cheaper Races

The method is not intended to rate claiming horses below $25,000 on the grass. Cheaper horses compete on the turf irregularly and infrequently, not at all at flagship tracks. The classified allowance pars invoked as a basis for the comparative turf-figure charts promoted here are not appropriate for evaluating lower-level claiming horses.

Constructing another set of turf-figure charts using maiden pars—which typically compare well with $20,000-$25,000 claiming horses—is possible, but impractical and unnecessary.

Claiming races below $25,000 on grass occur irregularly and can be analyzed reliably by depending on three factors, pedigree, relative class, and late speed (actual times).

Because cheaper claiming horses try the turf irregularly and infrequently, many older platers inexperienced on grass can be anticipated to move up boldly on the surface if bred for grass. Always look for that impressive turf sire, top and bottom, on top especially.

Among claiming horses bred for turf, identify any in peaking form and having a class edge. The class edge might consist of track class, or consistency against better claiming opposition at any track.

Years ago I spotted a $6500 claiming shipper from Pimlico entered against $18,000 claiming horses at Atlantic City—on the grass. The Pimlico shipper had outstanding turf breeding but had never attempted the grass in Maryland. Pimlico is leagues removed from Atlantic City. At 12–1, I backed the Pimlico shipper solidly, and it won impressively, by open lengths.

That same week, I had supported a pair of shippers from Detroit Race Course and middling claiming races when they appeared at Arlington Park on the turf against similar claiming types. Neither shipper had raced on the turf, but each possessed superb grass breeding. Both had been consistent types, having won numerous races on dirt. Clearly, the trainers had decided to run for the richer turf pots at Arlington with grass-bred hard-knockers they felt belonged. One of the shippers showed little, but the other won, at 40–1, no less.

In both cases pedigree cleared the path to the windows, supported by a careful class evaluation and attractive odds. That strategy applies broadly in low-priced claiming events on the grass. Try it.

Younger Horses

Needless to say (I trust), younger, inexperienced horses switching to turf should be evaluated primarily on pedigree. Regardless of dirt form, three-year-olds and juveniles bred for grass can be expected to win on grass, and do. Bets are recommended whenever the odds permit for each of the initial two grass starts.

As stated earlier, running style is also pertinent when considering young talent on the turf. Frontrunners and pace-pressers routinely expend too much early energy when first shifted to the turf, tire in the late stages, and lose, often at miserly odds. In races for three-year-olds and juveniles, prefer off-pace types and deep closers that are bred for grass. The rewards will be collected several times a season.

Once the more brilliant types learn how to conserve their speed and power on the grass, they figure, provided the pedigree is satisfactory on turf.

THE RELATIVE UNIMPORTANCE OF EARLY PACE

Consider, below, a fine point of pace analysis on the turf. It's an understandable source of confusion to figure handicappers and pace analysts everywhere.

Examine the last running line of the past performance tables for Sperry and Breakfast Table. The two were the high-rated contenders at a mile on the Hollywood Park grass, July 8, 1990. Respectively, the turf figures for the two: Sperry 108, Breakfast Table 110.

Careful pace analysts would probably prefer Sperry—the favorite at 2–1—notwithstanding the finishing figures, but would be wrong.

The pace analyst points out that Sperry tracked a 46.1 and 1:10 flat before finishing in 24.1 seconds June 10.

Breakfast Table followed the more leisurely 47 flat and 1:10.3 on June 4, 1989, before flying home in 24 seconds.

Presumably, Sperry can throttle back to a slower pace and outfinish Breakfast Table. Or if the pace quickens for Breakfast Table, the horse cannot finish as fast. The reasoning that is perfectly logical on the dirt is frequently flawed on the turf.

Both four-furlong fractions (46.1 and 47) are relatively slow, a vital consideration. The corresponding four-furlong par for $62,500 horses at a mile at Hollywood Park on the dirt is 45.3. Sperry may be attending a faster pace on grass than Breakfast Table, but both horses are traveling relatively slowly.

9th Hollywood

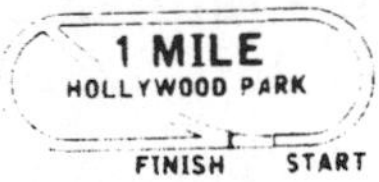

1 MILE. (Turf). (1.32⅘) CLAIMING. Purse $35,000. 4-year-olds and upward. Weight, 122 lbs. Non-winners of two races at a mile or over since May 20 allowed 3 lbs.; such a race since then, 6 lbs. Claiming price $62,500; for each $2,500 to $55,000, allowed 1 lb. (Races when entered for $50,000 or less not considered.)

***Sperry** — Ch. h. 7, by Stanford—Runctions, by Rasper II
VALENZUELA P A 116 — Br.—Oakshire Co Ltd (Eng) — 1990 6 1 3 1 $53,575
Tr.—Spawr Bill $62,500 — 1989 12 2 1 2 $68,100
Own.—ChristopoulosG-Gifford-Woo — Lifetime 49 7 10 6 $232,870 — Turf 39 6 10 5 $195,845

10Jun90-9Hol 1 Ⓣ:461 1:10 1:344fm 4¾ 116 43 42½ 42 1nk † ValenzuelPA8 62500 90-10 ‡Sperry,CarolinNorth,RcingRscl 12
†10Jun90—Disqualified and placed fourth; Came in stretch
25May90-5Hol 1 1/16 Ⓣ:474 1:111 1:41 fm*7-5 116 31 2½ 32½ 25½ ValenzuelPA9 62500 84-11 Cannon Bar, Sperry, Stanley 10
25May90—Wide backstretch
6May90-9Hol 1⅛ Ⓣ:472 1:11 1:464fm *3¼ 116 73½ 73¾ 42½ 22 ValenzuelPA2 70000 92-04 Simjour, Sperry, Cannon Bar 11
6May90—Boxed in 3/8-1/16
27Apr90-9Hol 1 Ⓣ:462 1:101 1:342fm 4 115 77 63½ 22 21 Meza R Q7 70000 91-08 Chief's Image, Sperry, Sabulose 9
31Mar90-5SA 1⅛ Ⓣ:464 1:11 1:474fm 3¾ 116 31 21½ 1½ 11¼ ValenzuelPA6 75000 86-09 Sprry,HotAndSmggy,MySnnyBy 10
3Mar90-5SA a6½f Ⓣ:21 :431 1:13 fm 12 116 810 76½ 56 35 ValenzuelPA3 70000 91-04 C. Sam Maggio,Litigated,Sperry 10
3Mar90—Bumped start
24Sep89-12Fpx 1 1/16 :453 1:11 1:422ft 7 117 21½ 3½ — — SibilR1 Ⓡ C B Aflbgh — — JstAsLcky,MghtSnow,RcttonSpn 3
24Sep89—Eased
28Aug89-5Dmr 1 Ⓣ:471 1:11 1:354fm 4 118 86¼ 75 63¾ 41¾ Stevens G L9 62500 90-09 Strt-Rt,CrolnNrth,HwVryTchng 10
28Aug89—Wide into stretch
16Aug89-3Dmr 1⅛ Ⓣ:472 1:121 1:493fm*9-5 117 43¾ 42½ 41¾ 56 Pincay L Jr3 80000 79-15 Just Bobby, Quavo, Argalaxy 7
4Aug89-7Dmr 1 Ⓣ:464 1:104 1:361fm 9¼ 114 57 65½ 54 33 Stevens G L3 85000 87-15 Rufjan, Individualist, Sperry 8
4Aug89—Steadied 1/16

Speed Index: Last Race: 0.0 3-Race Avg.: -3.0 8-Race Avg.: -2.5 Overall Avg.: -2.7
Jly 5 Hol 4f ft :492 H

Breakfast Table — B. h. 6, by Never Tabled—Briquette, by T V Lark
STEVENS G L 116 — Br.—Windy Hill T B A (Cal) — 1989 6 1 0 1 $27,600
Tr.—Mandella Richard $62,500 — 1988 7 1 1 0 $30,650
Own.—Taub S M — Lifetime 17 3 1 1 $71,275 — Turf 11 2 1 1 $58,250

4Jun89-9Hol Ⓣ:47 1:103 1:343fm 9¼ 115 21 2hd 1hd 11¼ Toro F4 Aw30000 91-10 BreakfastTable,ReveDore,Stlwrs 10
21May89-7Hol 1 1/16 Ⓣ:462 1:10 1:404fm 12 115 49 55½ 2hd 43¾ Toro F9 Aw30000 86-09 Desert Crest, Ramonda, Everso 9
13Apr89-8SA 1⅛ Ⓣ:46 1:112 1:474fm 19 116 21½ 21½ 24 37 Black C A7 Aw41000 81-12 SplendorCtch,RevDor,BrkfstTbl 10
12Mar89-3SA a6½f Ⓣ:22 :441 1:144fm 25 116 107¾ 86¾ 47 44¾ DlhoussyE2 Aw36000 88-13 BrveCpde,GoodDelivernc,Drmtis 10
12Mar89—Crowded final 1/8
18Feb89-7SA a6½f Ⓣ:214 :444 1:154gd 18 116 911 65½ 55½ 65½ McCrrnCJ1 Aw36000 74-20 GrndTier,Exceller'sSpcil,BrvCpd 10
20Jan89-5SA 1 1/16 :47 1:111 1:414ft 102 116 116¾ 95¾ 88¼ 811¾ Olguin G L 7 Aw38000 80-13 NoCnLos,FildOfViw,RcittionSpn 12
20Jan89—6 wide into drive
31Dec88-5SA 1 1/16 :47 1:11 1:424ft 48 117 41¼ 74¾ 910 1013¼ Solis A 11 Aw38000 73-10 GoldAnd,RcittionSpin,FildOfViw 11
22May88-7Hol 1⅛ Ⓣ:471 1:103 1:472fm 4¾ 117 33½ 21 33 57 StevensGL 6 Aw40000 84-09 StreetParty,Nilambr,BestSolution 8
24Apr88-9SA 1⅛ Ⓣ:482 1:123 1:501gd*9-5 118 53½ 73½ 64¼ 79 McCrrnCJ 8 Aw42000 67-25 Eliminante, Nilambar, All Cat 8
9Apr88-2SA 1⅛ Ⓣ:473 1:113 1:483fm 5¾ 118 99 96¼ 54 22½ McCrrnCJ1 Aw42000 81-08 RomnticPrinc,BrkfstTbl,StrtPrty 9
9Apr88—Wide into stretch

Speed Index: Last Race: +1.0 3-Race Avg.: -3.6 6-Race Avg.: -6.1 Overall Avg.: -7.4
Jly 3 Hol 7f ft 1:27 H ● Jun 28 Hol 6f ft 1:122 H Jun 22 Hol 6f ft 1:142 H Jun 15 SA 5f ft 1:01 H

Consider the early-energy output of the two: Sperry 50.89 percent and Breakfast Table 50.49 percent. The early-energy par on the dirt would be 51.80 percent, roughly eight to ten lengths faster. The same energy patterns are prevalent in the great majority of turf routes. Grass horses have lots left, as do *both* Sperry and Breakfast Table.

Thus the fastest finisher often wins, regardless of the early pace.

The point is this: unless the early pace has been extraordinarily fast, early pace is not relevant to figure handicapping on the turf.

As if to testify eloquently on the matter, Breakfast Table sat comfortably behind a 46.2 and 1:10.2 in the sample race, and finished again in exactly 24 flat, earning—again—a turf figure of 110. He paid a generous $12.40.

7505—NINTH RACE. 1 mile (turf). 4 year olds & up. Claiming prices $62,500-$55,000. Purse $35,000.

Index	Horse and Jockey	Wt.	PP	ST	¼	½	¾	Str.	Fin.	To $1
— —	Breakfast Table, Stevens	116	4	2	2^3	$2^{2½}$	$2^{1½}$	$1^{2½}$	$1^{2¾}$	5.20
7325	Sperry, P.Valenzuela	116	3	4	$3^{1½}$	3^1	3^1	2^1	$2^{2¾}$	2.30
7325	Lordalik, Davis	116	2	5	$5^{1½}$	4^{hd}	$4^{1½}$	$4^{1½}$	3^{nk}	3.10
7456	Cannon Bar, Delahoussaye	119	6	8	8	8	8	$6^{½}$	4^2	4.00
7361	Strung Up, Solis	116	5	7	$7^{2½}$	7^1	7^1	$5^{½}$	5no	16.10
7325	Fabulous Sound, Nakatani	113	1	3	1^2	$1^{1½}$	1^{hd}	$3^{½}$	6^1	5.90
7393	Stanley, Desormeaux	113	8	6	6^4	6^4	$6^{1½}$	7^{hd}	7^{nk}	18.90
6569	Jonleat, Sibille	116	7	1	$4^{½}$	$5^{1½}$	$5^{½}$	8	8	40.90

Scratched—Georgia River, Leasee.
Claimed—None.

4—BREAKFAST TABLE	12.40	5.60	3.20
3—SPERRY		3.60	2.60
2—LORDALIK			2.60

Time— 23 1/5, 46 2/5, 1.10 2/5, 1.34 2/5. Cloudy & firm. Winner—b.g.84 Never Tabled—Briquette. Trained by Richard Mandella. Mutuel pool—$365,177. Exacta pool—$529,519. Triple pool—$401,511.

BAPTISM

Opening Day, Del Mar, 1990, a racing day destined to live in gleeful memory for a handicapper who has long regarded the popular seaside oval near San Diego as a personal nemesis. On Day 1 of a season-long tryout (43 days) of my spanking-new turf figures, the numbers triumphed.

Del Mar, a peculiar track having sharp, improperly banked turns and an 840-foot stretch that contribute regularly to unfathomable biases and upsets on the mile dirt course, does redeem itself by carding a truly major turf program of stakes, assorted allowances, and high-priced claiming events. No fewer than eleven stakes on the grass are paraded before handicappers during the forty-three days. A shortened series of 7½-furlong grass runs around two turns spices the turf program, the only offering of races at the odd distance in southern California.

Granted easy access to Del Mar from the intertrack-wagering site at Santa Anita near my residence, I decided the 1990 summer season would be practically perfect for the inaugural full-season baptism-by-fire of the turf-figure methodology.

Could the figures beat the Del Mar grass season? By what margin? My friend and colleague Tom Brohamer agreed to play along using the same charts and figures. Brohamer had increasingly deserted turf races using conventional speed and pace methods, and thereby qualified as a particularly interested and observant critic, not to mention as solid a handicapper as exists.

The traditional opening-day feature at Del Mar is the Oceanside Stakes at a mile on grass for three-year-olds. It's become traditional too to split the race into two divisions, to accommodate the waiting list of grass horses. No four-horse feature here. On this day two divisions ran again, and in the first half I began to salivate over a closer with a tremendous figure advantage. I liked the second half too, and prepared to bet a pair of nonfavorites there.

In the second race, a nonwinners allowance affair for 3up that had not won $3000 twice other than maiden or claiming, the three high-figure horses looked like this in the past performances:

2nd Del Mar

1 1/16 MILES. (Turf). (1:40) ALLOWANCE. Purse $41,000. 3-year-olds and upward. Non-winners of $3,000 twice other than maiden, claiming or starter. Weights, 3-year-olds, 116 lbs.; older, 122 lbs. Non-winners of two races other than claiming at one mile or over since June 1 allowed 2 lbs.; of such a race other than maiden or claiming since then, 4 lbs. (Horses eligible only to the above conditions are preferred). (Winners that have started for a claiming price of $25,000 or less in their last three starts and maidens that are non-starters for a claiming price have second preference).

Racing Rascal				
SOLIS A				
Own.—Gatti R J				

Speed Index Last Race: -1.0   3-Race Avg.: -4.3   4-Race Avg.: -6.0   Overall Avg.: -2.8

Major Moment — Ch. c. 4, by Raise a Native—Olympic Moment, by Olympiad King
DESORMEAUX K J — 120 — Br.—Smith Helen & Alvarez J (Ky) — 1990 6 2 1 0 $47,150
Own.—Alvarez & Smith — Tr.—Sadler John W — 1989 4 M 1 0 $6,525
Lifetime 10 2 2 0 $53,675 — Turf 2 1 0 0 $22,900
24Jun90-9Hol 1 ①:463 1:102 1:344fm 6½ 116 75¼ 42 2hd 11½ DsormxKJ 9 Aw37000 90-10 MajorMoment,Rejim,SmrtDollrs 10
24Jun90—4-wide stretch
28May90-9Hol 1 1/16 :452 1:103 1:432gd 3¼ 116 43½ 23 22½ 23 DsormxKJ 4 Aw35000 80-21 LVoygur,MjorMomnt,Exclrbrtion 6
28May90—Veered out break
22Apr90-9SA a6½f ①:212 :434 1:131fm 10 120 31 32½ 31½ 43½ DsormxKJ 1 Aw34000 91-05 AbergwaunLad,MyNiriko,Patpsco 8
21Mar90-7SA 6½f :221 :452 1:164ft 9-5 120 51¾ 34 79¾ 716¼ McCrrnCJ 7 Aw34000 70-21 GoOnIn,SunStreak,LegalTenderII 7
21Mar90—Lugged in
8Mar90-6SA 6½f :222 :454 1:164ft 6½ 120 32 31½ 3nk 14½ DesormeuxKJ 6 Mdn 86-16 MjorMmnt,Spnsrshp,ClgryStmpd 7
8Mar90—Bumped 3/4, 5/8
2Feb90-3SA 6f :222 :46 1:114ft 8¼ 119 21 21 32 54½ Solis A 8 Mdn 73-23 ButfulMlody,LuckyLckyYo,Wrror 8
2Feb90—Lugged in 3/8
10Dec89-4Hol 1 :45 1:10 1:362ft 9¾ 118 2hd 21 23½ 25½ Solis A 10 Mdn 76-18 Ole',MajorMoment,L'AustYouth 10
10Dec89—Bumped 3/8
25Nov89-4Hol 6f :214 :442 1:082ft 38 119 41¾ 43½ 48½ 414 Solis A 1 Mdn 85-08 NvjoStorm,ScrtShw,LuckyLckyYo 8
2Sep89-4Dmr 6f :214 :444 1:093ft 5½ 117 1111 1111 1112 1112¾ Davis R G 8 Mdn 77-11 JklinPride,Geyser,BolshoiBginnr 12
5Aug89-2Dmr 6f :221 :452 1:10 ft 12 117 77 78¼ 89¾ 812 Davis R G 6 Mdn 76-15 Portal, Sun Streak, Gift Of Gold 10
5Aug89—Broke in, bumped
Speed Index: Last Race: 0.0 1-Race Avg.: 0.0 1-Race Avg.: 0.0 Overall Avg.: [illegible]
Jly 23 Dmr 4f ft :49 H Jly 18 SA 1 ft 1:424 H Jly 12 SA 5f ft 1:02 H Jly 6 SA 3f ft :354 H

Eratone — Ch. g. 5, by Exclusive Era—Last Bell, by Nicaray
STEVENS G L — 118 — Br.—Two Ten Tony Farm (Cal) — 1990 8 2 2 2 $54,350
Own.—Segal-Segal-Xitco — Tr.—Canani Julio C — 1989 7 2 0 1 $21,320
Lifetime 16 4 2 3 $75,670 — Turf 4 2 0 1 $41,950
13Jly90-9Hol 1⅛ ①:472 1:113 1:481fm *7-5 L 120 64 52¾ 1hd 13 Stevens G L 2 H25000 87-11 Eratone,Shirkee,SwingsFirstDnce 9
23Jun90-6Hol 1 1/16 ①:482 1:12 1:414fm 3 115 42½ 32½ 53 43½ BlckCA 1 Ⓢ Khaled H 82-14 RiverMstr,ElgntBrgin,StylishStd 5
18May90-8Hol 1⅛ ①:474 1:112 1:472fm 3½ 120 52½ 52 21½ 3nk Black C A 3 Aw37000 91-12 Kanatiyr,AdvocateTrining,Ertone 7
18May90—Jostled at break
3May90-9Hol 1 1/16 ①:463 1:102 1:404fm 7½ 116 74½ 62¾ 11½ 16 Black C A 6 Aw32000 91-10 Eratone, King Armour, Rejim 8
15Apr90-9SA 1 1/16 :47 1:113 1:423ft 4½ 116 85½ 65¼ 34½ 24½ Davis R G 9 c25000 85-12 TheMhrsCs,Erton,HurryAndSpdy 9
15Apr90—Wide
24Mar90-9SA 1 1/16 :464 1:12 1:434ft 4 116 63¾ 32½ 2½ 22 VlenzuelPA 7 c20000 82-21 Buckland'sHalo,Ertone,Vysotsky 11
24Mar90—Wide in stretch
8Mar90-5SA 7f :224 :452 1:231ft *2¾ 116 54 55 34½ 33 Davis R G 5 20000 84-16 Lark'sLegacy,RumboSet,Ertone 11
8Mar90—Broke slowly
28Jan90-1SA 6f :213 :451 1:11 ft 13 116 1113 1110 89½ 67 Davis R G 6 20000 74-19 InftnHdg,SprbMmnt,MrcAndM 11
28Jan90—Broke slowly
25Oct89-9SA 1 :461 1:112 1:371ft 4 116 54 4nk 3nk 11 Davis R G 3 Ⓢ 12500 83-21 Ertone,GreekTurf,Pirte'sAdvntur 8
25Oct89—4-wide into lane
15Oct89-4SA 6½f :213 :441 1:162ft 20 118 89¾ 87½ 89½ 812½ Black C A 1 Aw31000 75-13 BlueEydDnny,Portl,TimForShmns 9
15Oct89—Broke in a tangle
Speed Index: Last Race: -2.0 3-Race Avg.: -1.0 4-Race Avg.: -0.5 Overall Avg.: -1.7
Jly 22 Dmr 3f ft :362 H Jly 10 Hol 4f ft :482 H Jly 4 Hol 4f ft :48 H Jun 19 Hol 4f ft :481 H

The grass figures were:

Racing Rascal 116
Eratone 114
Major Moment 110

Exiting high-priced claiming races open to older horses, Racing Rascal qualified on class here, a point I trust experienced handicappers appreciate. Eratone looked cheaper, though far more impressive in four grass attempts, and had sparkled since claimed April 15 by Julio Canani, a claiming specialist in southern California. Major Moment fit the nonwinners conditions snugly and had just won smartly on the Hollywood Park turf.

At 10–1, a definite overlay, Racing Rascal beat Major Moment narrowly by a head. The $2 exacta paid $149.60, how generous! Eratone finished third. One-two-three, and like lightning the turf figures had crackled to a rapid start at old Del Mar.

Now to the fifth race, the top half of the Oceanside, and the prime bet of the afternoon. Without winning in three attempts on the turf, the colt Mehmetori had earned grass figures of 131 at 1⅛ miles, 112 at 1¹/₁₆ miles, and 110 at a mile, today's distance. No other contender had earned a 110 at any distance. The closest rival showed a 108 at 1¹/₁₆ miles.

The favorite, Robyn Dancer, rated poorly, getting a 103 (mile) and 98 in its previous pair of grass tries. It's instructive to examine Mehmetori's record in finer detail.

Handicappers should notice how impressively the colt has outrun its odds since being switched to the turf, not an uncommon form reversal.

The only hesitation involves today's distance. Can Mehmetori get up at a mile? Unless the pace appears to be unusually slow, the answer must be yes. Even at a mile, the final quarter-mile normally prevails on grass. Mehmetori's improving figures—110, 112, 131—suggest he might outclass this bunch clearly.

As for the six-week layoff, the workouts eradicate any doubts about form. It's an important point. Turf routers regularly return from extensive layoffs—far longer than six weeks—

and win. Why? The pace is relatively slow and the freshened horses do not tire as they might in a fast-paced dirt route.

An import that had won a listed stakes at seven furlongs in England ran a huge race here, but not big enough to resist a charging Mehmetori. The colt lagged far behind an ordinary pace of 46.4 and 1:11.1 before exploding under a clever gutty ride by jockey Julio Garcia. He won, paying $9.40.

FIFTH RACE
Del Mar
JULY 25, 1990

1 MILE.(Turf). (1.34$\frac{1}{5}$) 40th Running of THE OCEANSIDE STAKES (1st Division). $60,000 added. 3-year-olds. Non-winners of *$35,000 in 1990. By subscription of $75 each, which shall accompany the nomination, $300 to pass the entry box and $300 additional to start, with $60,000 added, of which $12,000 to second, $9,000 to third, $4,500 to fourth and $1,500 to fifth. Weight, 121 lbs. Non-winners of $60,000 at one mile or over allowed 3 lbs.; of such a race of $30,000 5 lbs.; of such a race of $22,000 or $17,000 any distance, 7 lbs. (Maiden and claiming races not considered). Highweights preferred. Starters to be named through the entry box Sunday, July 22, by the closing time of entries. A trophy will be presented to the owner of the winner. *A race worth $35,000 to the winner. Closed Wednesday, July 18, 1990 with 34 nominations.

Value of race $67,575; value to winner $40,575; second $12,000; third $9,000; fourth $4,500; fifth $1,500. Mutuel pool $467,270. Exacta pool $444,246.

Last Raced	Horse	M/Eqt.	A.	Wt	PP	St	¼	½	¾	Str	Fin	Jockey	Odds $1
10Jun90 ^{8}Hol^{2}	Mehmetori	Lb	3	114	9	8	10	10	$9^{1/2}$	5^{1}	1^{hd}	Garcia J A	3.70
20Jun90 ^{1}Eng^{9}	In Excess II		3	116	3	10	5^{2}	5^{1}	5^{hd}	4^{1}	$2^{1\,3/4}$	Stevens G L	3.70
4Jly90 ^{9}Hol^{2}	Predecessor	b	3	114	8	6	9^{6}	9^{4}	8^{1}	$6^{1/2}$	3^{hd}	Desormeaux K J	11.80
14Jly90 ^{9}Hol^{1}	Green's Leader	L	3	114	6	4	6^{1}	7^{1}	4^{1}	$3^{1/2}$	4^{2}	Davis R G	20.50
26May90 ^{8}Hol^{6}	Robyn Dancer	L	3	118	5	1	3^{1}	3^{1}	$2^{1/2}$	1^{hd}	5^{hd}	Valenzuela P A	3.10
9Jun90 ^{7}Hol^{5}	Old Alliance		3	117	2	3	$2^{1\,1/2}$	2^{1}	1^{hd}	2^{hd}	$6^{3/4}$	Pincay L Jr	9.20
7Jly90 ^{2}Hol^{1}	Cee's Tizzy		3	116	4	9	$8^{1\,1/2}$	$8^{1/2}$	7^{hd}	$7^{1\,1/2}$	7^{6}	Delahoussaye E	6.60
7Jly90 ^{5}Hol^{3}	Officer Hawk		3	116	1	2	$1^{1\,1/2}$	1^{hd}	$3^{1/2}$	$8^{2\,1/2}$	8^{3}	Solis A	10.50
9Jun90 ^{7}Hol^{6}	Shapiro's Hero	Lb	3	116	10	7	4^{hd}	4^{hd}	10	10	9^{1}	Pedroza M A	21.40
7Jly90 ^{5}Hol^{4}	Senegalaise	L	3	116	7	5	7^{1}	6^{hd}	6^{1}	$9^{1/2}$	10	Baze R A	30.20

OFF AT 4:24. Start good. Won driving. Time, :22$\frac{4}{5}$, :46$\frac{4}{5}$, 1:11$\frac{1}{5}$, 1:35$\frac{3}{5}$ Course firm.

$2 Mutuel Prices:			
9-MEHMETORI	9.40	4.60	3.20
3-IN EXCESS II		5.60	4.20
8-PREDECESSOR			5.20

$2 EXACTA 9–3 PAID $55.40.

Ch. c, (Feb), by Mehmet—Senori, by Jungle Savage. Trainer Mulhall Richard W. Bred by Vallone Mr–Mrs G (Ky).

MEHMETORI lagged far behind while trailing early, found room to come through between rivals coming into the stretch while closing strongly, threatened at the furlong marker, continued strongly in the final furlong and prevailed by a small margin. IN EXCESS II, checked off heels when full of run while in contention early along the inside after breaking slowly, battled for command in the drive and lost a close decision. PREDECESSOR, devoid of early speed, lost ground when fanned wide while rallying into the stretch and finished willingly for the show. GREEN'S LEADER, outrun early, moved up to engage for the lead after going six furlongs but weakened slightly late. ROBYN DANCER sat within close range of the lead, vied for the lead on the far turn and battled for command early in the drive before weakening. OLD ALLIANCE prompted the early pace, vied for the lead on the far turn and also battled for command early in the drive before weakening. CEE'S TIZZY, devoid of early speed after breaking slowly, was boxed in on the far turn and could not gain the needed ground in the drive. OFFICER HAWK set or forced the pace for a little more than six furlongs and gave way. SHAPIROS'S HERO, wide through the early stages while in contention, dropped back after six furlongs. SENGALAISE was wide on the backstretch.

Owners— 1, Arnold & Miller; 2, Munari J J; 3, Harbor View Farm; 4, Petropolis Stable Inc; 5, Herrick & No Problem Stable; 6, Juddmonte Farms; 7, Straub-Rubens Cecilia P; 8, Jones B C; 9, Shapiro-Stark-Stratton; 10, Siegel M-Jan-Samantha.

Trainers— 1, Mulhall Richard W; 2, Jackson Bruce L; 3, Barrera Lazaro S; 4, Sadler John W; 5, Vienna Darrell; 6, McAnally Ronald; 7, Russell John W; 8, McAnally Ronald; 9, Jumps Kenneth J; 10, Mayberry Brian A.

Batting two for two, by now, of course, I fully expected the figure horse in the second half of the Oceanside would complete the triumvirate. That colt flopped badly.

The winner went wire-to-wire following fractions of 49.0 and 1:12.2, not an "unusually slow" pace at Del Mar.

The late-speed and turf figures of the respective winners of the Oceanside looked like so:

Mehmetori	23.2	108
Forest Glow	23.3	106

Awaiting Mehmetori and a prime bet there, sad to admit I missed the opportunity presented by Racing Rascal and friends in the second race. Brohamer caught Racing Rascal small, but missed with an exacta box to Eratone. Both of us benefited from Mehmetori. My $200 prime bet netted $740.00, my fastest head start at Del Mar in years.

In evaluating the turf figures, prime bets will be $200 flat. Recreational bets will be $50, placed only when the odds demand the wager, however narrow the figure edge. Exotic keys will be treated separately, as they should.

On the second day at Del Mar, no turf races were programmed. Upsets dominated on the main track (one favorite survived), as they had on opening day (one favorite survived). The Pick 6 carryover for Day 3 surpassed a quarter-million dollars. I was not tempted. Only at Del Mar!!

Day 3

The two turf races today featured three-year-olds, the fifth race a nondescript group of $80,000 claimers going 1 1/16 miles. I found no bets, but finishers one-two deserve a longer look. Examine the records:

As I have argued repeatedly, three-year-olds are different. And so it is on the grass. Examine the pattern of turf figures earned by each of these contenders:

Noble Dr.			Short Timer		
June 17	GG	97	July 7	Hol	96
May 13	GG	105	May 23	Hol	98
			May 5	Hol	108
			April 4	SA	92

Which figure best represents the horse? The latest? The best? The typical figure?

In evaluating patterns of figures for older horses, the latest or most typical figure usually carries the cause. This controls for abnormally high figures in an otherwise common pattern, as reflected by Short Timer's turf record, where the 108 is atypical.

In evaluating three-year-olds, the top figure of the past ninety days deserves precedence. Now Short Timer's 108 and Noble Dr.'s 105 can be accepted as representative. The reasoning concedes that three-year-olds are consistently inconsistent. Fluctuations in the figures should be expected, as trainers continue to experiment with distance, class levels, and running styles.

That is, three-year-olds such as Short Timer and Noble Dr. must be conceded the possibility of matching their best recent figures. If the most recent figures are significantly lower, obviously the case weakens, as with both Short Timer and Noble Dr. At post, Short Timer was 9–2 and Noble Dr. 7–1. A third contender, Timeless Juan, figure of 104 last out, was offered at 3–1. I passed the top-figure horses here, but dared not take 3–1 against the pair.

Now to the seventh, for nonwinners of two races. The favorite here at 6–5 also showed the high turf figure at 108, second race back, a Grade 3 event. Examine the favorite's record and that of another contender.

Bimbo II's 108 and her May 12 figure were earned when the filly lagged early and finished fast. Last out, racing up close, the horse lost a length in the lane and earned a 103 following an "unusually slow" Hollywood Park pace.

With no early speed in today's field, Bimbo II might be placed forwardly again. If lagged, Bimbo II must then overtake a sluggish pace with a strong finish, a feat its record does not indicate it can accomplish. Maybe, but maybe not—and 6–5.

Orlanova is clearly an improving three-year-old, regally bred for grass and trained by the great turf horseman Charles Whittingham. The sire Conquistador Cielo has won with 30 percent of its first starters on the turf, a powerful statistic, and a convenient fact for handicappers to know. The maternal grandsire Nijinsky II is nothing less than the world's leading stakes sire, prepotent on turf.

When evaluating three-year-olds on the grass, if no horse has earned a figure of 110, examine the inexperienced grass runners. Look for a strong turf pedigree, à la Orlanova, and a successful grass barn, à la Whittingham. Prefer a come-from-behind running style and improving form, à la Orlanova as well.

The 110 figure represents a finish roughly a full second faster than the classified par. Three-year-olds en route to the stakes can match that number, though anything better will be hard to overhaul. Bimbo II's best was 108, a vulnerable figure.

A hesitation about Orlanova is the jockey. A weight fanatic, Whittingham here is using Vann Belvoir a sixteen-year-old apprentice in from Longacres, near Seattle. Jockeys are incidental to successful handicapping, but their value improves on the turf, where generally the pace is slow, the traffic congested, and the finish furious.

In southern California especially, talent on the turf is important among jockeys. A mistake at a crucial time normally spells defeat, as the opponent jockeys are highly talented. Belvoir was a negative, one reason Orlanova went off at 8–1.

I bet $50 to win, Orlanova.

On the far turn Belvoir steered Orlanova inside and wound up in tight quarters. He dropped back passing the quarter-pole, and appeared beaten.

Fortunately, Orlanova got clear outside in the upper stretch after regrouping, and ran down the meager opposition. Bimbo II had run rank early, and did not fire late. Orlanova paid a generous $18.60.

A third contender in the field is worth another look.

Cozzy — Gr. f. 3(Apr), by Cozzene—Hair Ribbon, by Ribero
SOLIS A — 116 — Br.—Baker Dr H (Ky) — 1990 9 1 1 1 $33,100
Tr.—Lewis Craig A — 1989 5 M 0 0 $2,375
Own.—Burnison E G — Lifetime 14 1 1 1 $35,475 — Turf 4 0 1 0 $7,850

14Jun90-8Hol 1⅛ (T):472 1:114 1:483fm 6 119 74½ 85½ 64½ 64½ Davis RG6 (F)Aw37000 80-15 Cat'sAir,PleasureBought,Raiatea 10
14Jun90—Wide trip
30May90-5Hol 1 1/16 (T):474 1:123 1:444fm 6¼ 119 96¼ 76 54½ 23½ Davis RG6 (F)Aw35000 67-26 Miss Tris,Cozzy,PleasureBought 10
30May90—Broke slowly
18May90-5Hol 1 (T):48 1:12 1:354fm 16 119 106¼ 86 54½ 52¼ Davis RG3 (F)Aw34000 83-12 DdHt,Tny'sTuton,MttnsAndMnk 10
18May90—Broke awkwardly
6May90-3Hol 1 :45 1:102 1:353ft 8½ 119 2hd 2hd 32½ 47½ Davis RG5 (F)Aw32000 78-12 Conteuse,PlsurBought,MdiclMrvl 6
11Apr90-8SA 1⅛ (T):463 1:104 1:472fm 72 113 52½ 41½ 74½ 77¾ SolisA4 (F)[R]Prvdncia 80-10 Mtrco,Somthngmrry,Njnsky'sLvr 9
28Mar90-6SA 1 :472 1:122 1:383ft 9¾ 117 1½ 2hd 2hd 11¾ Solis A7 (F)Mdn 74-18 Cozzy,WrCmmndrss,QckStpSlwpy 7
10Mar90-6SA 6f :22 :451 1:101ft 11 117 73 65½ 68¾ 511½ ValenzuelPA9 (F)Mdn 73-16 MediclMrvl,BstOfTst,SyrinWintr 10
10Mar90—Wide 3/8 turn
24Feb90-4SA 1 1/16 :481 1:123 1:453ft 8½ 117 52¼ 53½ 65¾ 79¾ Solis A4 (F)Mdn 65-22 Conts,ArlngtonEght,MySongFrY 10
24Feb90—Rank; steadied
10Feb90-4SA 6f :214 :45 1:113ft 44 117 85¼ 35 35 34¼ Solis A9 (F)Mdn 74-20 Phil's Illusion, Orlanova, Cozzy 12
25Nov89-6Hol 6f :213 :444 1:094ft 60 1135 88 75¾ 55 45¼ Nakatani CS8 (F)Mdn 87-08 Wakia, Phil's Illusion, Azusa 11
Speed Index: Last Race: -5.0 3-Race Avg.: -5.6 4-Race Avg.: -6.7 Overall Avg.: -8.0
Jly 21 Dmr 7f ft 1:283 H Jly 14 Hol 6f ft 1:14 H Jly 8 Hol 6f ft 1:142 H Jly 3 Hol 3f ft :38 H

Last out Cozzy earned a 107 at Hollywood Park. But the race is not ratable, Cozzy having finished sixth of ten, beaten 4½ lengths—not a good race. Her second two back, May 30, is a ratable (good) race. Cozzy gets 94 there. Prefer to rate good races, when horses fire, and not lackluster performances when figures can be inflated by the strong performances of other horses. Deep closers, in particular, often reveal misleadingly strong figures while well-beaten. They merely are dragged along by the strenuous efforts of classier horses. Do not be fooled.

Day 4

The high-rated contender and its main opposition are presented below. It's a nonwinners allowance contest, 1⅛ miles on grass, for nonwinners other than maiden or claiming, 3up.

Predecessor — B. c. 3(Apr), by Affirmed—Cornish Colleen, by Cornish Prince
DESORMEAUX K J — 120 — Br.—Harbor View Farm (Ky) — 1990 9 0 3 3 $56,575
Tr.—Barrera Lazaro S — 1989 5 1 1 0 $29,248
Own.—Harbor View Farm — Lifetime 14 1 4 3 $85,823 — Turf 9 0 3 3 $59,898

25Jly90-5Dmr 1 (T):464 1:111 1:352fm 12 114 94¾ 83¼ 62¾ 31¾ DsrmxKJ8 [R]Ocnsde 95-05 Mehmetori,InExcessII,Prdcssor 10
25Jly90—Run in divisions; Raced wide
4Jly90-9Hol 1 1/16 (T):473 1:12 1:432fm 2¼ 119 87 21½ 21½ 2no StevensGL5 Aw37000 78-16 ForestGlow,Predecessor,BrtonDn 9
4Jly90—Bumped break
22Jun90-7Hol 1 1/16 (T):472 1:112 1:413fm 5¼ 114 54½ 52 21½ 22 StevnsGL3 [R]Str Dst 85-15 TightSpot,Predcssor,KptHisCool 7
10Jun90-8Hol 1⅛ (T):474 1:113 1:474fm 36 113 1hd 11½ 1½ 43½ DsrKJ8 Cnma H 85-10 Jovial,Mehmetori,Itsllgreektome 10
10Jun90—Grade II
23May90-8Hol 1 (T):463 1:103 1:352fm 4¼ 115 77 64¼ 64¼ 33¾ Davis R G7 Aw37000 83-13 OldAllince,CollegeGreen,Prdcssor 7
23May90—Wide backstretch
5May90-9Hol 1 1/16 (T):464 1:101 1:403fm 8¼ 119 2½ 2½ 21½ 22 Garcia J A7 Aw32000 90-08 ThPrmMnstr,Prdcssr,HtchccWds 8
26Apr90-8Hol 1 (T):464 1:103 1:344fm 28 119 73¾ 75¾ 75½ 36¼ Garcia J A3 Aw32000 84-10 CockO'Hoop,Pictoril,Predecssor 11
26Apr90—Bumped at break

14Apr90-7SA 1 :45³ 1:10³ 1:37 ft 24 120 71³ 7⁹ 71⁰ 59¾ Flores D R⁸ Aw37000 72-17 Big Bass, Toby Jug, Honor Clef 8
  14Apr90—Wide throughout
28Mar90-8SA a6½f ⑦:21 :43¹¹:134fm 10³ 115 10⁹¾12¹⁰12⁹½12¹⁰½ Black C A² Bldwn 82-08 FrmWy,ImTheIcemn,RobynDncr 12
  28Mar90—Steadied late
5Nov90-6GP 1 ⑦:49¹¹:12²1:37 gd 9½ 115 2¹ 2³ 64¾ 55½ Stevens G L¹ Manila 84-15 Somethingdifferent,Litunin,Swdus 8
  Speed Index—Last Race: 0.0   3-Race Avg.: -2.0   8-Race Avg.: -3.0   Overall Avg.: -4.5
  Jly 20 Hol 5f ft 1:00³ H   Jly 13 Hol 5f ft 1:00² H   Jun 30 Hol 4f ft :48² H   Jun 18 Hol 5f ft :59³ H

Aksar   B. c. 3(Feb), by Sharpen Up—Akila, by Top Ville
                                    Br.—H H Khan (Ky)   1990 2 1 0 1 $22,800
  STEVENS G L   120   Tr.—Jackson Bruce L   1989 1 M 0 0
  Own.—Munari J Je   Lifetime 3 1 0 1 $22,880   Turf 3 1 0 1 $22,880
16Apr90-4Longchamp(Fra) a1⅜ 2:27 yl 5¾ 128 ⑦ 32¾ Cruz A S Px Nils(Gr2) Intimiste, Gargarin, Aksar 6
29Mar90-3StCloud(Fra) a1⅜ 2:15 gd 10 123 ⑦ 11¼ CrAS Px Ksmndo(Mdn) Aksar,Kandyar,JohnnyMountain 11
9Nov09-3Evry(Fra) a1 1:47 yl *2¾ 123 ⑦ 7¾¾ CrAS Px PcdCqbs(Mdn) ValFleuri,Mumexis,SantiagoRob 16
  Speed Index—Last Race: (—)   3-Race Avg.: (—)   12-Race Avg.: (—)   Overall Avg.: (—)
  Jly 23 Dmr ⑦ 5f fm 1:03¹ H (d)   Jly 16 SA 7f ft 1:27³ H

Can the French import Aksar, away 3½ months, handle a colt showing turf figures of 105 (July 25) and 108 (June 22)?

Unless the local contenders reveal figures upwards of 110, European imports can be expected to outclass them under non-winners allowance conditions, maybe by a landslide. European grass racing is so superior to that of the States, imports placed in graded or listed stakes of France, England, Ireland, or Italy can readily shine in U.S. overnight races, notwithstanding long layoffs or inexperience with the footing or distance.

With Predecessor at 7–5 and Aksar at 5–2 on the morning line, a prime bet loomed a possibility, so I negotiated the short trip to the intertrack site.

The bettors were not fooled. Aksar went off at 6–5, Predecessor at 2–1. No bet. Exactas were underlays too.

Predecessor got an extra-slow pace on the solo lead, and a rank Aksar could not catch up late, missing by a long length. Saved by the price, a frequent scenario!

In the Grade 2 feature at 1¹⁄₁₆ miles on the turf, the co-figure stickouts at 114 were prior Grade 2 winners Royal Touch and Invited Guest. One of the two low-rated mares in the field, figure 105, rallied late to upset, paying $47.20.

Day 5

The first Sunday afternoon, the seventh race and final leg of a Pick 6 carryover of $1.1 million (a North American record) was carded at nine furlongs on the grass. Excepting a first starter that surprised at $30.00, the first five legs of the Pick 6 proved formful this day after only five favorites—three of them odds-on—had scored during Del Mar's first four days of racing. Yours truly had deposited a $192 ticket and had reached the seventh race "alive."

This turf race was contentious. In descending order, examine the figures of six contenders. Another contender was a Grade 3 winner of England, trained by the outstanding Neil Drysdale.

River Warden	112
Exclusive Partner	112
Dream of Fame	114
The Medic	110
Companion	113
Silent Prince II	110

On the Pick 6 ticket, I had coupled Dream of Fame (entry mate of River Warden), the high-figure horse at 114, and Drysdale's import. I had entertained including Companion, but eliminated the horse finally when another contender in an earlier race drew in from the also-eligible list—and won. Examine Companion's record:

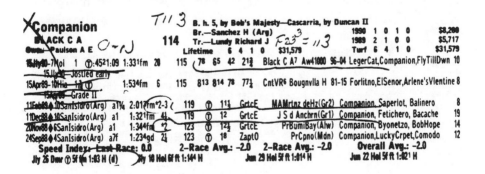

I preferred the import from England to this five-year-old from Argentina. In addition, Companion had outrun its 20–1 odds July 15 after a layoff extending fifteen months, and might be on a bounce pattern here.

The Del Mar bettors preferred Companion against the field at 5–2, and the Argentinian responded with a tremendous finish to overhaul a strong-running Exclusive Partner inside the sixteenth-pole. I should have trusted my own figures and included the horse, naturally. The forty "live" Pick 6 tickets were redeemed for $55,000 each, with $3.5 million in the pool.

More than 1200 tickets shared the Pick 5 consolation which paid $588.40.

Day 6

A handful of figure-handicapping lessons await practitioners who try their hand at the $80,000 claiming race below. Examine the records and figures of the four contenders displayed. Which horse figures best? How should the race be played?

```
Princess Raya                    Ch. m. 5, by Bold Tropic—Mountain Nectar, by Cox's Ridge          8-1
MEZA R Q                         Br.—Miller A (Ky)                       1989 12 4 3 0   $79,950
                           116   Tr.—Bunn Thomas M Jr         $80,000    1988  6 0 0 1    $8,325
Own.—Bernheim-Hecht-Kohn         Lifetime 21 5 3 1 $101,375              Turf  9 3 2 0   $69,650
8Dec89-9Hol  1 1/16 T:46 3 1:10 4 1:41 2 fm 14   112  2 5  2 3  2hd 1 3/4  Meza R Q 4 F 125000 87-13 PrincessRy,ImprilStr,EdgOfHvn 10
23Nov89-9Hol 1 1/16 T:46 1 1:10 2 1:41 4 fm 13   116  3 4  3 1 1/2  1 1/2  2nk  BoulngerG 5 F 80000 85-15 ScrmngSu,PrncssRy,SuprJourny 12
10Nov89-5SA  1 1/8 T:45 2 1:09 4 1:46 3 fm 14    115  3 3/4 3 1 1/2 4 1 1/2 7 3 3/4  Sibille R 1 F 105000 95-01 EdgeOfHeaven,Cifra,RedTheCrds 8
21Oct89-7SA  a6 1/2 f T:21 1 :43 1:13 1 fm 17    119  9 5 3/4 9 5 3/4 9 6 3/4 8 2 3/4  Meza RQ 4 F Aw34000 99 — Kiwi, Dancitus, La Tropicana 11
8Oct89-5SA   a6 1/2 f T:21 3 :43 1:13 1 fm 7     118  8 4 3/4 8 5 1/4 7 5 1/2 7 2 3/4  Toro F 8 F 100000 90-07 TblFrolc,Dot'sL'Ntrl,AttndToDtl 10
      8Oct89—Wide crossing dirt
9Sep89-8Dmr  1 1/16 T:47 1 1:11 1 1:42 4 fm 16   115  6 6  7 5 3/4 11 8 3/4 11 14 1/2  BzeRA 4 F R Osnts H 71-14 Nikishk,DringDoon,GoldFircrckr 11
26Aug89-7Dmr 1 T:48 1:12 3 1:36 4 fm 4 1/2      118  1hd 1hd 1 1 1/2 1 1 1/2  Baze RA 3 F Aw30000 87-16 PrncssRy,DucklngPrk,DnsusDLn 10
11Aug89-7Dmr 1 1/8 T:48 1 1:13 2 1:51 3 fm 4 1/2  118  8 5 1/4 4 2  4 1 1/2 2 3/4  StvnsGL 7 F Aw35000 74-25 Felidia,PrincessRay,RpAtTheDoor 9
      11Aug89—Took up 1/8
23Jly89-9Hol 1 1/16 T:47 1 1:11 4 1:42 3 fm 10   111 5  2 1/2 1hd 1hd 1 1/2  Garcia H J 4 F 50000 81-12 PrincessRy,Codex'sBride,Goldrry 6
23Jun89-3Hol 1 1/8 :47 3 1:12 1 1:51 1 ft 2 3/4   116  2 1  1 1 1/2 1 5  1 6 1/2  StevnsGL 1 F c16000 81-15 PrncssRy,UpToHrTrcks,LpOfLxry 6
  Speed Index: Last Race: 0.0     3-Race Avg.: -1.3     7-Race Avg.: -3.4     Overall Avg.: -3.2
Jly 24 Dmr 5f ft 1:02 H     Jly 21 Dmr 3f ft :38 2 B     Jly 13 Hol 6f ft 1:18 H     Jly 6 Hol 6f ft 1:17 H

*Belle Poitrine                  B. m. 6, by Dominion—Hardirondo, by Hardicanute                    9-5
VALENZUELA P A                   Br.—Ferguson Mrs A (Ire)                1990  8 2 3 1   $75,000
                           118   Tr.—Vienna Darrell           $80,000    1989  5 1 1 0   $33,950
Own.—Forgnne-Klin-RnchSnMglEtl   Lifetime 22 8 4 1 $136,932              Turf 21 7 4 1  $112,182
13Jun90-9Hol 1 1/16 T:46 4 1:10 3 1:41 4 fm *7-5  119  2 1/2 2hd 1 1/2 1 2 1/2  VlenzuelPA 4 F 80000 86-14 BellePoitrine,RdThCrds,ImprilStr 7
      13Jun90—Veered out break
20May90-6Hol 1 1/8 T:46 2 1:10 3 1:48 1 fm *8-5  116  3 2 1/2 2 1/2 2 1/2 1 1 3/4  VlenzuelPA 4 F 80000 87-08 BellePoitrine,Dncingintheprk,Trin 8
28Apr90-9Hol 1 1/16 T:47 1:11 1 1:42 fm 4        116  4 2 1/2 6 2 1/4 5 2 1/2 2 1 1/2  VlenzuelPA 3 F 80000 83-15 Nimes, Belle Poitrine, Seaside 12
      28Apr90—Lacked room 1/4
14Apr90-5SA  1 T:46 1:10 1:35 2 fm 7             116  6 9  6 6 1/2 5 3 1/2 2hd  VlenzuelPA 4 F 80000 86-14 Nimes,BellePoitrine,CasPetrone 10
      14Apr90—Broke slowly
25Mar90-9SA  1 T:47 4 1:11 4 1:36 2 fm 4 1/2     116  5 3 1/2 7 6  8 7 1/4 8 9  VlenzuelPA 4 F 80000 72-15 Casa Petrone, Brasilia,RegalFawn 8
      25Mar90—Lugged in drive
28Feb90-5SA  1 T:46 3 1:10 4 1:36 fm *3          117  6 5 1/2 7 5  5 3  2 1/2  VlenzuelPA 3 F 80000 82-17 CsPetron,BllPoitrin,Dot'sL'Nturl 10
      28Feb90—Wide into stretch
```

Almost two decades ago Andrew Beyer noted the best use of speed figures was to predict which claiming horses can win on the rise in class. He might have added a second wonderful application; namely, identifying phony favorites.

Belle Poitrine (9–5) rates poorly in this field and can be summarily eliminated. When favorites reveal weak figures, dirt or grass, throw them out unmercifully. With a 98 while winning June 13, Belle Poitrine ranks at least four lengths in arrears of the contention here.

On the numbers, Softscape sticks out here, doesn't she? Yes, absolutely!

Following a freshening layoff, such as thirty to ninety days, figure handicappers can prefer the top figure of the previous three or four. If not outclassed, numerous grass horses run well following a freshening respite. Do not concentrate on the race preceding the layoff, which often rates poorly. Softscape earned just a 98 that day, May 31, at Hollywood Park.

But on May 16, versus the nice stakes mare Rosadora, Softscape gained seven lengths in the late stages of a restricted nine-furlong stakes, late speed of 35.3, figure of 119 at Hollywood Park. This is the figure to use, and it towers above the others here.

If further evidence is needed, and sometimes it is, on April 11 at Santa Anita, Softscape again finished in 35.3, earning another 119. Case closed. At 9–2, a prime bet is well-deserved here. The overlay results from the phony favorite, always an enticing situation, provided the alternative is plain.

I bet $200 to win on Softscape, my second prime wager of the season. In addition, I took $20 exactas with Softscape on top of Princess Raya and Seaside.

Softscape did not disappoint, finishing smartly from far behind under Gary Stevens, and paying $11.40. The exacta was completed by Dancinginthepark, figure of 105. Belle Poitrine finished fifth of nine.

The keys here involve (a) tossing the false favorite having a low figure, and (b) locating the representative figure of Softscape. Handicappers tied too tightly to the last running line, the race preceding a layoff, misjudged the form cycle and missed a generous opportunity.

Week 2

The filly Rosie Potts (114) looked to have a nonwinners-twice allowance lot at a real disadvantage to begin the second week of action. She ran third, losing to the Spectacular Bid filly, Spectacular Face (107). The greatest racehorse of the 1980s has flopped at stud, but as handicappers realize, not on the turf, where his get win 23 percent, including 22 percent of the first starters.

Spectacular Face was hardly a first-timer on grass, but the result chart is worth a brief consultation.

SEVENTH RACE
Del Mar
AUGUST 1, 1990

1 1/16 MILES.(Turf). (1.40) ALLOWANCE. Purse $41,000. Fillies and mares. 3-year-olds and upward which are non-winners of $3,000 twice other than maiden, claiming or starter. Weights, 3-year-olds, 116 lbs.; older, 121 lbs. Non-winners of two races other than claiming at one mile or over since June 1 allowed 2 lbs.; of such a race other than maiden or claiming since then, 4 lbs.; since April 23, 6 lbs. (Horses eligible only to the above conditions are preferred.) (Winners that have started for a claiming price of $25,000 or less in their last three starts and maidens that are non-starters for a price have second preference.)

Value of race $41,000; value to winner $22,550; second $8,200; third $6,150; fourth $3,075; fifth $1,025. Mutuel pool $337,831. Exacta pool $315,447.

Last Raced	Horse	M/Eqt.A.Wt	PP St	1/4	1/2	3/4	Str	Fin	Jockey	Odds $1
21Jly90 9Hol2	Spectacular Face	L	4 115	2 7	7	7	7	7¹	1¾	Black C A	4.90
6Jly90 7Hol6	Dame Rousara	L	3 110	6 3	41½	41½	41	3hd	21½	Garcia J A	2.10
28Jun90 8Hol3	Rosie Potts		4 117	7 4	61	61	61	4½	3½	Pincay L Jr	2.70
21Jly90 9Hol4	Miss Tris	b	3 114	4 1	1hd	21	11	12	42	Stevens G L	8.60
14Jun90 G1	Roberta	Lb	4 119	1 6	3½	31	31	21	51	Hansen R D	28.30

8Jly90 ‹	4	Let Fly	L	3	115	3	5	5^1	5^{hd}	$5\frac{1}{2}$	6^{hd}	6no	Baze R A	5.00
12Jly90	11	Raiatea	b	3	109	5	2	$2^{1\frac{1}{2}}$	1^1	$2\frac{1}{2}$	$5\frac{1}{2}$	7	Belvoir V^5	6.70

OFF AT 5:13. Start good. Won driving. Time, :24⅘, :49⅕, 1:13⅖, 1:37⅘, 1:43⅗ Course firm.

$2 tuel Prices:

3–SPECTACULAR FACE	11.80	4.40	2.80
6–DAME ROUSARA		4.00	2.80
7–ROSIE POTTS			2.60

$2 EXACTA 3–6 PAID $56.20.

Gr. f, by Spectacular Bid—Lady Face, by Proud Clarion. Trainer Mandella Richard. Bred by Franks & Hancock (Ky).

SPECTACULAR FACE, a bit rank and far back early after being bumped in the initial strides, generated the needed kick in the last quarter, had to look for a clear path in traffic early in the drive, got through between rivals in midstretch and was up in time for a good come from behind win despite the leisurely early pace. DAME ROUSARA, patiently handled while being outrun early but never far back, finished willingly to gain the place. ROSIE POTTS, devoid of early speed, entered the stretch five wide and rallied for the show. MISS TRIS set or forced the pace from the beginning and weakened in the last furlong. ROBERTA, close up early after being bumped in the opening strides, weakened in the final furlong. LET FLY, outrun early, lacked the needed response in the last quarter. RAIATEA lugged out from the start, raced near or on the lead through the early stages, gave way and was four wide into the stretch. SHE'S A V.P. (1A), COUPLED WITH RAIATEA (1), WAS SCRATCHED BY THE STEWARDS.

Owners— 1, Fares Farms; 2, ClvrRcgSt(Ls)-Alxndr-BkrEtal; 3, Frontiere Georgia; 4, Browne M F; 5, Klinger & Two Rivers Farm; 6, The Anvil; 7, Moss Mr-Mrs J S.

Trainers— 1, Mandella Richard; 2, Drysdale Neil; 3, Sadler John W; 4, Lukas D Wayne; 5, Mason Lloyd C; 6, Sherman Art; 7, Whittingham Charles.

Corrected weight: Spectacular Face 115 pounds. **Overweight:** Rosie Potts 2 pounds; Miss Tris 2; Let Fly 3.

Scratched—Bel Darling (28Jun90 ^{8}Hol^8); She's A V. P. (6Jly90 ^{7}Hol^5).

Did handicappers notice the early pace? It's doggedly slow.

How about Spectacular Face's position after six furlongs? The filly is last, behind a 1:13.2. She's still last at the stretch call, and looking for room besides.

The lesson is plain. Handicappers must be careful about the pace analysis on turf that suggests a slow pace will favor front-runners or pace-pressers. It ain't necessarily so. Turf racing and dirt racing differ dramatically on the matter, and this race illustrates that well. The fastest finishers and best horses are always dangerous on the turf, regardless of the probable pace.

To be sure, frontrunners can be advantaged by a doggedly slow pace on the grass. But the horses should be as classy as the closers they must resist, should have demonstrated endurance and willingness on grass before, and should not reveal short or questionable form.

In addition, some turf horses rally best as one-run horses. They lag, then explode late, or they do not win. Prior to this race, Spectacular Face had repeatedly moved into contention at the prestretch call, but had been outrun in the lane. Here the filly stayed back until the eighth-pole, ran one-eighth of a mile, and got up despite a tardy pace. On the turf it happens all the time.

The next day would bring a prime bet on the grass in a six-horse featured allowance race. The handicapping is tricky, however, and not many figure handicappers or class handicappers can be expected to unravel this one.

8th Del Mar

1 MILE. (Turf). (1.34⅘) ALLOWANCE. Purse $55,000. Fillies and mares. 3-year-olds and upward which are non-winners of $19,250 other than closed or claiming at one mile or over since July 24, 1989. Weights, 3-year-olds, 116 lbs. Older, 122 lbs. Non-winners of such a race since May 1, 1989 allowed, 2 lbs. Such a race in 1989 allowed, 4 lbs. Such a race any distance since July 24, 1989 allowed, 6 lbs.

*Triomphe

Ch. m. 7, by Nebleys—Sensitive Elizabeth, by Sensitivo
BAZE R A 116 Br.—Haras Blackie (Chile) 1989 10 0 1 3 $7,800
Tr.—Dorfman Leonard 1988 5 1 0 1 $5,551
Own.—Hill S R Lifetime 44 8 7 9 $36,657 Turf 41 8 7 9 $36,482

8Dec89-9Hol 1⅛ Ⓣ:46³1:10⁴1:41²fm 48 117 7¹¹ 9⁸½ 7⁴½ 6²½ Baze R A⁸ Ⓕ 150000 84-13 PrincessRy,ImprilStr,EdgOfHvn 10
24Oct89-8Kee a1⅛ Ⓣ 1:45¹fm 9½e 112 1² 1½ 2² 3⁴½ JhnsnPA⁸ ⒻAw26000 91-04 TimelyII,SplitSentence,Triomph 10
27Aug89-11RD 1⅛ Ⓣ:48¹1:12³1:42³fm*3-2 115 1¹½ 1hd 3¹½ 3⁷½ Mella SA² ⒻAw12000 86-06 Kickshw,PhonixSunshin,Tromph 10
13Aug89-4RD 1⅛ Ⓣ:47 1:11¹1:42 fm*3-5e 116 2¹ 2hd 1¹½ 2½ Mella SA² ⒻAw12000 96-03 SplitSntnc,Triomph,NoAccountnt 9
2Aug89-3RD 1⅛ Ⓣ:46⁴1:12¹1:42³fm 7e 116 2² 1¹ 3½ 3²½ Mella SA⁹ ⒻAw12000 92-05 LdyLush,SplitSentence,Triomphe 9
13May89-9Hol 1¼ Ⓣ:47²1:13¹1:48²fm 37 108⁵ 2hd 2¹ 6⁸½ 7¹⁵ Garcia H J³ Ⓕ 90000 71-10 Cifra, Our Lutka, Velvet Blue 8
9Apr89-8GG 1⅜ Ⓣ:48²1:38 2:16³fm 6½ 115 2³ 2² 2⁵ 5⁹¾ Hansen RD⁵ ⒻHcp0 72-21 Rakau Polly, Situada, Marraine 6
18Mar89-5SA 1 Ⓣ:47 1:11⁴1:36⁴fm 21 115 1hd 2hd 7⁴½ 8⁸ Black C A⁹ Ⓕ 100000 79-11 Ironcombe, Belle Poitrine, Cifra 10
3Mar89-8SA 6½f :21⁴ :44³ 1:16²gd 24 114 5⁵ 6¹⁰ 6⁸½ 6¹⁵ StvnsGL⁶ ⒻAw55000 73-19 Survive, Invited Guest, SarosBrig 6
20Jan89-8SA 1 :44⁴ 1:09² 1:34⁴ft 24 114 6⁶ 10¹² 10²³ 10²⁸½ Meza RQ⁷ ⒻAw60000 65-13 JunglDwn,AnglinBllrin,CritTostd 10
20Jan89—Rank, steadied 7/8

Speed Index: Last Race: -3.0 3-Race Avg.: -5.3 8-Race Avg.: -7.0 Overall Avg.: -8.6
Jly 31 Dmr 4f ft :48³ H Jly 26 Dmr Ⓣ 6f fm 1:16³ H (d) Jly 19 Hol 5f ft 1:03 H Jly 6 Hol 6f ft 1:16 Hg

Paper Princess

Ro. f. 4, by Flying Paster—Hattab Gal, by Al Hattab
PINCAY L JR 118 Br.—Winchell V H (Cal) 1990 6 3 1 2 $146,100
Tr.—McAnally Ronald 1989 11 3 4 2 $98,325
Own.—Rechna-VHWSt-WhthmEtal Lifetime 17 6 5 4 $245,025 Turf 9 4 3 1 $170,250

23Jun90-8Hol 6f Ⓣ:22¹ :44²1:08²fm 9-5 119 5⁴½ 4⁴½ 4²½ 1nk PcLJr¹ ⒻⓈValkyr H 97-03 PperPrincss,PrincssRoylty,Surviv 6
20Apr90-8SA a6½f Ⓣ:21 :43¹1:12⁴fm*3-2 115 6⁶ 4⁵ 2³ 1½ McCrrC² ⒻⓇMtWls 97-03 PprPrncss,WrnngZon,TrpclStphn 8
21Mar90-5SA 1 Ⓣ:45⁴1:10 1:34²fm 4 117 3³ 3²½ 1hd 2¾ McCrrCJ⁵ ⒻAw54000 90-09 RluctntGst,PprPrncss,BrghtAsst 10
21Mar90—Lugged in late
22Feb90-8SA 1 :46² 1:11¹ 1:36⁴ft *4-5 115 4² 2½ 2½ 3³½ McCrrCJ⁵ ⒻAw55000 79-23 Voila,SugarplumGal,PperPrincess 6
22Feb90—Wide 7/8 turn
26Jan90-3SA a6½f Ⓣ:21¹ :43¹1:13³fm*7-5 115 7⁷½ 6³½ 1½ 1²½ McCrrCJ⁷ ⒻAw42000 93-07 PaperPrincess,YingN'Yang,Rack 10
5Jan90-3SA 1 Ⓣ:46 1:09²1:34²fm *2 115 5³½ 5³ 5² 4² McCrrCJ⁷ ⒻAw47000 89-07 ‡ExcellentLdy,Dncitus,YingN'Yng 8
5Jan90—Placed third through disqualification; Jostled 1/16
6Dec89-5Hol 1 Ⓣ:47³1:14¹1:35²fm *2½ 115 3² 3¹½ 5½ 5² McCrrCJ⁴ ⒻAw32000 85-13 HthrAndRos,GoldFircrckr,Dncitus 6
6Dec89—Wide into stretch
8Nov89-8SA 1⅛ :46⁴ 1:10² 1:42¹ft 2¾ 117 1¹ 1hd 2hd 3²½ McCrrCJ⁴ ⒻLdVstH 91-09 ApprdTFl,AffrmdClssc,PprPrncss 7
8Nov89—Grade III
13Oct89-8SA 1 :44³ 1:09⁴ 1:36¹ft *1 115 4⁸ 2² 1hd 1²½ McCrrCJ⁶ ⒻAw37000 86-19 PprPrncss,BlckStckngs,SngngPrt 6
13Sep89-5Dmr 1 Ⓣ:47 1:11³1:36¹fm *2 114 5⁴½ 5¹½ 2¹ 1¹ McCrrCJ⁹ ⒻAw36000 90-16 PprPrncss,MjstcSond,MroonBck 10

Speed Index: Last Race: -1.0 3-Race Avg.: -2.3 4-Race Avg.: -0.2 Overall Avg.: +0.6
Jly 20 Hol 7f ft 1:24⁴ B ● Jly 14 Hol 6f ft 1:10⁴ H Jly 8 Hol 5f ft 1:00⁴ H Jun 21 Hol 3f ft :36² B

Formidable Lady

B. f. 4, by Silver Hawk—Hey Mama, by High Tribute
VALENZUELA P A 120 Br.—Jones B C (Ky) 1990 6 1 1 0 $53,875
Tr.—Gonzalez Juan 1989 5 2 2 1 $119,150
Own.—FastFriendsSt-LevetonEtAl Lifetime 18 4 5 2 $246,175 Turf 9 2 3 1 $149,700

11Jly90-8Hol 1 Ⓣ:47³1:11³1:35³fm *2½ L 116 2³ 3¹½ 4²½ 4¾ VlnzlPA² ⒻAw60000 85-14 JblinBrown,WrningZone,LightIce 5
20May90-8GG 1⅛ Ⓣ:47³1:12 1:44 gd 3½ 120 5⁷½ 8⁵½ 7⁶ 6⁵ WrrRJ⁷ ⒻⓇStrBlfH 87-11 ArtCollg,AmyLous,BrssSssNClss 10
15Apr90-8SA 1 Ⓣ:45³1:09¹1:33¹fm 20 115 8¹¹ 8¹⁰ 8¹¹ 8⁹½ BlcCA⁵ⒻBd Br CpH 88-07 Saros Brig, Run To Jenny, Fieldy 8
15Apr90—Grade III; Wide
31Mar90-8GG 1⅛ Ⓣ:46²1:10²1:42³fm 4½ 117 3⁷ 3⁴½ 2³ 2² WrrRJJr⁴ ⒻGldPpH 97-05 SrosBrig,FormidblLdy,JblnBrown 7
31Mar90—Grade III
24Feb90-7SA 1 Ⓣ:46³1:10³1:34⁴fm 7 116 3²½ 3¹ 3¹½ 1½ VlnzlPA⁶ ⒻAw47000 89-11 FormidblLdy,GoldFircrckr,Conclr 9
12Feb90-3SA 1 :46³ 1:11³ 1:37³ft 4¼ 116 4⁴ 4⁴ 4⁶½ 4⁹ VlnzlPA¹ ⒻAw47000 70-25 FantsticLook,Felidi,HiddenGrden 6
12Feb90—Wide final 3/8
11Jun89-8GG 1⅛ Ⓣ:48²1:13 1:49⁴fm*6-5 122 2² 2¹½ 2¹½ 3³½ GrydrAT² ⒻCal Oks 95-09 GnrlChrg,TppngTdor,FormdblLdy 7
28May89-8Hol 1⅛ Ⓣ:46¹1:10²1:40¹fm 3½ 118 2³ 2¹½ 2²½ 2⁴ VllPA¹ ⒻHnymn H 89-09 HotOptn,FrmdblLdy,BlckStckngs 6
28May89—Grade III
13May89-8Hol 1 Ⓣ:45³1:09⁴1:34 fm 4½ 119 6³¾ 6³ 5²½ 2²½ BlackCA⁹ ⒻSenorita 91-10 RluctntGst,FormdblLdy,GnrlChrg 9
12Apr89-8SA 1⅛ Ⓣ:47 1:13 1:50³fm 6½ 117 3¹½ 1½ 1²½ 1¹½ StsGL⁶ ⒻⓇPrvdncia 74-26 FormidbleLdy,GenerlChrge,Kelly 10

Speed Index: Last Race: -1.0 3-Race Avg.: -2.6 9-Race Avg.: -0.3 Overall Avg.: -0.8
Jly 28 Dmr 5f ft :59⁴ H Jly 22 Dmr 6f ft 1:12² H ● Jly 9 Hol 3f ft :35³ H ● Jly 2 Hol 1 ft 1:38² H

Down Again
B. m. 6, by Encino—Dawn Is Breaking, by Import
BLACK C A **122**
Br.—Schibbye & Nebbiolo Place (Ky) 1990 5 1 0 0 $54,500
Tr.—Cross Richard J 1989 15 2 4 4 $254,180
Own.—Buss-Robinson-SummaStble
Lifetime 49 10 11 8 $578,021 Turf 47 10 11 7 $569,696

11Jly90-8Hol 1 Ⓣ:4731:1131:353fm 3 114 44 41½ 31 5¾ BlackCA1 ⒻAw60000 85-14 JblinBrown,WrningZone,LightIce 5
11Jly90—Lacked room 3/8
15Jun90-8Hol 1 1/16 Ⓣ:4741:12 1:412fm 5½ 114 42½ 52 53¾ 54½ BlackCA4 ⒻAw60000 83-11 T.V.OfCrystl,JblnBrwn,SwtRbrtII 6
15Jun90—Boxed 5/16 - 3/16
25Feb90-8SA 1 Ⓣ:4541:0941:341fm 20 118 67 54 74¼ 95½ BlcCA1 ⒻBna VstaH 87-08 Saros Brig,RoyalTouch,Nikishka 10
25Feb90—Grade III; Stumbled start
14Feb90-8SA a6½f Ⓣ:204 :43 1:13 fm 16 117 79 66 2½ 1½ BlcCA3 ⒻMnrva H 96-04 Down Again, Sexy Slew,HotNovel 9
14Feb90—Grade III
31Jan90-8SA a6½f Ⓣ:214 :4341:14 fm 3¾ 117 33½ 31½ 31½ 54½ Davis RG1 ⒻAw52000 86-09 DncngTrbt,Annoconnor,CollctvJy 6
30Dec89-7SA a6½f Ⓣ:212 :4311:124fm*7-5 121 54 53¼ 32 22 McCrrCJ7 ⒻAw55000 102 — Josette, Down Again, HastyPasty 7
5Nov89-8SA 1 Ⓣ:4511:0831:332fm 4½ 119 67 75 85¾ 75 BzRA8 ⒻL R Rwn H 99 — BabaCool,Davie'sLamb,StylishStr 9
5Nov89—Very wide 3/8
22Oct89-6Lrl 6f Ⓣ:23 :4731:14 sf 13 121 66 56½ 1hd 41¾ Toro F4 Lrl Dash 70-28 Cricket Ball,Oraibi,PointOfLight 14
11Oct89-8SA a6½f Ⓣ:212 :43 1:124fm *2¾ 119 85½ 54½ 32 2nk McCrrCJ4 ⒻAtnDsH 95-05 WrnngZon,DwnAgn,StrmyBtVld 11
19Aug89-8Dmr 1⅛ Ⓣ:4821:1221:484fm*8-5e 114 66½ 65 52¼ 42 StsGL6 ⒻRamona H 87-11 BrownBess,DaringDoone,Galunpe 7
19Aug89—Grade I; Very wide 3/8
Speed Index: Last Race: -1.0 3-Race Avg.: -4.0 5-Race Avg.: -3.0 Overall Avg.: -2.0
Jly 30 Dmr 5f ft 1:021 Hg Jly 25 Dmr 5f ft 1:001 Hg Jly 20 Hol 4f ft :482 Bg Jly 7 Hol 5f ft 1:004 Hg

***Sonilla**
B. m. 5, by Son of Shaka—Il Piccolo, by Ribston
DELAHOUSSAYE E **116**
Br.—Apostolides Miss J (Eng) 1990 1 1 0 0 $19,250
Tr.—Mettee Richard C 1989 15 4 1 1 $37,879
Own.—Greenwood G C
Lifetime 34 8 1 3 $72,484 Turf 34 8 1 3 $72,484

28Jun90-5Hol 1⅛ Ⓣ:47 1:11 1:41 fm 14 116 76½ 85½ 63 11½ Black C A9 Ⓕ 62500 90-08 Sonilla,MjesticSound,CsPetrone 10
28Jun90—5 Wide stretch
10Nov89♦5Redcar(Eng) 7f 1:261gd 11 127 Ⓣ 1013 WllmsJ Redcar Nov H Brizincote,ShrpJustice,NwMxico 26
21Oct89♦6Newmarket(Eng) 6f 1:12 gd 9 114 Ⓣ 85¾ WllsJ Phntom Huse H BeFresh, Macrobian, Quiche 24
14Oct89♦3Ascot(Eng) 5f 1:014gd 6½ 117 Ⓣ 74¾ WilliamsJ Bovis H LgnBch,CmbrnWltzr,CrftExprss 16
6Oct89♦2Newmarket(Eng) 6f 1:134gd 5½ 118 Ⓣ 1nk WllsJ Snwdns Marque H Sonilla,YoungTearawy,SloeBerry 13
20Sep89♦5Ayr(Scot) 7f 1:293sf 9 123 Ⓣ 1¾ WllsJ LdbrksStrthcldH Sonilla, Rambo's Hall,Ned'sAura 14
14Sep89♦6Doncaster(Eng) 7f 1:273gd *4 118 Ⓣ 41½ WillimsJ Kayto H Superoo,DonovnRose,Bournville 18
7Sep89♦1York(Eng) 7f 1:241gd 14 122 Ⓣ 11½ WillmsJ QuintinGilbeyH Sonilla,Ned'sAura,HighestPraise 16
28Aug89♦5Chepstow(Eng) 7f 1:214gd 14 130 Ⓣ 12 WllsJ John H Watts H Sonilla,Humlong,Mine'sADouble 20
Speed Index: Last Race: -2.0 1-Race Avg.: -2.0 1-Race Avg.: -2.0 Overall Avg.: -2.0
Jly 26 Dmr Ⓣ 5f fm 1:023 B (d) Jly 18 Hol 5f ft 1:004 B ● Jly 8 Hol 3f ft :354 H Jun 23 Hol 4f ft :474 H

***Run To Jenny**
B. f. 4, by Runnett—Loch Leven, by Le Levanstell
STEVENS G L **116**
Br.—Graigueshoneen Stud (Ire) 1990 3 2 1 0 $83,450
Tr.—Jackson Bruce L 1989 8 0 1 3 $37,161
Own.—Munari J J
Lifetime 16 3 3 4 $188,279 Turf 16 3 3 4 $188,279

15Apr90-8SA 1 Ⓣ:4531:0911:331fm 5½ 116 46 43 43½ 2½ StsGL3 ⒻBd Br CpH 96-07 Saros Brig, Run To Jenny, Fieldy 8
15Apr90—Grade III
28Mar90-5SA 1 Ⓣ:4631:1121:361fm *1 119 76 63½ 41½ 11 StvnsGL8 ⒻAw42000 82-18 RnTJnny,ElgncInDsgn,SpctclrFc 10
9Mar90-7SA 1 Ⓣ:48 1:12 1:362fm*4-5 114 96¾ 64½ 43 11½ StevensGL1 Aw37000 81-18 RunToJnny,Prtndr'sGold,Mr.Szzlr 9
9Mar90—Wide in stretch
23Sep89♦6Curragh(Ire) 7f 1:263yl 8 117 Ⓣ 58½ QntnR McDnghBland Pirouette, Careafolie, Rain Burst 9
2Sep89♦4Haydock(Eng) 6f 1:123gd 100 128 Ⓣ 813 DttrL LdbrkSprntCp(Gr1) Dnehill,CricketBll,APryrForWings 9
27Aug89♦2Leopardst'n(Ire) 7f 1:28 gd 6 119 Ⓣ 33 CrineS BrrnstwnStdGld TwilightAgena,ClostL,RunToJnny 8
7Aug89♦5Leopardst'n(Ire) 1 1:384gd*8-5 122 Ⓣ 57¾ CrineS ⒻBrwnstwnStd Awyd,UpwrdTrnd,FrndlyPrsusion 6
22Jly89♦5Leopardst'n(Ire) 7f 1:252gd*6-5 119 Ⓣ 21½ Roche C Bllycrs Milieu,RunToJenny,BlasteaHeath 8
21Jun89♦3Ascot(Eng) 1 1:393fm 20 126 Ⓣ 76½ •KinnMJ ⒻCrntn (Gr1) GoldnOpinon,MgcGlm,GustArtst 12
•21Jun89—Dead heat
27May89♦4Curragh(Ire) 1 1:382gd 33 126 Ⓣ 32¾ EddrPA ⒻIrsh 1000Gns(Gr1) Ensconse,Aldbourne,RunToJnny 13
Speed Index: Last Race: +3.0 3-Race Avg.: +0.6 3-Race Avg.: +0.6 Overall Avg.: +0.6
Jly 26 Dmr Ⓣ 4f fm :481 H (d) ● Jly 18 SA 7f ft 1:272 H Jly 11 SA 6f ft 1:164 H Jly 4 SA 5f ft 1:033 B

This classified event bars any horse that has won a winner's share of $19,250 (purse of $35,000) for a year. This can be considered a highly restricted race—as anything that has done anything in a year is ineligible—fair game for a wide array of horses, including high-priced claiming horses. The figures called the outcome cold.

The public strongly favored Run To Jenny at even money, presumably because the Irish filly had finished second in a graded stakes April 15 at Santa Anita. That day Run To Jenny finished in 23.2, at a mile, but Santa Anita's grass course is extremely glib. The figure is a mere 105.

In its previous pair of miles at Santa Anita, victories both, Run To Jenny earned turf figures of 98 and 102, respectively, hardly the stuff of even-money shots. The stakes placing notwithstanding, this filly's class and late speed are still open to debate.

The high-figure horse, by some seven lengths, no less, is the English import Sonilla. From far back at Hollywood Park on June 28, Sonilla finished the final five-sixteenths at 1¹⁄₁₆ miles In 29 flat. The figure is 120; solid!

Away thirty-two days after a big win following a long layoff, Sonilla may be on a bounce pattern here, but the figure is hard to resist and the odds at post were an irresistible 8–1.

Handicappers who want to suggest Sonilla is outclassed here, exiting a $62,500 claiming race, are badly mistaken. Under highly restricted classified conditions, high-priced claiming winners qualify on class. I implore handicappers to understand that proposition. It's basic to effective handicapping.

Not only is Sonilla well-qualified under today's conditions, she enjoys a significant figure edge on the opposition, including Run To Jenny, a strongly overbet proposition here. Whether a prime bet is warranted or not, Sonilla is a bettable overlay in this contest, in stark contrast to the unbettable underlay that Run To Jenny represents.

Bowing to the figures, I risked a prime amount here. Run To Jenny did not receive a particularly heady ride from national leader Gary Stevens, who used the filly early and wide rounding the far turn, which helped Sonilla's late challenge. It was a long steady run, nothing explosive, but Sonilla got there. She returned $18.00, a sweet testimonial to the turf figures.

I am delighted to present the official result chart.

EIGHTH RACE
Del Mar
AUGUST 2, 1990

1 MILE.(Turf). (1.34⅕) ALLOWANCE. Purse $55,000. Fillies and mares. 3-year-olds and upward which are non-winners of $19,250 other than closed or claiming at one mile or over since July 24, 1989. Weights, 3-year-olds, 116 lbs. Older, 122 lbs. Non-winners of such a race since May 1, 1989 allowed, 2 lbs. Such a race in 1989 allowed, 4 lbs. Such a race any distance since July 24, 1989 allowed, 6 lbs.

Value of race $55,000; value to winner $30,250; second $11,000; third $8,250; fourth $4,125; fifth $1,375. Mutuel pool $283,075. Exacta pool $247,372.

Last Raced	Horse	M/Eqt.A.Wt	PP	St	¼	½	¾	Str	Fin	Jockey	Odds $1
28Jun90 5Hol1	Sonilla	L 5 116	5	4	5hd	6	6	3hd	1½	Delahoussaye E	8.00
23Jun90 8Hol1	Paper Princess	L 4 118	2	2	2½	21	2½	21½	2½	Pincay L Jr	1.90
15Apr90 8SA2	Run To Jenny	L 4 116	6	5	6	51½	1hd	1hd	32	Stevens G L	1.20
11Jly90 8Hol5	Down Again	6 122	4	6	3hd	4hd	51½	4hd	4no	Black C A	6.90
11Jly90 8Hol4	Formidable Lady	L 4 120	3	1	41½	3hd	4hd	51½	56½	Valenzuela P A	6.60
8Dec89 9Hol6	Triomphe	L 7 116	1	3	11½	11	31	6	6	Baze R A	47.30

OFF AT 5:47. Start good. Won driving. Time, :24⅘, :48⅘, 1:12⅗, 1:36⅗ Course firm.

$2 Mutuel Prices:				
	5–SONILLA	18.00	5.60	2.80
	2–PAPER PRINCESS		3.20	2.20
	6–RUN TO JENNY			2.40

$2 EXACTA 5–2 PAID $50.60.

B. m, by Son of Shaka—Il Piccolo, by Ribston. Trainer Mettee Richard C. Bred by Apostolides Miss J (Eng).

SONILLA, devoid of early speed, came into the stretch four wide, generated the needed rally and was up in time. PAPER PRINCESS, close up early, got the lead between calls in the final furlong but could not outfinish SONILLA. RUN TO JENNY, devoid of early speed, made a move on the backstretch to reach the front approaching t he far turn but then weakened slightly in deep stretch. DOWN AGAIN, close up early after breaking slowly, was boxed in on the far turn and lacked the necessary response in the drive. FORMIDABLE LADY, in contention early, also lacked the necessary response in the drive. TRIOMPHE established the early pace and faltered.

Friday on the turf a three-year-old and four-year-old showing one start apiece on grass met as the top-figure contenders under nonwinners-once allowances. Which do handicappers prefer?

High Rank — B. g. 3(Mar), by Lord at War (Arg)—Queen to Conquer, by King's Bishop — 6-5
VALENZUELA P A — 116 — Br.—Wimborne Farm Inc (Ky) — 1990 6 1 2 1 $36,900
Own.—ClrRcg(Ls)–Whttghm–UnrEtl — Tr.—Whittingham Charles — Turf 2 0 1 1 $12,200
Lifetime 6 1 2 1 $36,900

20Jly90-9Hol 1⅛ Ⓣ:482 1:124 1:49 fm *3-2 119 33½ 31 11 2¾ VlenzuPA 5 Aw37000 82-16 Barton Dene, High Rank, Raggle 5
20Jly90—Lugged in
27Jun90-4Hol 1 1/16 :471 1:12 1:43 ft 2½ 116 31½ 3½ 1½ 14 Valenzuela PA 3 Mdn 85-17 HighRnk,DsrtRumor,PndltonRidg 5
27Jun90—Lugged in
13May90-6Hol 1 1/16 :46 1:102 1:421 ft 5½ 116 67½ 53¼ 21½ 21¼ Valenzuela PA 9 Mdn 88-17 BelAirPstr,HighRnk,PrlssCurrnt 10
13May90—Boxed in 3/16
14Apr90-2SA 1⅛ Ⓣ:454 1:092 1:474 fm 6¾ 117 713 713 612 34 DelahoussyeE9 Mdn 82-14 OfficerHwk,ScrtWitnss,HighRnk 12
14Apr90—Lugged in badly
18Mar90-4SA 1 1/16 :473 1:124 1:45 ft 5½ 117 97¼ 812 79¼ 716¼ Davis R G1 Mdn 62-16 ChiefOnTheRun,RiverDcr,BtsCstl 9
24Feb90-6SA 6f :214 :45 1:104 ft 62 118 99¾ 88½ 79¾ 68½ Davis R G10 Mdn 73-16 StrOfRlty,‡CndymnB,LIBtO'Lrcn 11
24Feb90—Placed fifth through disqualification

Speed Index: Last Race: –2.0 2–Race Avg.: –3.0 2–Race Avg.: –3.0 Overall Avg.: –5.3
Aug 1 Dmr 3f ft :372 H Jly 27 SLR tr.t 3f ft :364 H Jly 15 Hol Ⓣ 5f fm 1:022 H (d) Jly 5 Hol 3f ft :371 H

Maison Maestro — B. c. 4, by Mamaison—Raja's Song, by Raja Baba — 4-1
SOLIS A — 118 — Br.—Daley R–Jean–M (Ky) — 1990 3 1 2 0 $20,000
Own.—Harrington L D — Tr.—Mitchell Mike — 1989 10 0 1 2 $14,450
Lifetime 15 2 4 2 $50,950 — Turf 3 0 1 0 $8,100

23Jly90-9Hol 1 1/16 Ⓣ:48 1:114 1:421 fm 11 L 116 63¾ 64¾ 52¾ 2no Solis A 8 Aw37000 84-11 Agiwin,MaisonMestro,FinlForecst 9
23Jly90—4-wide into lane
22Jun90-1Hol 1 :452 1:102 1:361 ft 5¼ 115 64½ 42½ 1hd 14 DelhoussyeE 5 20000 83-18 MaisonMestro,LeTche,BerInMind 9
22Jun90—Bumped at break
13Jun90-1Hol 7f :214 :442 1:223 ft 4¾ 116 77 88½ 55½ 23½ DelhoussyE 5 c12500 88-06 McrthrFc,MsonMstro,GoStdyLd 12
13Jun90—Bumped hard 3/8
19Nov89-5Hol 6½f :22 :443 1:16 ft 6½ 115 74¼ 97¾ 98¼ 69¾ Toro F 10 16000 85-09 HsLgcy,RstyAtttd,Amnothrbrthr 10
19Nov89—Wide final 3/8
14Oct89-1SA 6½f :214 :444 1:163 ft 3 116 66½ 66 35½ 36 Toro F 6 16000 81-15 GoStdyLd,FrstLoylty,MsonMstr 10
14Oct89—Rough start
10Sep89-2Dmr 6f :214 :443 1:093 ft *2¼ 116 129¼ 128¾ 117¾ 75¼ Toro F 9 25000 85-09 SrosNightWnd,FntstcHop,Ldyzd 12
10Sep89—9 wide into drive
25Aug89-7Dmr 6f :22 :443 1:083 ft 7 116 84¼ 44 44 55 Toro F 2 40000 90-14 FiestDlSol,OlympicBrt,Brillintizd 12

As class handicappers appreciate, three-year-olds are highly preferable to 4up under nonwinners-once or -twice allowance conditions. Anyone who does not understand that should retreat to square one. They cannot receive much nourishment from their figures anyway.

On cold dope here, High Rank at 106 July 20 probably should be expected to overtake Maison Maestro at 108 July 23. Reason: the younger horse has every right to improve, as the older horse does not.

Yet High Rank is 6–5 and cannot be backed. Can Maison Maestro at 4–1? In combination with the strong debut on the grass, the odds permits a wager here on the figure horse. But not a prime bet, please. I bet $50.

The pair engaged one another in a long stretch duel, Maison Maestro getting the slight edge a furlong out. But High Rank did improve, and did prevail inside the sixteenth-pole, scoring by a neck. The four-year-old, claimed for $12,500 as recently as June 13, hung near the wire.

The fifth race on Saturday was carded at the unfamiliar 1³⁄₈ miles. To illustrate a few key points with turf figures, I present the high-figure horses and the most interesting long shot. Smoke the contenders over and pick a probable winner.

5th Del Mar

1 ⅜ MILES. (Turf). (2.13⅘) CLAIMING. Purse $38,000. 3-year-olds and upward. Weights, 3-year-olds, 116 lbs.; older, 122 lbs. Non-winners of two races at one mile or over since June 15, allowed 2 lbs.; of such a race since then, 4 lbs.; since April 23, 6 lbs. Claiming price $62,500; for each $2,500 to $55,000, allowed 1 lb. (Maiden and races when entered for $50,000 or less not considered.)

Novelty

B. g. 7, by Ack Ack—Design, by Tom Rolfe

My Sonny Boy — Ch. h. 5, by Te-Agori-Mou—My Mary, by Rising Market
MEZA R Q — 116 — Br.—Old English Rancho (Cal) — 1990 8 0 3 1 $37,025
Tr.—Spawr Bill $62,500 — 1989 9 2 3 1 $45,085
Own.—Sell C R — Lifetime 19 2 7 3 $86,250 — Turf 11 2 3 1 $64,500

16Jun90-9Hol 1½ Ⓣ:4922:0342:274fm 2¼ 117 56 41¾ 31 21½ Pincay L Jr1 c62500 80-13 Novelty,MySonnyBoy,RoundRiver 8
16Jun90—Boxed in 1/4, 1/8
3Jun90-6Hol 1⅛ Ⓣ:4921:1231:483fm 3 117 52¼ 52¾ 3½ 43¾ Pincay L Jr2 80000 81-07 Mshkr,HtAndSmggy,SngsFrstDnc 7
3Jun90—Rank 7/8 turn
19May90-9Hol 1¼ Ⓣ:4811:3622:003fm 6¾ 117 38 53¼ 42¼ 22 Pincay L Jr6 80000 88-10 Rosen, My Sonny Boy, Novelty 8
6May90-9Hol 1⅛ Ⓣ:4721:11 1:464fm 5 117 86 85¼ 84 55¼ Pincay L Jr11 80000 89-04 Simjour, Sperry, Cannon Bar 11
6May90—Wide
20Apr90-5SA 1⅛ Ⓣ:4611:1021:464fm 3¾ 118 78¼ 65 42½ 21¼ Pincay L Jr2 80000 90-09 DaysGoneBy,MySonnyBoy,Leasee 8
20Apr90—Jumped track late
31Mar90-5SA 1⅛ Ⓣ:4641:11 1:474fm 4 117 74½ 75 54 31¾ Pincay L Jr3 80000 84-09 Sprry,HotAndSmggy,MySnnyBy 10
9Mar90-5SA 1¼ Ⓣ:46 1:3612:01 fm 6¾ 117 67½ 61¾ 33 42¾ Pincay L Jr8 80000 80-18 DkothThunder,LtestRls,RivrMik 10
9Mar90—Bumped start
14Feb90-5SA 1 Ⓣ:4711:11 1:35 fm 26 114 118½118¼ 78 610 Hawley S9 85000 78-12 Bruho, Strogien, Band Leader 11
4Aug89-5Dmr 1⅛ Ⓣ:48 1:1311:503fm 8¼ 121 64¾ 1hd 11½ 12½ StevensGL6 Aw35000 80-15 MySonnyBoy,CrolnNrth,KngTfn 10
25Jly89-10LA 1$\frac{1}{16}$:451 1:111 1:431ft 4¾ 117 74½ 72¾ 56½ 34 PattonDB3 W Knott 85-15 MghtSnow,CrnkyKd,MySonnyBy 7

Speed Index: Last Race: –7.0 3–Race Avg.: –7.0 9–Race Avg.: –5.8 Overall Avg.: –5.3
Jly 23 Hol 3f ft :373 H Jly 16 Hol 5f ft 1:03 H Jly 9 Hol 4f ft :511 H Jun 13 Hol 4f ft :472 H

***Simjour** — Ch. c. 4, by Adenijah—Sellasia, by Dankare
Br.—H H Aga Khan (Ire) — 1990 4 1 0 0 $19,250
DESORMEAUX K J — 117 — Tr.—Vienna Darrell $60,000 — 1989 5 1 1 1 $11,847
Own.—Red Baron's Barn — Lifetime 10 3 1 1 $34,507 — Turf 10 3 1 1 $34,507

1Jly90-5Hol 1 Ⓣ:4621:0941:34 fm 11 L 117 1014 1012 1012 79¾ Pincay L Jr6 80000 84-08 BrvCpd,PtchGrndfg,HtAndSmgg 10
1Jly90—4 wide stretch
16Jun90-7Hol 1⅛ Ⓣ:4741:1131:471fm 5¾ 117 76½ 86 76¾ 78¾ Pincay LJr5 Aw41000 83-13 Kaboi, Polar Boy, Record Boom 9
16Jun90—Wide stretch
19May90-6Hol 1¼ Ⓣ:4821:3622:003fm 6¾ 114 811 63¾ 86¾ 97 Garcia J A2 200000 83-10 RoylRech,LiveThDrm,RcordBoom 9
19May90—Rank early
6May90-9Hol 1⅛ Ⓣ:4721:11 1:464fm 14 116 63 63¼ 2½ 12 DesormuxKJ4 80000 94-04 Simjour, Sperry, Cannon Bar 11
6May90—Wide in drive
13Jly89♦3Kempton(Eng) 1½ 2:313fm 3 133 Ⓣ 46 Cook P Oak H BayBird, TuppennyRed, AlSkeet 5
6Jly89♦3Haydock(Eng) 1½ 2:303gd 10 122 Ⓣ 33¼ CchrR HydkPkJlTrphy Alphabel, ReliefPitcher, Simjour 5
22Jun89♦6Ascot(Eng) 1½ 2:291fm 6 126 Ⓣ 69¼ CuthnS KngGrge V H Crlngford,RddyLcky,CossckGrd 14
19May89♦2Newbury(Eng) 1½ 2:313gd 3¼ 125 Ⓣ 2¾ Reid J Ultramar H Keswa, Simjour, Tempering 8
13Apr89♦4Brighton(Eng) 1 1:373gd *9-5 123 Ⓣ 1½ Reid J Evening Argus H Smjour,SrousTroubl,GoodPrtnrs 17
17Oct88♦7Chepstow(Eng) 7f 1:273sf 10 119 Ⓣ 17 NsW WhtbryMnoGrad Simjour,PleeRebl,SwingingNoJo 20

Speed Index: Last Race: –8.0 3–Race Avg.: –6.3 4–Race Avg.: –5.2 Overall Avg.: –5.2
Jly 30 Dmr 6f ft 1:134 H Jly 25 Dmr 5f ft 1:021 H Jun 11 Hol 6f ft 1:132 H Jun 6 Hol 5f ft 1:014 H

Great Relations — B. c. 4, by Care—Northern Oasis, by Damascus
Br.—Singer C B (Ky) — 1990 7 1 0 2 $35,775
PINCAY L JR — 116 — Tr.—Fanning Jerry $62,500 — 1989 5 1 1 0 $4,740
Own.—Singer C B — Lifetime 14 2 2 2 $43,308 — Turf 13 2 2 2 $43,308

22Jly90-7Hol 1½ Ⓣ:50 2:0332:271fm 10 L 116 69½ 55 34½ 36 DelhoussyeE6 80000 79-12 Putting, Novelty, Great Relations 6
1Jly90-7Hol 1$\frac{1}{16}$ Ⓣ:46 1:10 1:411fm 22 L 118 76½ 63½ 64½ 53¼ Meza R Q 3 Aw38000 86-08 Cannon Man,PureGenius,LazyBoy 9
1Jly90—Broke slowly
3Jun90-6Hol 1⅛ Ⓣ:4921:1231:483fm 5¼ 116 1hd 11½ 2hd 56¾ DelhoussyeE 6 70000 78-07 Mshkr,HtAndSmggy,SngsFrstDnc 7
3Jun90—Broke slowly
19May90-9Hol 1¼ Ⓣ:4811:3622:003fm 10 119 713 65¾ 54¾ 54½ DelhoussyeE2 80000 85-10 Rosen, My Sonny Boy, Novelty 8
23Apr90-5SA 1½ Ⓣ:47 2:01 2:26 fm 2½ 119 2½ 21 31½ 58¾ McCarron CJ1 62500 75-13 Putting, Ostoyal, Latest Release 6
23Apr90—Lugged in drive
15Apr90-5SA 1¼ Ⓣ:4541:3511:594fm*8-5 119 99½ 53 32 1½ StevensGL8 Aw37000 89-07 GretRltions,Mr.Sizzlr,ChstnutFrz 11
15Apr90—Broke slowly,wide

Distance is the crucial consideration. At classic distances, horses must be rated using races at classic distances. Middle distances are not sufficiently related to longer distance to make those figures transportable.

Technique changes too. At classic distances—1¼ miles and beyond—no adjustment for pace is warranted. Extra slow pace fractions will be the norm. Regardless, the ability to finish well counts most.

Correct technique is the key to the contest at hand. Novelty earns a 113 on July 22, My Sonny Boy a 112 on June 16, and Great Relations a 111 on July 22. Handicappers should also be aware that smaller numerical differences are more meaningful at longer distances. One length at 1⅜ miles is more definitive than a length at 1¹⁄₁₆ miles.

Novelty rates roughly a half-length superior to My Sonny Boy here. Odds on both are 5–2, the co-favorites.

Now examine Simjour. The big win at Hollywood Park on May 6 stands out, as does the dulling form since. On May 6, Simjour earned a splendid figure of 124. But the distance is 1⅛ miles, and the figure does not transfer to 1⅜ miles. The longer distance robs most horses of the punching power they retain at shorter distances.

Following a milkwagon pace, set by My Sonny Boy, and tracked by Novelty, the pair fought furiously throughout the stretch. Novelty got up in the last stride, winning by a nose. He paid $7.00.

Later on Saturday, at a mile, a nonwinners-four-times allowance, I liked Rogue's Realm, who had a two-length edge on the figures, had won at Del Mar last season, and was offered at 7–2. He finished a nonthreatening third.

The pair of turf races on Sunday were distinguished by high-figure stickouts, a 10-point and a 12-point advantage to a contender in each. I knew a prime bet would be registered in the fifth, but the odds would play a decisive role in the eighth.

Examine the favorite and top-figure contender for the fifth, an $80,000 claiming event at 1¹⁄₁₆ miles, 3up.

```
8Jly89-9Hol   1½ ①:5031:1421:494fm *2   116  2½  2½  1hd 1hd  Baze R A 2     80000 79-12 GrnJudgmnt,JustBobby,McCubbn 5
25Jun89-8GG    1½  :454 1:084 1:411ft   13   115  813 811 7½ 57½  Lmbrt J ‖AU Rvr H  86-14 BigChill,SuperSurgeon,RovingFre 8
18Jun89-3GG    1½ ①:4641:1211:432fm*9-5  118  2nd 2½ 1hd 31½  Gonzalez RM 1 HcpO  95-11 CttngWnd,DblnO'Brn,GrnJdgmnt 6
      Speed Index: Last Race: -1.0    3=Race Avg.: -1.3   9=Race Avg.: -1.1    Overall Avg.: -1.0
Jly 30 Dmr 6f fm 1:173 H (d)   Jly 24 Dmr 4f ft :482   Jly 1 BM 5f ft 1:01 H   Jun 25 BM 5f ft 1:001 H
```

Treig O-N   πₑ²
DESORMEAUX K J 115
Own.—Keck H B O-N

Dk. b. or br. c. 4, by Forli—Pailleron, by Majestic Light
Br.—Keck H B (Ky)
Tr.—Whittingham Charles $95,000

| | 1990 | 10 | 1 | 0 | 3 | $41,325 |
| | 1989 | 6 | 1 | 0 | 0 | $21,475 |

Lifetime 29 3 0 3 $70,200 F28 = R² Turf 13 2 0 3 $62,800

```
22Jly90-10Hol  1½ ①:4741:1111:404fm  13  116  75½ 74½ 2½ 11½  Desormux K J3  62500 91-12 Treig, Hot And Smoggy, Neskimo 8
      22Jly90—4-wide stretch
1Jly90-5Hol    1 ①:4621:0941:34 fm  29  116  77½ 76½ 812 910½  Sibille R7  75000 84-08 BrvCpd,PtchGrndfg,HtAndSmgg 10
      1Jly90—5 wide stretch                                        F24 = 110
27May90-9Hol   1 ①:46 1:1011:344fm  8½  112  71½ 65 53½ 52½  Desormux K J6  90000 86-10 SilverCircus,DaysGoneBy,Lordlik 7
16May90-9Hol   1 ①:46 1:1021:334fm  6½  114  8⁴ 87½ 77 35½  Solis A8  75000 90-06 Carolina North, Neskimo, Treig 8
27Apr90-9Hol   1 ①:4621:1011:342fm *4  116  65 53 64½ 65½  Valenzuela PA9  80000 87-08 Chief's Image, Sperry, Sabulose 9
      27Apr90—Wide into stretch
1Apr90-5SA     a6½f ①:204 :4321:134fm 9½  118  101310¹¹ 86½ 32  Valenzuela PA7  80000 90-08 Paisano Pete, Dr. Brent, Treig 12
19Mar90-5SA    a6½f ①:212 :4331:13 fm  21  118  10⁹½10⁸½ 66 32¾  Valenzuela PA1  80000 93-05 Paisano Pete, Lordalik, Treig 10
      19Mar90—Lugged in late
18Feb90-5SA    1½ :471 1:364 2:022sy  6  115  33½ 618 733 —  McCarron C J4  80000 — — Kadial, Stop TheStage,JustBobby 7
      18Feb90—Eased
27Jan90-7SA    1½ ①:4631:1011:47 fm  5  116  31 32 42½ 63  Vlenzul PA4 Aw42000 87-10 DremOfFme,Shotiche,LtestReles 10
      27Jan90—Steadied 1/16
11Jan90-8SA    1½ ①:4531:0931:46 fm  26  116  43 31½ 33½ 43¾  McCrrn C J8 Aw42000 91-05 SuperMy,SuperRdy,BrokThMold 10
      Speed Index: Last Race: +3.0    3=Race Avg.: -2.3   7=Race Avg.: -3.2    Overall Avg.: -3.0
Aug 2 Dmr 5f ft 1:004 H   Jly 29 Dmr 3f ft :352 H   Jly 20 Hol 3f ft :364 H   Jly 15 Hol 5f ft 1:003 H
```

Other contenders and the figures were:

Hot And Smoggy	112
Patchy Groundfog	110
Breakfast Table	110
Racing Rascal	110

At 122, Treig towered above the field on the figures, and when the horse came flying to the wire in front at $21.00 (9½-to-1) I got even more excited about these numbers. The second-high figure horse finished second in the race, producing an exacta of 66–1, which I inconveniently overlooked. The prime bet, nonetheless, felt exhilarating.

In the featured La Jolla Handicap (Grade 3) for three-year-olds, at 1¹/₁₆ miles, Itsallgreektome stood apart whether handicappers relied upon its figure at 1⅛ miles (122), the last running line, at 1¹/₁₆ mile (116), two races back, or at a mile (112), three races ago.

Regardless, when the gelding was strongly backed to 9–5, I backed away. I wanted 2–1 minimum and never saw that line since early in the wagering. Itsallgreektome lost by a nose that would have disappeared in the next stride. The winner was the His Majesty colt Tight Spot (108), who had won its first turf start wire-to-wire last out, and repeated by pressing the pace and drawing clear into the stretch this time.

I might have bemoaned a key bet on Itsallgreektome, but discretion once more proved the better part of valor at the races.

On Monday I liked the high-rated filly in the turf feature, for nonwinners three times other than maiden or claiming, well enough to risk another prime wager, but Girl of France (119) proved fourth best only. The winner rated 110 on the numbers.

The ledger after two weeks and eighteen turf races told a fabulous tale. The cold dope showed 7 of 18 winners, or 39 percent. Amount bet had been $36, but the return was $107.40, an ROI of 300 percent.

Prime bets had proved even more remarkable. Four of five had won, at average odds of 6.3-to-1. A $200 wager to win on each of the five prime horses would have netted $4980.00. If this kind of thing continued, the new turf figures would have become part and parcel of everyman's handicapping equipment, and Del Mar would have been humbled at last.

Week 3

The third week in review began as the second ended, on a downbeat for the top-figure horse. These were three-year-olds that had not won two races. For the leading two contenders, I present the previous two turf figures.

Pro For Sure	1M	110
	1$^{1}/_{16}$M	98
Pictorial	1$^{1}/_{16}$M	108
	1M	113

Pictorial was returning from a three-month respite and was running on Lasix for the first time. She was 3–1.

Pro For Sure was beaten a nose last out, July 25, at Del Mar. She was favored at 8–5.

I accepted the second figure back for Pictorial as a best estimate, passing the race preceding the vacation.

I would not take Pro For Sure at 8–5 here regardless, but the pattern of figures can be a positive sign among improving three-year-olds. Second start on the grass, Pro For Sure had improved six lengths. That kind of improvement normally continues, provided the three-year-olds are brought back within a few weeks under comparable conditions. A next step up in class is perfectly acceptable, of course, following a win.

Pro For Sure won rather handily here, virtually wire-to-wire in good time. Pictorial was third, headed for second.

The fifth race on Thursday shaped up as a muddled event at a mile for fillies and mares, 3up. No real surprise, the top-figure horse finished fourth. The second-rated contender won, wire to wire, at 2.4–1.

The nonwinners-twice feature delivered a bettable proposition. The figures did not separate the top two contenders, but the odds did:

Really Brilliant	112	5–1
Eratone	112	7–5

I backed Really Brilliant at the odds, and that colt finished ahead of Eratone by a length. Unfortunately, Chief's Image (106) won by three-quarters, flying in late under Eddie Delahoussaye, the best finisher from the rear in the game.

If exactas are played here, boxing the two top-rated horses, Really Brilliant should be used on top multiple times, Eratone on top much less, perhaps as a saver (of capital) only. The opposite tactic, Eratone on top, produces an underlay combination, which is poor procedure.

In the lone turf race on Friday, the high-figure horse Neskimo (112) finished second to a gelding returning from a 3½-month vacation. At 9–5 odds, Neskimo was not bettable. Nothing else qualified for a wager either.

To begin the weekend, in the fifth race Saturday the two top-rated horses at 104 ran one-two at a middle distance for nonwinners other than maiden or claiming. One was 5–2, the other 2–1, a no-bet situation. The exacta was not bettable either. It paid $15.20, less than 3–1 for a two-horse box.

An intriguing proposition in the field was Woodley's Fee, which looked like so:

Unraced on turf, Woodley's Fee is a daughter of Seattle Slew. That sire wins with 20 percent of his starters on grass, and with 12 percent of his first starters.

Favored for its inaugural two starts at three, Woodley's Fee cracks its maiden on the fifth try, at a one-turn mile at Hollywood Park, when not expected to win. The filly scores by five with a running style that might transfer effectively to the deeper grass.

As a maiden-claiming graduate moving into the allowances, Woodley's Fee is a 20–1 shot on the morning line. The bettors, however, showed greater respect. Woodley's Fee was 8–1 nearing post time. Price is essential here, and the odds look marginal. I passed. Woodley's Fee ran well enough, finishing fourth, beaten 4½ lengths.

The feature on Saturday offered the only prime bet of the week. It was the Escondido Handicap, a $75,000 pot for 3up at the peculiar 1⅜ miles. On the numbers, River Warden stood out, as did its relative class at this distance. Examine River Warden's record briefly:

I have already cautioned handicappers not to use figures at middle distances to project figures at classic distances. Considerable research persuades us the distances are distinct, the races won by distinct populations of horses.

But a variation of the guideline can present an opportunistic moment. River Warden earned a huge figure of 130 at nine furlongs at Del Mar July 29, but the four-year-old already has proved itself at classic distances. That kind of figure transfers swimmingly, especially in an improvement pattern, such as River Warden shows following its layoff March 24.

Today's conditions specified, ". . . for nonwinners of $35,000 at a mile or over in 1990." A soft spot for the likes of River Warden, a Grade 2 winner at three in France.

The odds proved irresistible, at 6–1.

A prime wager drifted down the drain when the field swung into the upper stretch. Jockey Russell Baze, moving up and surveying a struggling field in front of him, attempted to split horses, but was forced to check sharply. The rider might have gone around, but did not. The horse regained stride and finished eagerly, but much too late.

Would River Warden have won? The result chart is very suggestive, and expresses my sentiment exactly.

8143—EIGHTH RACE. 1⅜ miles (turf). 3 year olds & up. 37th Running Escondido Handicap. Purse $75,000.

Index	Horse and Jockey	Wt.	PP	¼	½	¾	1	Str.	Fin.	To $1
7604	Rial, Fernandez	112	5	4	$5^{1/2}$	6^{4}	6^{5}	$3^{1/2}$	1^{hd}	28.70
7604	Mashkour, Solis	113	6	6	6^{5}	5^{2}	$5^{1 1/2}$	$2^{1 1/2}$	$2^{1 3/4}$	3.80
7604	Valdali, Delahoussaye	116	4	5	4^{1}	$4^{1/2}$	4^{hd}	$1^{1/2}$	3no	1.60
8043	River Warden, Baze	115	1	7	$7^{1 1/2}$	7^{2}	7^{4}	6^{2}	4^{1}	6.10
7583	Great Communicator, Sibille	119	2	2	$2^{1 1/2}$	$2^{1 1/2}$	$2^{1 1/2}$	$5^{1/2}$	$5^{1 1/4}$	3.00
7550	Miserden, Flores	111	3	1	1^{1}	$1^{1/2}$	$1^{1/2}$	4^{1}	6^{4}	14.90
8043	Colson, P.Valenzuela	116	7	3	3^{4}	3^{3}	3^{1}	7^{6}	7^{5}	8.80
7605	Law Journal, Berrio	107	8	8	8	8	8	8	8	63.70

Scratched—Lowell.

5—RIAL	**59.40**	**21.20**	**5.80**
6—MASHKOUR		**5.60**	**3.00**
4—VALDALI			**2.40**

Time—24 3/5, 48 2/5, 1.13, 1.37 1/5, 2.14 3/5. Cloudy & firm. Winner—BH 85 Family Crest-Rupia. Trained by Vincent Clyne. Mutuel pool—$418,217. Exacta pool—$388,417. Triple pool—$388,954.

$2 EXACTA (5-6) PAID $222.40
$3 DAILY TRIPLE (1-2-5) PAID $1,417.20

RIAL, difficult to handle from the start, was rank while being outrun, was steadied and shuffled back on the clubhouse turn, lost ground on the final turn while gaining, began the stretch drive four wide, lugged inward in the drive, brushed with Mashkour in deep stretch and just got up in closing yards. MASHKLUR, patiently handled while being outrun early, rallied to bid for command turning into the stretch for the drive, had the lead between calls in the final furlong, came out and brushed with Rial in deep stretch and could not quite outfinish that rival. VALDALI, also patiently handled while being outrun early, got through along the inner rail to wrest the advantgage just before reaching the quarter pole on the last turn but weakened late. RIVER WARDEN, far back early, closed strongly to get closer turning into the stretch for the drive, was steadied when boxed in coming into the stretch, then was coming on strongly late after getting a clear path. LOWELL (7) was withdrawn. All wagers on him in the regular, exacta and late double pools were ordered refunded and all of his late triple selections were switched to the favorite, Valdali (4)

In general, trips are vastly overrated in turf racing. Swinging wide on the far turn usually is meaningless. So is steadying and checking on the far turn, a common occurrence. The horses normally can get clear by the upper stretch, and still have ample time to fly to the wire first.

Two trips are troublesome. Any horses obviously rank en

route to the clubhouse turn remains in serious danger of squandering too much energy too soon. Some of these rank contenders do settle into a relaxed stride on the clubhouse turn, or early on the backside. But those that do not relax do not often win.

Once closers have been set down, either into the upper stretch, as with River Warden, or in mid-stretch, checking and altering course results in defeat. Stride can be regained, but momentum has been surrendered and other contenders are now rallying hard. It's difficult to regain stride, momentum, and advantage in time to win.

Going wide does not matter much, unless the horses are being used hard simultaneously. Usually closers will move up wide but under the jockey's control. The horses have not yet been set down. Once the stretch path has been cleared, the rider sets his mount down seriously. Most of the best horses get there.

A premature move is the much more serious mistake on the grass. A big move approaching the far turn or around the far turn regularly dissipates by mid-stretch or later. The tiring horse is overrun by a more patient horse and rider. It happens all the time, one reason apprentices and whoop-de-do jockeys seldom bring back winners on the turf. A patient ride beats a hustling ride on the turf nine times of ten.

On Sunday the three turf races were stakes, split halves of the San Clemente Handicap, for three-year-old fillies, and the Grade 1 Eddie Read Handicap, for 3up, the West Coast prep for the Arlington Million.

In both divisions of the San Clemente, the figure horse finished third. I supported Bidder Cream in the second half at 9–1. He broke slowly, relaxed, and rallied, but not strongly enough.

The Grade 1 Eddie Read shaped up as a contentious race, meaning the probabilities were well-distributed among several contenders. Below is the high figure for each contender when its previous three starts are considered, and the public odds on each near post.

Golden Pheasant	129	2–1
Fly Till Dawn	123	12–1
Saratoga Passage	124	5–1
Classic Fame	124	2–1
Companion	119	6–1

The top figure Golden Pheasant was returning from a layoff and was prepping for the Arlington Million. Saratoga Passage had won the Eddie Read in 1989, earning another 124 that day. Following a pair of improving efforts at Hollywood Park, Saratoga Passage appeared to be approaching its sharpest form. Companion had won two improving races, the last a smasher at Del Mar two weeks ago, and figured to improve again. But how much?

Contentious races can be characterized by unanswered questions, and this was no exception. Dick Mitchell has argued ad nauseam that when analyzing contentious races, handicappers must take the odds in the end. It's irrefutable advice.

As the probabilities are close, but the prices far apart, the advantage goes to the high-odds horses. Favorites and low-priced contenders (below 7–2) are tossed unceremoniously, unless combined in saver exactas. Long-priced horses (8-to-1 and up) can be backed to win and keyed top and bottom in generous exactas.

Anyone who followed that strategy in the Eddie Read cashed in, as the outsider Fly Till Dawn set a sluggish solo pace and took the field all the way, nosing Classic Fame to win.

I had passed the race, not liking Fly Till Dawn on the front end at Del Mar against ranking horses. But the fractions played out as 24.3, 48.3, and 1:12.2. A good horse then dug in and had enough stamina and competitive drive to survive.

On Monday of Week 3 the high-figure horse in the third also outclassed the nonwinners-once allowance conditions so obviously that the Danzig filly was certain to go as an underlay to win.

She was offered at even money. No bet.

But the exacta here afforded handicappers the chance to convert an underlay to an overlay. The second choice in the wagering at 2–1 had earned a weak turf figure of 96. She was a frontrunner to boot, and might tire earlier on Del Mar's deeper lawn. Below are the past performances for the favorite and second choice.

Kissogram Girl Dk. b. or br. f. 3(Feb), by Danzig—Foreign Courier, by Sir Ivor
DELAHOUSSAYE E 117 Br.—Gainsborough Farm Inc (Ky) 1990 1 0 0 1 $5,400
Own.—MktmShkhMktmRshdAl Tr.—Drysdale Neil— 1989 3 1 0 0 $4,752
Lifetime 4 1 0 1 $10,152 Turf 4 1 0 1 $10,152
29Jly90-9Dmr 1 1/16 Ⓣ:48 1:12⁴1:43⁴fm 8 1/2 117 9 7 1/4 8 5 1/4 5 3 3 1 1/2 DlhssyE4 ⒻAw36000 86-09 Intercivet, Beata, Kissogram Girl 9
29Jly90—Wide in drive
14Oct89◆4Ascot(Eng) 5f 1:02 gd 2 3/4 120 Ⓣ 8 21 SnbrWR Crnwlls(Gr3) Argntm,Smthngdffrnt,DncngMsc 9
4Oct89◆4Newmarket(Eng) 6f 1:14²gd 6 1/4 123 Ⓣ 8 5 SbrWR ⒻChvlyPk(Gr1) DdCrtn,LnofThndr,ChmsofF·dm 11
29May89◆1Sandown(Eng) 5f 1:02 fm *2-5 123 Ⓣ 1 2 SbrWR ⒻFreemans(Mdn) KssogrmGrl,InThPprs,BrghtFlowr 7
Speed Index: Last Race: -5.0 1-Race Avg.: -5.0 1-Race Avg.: -5.0 Overall Avg.: -5.0
Aug 7 Dmr 6f ft 1:15³ H Jly 25 Dmr 4f ft :48 H Jly 20 Hol 1 ft 1:42³ H Jly 10 Hol 6f ft 1:16² H

Priceless Lady B. f. 3(Apr), by Secretariat—Nervous Pet, by Nervous Energy
DESORMEAUX K J 120 Br.—Mabee Mr-Mrs J C (Ky) 1990 5 1 2 1 $23,550
Own.—Golden Eagle Farm Tr.—Mandella Richard Turf 2 1 1 0 $16,750
Lifetime 5 1 2 1 $23,550
20Jly90-8Hol 1 1/16 Ⓣ:47¹1:10⁴1:41⁴fm 10 115 1 1 1hd 1 1/2 2 1 1/2 DsrmxKJ5 ⒻAw37000 84-16 HrdlyHerd,PricelssLdy,CshInNow 8
17Jun90-6GG 1 Ⓣ:48¹1:13¹1:39¹fm 7 3/4 117 1 1/2 1 2 1 3 1 4 1/2 Patterson A7 ⒻMdn 76-18 PriclssLdy,AnyTimNow,Krskrossd 9
27May90-3GG 6f :21³ :44³ 1:11 sy *8-5 117 3 4 4 5 4 6 1/2 4 11 1/2 Patterson A5 ⒻMdn 71-19 TrnToHvn,RoylCmpttn,AnyTmNw 7
27May90—Bumped in drive
15Apr90-1GG 6f :21⁴ :44⁴ 1:09⁴ft 4 3/4 117 1 1 1 1/2 3 1/2 3 3 1/4 Patterson A6 ⒻMdn 86-13 PrinclyHug,Tiffny'sGm,PrclssLdy 6
18Mar90-5GG 6f :22 45 1:11²ft 5 3/4e 117 2 1 2 1 2 1 1/2 2 2 PattersonA10 ⒻMdn 79-13 LvThtSng,PrclssLd,Asltn sAngis 11
Speed Index: Last Race: 0.0 2-Race Avg.: -4.5 2-Race Avg.: -4.5 Overall Avg.: -5.6
●Aug 6 Dmr 6f ft 1:11² H Jly 14 Hol 7f ft 1:26⁴ H Jly 8 Hol 4f ft :48³ H

In these situations, handicappers are rightly recommended to eliminate the overbet second choice in exacta combos. Cover instead any three-year-old possessing (a) excellent turf breeding and (b) superb odds.

Today's field offered a 70–1 shot from England and a 25–1 shot showing one decent grass race. The strong favorite won as expected. But when the 25–1 shot headed a 5–1 third choice for the place, the $2 exacta returned $98, or 48–1. The $4 two-horse two-hole investment returned odds of 24–1, a nice overlay in the two-hole, to be sure.

In the featured allowance race at a mile, a Wayne Lukas colt showing a 102 in seventeen grass attempts sped to the front and returned to the winner's circle sporting a 109 figure. The impressive stretch run smacked of a horses-for-courses exhibition. Maybe Lukas would wheel Santa Tecla back before Del Mar closes.

Poorly suited to the mile, the high-figure horse rallied from last to second. He needed extra distance.

Week 4

And on the fourth go-round practically every other turf race was won and lost by the numbers. The first hope was former winner Softscape, a stickout on the figures, but an unfortunate loser nonetheless. Softscape was knocked into the rail during the run to the clubhouse turn. The rider took up and back sharply.

Odds of 9–5 prevented a prime bet on Softscape, but the horse keyed exactas and a sweet Pick 3 for me, which blew.

The next afternoon another favorite, the 2–1 Past Remembered, won a close decision. It was an allowance race for non-winners-twice other than maiden, claiming, or starter. The past performances are worth scouring:

The crucial consideration regards the ratable races. Last out, Past Remembered lost as the 4–5 standout, earning a 107. Two back the filly lost at 6–5 by a neck, earning a 122. Three back the horse got a 110 while beaten a length as a nonfavorite.

Which figure should be used today?

Either of the top two figures qualified to beat this bunch. These should be accepted, the last line discounted. A dull line can be tolerated in a sharp, consistent pattern. This is especially true on the grass, where the absence of a rapid pace sustains positive form for longer periods.

Of Past Remembered, notice the attractive workouts following the dull race July 21. Form remains intact. Especially sharp workouts are unnecessary, but reassuring. Likewise, the wide trip is not the forgiving element here, but supports the general case.

Keep in mind that a dull race in a sharp context is forgivable, particularly on the turf. Two dull races in succession are not forgivable. And a single dull line in a declining pattern is bad news. That is not the situation here.

At 2–1 I took Past Remembered seriously enough here, but did not offer a prime amount. The filly trailed the pace by a shorter margin than normally, and prevailed in a long hard drive.

The other interesting contest of the week occurred in Saturday's feature, a Grade 1 event for older fillies and mares at nine furlongs. Years ago I urged handicappers to favor Grade 1 horses in Grade 1 races. The guideline holds firm on the turf. Below, examine the past performances of four contenders.

Reluctant Guest
DESORMEAUX K J 117
Own.—Folsom R S

Brown Bess
KAENEL J L 122
Own.—Calbourne Stable

Double Wedge 114
DAVIS R G
Own.—Gann, E A

30Jun90-8Hol 1⅛ Ⓣ:464 1:10 1:47 fm *2½ 115 52¼ 53½ 54 43½ StsGL4 ⒻBv Hls H 89-07 ButfulMlody,RlctntGst,StylshStr 6
30Jun90—Grade I; 4-wide stretch
27May90-8Hol 1⅛ Ⓣ:474 1:114 1:474fm 2½ 112 63½ 62¾ 2½ 12 DsRG4 ⒻGmly H 89-10 DoublWdg,StylshStr,ButfulMlody 6
27May90—Grade I; 4-wide stretch
12May90-8GG 1⅜ Ⓣ:483 1:382 2:153fm 5 112 43½ 31½ 3½ 2¾ DsRG5 ⒻYrba BnaH 92-09 Petitelle,DoubleWedge,BrownBss 5
31Mar90-8SA 1¼ Ⓣ:45 1:34 1:582fm 30 111 2½ 42 32 3hd DsRG4 ⒻSta Brb H 96-09 BrownBess,RoylTouch,DoublWdg 5
31Mar90—Grade I; Troubled trip
22Feb90-8SA 1 :462 1:111 1:364ft 6 116 69½ 67 57 58½ DlhssyE6 ⒻAw55000 74-23 Voila,SugarplumGal,PperPrincess 6
22Feb90—Broke slowly
26Jan90-8SA 1 Ⓣ:453 1:093 1:342fm 7¾ 115 76 65 65½ 77¼ McCrrCJ6 ⒻAw60000 84-09 Oeilladine,Agirlfromars,BabaCool 8
14Jan90-7SA 1⅛ Ⓣ:47 1:112 1:48 gd*2-3e 116 21 2hd 21½ 22¼ DlhssyE3 ⒻAw60000 83-15 GenrlChrg,DoublWdg,SugrplumGl 6
26Dec89-7SA 1 Ⓣ:463 1:102 1:334fm 4 116 54½ 52½ 42 22½ DlhssyE9 ⒻAw60000 99 — Oeilldine,DoubleWdg,SugrplumGl 9
17Nov89-5Hol 1 Ⓣ:463 1:101 1:342fm 2¾ 116 2½ 11½ 1½ 42 DlhssyE5 ⒻAw45000 90-09 InvitedGuest,RintrRngd,Dvi'sLmb 6
5Nov89-8SA 1 Ⓣ:451 1:083 1:332fm 11 115 55½ 33 41¾ 41¼ ToroF1 ⒻL R Rwn H 103 — BabaCool,Davie'sLamb,StylishStr 9
5Nov89—Bumped 1/8

Speed Index: Last Race: -4.0 3-Race Avg.: -1.3 9-Race Avg.: -0.7 Overall Avg.: -1.0
Aug 15 Dmr Ⓣ 5f fm 1:04 H (d) Aug 9 Dmr Ⓣ 6f fm 1:154 H (d) Aug 2 Dmr Ⓣ 7f fm 1:27 H (d) ●Jly 26 Dmr Ⓣ 6f fm 1:142 H (d)

***Jabalina Brown *** — **B. m. 5, by Dark Brown—Destination, by Logical**
GARCIA J A — **114** — **Br.—Haras Rosa del Sur (Arg)** — **1990 7 2 1 1 $135,450**
Tr.—McAnally Ronald — **1989 7 2 1 0 $77,300**
Own.—Haras Rosa del Sur — **Lifetime 22 7 4 1 $241,624** — **Turf 18 5 4 1 $190,617**

28Jly90-8Dmr 1 1/16 Ⓣ:481 1:121 1:423fm 23 112 76½ 75 52½ 1nk GrcJA1 ⒻPalomar H 94-08 JabalinaBrown,StylishStr,Nikishk 8
28Jly90—Grade II
11Jly90-8Hol 1 Ⓣ:473 1:113 1:353fm 5¾ 116 33 2½ 2½ 1no AlmeidG4 ⒻAw60000 86-14 JblinBrown,WrningZone,LightIce 5
11Jly90—Lugged out early
15Jun90-8Hol 1 1/16 Ⓣ:474 1:12 1:412fm 7¾ 116 52½ 31½ 22½ 23½ AlmeidG6 ⒻAw60000 84-11 T.V.OfCrystl,JblnBrwn,SwtRbrtII 6
12May90-8GG 1⅜ Ⓣ:483 1:382 2:153fm 12 111 55½ 53¼ 45½ 45¼ AldG2 ⒻYrba Bna H 88-09 Petitelle,DoubleWedge,BrownBss 5
31Mar90-8GG 1 1/16 Ⓣ:462 1:102 1:423fm 17 114 716 711 57½ 34½ AldG6 ⒻGldn Ppy H 94-05 SrosBrig,FormidblLdy,JbinBrown 7
31Mar90—Grade III

Grass champion Brown Bess heads the field, but becomes a fast toss-out today. The eight-year-old had not looked the part in 1990 in four races at Santa Anita and Golden Gate Fields. Not unimportantly, the figures told the same tale. A 112 at Santa Anita on March 11 (Grade 1) was Brown Bess's best of season, a low mark for a champion.

Of the other three, two carry Grade 1 credentials and the high figures too. Jabalina Brown earned a 116 in the Grade 2 Palomar at Del Mar by a neck July 28, and a 119 overnight July 11. The mare, now five, has never been tested under Grade 1 conditions. Reluctant Guest (120) and Double Wedge (122) deserve the nod.

The two Grade 1 graduates did not disappoint, finishing well clear of the others. Double Wedge outran Reluctant Guest in the late stages, flattering the figures. She paid $12.80.

The next afternoon the Del Mar Derby, on the grass, was marred by an untoward incident out of the gate and toward the clubhouse turn. Eventual winner Tight Spot, not the figure horse by a few lengths, came over early from her outside post and bothered several contenders. Tight Spot was disqualified to last.

Encamped with colleague Tom Brohamer for the week in Las Vegas, where we suffered an unusual pasting at the race books, I am delighted to report the turf figures saved us from disaster. The figures toppled Saratoga reliably, and generated profits at Monmouth Park, Pimlico, and Atlantic City as well.

At Saratoga the prime bet of the week on the turf lost by a neck in excellent time only because the Grade 1 filly Lady In Silver—Prix Diane in France and second to Steinlen as a three-year-old filly in the 1989 Arlington Million—popped up in an allowance race for nonwinners three times other than maiden or claiming, and popped back into form. Our good thing, Plenty of Grace, had moved to the lead strongly entering the stretch and dug in when challenged by the division leader, but got beat regardless.

At times this can be a bewildering pastime.

Week 5

As the fifth week of racing proceeded, mysteriously, the crowd appeared to possess my newly minted turf ratings. On Wednesday, Thursday, Friday, and Saturday, the top figure horses, six of them, went to the gate as favorites below 2–1.

Three won, three lost, a virtual push. Interestingly, the trio of losers were defeated by a phenomenon not altogether uncommon at mid-meeting on a turf course hospitable to deep closers.

Examine the result chart below:

FIFTH RACE
Del Mar
AUGUST 18, 1990

1 ⅛ MILES.(Turf). (1.46⅗) CLAIMING. Purse $42,000. 3-year-olds and upward. Weights, 3-year-olds, 116 lbs.; older, 122 lbs. Non-winners of two races at a mile or over since July 1 allowed 2 lbs.; of a race since then, 4 lbs.; since June 1, 6 lbs. Claiming price $80,000; if for $75,000 allowed 2 lbs. (Maiden and races when entered for $70,000 or less not considered.) (Non-starters for $25,000 or less in their last three starts preferred.)

Value of race $42,000; value to winner $23,100; second $8,400; third $6,300; fourth $3,150; fifth $1,050. Mutuel pool $505,115. Exacta pool $566,147.

Last Raced	Horse	M/Eqt.	A.Wt	PP	St	¼	½	¾	Str	Fin	Jockey	Cl'g Pr	Odds $1
5Aug90 ^{5}Dmr^{2}	Hot And Smoggy	LBb	6 116	8	1	$1^{1½}$	1^{1}	1^{1}	1^{hd}	1^{hd}	Black C A	80000	5.10
4Aug90 ^{5}Dmr^{1}	Novelty	LB	7 116	3	2	2^{hd}	$2^{½}$	$2^{1½}$	2^{hd}	2^{hd}	Solis A	80000	7.70
10Aug90 ^{7}Dmr^{4}	Days Gone By	LB	6 116	7	6	$3^{1½}$	$3^{1½}$	$3^{½}$	$3^{3½}$	3^{3}	Baze R A	80000	4.30
5Aug90 ^{5}Dmr^{1}	Treig	B	4 120	5	7	$6^{1½}$	5^{1}	5^{1}	$4^{½}$	$4^{½}$	DesormuxKJ	80000	2.50
4Aug90 ^{11}LA^{7}	Fairly Affirmed	LBb	6 117	2	4	$4^{½}$	$4^{1½}$	$4^{1½}$	$5^{2½}$	5^{2}	Pincay L Jr	80000	36.30
1Aug90 ^{5}Dmr^{1}	Dakotah Thunder	LB	4 116	4	3	5^{1}	6^{1}	7^{hd}	$8^{1½}$	6no	Garcia J A	80000	8.70
4Aug90 ^{3}Dmr^{2}	Cranky Kid	LBb	5 120	6	9	9	9	9	6^{hd}	$7^{2¼}$	DelhoussyeE	80000	6.50
5Aug90 ^{5}Dmr^{6}	Racing Rascal	LBb	4 120	1	5	7^{hd}	7^{hd}	$6^{½}$	$7^{½}$	$8^{2¾}$	Meza R Q	80000	8.10
4Aug90 ^{5}Dmr^{4}	Simjour	LB	4 114	9	8	$8^{1½}$	$8^{2½}$	8^{2}	9	9	Davis R G	75000	13.70

OFF AT 4:16. Start good. Won driving. Time, :25⅗, :49⅘, 1:13⅘, 1:38⅕, 1:50⅖ Course firm.

$2 Mutuel Prices:			
8–HOT AND SMOGGY	12.20	5.40	3.40
3–NOVELTY		8.00	4.40
7–DAYS GONE BY			4.00

$2 EXACTA 8–3 PAID $94.00.

Ch. h, by Singular—Marselar, by Selari. Trainer Stute Melvin F. Bred by Siegel Jan (Fla).

HOT AND SMOGGY made the early pace, battled for command all the way down the stretch while inside NOVELTY and DAYS GONE BY and prevailed by a small margin in a game effort. NOVELTY prompted the early pace, battled for command all the way down the stretch while between HOT AND SMOGGY and DAYS GONE BY and gave his all only to lose a close decision. DAYS GONE BY, close up early, battled for command through the stretch while outside HOT AND SMOGGY and NOVELTY and also gave his all only to lose a close decision. TREIG, devoid of early speed, failed to generate the needed rally. FAIRLY AFFIRMED, in contention early, lacked the needed response in the drive. DAKOTAH THUNDER had no apparent mishap. CRANKY KID was four wide into the stretch. RACING RASCAL lacked early speed and failed to menace.

The figure horses here were Treig and Novelty, not the winner Hot And Smoggy. Though frequently close, Hot And Smoggy had not won in two seasons and sixteen starts. But now it stole away on a solo lead in milkwagon fractions: 25.3, 49.4, and 1:13.4 through six furlongs. Unchallenged to the mile at 1:38.1, Hot And Smoggy dug in late and finished the final furlong in 12.1, heading Novelty.

That was last week. This week two upsets followed the same tardy pace, each surprise ending paying greater than 20–1.

On grass courses that favor closers, the jockeys learn soon enough to slow the pace as much as possible. Eventually the early pace proceeds at a virtual gallop. If a decent horse gets clear on this kind of lead, and relaxes (an important consideration), it can sprint to the wire late. Ordinary horses cannot catch up.

Over six furlongs at 1:13.4, Hot And Smoggy dispensed only 49.79 percent of its energy August 18, a decidedly low output. It ran for three furlongs only, but had lots in reserve for that long burst.

This does not mean the course is suddenly favoring frontrunners. When the early pace again picks up, again the closers dominate. But turf races can be stolen on the front at times. It's extremely difficult for handicappers to recognize the opportunity. Even when a lone frontrunner can be spotted in the past performances, the fractional times will be difficult to predict, as the typical pace on grass is slow enough. Moreover, even when the pace is doggedly slow, as with Hot And Smoggy, the frontrunner must proceed while relaxed. If the jockey has strong-armed the animal to slow matters down, arousing a struggle by the horse to run through the hold, all will be lost regardless. That squanders excessive energy, and fractional times notwithstanding, those hard-held frontrunners almost always collapse.

Handicappers alert to the circumstances should not conclude the course is now favoring early speed, unless the pace has been par or faster than par, and frontrunners—especially unexceptional frontrunners—have been suddenly lasting.

It was Sunday when at last a top-figure horse did not go postward an underlay. It was the featured Del Mar Oaks (Grade 3), offering $150,000-added to three-year-old fillies. The high-figure filly was not only not favored, it was one of the sweetest bets of the season. I present that filly and the entry favored by the crowd:

```
Slew Of Pearls                          B. f. 3(Feb), by Tsunami Slew—Cassock of Pearls, by Czaravich
  BLACK C A                       117   Br.—Whelan D J & Elizabeth (Ky)              1990  6 1 1 3    $102,000
Own.—Royal Lines                        Tr.—Gregson Edwin                            1989 10 3 1 1    $127,318
                                      Lifetime  16 4 2 4  $238,121                   Turf 11 3 2 4    $214,281
12Aug90-2Dmr  1  Ⓣ:474 1:114 1:362fm *2¼ B 116  63¾ 52½ 31  31   BlcCA7 ⒻSn ClmteH 91-06 Nijinsky'sLovr,BimboII,SlwOfPrls 9
   12Aug90—Run in divisions
1Jly90-8AP  1⅛ Ⓣ:482 1:13  1:491fm  7½    116  86  73¼ 63¼ 31¾  BlcCA6 ⒻPucker Up 96-08 SothrnTrdtn,VrgnMchl,SlwfPrls 11
   1Jly90—Grade III; Steadied turn
2Jun90-8Hol  1 1/16 Ⓣ:464 1:104 1:412fm  5½  117  74¾ 73¼ 53½ 31¾  DsrKJ5 ⒻHnymn H 86-12 Mterco,AnnulReunion,SlewOfPrls 9
   2Jun90—Grade III; Wide
29Apr90-8GG  1⅛ Ⓣ:491 1:143 1:512fm  2     116  32½ 32½ 1hd 2½   HnsnRD1 ⒻCal Oaks 89-09 FreyStrk,SlewOfPerls,AlohCorrin 5
8Apr90-8GG  1 1/16 Ⓣ:484 1:131 1:442fm  2¼   121  43  32  1hd 1nk  HnsnRD6 ⒻSngstrss 90-09 SlewOfPrls,TstfulT.V.,ClssyVigor 7
   8Apr90—Bore in
12Jan90-10Crc a1⅛ Ⓣ         1:482fm *2½    122  42½ 42  33½ 53   McClWH1 ⒻTrpPOs 73-24 JoyceAzlen,ColonilRunnr,Ct'sAir 13
30Dec89-10Crc 1 1/16 Ⓣ:48 1:121 1:443gd *2¼ 120  72¼ 63  47½ 45¼  McClWH7 ⒻMiramr 71-22 JoycAzln,SouthrnTrdton,SuprFn 14
   30Dec89—Steadied
4Nov89-7Aqu  1⅛ Ⓣ:494 1:154 1:561sf  *2    121  98  63  33  33½  CarrD4 ⒻMiss Grillo 65-31 Svn,Rootntootnwootn,SlwofPrls 11
   4Nov89—Grade III; Bumped start
21Oct89-8Lrl  1 1/16 :474 1:132 1:46 ft  4¾  119  63½ 44  612 719¼ Carr D9 ⒻSelima 64-15 SweetRoberta,Habar,WveringGirl 9
   21Oct89—Grade II
1Oct89-10Pim  1  Ⓣ:483 1:132 1:4[illegible] yl 9-5 117 97¾ 52½ 12  12¼  CrrD10 ⒻQunEmprs 70-27 SlwofPrls,IrishActrss,VirgnMchl 12
  Speed Index:  Last Race: -3.0     3-Race Avg.: -0.3     9-Race Avg.: -2.3      Overall Avg.: -4.2
Aug 20 Dmr Ⓣ 5f fm 1:013 H (d)  Aug 9 Dmr Ⓣ 4f fm :493 H (d)  Aug 3 Dmr 1 ft 1:394 H  ●Jly 28 Dmr 7f ft 1:26 H

Bel's Starlet                           Ro. f. 3(Jan), by Bel Bolide—Vigor's Star, by Vigors
  DESORMEAUX K J                  115   Br.—Mabee Mr-Mrs J C (Cal)                   1990  4 0 1 1     $35,550
Own.—Golden Eagle Farm                  Tr.—Mandella Richard                         1989  7 2 3 0    $132,365
                                      Lifetime  11 2 4 1  $167,915                   Turf  1 0 1 0     $15,000
12Aug90-5Dmr  1  Ⓣ:48 1:114 1:361fm  7¾ B  114  63  53  31½ 2no  BlcCA1 ⒻSn ClmteH 93-06 LonelyGirl,Bel'sStrlet,BidderCrm 9
   12Aug90—Run in divisions; Troubled trip
22Jly90-3Hol  6f :212 :441 1:092ft   5       111  42¼ 31½ 31½ 33¼  Davis RG1 ⒻAw37000 90-10 Dvil'sOrchid,PlumPoppy,Bl'sStrlt 6
17Jan90-8SA   1  :463 1:12 1:383gd   3¼e     118  84¾ 63  42  45   DvsRG7 ⒻⓇLa Cntla 69-26 FtToScout,AnnulRunon,NsrsPrd 10
   17Jan90—Broke slowly
3Jan90-8SA   7f :22 :443 1:221ft     4½      121  42½ 42  21½ 46½  McCrr7 ⒻⓈClBrdrs 85-12 Mterco,MissFireDncr,ForMyMom 9
   3Jan90—Broke slowly
15Nov89-8Hol  6½f :221 :45 1:163ft   2½      119  31  2hd 1hd 42¼  DvisRG3 ⒻMoccasin 90-10 Owiseone, Ten K, Dramatic Joy 4
9Oct89-8SA   1 1/16 :454 1:104 1:443ft  3¾   115  42  21  21  23   DsRG4 ⒻOak Leaf 75-19 DominntDncer,Bel'sStrlet,Mterco 7
   9Oct89—Grade I
11Sep89-8Dmr  6f :213 :442 1:09 ft   *7-5    117  2½  11½ 14  17½  DvsRG2 ⒻⓈC T B A 93-09 Bel'sStarlet,Shinko'sLss,‡Shnnon 8
19Aug89-3Dmr  6f :22 :451 1:101ft    4¾      118  63¾ 31½ 32  23½  Davis RG3 ⒻAw32000 83-14 TenK,Bel'sStarlet,PamperedSteel 6
   19Aug89—Bumped 3/8
2Aug89-8Dmr  6f :213 :442 1:094ft    7½      115  53¼ 43½ 35½ 58¼  Davis R G2 ⒻJr Miss 81-15 AWldRd,DomnntDncr,Tny'sTton 11
18Jun89-8GG  5½f :211 :44 1:031ft    3½      114  32  31½ 22  23   CpTM5 ⓈQuickstep 91-19 DominantDncer,Bel'sStrlet,Obrut 9
  Speed Index:  Last Race: -1.0     1-Race Avg.: -1.0     1-Race Avg.: -1.0      Overall Avg.: -1.0
Aug 23 Dmr Ⓣ 3f fm :371 H   ●Aug 9 Dmr Ⓣ 4f fm :48 B (d)   Aug 4 Dmr 6f ft 1:122 H   Jly 20 Hol 3f ft :383 B

Annual Reunion                          Dk. b. or br. f. 3(Mar), by Cresta Rider—Love For Life, by Forli
  VALENZUELA P A                  117   Br.—Mabee Mr-Mrs J C (Ky)                    1990  6 1 2 1     $79,050
Own.—Golden Eagle Farm                  Tr.—Jones Gary                               1989  7 2 1 1    $130,000
                                      Lifetime  13 3 3 2  $290,050                   Turf  1 0 1 0     $20,000
8Jly90-8Hol  1⅛ :47 1:113 1:494ft   *2e L  121  66½ 64¼ 68  610½ DsrKJ6 ⒻHol Oaks 74-19 Patches, Jefforee, PamperedStar 8
   8Jly90—Grade I; Wide trip
2Jun90-8Hol  1 1/16 Ⓣ:464 1:104 1:412fm  9    119  21½ 2hd 11  2hd  VllPA9 ⒻHnymn H 88-12 Mterco,AnnulReunion,SlewOfPrls 9
   2Jun90—Grade III
13May90-8GG  1 1/16 :46 1:101 1:414ft  *4-5   119  54  3½  21  11½  HnsRD4 ⒻMoraga H 89-17 AnnualReunion,TimelyWlk,LetFly 9
   13May90—Wide backstretch
17Mar90-8SA  1 1/16 :462 1:104 1:43 ft  13     117  55  55  69  610¼ BlnrG2 ⒻS A Oaks 78-13 HilAtlntis,BrightCndls,FtToScout 6
   17Mar90—Grade I; Wide
12Feb90-8SA  1 1/16 :464 1:114 1:453ft  *3-2   117  65  55  44½ 32¼  BlnrG2 ⒻⓇSta Ysbl 73-25 BrghtCndls,HvnForBd,AnnulRnon 7
   12Feb90—Lost rein 1/8
17Jan90-8SA  1  :463 1:12 1:383gd  3¼e       114  96¼ 52½ 31½ 2¾   BlnrG5 ⒻⓇLa Cntla 73-26 FtToScout,AnnulRunon,NsrsPrd 10
   17Jan90—Wide final 3/8
3Dec89-8Hol  1  :451 1:101 1:353ft  38        120  97¼ 74¾ 42½ 21½  BlnrG4 ⒻHol Strlt 84-17 ChvlVolnt,AnnlRnon,SpclHppnng 9
   3Dec89—Grade I; Wide
16Nov89-8Hol  1 1/16 :463 1:121 1:45 ft  6     117  67¼ 43  24  1hd  BolngrG6 ⒻAw28000 75-25 AnnulReunion,NsersPride,Horsch 7
   16Nov89—Wide final 3/8
14Oct89-7SA  6f :214 :451 1:103ft  2          118  57  56  58  510½ Baze RA3 ⒻAw31000 74-15 DrmticJoy,SrosTresur,KrryPippin 7
   14Oct89—Bumped start
3Sep89-8Dmr  1  :443 1:09 1:35 ft  46         114  813 913 921 927¼ OlrsF6 ⒻDmr Deb 64-09 RueDPlm,DominntDncr,ChvlVolnt 9
   3Sep89—Grade II
  Speed Index:  Last Race: 0.0      1-Race Avg.: 0.0      1-Race Avg.: 0.0       Overall Avg.: -5.0
●Aug 20 Dmr Ⓣ 6f fm 1:134 H (d)  Aug 13 Dmr Ⓣ 6f fm 1:152 H (d)  Aug 6 Dmr Ⓣ 5f fm 1:012 H (d)  Jly 31 Dmr 4f ft :481 H
```

When favored at Del Mar August 12 in the ungraded, un-listed San Clemente Stakes, Slew Of Pearls finished third, beaten a length, earning a figure of 102.

In first starts on the grass, entrymates Bel's Starlet (105) and Annual Reunion (104) had earned stronger figures, respectively.

Shouldn't handicappers prefer the entry over Slew Of Pearls in the Grade 3 Oaks?

Not a bit.

In the Grade 3 Pucker Up at Arlington Park July 1, Slew Of Pearls had earned a turf figure of 114 at nine furlongs. On June 2, at Hollywood Park, another Grade 3 turf stakes, Slew Of Pearls had earned a 108. Either figure headed the field, and the 114 towered above the opposition here.

A little handicapping helped to explain the 102 in the San Clemente. First, Slew Of Pearls had rallied boldly along the in-side in the upper stretch, but stopped abruptly after looking like a winner. The trainer later said the filly was short of form that day, but she might also have refused to slip through what was a narrow opening along the rail.

The acceleration that had proceeded the strange, sudden stop was undeniable.

Moreover, trainer Gregson moves cautiously with better horses. The San Clemente was obviously a prep for the more important Del Mar Oaks, not an unimportant consideration. If Slew Of Pearls could run back to either of her prior graded-stakes figures, she represented a double-advantage horse. That is, either of its top two figures were stronger than any figure of the other contenders.

Especially when evaluating three-year-olds, but all the time, handicappers can rely on the pattern of figures in the last se-quence of races, as many as six, to predict what should most likely happen today. Flexible thinking not only beats rigid rules, it also beats mechanical figure handicapping much of the time.

Slew Of Pearls was sent to the post in the Oaks an 8½-to-1 shot, a definite overlay.

She lagged early, exploded around the far turn. By the eighth-pole, Slew Of Pearls had charged to the front and merely cakewalked to the wire, clearly en route to Grade 1 competition.

She paid a generous $19.00.

The following afternoon, Monday, the high figure horse in the single grass event held an irresistible 10-point (five lengths) advantage against claiming opposition. As the horse had been 23–1 last out, I hoped for a minor score. Here are the past performances.

5th Del Mar

1 MILE. (Turf). (1.34⅕) CLAIMING. Purse $38,000. Fillies and mares. 3-year-olds and upward. Weights, 3-year-olds, 116 lbs.; older 122 lbs. Non-winners of two races at a mile or over since July 1 allowed 2 lbs.; such a race since then, 4 lbs.; since June 1, 6 lbs. Claiming price $62,500; for each $2,500 to $55,000 allowed 1 lb. (Maiden and races when entered for $50,000 or less not considered).

Bold Costa — B. f. 4, by Bold Forbes—La Costa Caper, by Pretense
BAZE R A — 120 — Br.—Glencrest Farm &RandallMay (Ky) — 1990 5 1 1 1 $31,200
Own.—Dame' Construction Co Inc — Tr.—Knight Terry $62,500 — 1989 13 4 2 2 $69,900
Lifetime 26 6 5 6 $136,040 — Turf 9 4 1 2 $68,550

15Aug90-5Dmr	1 1/16	Ⓣ:48³ 1:12³ 1:43¹fm	25	L	116	5³½	4²	1½	1¹¾	Baze R A⁷	Ⓕ55000	91-09	BoldCosta,FrauleinMri,Softscpe	10
15Aug90—Jostled start														
30Jun90-10Aks	1 1/16	:46² 1:11² 1:45 ft	*8-5		116	3⁶	3⁵	2⁵	2¹⁰	WllsRD¹	ⒻAw14000	79-15	StiffQuestion,BoldCost,AWildPst	7
23Jun90-11Aks	1 1/16	:47¹ 1:12³ 1:46 ft	21		115	2½	2¹	6⁷½	8¹⁰¼	GrrTG³	ⒻBudBrdCp	74-23	FigsWvng,Luthr'sLnch,DrmyMm	11
7Apr90-7GG	1	Ⓣ:46⁴ 1:11¹ 1:36⁴fm	5¾		117	8⁷	8⁶	7⁹	6⁷	DcyTT⁶	ⒻChpl Drms	81-13	VrietyBby,HthrAndRos,ArtCollg	10
6Jan90-6BM	1 1/16	Ⓣ:47¹ 1:12¹ 1:44³gd	4½		116	5⁴½	4¹¾	2½	3¾	DcTT¹⁰	ⒻC D Hpr H	81-21	AssumedTrits,Superfoi,BoldCost	11
24Dec89-8BM	1 1/16	Ⓣ:47¹ 1:12³ 1:45 fm	*4-5		118	3⁶½	2hd	1½	1¹½	Doocy T T³	ⒻHcpO	80-22	BldCst,WhmsclLdy,BrssSssNClss	6
26Nov89-7BM	1 1/16	:46¹ 1:11¹ 1:45³gd	6¼		114	6⁷½	7⁹¾	8⁹¾	8⁹¾	DocyTT⁴	ⒻCarmel H	59-29	LdyMichele,TchYou,CollctivJoy	11
5Nov89-8BM	1 1/16	:46² 1:10³ 1:43²ft	5		114	4³	3¹½	2¹	3¹½	DcTT³	ⒻPalo Alto H	78-23	PersonlVictory,BbRoug,BoldCost	7
11Oct89-8BM	1 1/16	Ⓣ:47 1:11⁴ 1:44³fm	*6-5		114	2⁴	2⁴	1²	1³	DoocyTT²	ⒻAw19000	80-19	BoldCosta,LovelyRuler,ClenLines	6
29Sep89-1BM	1 1/16	Ⓣ:48 1:12⁴ 1:44⁴fm	4		114	1³	1²	1⁶	1⁷	DoocyTT⁶	ⒻAw18000	79-21	BoldCost,MoonltDsrt,NcholsnMn	7

Speed Index: Last Race: 0.0 3–Race Avg.: -1.3 6–Race Avg.: -0.5 Overall Avg.: -2.3
Aug 10 BM 4f ft :49² H Aug 1 Aks 6f ft 1:16² B Jly 25 Aks 5f ft 1:03² B Jly 15 Aks 6f ft 1:16³ B

Bold Costa won as powerfully as the figures suggested, but against a truly lackluster field. Everyone jumped on this filly's bandwagon today. She paid $3.80. No bet.

In a week jammed with underlays, the lonely overlay won as much the best. One wager, one victory. A very good week, to be sure.

Week 6

With two weeks remaining and the turf figures comfortably ahead, I decided to limit prime bets to outstanding figure horses that were also outstanding overlays.

During the preceding three weeks, the top figure horses had won 8 of 22 races, 36 percent. Eliminating one odds-on underlay, average odds on winners was 3.1-to-1. The ROI was a sweet .74.

Five-week totals were impressive. Of 39 figure horses, 14 had won, 37 percent. Average odds on winners was 4.3-to-1, an ROI of .74—sweet!

Week 6 featured Labor Day weekend and the simulcast of the Arlington Million, a race that has proved especially rewarding for this punter. I felt With Approval would be the horse to beat in 1990, and looked forward to calculating the race figures.

Figure horses went down to defeat earlier that week and even that day, as a 10–1 overlay making its first grass start (son of Lyphard's Wish) ran third in a nondescript allowance field.

When the wagering on the Million began at Del Mar, With Approval was 2–1 first click. A win bet had to be discarded, as the race looked relatively contentious. A useful strategy in contentious races identifies the leading four or five contenders and supports any at 8–1 or greater.

Examine the four contenders I had isolated while doing the homework:

***Steinlen** — B. h. 7, by Habitat—Southern Seas, by Jim French
SANTOS J 126 — Br.—Allez France Stables (Eng) — Tr.—Lukas D Wayne
Own.—Wildenstein Stable — Lifetime 42 20 10 6 $3,120,100
1990 7 3 2 1 $720,104
1989 11 7 3 1 $1,521,378
Turf 41 20 10 6 $3,120,100

12Aug90-8Sar 1⅛ Ⓣ:4641:1041:482gd*1-3 126 2½ 2hd 12 22 StsJA5 B Baruch H 86-11 Who's to Pay,Steinlen,RiverofSin 5
12Aug90—Grade II
21Jly90-8Atl 1 3/16 Ⓣ:4841:1141:52 fm*8-5 L 124 11 1½ 11½ 13¾ SntsJA7 Casar Int H 103-10 Steinlen, Capades, Alwuhush 8
21Jly90—Grade II
4Jly90-8Hol 1⅛ Ⓣ:4641:1021:474fm*8-5 L 125 21 2hd 1½ 2¾ PncLJr5 Amrcn H 88-16 ClassicFme,Steinlen,PlesntVriety 7
4Jly90—Grade II
28May90-8Hol 1¼ Ⓣ:4831:3742:03 gd 3¾ 124 25 21 21 1nk PncLJr3 Hol Tf H 78-22 Steinlen, Hawkster, Santangelo 6
28May90—Grade I
13May90-8Hol 1⅛ Ⓣ:4841:1211:47 fm 9-5 126 21 1hd 2hd 32 SntsJA5 Jn Hnry H 91-09 GoldenPhesnt,ClssicFme,Steinlen 5
13May90—Grade II; Lost whip
8Apr90-8SA 1 Ⓣ:45 1:09 1:332fm *1 125 42 32½ 21 1hd SntsJA5 El Rncn H 96-05 Steinlen, Bruho, Wonder Dancer 6
8Apr90—Grade II
4Mar90-5SA 1 Ⓣ:45 1:09 1:342fm*6-5 126 48 57¼ 54½ 74¾ SntsJA7 Arcadia H 86-18 Prized, Happy Toss, On TheMenu 9
4Mar90—Grade III
4Nov89-7GP 1 Ⓣ:4721:1121:371gd 9-5 126 52½ 63¼ 21 1¾ SntsJA2 Br Cp Mile 88-13 Steinlen, Sabona, MostWelcome 11
4Nov89—Grade I; Rough trip-drvg
21Oct89-8Kee 1⅛ Ⓣ:4831:1321:522yl *1-3 126 53½ 51¾ 1hd 1hd StsJA4 Kee Brd Cp 80-20 Steinlen, Crystal Moment,Fosen 10
21Oct89—Grade III
3Sep89-8AP 1¼ Ⓣ:4911:3912:033fm 5¼ 126 22 32 3½ 1½ SntosJA4 A Million 76-25 Steinlen,LdyinSilver,YnkeeAffir 13
3Sep89—Grade I

Speed Index: Last Race: -3.0 3–Race Avg.: +4.6 10–Race Avg.: +2.1 Overall Avg.: +2.1
●Aug 29 Bel 4f gd :47 B Aug 9 Sar tr.t 4f ft :532 B Jly 31 Sar tr.t 4f ft :502 B Jly 15 Hol 5f ft :593 B

Golden Pheasant — Ro. c. 4, by Caro—Perfect Pigeon, by Round Table
STEVENS G L 126 — Br.—Carelaine&VintgeMedowFrms (Ky) — Tr.—Whittingham Charles
Own.—Gretzky & Summa Stable — Lifetime 10 4 3 1 $365,470
1990 4 2 0 1 $190,500
1989 6 2 3 0 $174,970
Turf 10 4 3 1 $365,470

12Aug90-8Dmr 1⅛ Ⓣ:4831:1221.481fm 2½ B 122 53½ 64 43 31¾ StnsGL3 E Read H 95-06 FlyTillDwn,ClssicFme,GoldnPhsnt 8
12Aug90—Grade I
28May90-8Hol 1¼ Ⓣ:4831:3742:03 gd *1 122 36 32½ 34½ 45¾ McCrrCJ5 Hol Tf H 72-22 Steinlen, Hawkster, Santangelo 6
28May90—Grade I
13May90-8Hol 1⅛ Ⓣ:4841:1211:47 fm*7-5 120 44 41¾ 3½ 11¾ McCrrCJ3 Jn HnryH 93-09 GoldenPhesnt,ClssicFme,Steinlen 5
13May90—Grade II, Bumped start
22Apr90-5SA 1⅛ Ⓣ:4541:0931:454fm*4-5 116 109¼ 88 22 11¾ McCrrnCJ1 Aw42000 96 — GoldenPhesnt,FlyTillDwn,Kntiyr 10
22Apr90—Broke slowly; wide
8Oct89♦5Longchamp(Fra) a1½ 2:304gd 10 123 Ⓣ 14 CrzAS ArcdeTriomphe CrrollHouse,Beher,SintAndrews 19
17Sep89♦4Longchamp(Fra) a1½ 2:322yl 7 123 Ⓣ 11½ Cruz A S Prix Neil (Gr 2) GoldenPhesnt,FrnchGlory,Nnwin 8
2Jly89♦4StCloud(Fra) a1½ 2:354gd 7¾ 121 Ⓣ 2hd CrAS GndPx de StClf(Gr 1) Sherrif'sStr,GoldenPhsnt,Bcytino 6
11Jun89♦7Chantilly(Fra) a1½ 2:334gd*9-5 121 Ⓣ 2no CruzAS Prix du Lys (Gr 3) HrvestTime,GoldenPhsnt,Spirits 8
9May89♦3Chester(Eng) a1½ 2:341gd 6 123 Ⓣ 22½ RbrtsM Chester Vase (Gr 3) OldVic,GoldenPheasant,Warrsnan 5
14Apr89♦1Newbury(Eng) 1⅜ 2:31 sf 4 126 Ⓣ 1¾ RbrtsM Spring (Mdn) GoldenPhesnt,FirProspect,Cmbo 8

Speed Index: Last Race: +1.0 3–Race Avg.: -1.0 4–Race Avg.: -1.7 Overall Avg.: -1.7
●Aug 30 AP Ⓣ 4f fm :51 B Aug 25 Dmr Ⓣ 1f fm 1:393 H (d) Aug 20 Dmr Ⓣ 5f fm 1:044 B (d) Aug 9 Dmr Ⓣ 5f fm 1:01 H (d)

With Approval *T11 8*
PERRET C *4-N* 126
Own.—Kinghaven Farms

Ro. c. 4, by Caro—Passing Mood, by Buckpasser
Br.—Kinghaven Farms Ltd (Ont-C)
Tr.—Attfield Roger
Lifetime 20 13 3 0 $2,141,540 *30 = 110*

1990	8	5	1	0	$321,840		
1989	10	6	2	0	$1,772,150		
Turf	8	7	1	0	$1,532,760		

18Aug90-8WO 1¼ ①:46 1:1121:421fm*1-6e 126 46 43½ 2½ 1½ SymourDJ⁸ Aw35200 84-16 WthApprovl,BrvrByThDy,Asturno 8
28Jly90-8Bel 1½ ①:5122:0332:28 fm*1-2 124 42½ 2nd 2nd 22¾ RrRP⁶ Sword Dncr 87-13 ElSenor,WithApproval,HodgesBy 7
28Jly90—Grade I
7Jly90-9Bel 1⅜ ⊺:4831:3632:121fm*2-3 122 2½ 1hd 11 11½ Perret C³ Tidal H 102-05 WithApproval,Alwuhush,GreenBrb 5
7Jly90—Grade II
17Jun90-8Bel 1⅜ ⊺:4711:34 2:101fm*6-5 118 (33½ 21 1hd 11¾ PerrtC⁵ Bwl Grn H 112 — WithApproval,CheninBlnc,ElSenor 9 *F36 = 29² = 118*
17Jun90—Grade II
3Jun90-9WO 1⅛ ⊺:4811:1131:413fm*2-5 126 74¾ 64¾ 34 13½ SrDJ³ ⓢConnght Cp 102 — WthApproval,TotofRum,ShpodyBy 9
3Jun90—Grade III-C
12May90-10Pim 1¼ :464 1:103 1:53 ft 9¾ 118 46 55 813 917 RrRP³ Pim Specl H 84-16 CriminalType,Ruhlmnn,DeRoche 10
12May90—Grade I
24Apr90-9Kee 1⅛ ①:4841:1331:432fm*3-5 115 33 2nd 11½ 12½ RomeroRP³ Aw26900 98-03 WithApproval,RingrsChnc,Rngrmn 7
7Mar90-8GP 7f :224 :46 1:234ft *1 122 95¾ 76½ 67½ 65¼ SymourDJ⁵ Aw24000 82-16 Crborndm,TwcTooMny,Shttlmn 10
7Mar90—Brushed
20Aug89-8WO 1½ ①:4832:0422:29 fm*3-5 126 43½ 1hd 16 17½ SrDJ³ ⓢBreeders 95-05 WithApprovl,MostVlnt,TldSlmnc 13
20Aug89—Grade I-C
30Jly89-8FE 1⅛ :493 1:142 1:564ft *4-5 126 21½ 3½ 2nd 1hd SrDJ⁵ ⓢPrn OWales 96-14 WithApprovl,DomscDn,MostVlint 5
30Jly89—Grade I-C
Speed Index: Last Race: 0.0   3-Race Avg.: +2.3   7-Race Avg.: +3.1   Overall Avg.: +3.0
Aug 30 WO (5f ft 1:014 B)   Aug 15 WO 5f ft 1:002 B   ●Aug 9 WO 4f ft :472 B   ●Jly 25 WO 5f ft :593 B

Prized *3-N* *T111*
DELAHOUSSAYE E 126
Own.—Clever-Meadowbrook et al

Dk. b. or br. c. 4, by Kris S—My Turbulent Miss, by My Dad George
Br.—Meadowbrook Farms Inc (Fla)
Tr.—Drysdale Neil
Lifetime 13 8 2 2 $2,157,305 *24 += 94*

1990	2	2	0	0	$247,000
1989	7	4	0	2	$1,888,705
Turf	3	3	0	0	$1,147,000

25Mar90-8SA 1½ ①:4541:5912:251fm*8-5 126 25 35½ 34½ 1½ DlhssE¹ Sn Ls Ry 88-15 Prized, Hawkster, FranklyPerfect 6
25Mar90—Grade I   *F22⁵ = 111*
4Mar90-5SA 1 ①:45 1:09 1:342fm 3½ 124 915 89 44½ 11 DlhssE² Arcadia H 91-18 Prized, Happy Toss, On TheMenu 9
4Mar90—Grade III   *F23⁵ = 106*
4Nov89-9GP 1½ ①:4832:0332:28 (gd)8¾ 122 42½ 43½ 31 1hd DlhssE⁸ Br Cp Turf 85-13 Prized, Sierra Roberta, Star Lift 14
4Nov89—Grade I
7Oct89-8Bel 1½ :483 2:05 2:291ft 5 121 25 59 514 424½ DlhssE⁷ J C Gold Cp 50-23 EsyGoer,Cryptoclernce,ForvrSilvr 7
7Oct89—Grade I
10Sep89-9WO 1¼ :462 1:36 2:02 ft 2½ 123 56 32 31 1½ DlssE¹ Molson M'ln 96-12 Prized,CharlieBarley,DomascaDan 8
10Sep89—Grade I-C
23Jly89-8Hol 1¼ :473 1:362 2:014ft 5 120 44 22½ 24 1¾ DlhssyE⁵ Swaps 83-18 Prized, Sunday Silence, Endow 5
23Jly89—Grade II; Wide
3Jly89-8Hol 1¼ :463 1:102 1:482ft *2½ 116 96½ 76½ 44½ 32½ DlhssyE² Slvr Scr H 93-10 RiseAStnz,BrokeTheMold,Prized 12
3Jly89—Grade II; Bobbled start
8Mar89-8SA 1⅛ :46 1:103 1:484ft 3¾ 116 67½ 73¾ 22½ 11¾ DlhossyE⁵ ⓝBrdbry 85-15 Prized,CroLover,ExemplryLeder 10
7Jan89-11Crc 1⅛ :494 1:142 1:522ft 6¼ 114 33 32½ 35½ 37¾ BrenR³ Trp Pk Dby 80-13 BigStnley,AppelingPlesure,Prized 8
7Jan89—Grade II; Bumped st
25Dec88-7Crc 1⅛ :491 1:143 1:54 ft 2 117 1½ 11½ 14 18 Breen R¹ Aw14900 80-18 Prized,Drby'sSecret,ClssicExmple 7
Speed Index: Last Race: +3.0   3-Race Avg.: +3.3   3-Race Avg.: +3.3   Overall Avg.: 1.4
Aug 30 AP ① 4f fm :54 B   Aug 23 Dmr ① 4f fm 1:43 H   Aug 17 Dmr 1 ft 1:39 H   Aug 11 Dmr 7f ft 1:29 H

On cold dope, final separations here proved difficult, but the champion Steinlen shaped up as a very probable underlay. Inconsistent throughout 1990, Steinlen had bounced back strongly from prior defeats and had looked sensational in winning the Ceasar's International in track-record time.

But the champ had followed that supreme effort with his poorest turf showing ever—a figure August 12 of 90. As figure handicappers realize, even top horses will regress following supreme performances, but not this badly. Steinlen was unlikely to bounce back a third time in the 1990 Million, and certainly could not be bet as the favorite.

I had been mistaken twice before in 1990 about Steinlen's decline, but felt confident on the matter again.

Prized entered the fray following a layoff of five months and figured three lengths softer than either With Approval or Golden Pheasant. In addition, Prized had recorded three turf figures—three winning races—that were amazingly ordinary. Even his 1989 Breeders' Cup victory (106) had occurred against an unusually undistinguished field.

The layoff looked problematic as well, and if Neil Drysdale were not the extraordinary trainer of the colt, I would have dismissed Prized out of hand. As events proceeded, the odds dipped too low to rely on a possibly unready horse at a classic distance with a million dollars up.

Near post time the odds were:

Golden Pheasant	6–1
With Approval	5–1
Prized	8–5
Steinlen	2–1

With Approval appeared on the track in front wraps, a surprise to me. Golden Pheasant had finished the final three furlongs of two nine-furlong races in less than 35 seconds, powerful runs. Yet finishes at middle distances are not interchangeable with finishes at classic distances. It's really a different world, notably under Grade 1 conditions.

Golden Pheasant's loss in the Eddie Read at Del Mar (Grade 1) August 12 did not bother me. Trainer Charlie Whittingham prepares stakes horses for major objectives better than any horseman in history. Whittingham did not care about winning the Eddie Read with a strenuous effort that might have depleted too much energy too soon for a layoff returnee. But the unknown cause of the layoff following the upset at Hollywood Park on Memorial Day provided its own hesitation.

In addition, how good exactly is Golden Pheasant? Plastered in the Arc at 10–1 as a three-year-old, the Caro colt did take the twelve-furlong Grade 2 Neil stakes at Longchamp, limited to three-year-olds. More impressively, Golden Pheasant had come within a head at 7–1 of winning France's Grade 1 St. Cloud stakes, offering $433,500 to three-year-olds and up.

Without a stick-out overlay in the win pool, With Approval and Golden Pheasant could be combined to advantage in the exacta pool. Exacta probables at Del Mar showed the combination returning a lusty 60–1.

I boxed the pair of figure horses in multiple exactas. Original plans to use each of the leading pair on top of Prized and Steinlen were shelved at the odds—underlays all.

With Approval tracked Steinlen and another frontrunner until they began to bend into the stretch, and then flew by Steinlen with sudden, surprising ease.

Golden Pheasant followed With Approval into the stretch. He then found that extra gear only champions can find, and inside the sixteenth-pole passed With Approval under a steady hand ride from jockey Gary Stevens.

The two outran the field by many lengths, and the best horse won. Golden Pheasant paid $15.20 at Arlington Park and $14.00 at Del Mar. The Del Mar exacta returned $103.20, or 50–1.

It would be quite a nice day at the races, after all.

The next afternoon, Labor Day, the feature provided one of those situations handicappers relish. It was the Del Mar Handicap (Grade 2), 3up, offering $300,000-added at the unusual 1⅜ miles. And it was a two-horse race, at least as far as the figures indicated.

Examine the two top contenders:

8th Del Mar

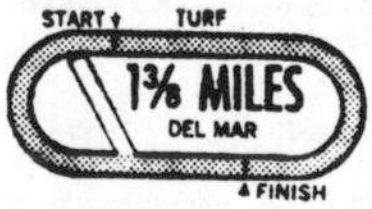

1 ⅜ MILES. (Turf). (2.13⅗) 51st Running of THE DEL MAR HANDICAP (Grade II). Purse $300,000. 3-year-olds and upward. By invitation with no nomination or starting fee. The winner to receive $165,000 with $60,000 to second, $45,000 to third, $22,000 to fourth and $7,500 to fifth. Weights to be published Monday, August 27. The Del Mar Thoroughbred Club will invite a field of highest weighted horses to accept. In the event that one or more of these decline, those weighted below them as provisional invitees will be invited in weight order to replace them. The field acceptances will be drawn by the closing time of entries, Saturday, September 1. A trophy will be presented to the owner of the winner. Invitations issued Monday, August 27.

Live The Dream B. c. 4, by Northern Baby—Became a Lark, by T V Lark
SOLIS A 118 Br.—Bradley-Chndler-Whittinghm (Ky) 1990 7 1 2 1 $137,050
Own.—Bradley-Brdley(Lse)-Chndler Tr.—Whittingham Charles 1989 14 4 2 1 $257,900
Lifetime 21 5 4 2 $394,950 Turf 16 5 4 1 $388,050

23Jly90-8Hol 1½ Ⓣ:49 2:01^{4}2:25^{3}fm 5½ 116 $2^{1\frac12}$ 2^1 $2^{1\frac12}$ $2^{\frac12}$ Solis A^3 Sunset H 92-11 PetiteIle,LiveTheDrem,SoftMchin 9
23Jly90—Grade II
29Jun90-7Hol 1$\frac{1}{16}$ Ⓣ:47^{1}1:11^{1}1:41^{3}fm 8¾ 116 $4^{6\frac12}$ 3^2 2^1 1^{nk} Solis A^3 Ⓡ Fiesta H 87-13 LvThDrm,FlyTllDwn,ExclsvPrtnr 12
19May90-6Hol 1¼ Ⓣ:48^{2}1:36^{2}2:00^{3}fm 3¾ 120 3^5 $2^{1\frac12}$ 2^2 $2^{1\frac34}$ Solis A^7 275000 88-10 RoylRech,LiveThDrm,RcordBoom 9
22Apr90-8SA a1⅜ Ⓣ:48^{2}2:25^{2}2:46^{3}fm 22 116 $7^{7\frac14}$ 6^9 5^6 6^6 Solis A^2 S J Cp Iv H 106 — Delegant, Valdali, Hawkster 7
22Apr90—Grade I; Rank 3 1/2
19Feb90-8SA 1½ Ⓣ:49^{3}2:03^{1}2:28 gd 10 118 5^5 $4^{1\frac34}$ $7^{3\frac12}$ $8^{5\frac34}$ SlsA^{10} Sn Ls Obp H 68-26 FrnklyPerfct,Dlgnt,JustAsLucky 12
19Feb90—Grade III; Wide
4Feb90-8SA 1¼ :47^2 1:36^4 2:01^{2}gd 6¾ 118 5^4 $9^{5\frac34}$ $9^{7\frac34}$ $9^{13\frac14}$ VlnlPA^6 C H Strub 74-18 FlyngContnntl,QtAmrcn,Hwkstr 10
4Feb90—Grade I; Wide stretch
21Jan90-8SA 1⅛ Ⓣ:46^{3}1:34^{4}1:58^{1}fm *2¼ 119 $6^{3\frac34}$ 7^4 6^6 $3^{4\frac12}$ McCrrCJ^5 Sn MrcsH 92-03 Putting,ColwyRlly,LiveTheDrem 13
21Jan90—Grade III; Shuffled back

10Dec89-8Hol 1½ ⓣ:50³2:03¹2:26³fm 7¾ 122 7⁶ 6³½ 5⁵ 4⁵ Solis A⁴ Hol Trf Cp 83-12 FrnklyPrfct,YnkAffir,PlsntVrity 10
10Dec89—Grade I
19Nov89-8Hol 1⅛ ⓣ:47 1:10¹1:47 fm 14 122 7⁸ 7⁷½ 5² 1hd Solis A⁶ Hol Dby 93-09 LiveTheDrem,ChrliBrly,RivrMstr 13
19Nov89—Grade I; Checked, wide
28Oct89-8SA 1¼ ⓣ:46²1:34²1:58 fm 18 110 3¹½ 4¹ 4¹¼ 1no DvsRG² ⓢH P Rsl H 106 — LvThDrm,Bosphorus,SkpOtFront 8
28Oct89—Blocked into drive
Speed Index: Last Race: -8.0 1—Race Avg.: -8.0 1—Race Avg.: -8.0 Overall Avg.: -0.9
Aug 30 Dmr ⓣ 5f fm 1:03² H (d) Aug 25 Dmr ⓣ 1 fm 1:39³ H (d) ●Aug 20 Dmr 1 ft 1:38 H Aug 15 Dmr 6f ft 1:14³ H

Mehmetori Ch. c. 3(Feb), by Mehmet—Sonori, by Jungle Savage
GARCIA J A 107 Br.—Vallone Mr-Mrs G (Ky) 1990 10 2 1 0 $95,350
Own.—Arnold & Miller Tr.—Mulhall Richard W Turf 5 1 1 0 $73,075
Lifetime 10 2 1 0 $95,350
19Aug90-8Dmr 1⅛ ⓣ:48³1:13¹1:49³fm 6¾ LB 122 10¹⁴10⁸¾ 7⁷¾ 6⁵¼ GrciJA 7 Dmr Iv Dby 84-08 ‡TightSpot,Itsllgrktom,Prdcssor 10
19Aug90—Grade II; Broke slowly; Placed fifth through disqualification
25Jly90-5Dmr 1 ⓣ:46⁴1:11¹1:35²fm 3¾ L 114 10⁸¾ 9⁴¼ 5¹¾ 1hd Garcia JA 9 ⓢOcnsde 97-05 Mehmetori,InExcessII,Prdcssor 10
25Jly90—Run in divisions
10Jun90-8Hol 1⅛ ⓣ:47⁴1:11³1:47⁴fm 13 113 10⁹½10⁸½ 6²¾ 2¹ GrciJA 1 Cnma H 88-10 Jovial,Mehmetori,Itsllgreektome 10
10Jun90—Grade II; Wide in stretch
26May90-8Hol 1 1/16 ⓣ:46¹1:09³1:40¹fm 12 114 9⁹ 9⁷¼ 8⁴¾ 5³ BlcCA¹ W Rogers H 91-06 Itsallgreektome,Warcraft,BllCove 9
26May90—Grade III
5May90-6Hol 1 ⓣ:45⁴1:09²1:34³fm 100 112 9⁸½ 8⁶½ 6²¾ 5¹ PttDB 1 Splt Br CpH 90-08 Itsllgreektome,Wrcrft,RobynDncr 9
5May90—Blocked late
14Apr90-7SA 1 :45³ 1:10³ 1:37 ft 16 118 8¹⁷ 8⁹½ 4⁸ 4⁶¼ Baze R A 3 Aw37000 76-17 Big Bass, Toby Jug, Honor Clef 8
14Apr90—Bumped 3/16
17Mar90-7SA 1 1/16 :47⁴ 1:12² 1:43³ft 8¼ 118 6⁵ 6⁶¼ 5⁵¼ 8⁹¼ McCrrnCJ 8 Aw37000 76-13 HwiinPss,FuturCrr,NuitsSt.Gorgs 8
17Mar90—Bobbled start
4Mar90-4SA 7f :22⁴ :46¹ 1:25 ft 2¾ 118 8⁴¾ 5³¼ 3¹ 1¹ McCarron C J 5 Mdn 78-19 Mehmetori,FestivColony,RsSyng 12
4Mar90—Bumped 3/16
4Feb90-2SA 6½f :21⁴ :45¹ 1:17 m 4½ 118 6³½ 7⁵¼ 6⁶ 5⁵½ DelahoussyeE⁹ Mdn 79-15 H'sLkThWnd,SportsVw,FutrCrr 10
4Feb90—Broke slowly
14Jan90-6SA 6f :22² :45³ 1:10³m *2¾ 118 8¹³ 8¹³ 5⁹¼ 4⁴¼ DelahoussyeE³ Mdn 78-14 HonorClef,Cox'sEnchnt,SpnishStl 9
Speed Index: Last Race: -7.0 2—Race Avg.: -9.0 2—Race Avg.: -9.0 Overall Avg.: -4.8
●Aug 26 Dmr 4f ft :46 H ●Aug 12 Dmr 6f ft 1:10 H Aug 2 Dmr 4f ft :48³ H Jly 18 Hol 6f ft 1:13³ H

The crucial consideration here is our opening-day benefactor Mehmetori, flashing on the board at a delightful 11–1.

On June 10, over nine furlongs in the Grade 2 Cinema at Hollywood Park, Mehmetori had earned an awesome figure, a 131, virtually off the scale.

The colt represented a key bet July 25 at Del Mar, scoring at 7–2 at a flat mile, getting a 108.

The Del Mar Derby can be tossed, the outside horses having come over on the field just after the start, causing severe interference to many contenders, including Mehmetori.

Mehmetori stood at 11–1 in the Del Mar Handicap because it would be a three-year-old testing older. In fact, older horses hold the advantage against three-year-olds in stakes and handicaps, but the exceptions in the fall will be several, and this lineup would not scare impressive sophomores a bit.

Of the older contenders, only Live The Dream looked the part of the Grade 1 article. At three he had won the Hollywood Derby with a strong figure (124), and had finished close enough against ranking older stars such as Frankly Perfect and Yankee Affair.

Live The Dream had performed consistently well in 1990 too, including a figure of 114 at a mile and a half in the Grade 1 Sunset at Hollypark. This guy relished marathon distances.

That was the real rub with Mehmetori. His 131 had been earned at a middle distance, and middle-distance figures do not transfer well to classic distances. On the other hand, his sire, Mehmet, had an average winning distance among its progeny of 7½ furlongs, indicative of numerous marathon winners.

Mehmetori would probably not flatten badly at 11 furlongs, but could it handle Live The Dream in the lane?

Live The Dream was the crowd's choice at 2–1. The situation proved irresistible. Mehmetori might be backed solidly to win, and protected on the underside of exactas having Live The Dream on top. I took both propositions aggressively, offering a prime amount on the 11–1 shot and protecting with multiple exacta boxes on the pair.

Mehmetori lagged behind, in the customary manner, and unleashed a huge accelerating move into the far turn. The three-year-old circled the field in a twinkle and reached the front entering the stretch.

From a few lengths behind the pacesetters, Live The Dream had moved up too, and the pair were abreast approaching the eighth pole.

Mehmetori actually forged in front, but briefly. The older Live The Dream responded in kind, gaining momentum and force with every stride. The two battled the length of the stretch, but the three-year-old could not keep up late. It would be Live The Dream by 1½ lengths.

The rider here had moved a bit soon, but I suspect the ending would have been the same regardless. The older horse was simply the better horse at 1⅜ miles. The exacta paid a respectable $69, but if the three-year-old had won, it would have been a minor coup.

It's the ones that get away that prevent the most rapid kind of progress in this unbelievable field.

Week 7

Getaway week proved inopportune, the figure horses registering in 4 of 13 races (31 percent), but without an attractive overlay.

The best chance for a small score reared up in the second race of the week. It was an advanced nonwinners allowance contest, for nonwinners three times other than maiden or claiming. The top figure horse would be facing an odds-on favorite exiting classier races, but with a softer figure.

The conflicting data provide a subtle lesson in handicapping. Examine the records of the two:

7th Del Mar

Elsewhere I have cautioned that under nonwinners three times allowances, handicappers should favor horses that already have impressed in open and listed stakes, but discount horses that already have competed in claiming races.

Tatsfield, however, has finished close in the kind of high-priced claiming races regularly stocked by the graduates of advanced allowances that cannot compete successfully in stakes. In the $100,000 claiming route on grass August 5, his figure was an impressive 114.

Kanatiyr has never been entered to be claimed, has notched two allowance conditions, and has finished second twice in good time in races similar to today's. Yet his stakes record is unpersuasive and his figures in recent placings have been 105, 106.

Is Kanatiyr superior to Tatsfield? Or is Kanatiyr a fake, vulnerable to the kind of lofty claiming opposition familiar to Tatsfield?

It's a tough call on cold dope.

The betting, however, solves the dilemma. Kanatiyr is 3–5, Tatsfield 8–1. The money goes to Tatsfield without hesitation, a position I trust practiced handicappers will appreciate.

As events proceeded, Tatsfield took the lead turning into the stretch, but was quickly pressed by charging Kanatiyr. Tatsfield could not hold the classier Kanatiyr, after all. The favorite drew clear handily, won by a couple of lengths.

The exacta was available here, and by all means a box between the two, or a saver ticket with Kanatiyr atop Tatsfield makes sense, in theory at least. But the Kanatiyr-to-Tatsfield combination was projected to return a pitiable $15, or 6½-to-1, less than Tatsfield's odds to win. No bet.

The final bet of the season was among the easiest. It was a starter's handicap, for fillies and mares, 3up, having a specified starting price of $50,000 in 1990.

I have presented the past performances for the reader's review, along with the turf figures of all starters. The top figure horse went to the post at 8–5, a favorite. The exacta is available. How should the race be played?

9th Del Mar

1 1⁄16 MILES. (Turf). (1.40) SANDCASTLE HANDICAP. Purse $55,000 Added. Fillies and mares, 3-year-olds and upward which have started for a claiming price of $50,000 or less in 1990. By subscription of $50 each which shall accompany the nomination, $150 to pass the entry box, with $55,000 Added, of which $11,000 to second, $8,250 to third, $4,125 to fourth and $1,375 to fifth. Weights Monday, September 3, 1990. Starters to be named through the entry box Saturday, September 8 by closing time of entries. Closed, Friday, August 31, 1990 by 12 noon with 16 nominations. (Non-starters since July 24 other than races at Del Mar will be preferred.) (High-weights second preference.) *Claimed horses do not have to re-establish eligibility.

Panic Stricken
MERCADO P **112**
Own.—Clamage R S
Ro. f. 4, by Northern Jove—Thunder Chick, by Sham
Br.—Sunrise Thrbrd Stables Inc (Fla) 1990 14 2 5 1 $17,694
Tr.—Sticka Ron 1989 2 M 0 0
Lifetime 29 2 5 2 $19,944 Turf 9 2 3 1 $16,030

23Aug90-8Dmr 1⅛ Ⓣ:4831:1331:511fm 37 B 122 96½ 94½ 74½ 74¾ MercdoP3 ⒻAw36000 77-18 Jstonofthgrls,C'sSong,Wodly'sF 10
23Aug90—Took up 1/16
25Jun90-10GG 1 1/16 Ⓣ:4811:12 1:441fm 4½ 114 65½ 55 33½ 21 GuerreroA10 Ⓕ 22500 90-09 ShrryLynnB.,PnicStrckn,Goldrry 11
14Jun90-9GG 1 1/16 Ⓣ:48 1:12 1:451fm 6½ 118 85½ 62 21 2nk GrrdoOL 5 ⒻAw21000 86-14 Robert,PnicStricken,CptiveBride 8
31May90-5Hol 1 1/16 Ⓣ:4711:1141:443fm 37 113 913 912 912 98¼ Garrido OL 5 Ⓕ 55000 64-23 Trin,ImperialStar,ReadTheCards 10
19May90-12TuP 1 1/16 Ⓣ:50 1:15 1:48 fm 5 122 67 53½ 2hd 2hd Garrido O L 4 ⒻSplW 73-27 Chateau Bell,PanicStricken,Weep 8
19May90—Came in late
12May90-9Hol 1⅛ Ⓣ:4731:1121:481fm 9½ 119 54½ 54½ 68 613¾ GrrdoOL 5 ⒻAw32000 73-10 TafftShwl,MjesticSound,StrPster 7
12May90—Wide early
15Apr90-11TuP 1 1/16 :472 1:112 1:443ft 12 117 119¾ 107¼ 87¾ 84¼ Garrido O L 4 ⒻInvH 80-22 Waltzing Fran, Weep, Riches 12
30Mar90-10TuP 7f Ⓣ:231 :4641:25 fm 2¾ 114 710 45½ 2hd 13 GrridoOL 1 ⒻAw4900 90-10 PnicStrickn,Rhondlng,Chrs'sDbut 8
25Mar90-9TuP 1 Ⓣ:4741:1241:383fm 6½ 112 79¾ 64¾ 52¾ 31 Garrido O L 8 Aw4900 85-14 CptnGun,LckyStblBoy,PncStrckn 8
15Mar90-10TuP 1 :462 1:11 1:37 ft 15 108 1hd 31 32 53½ Gann S L 2 Aw4700 85-13 JlousScrt,NorthrnCt,LckyStblBoy 7
Speed Index: Last Race: +2.0 2–Race Avg.: 0.0 2–Race Avg.: 0.0 Overall Avg.: –3.7
●Sep 6 SLR tr.t 4f ft :473 H Sep 1 SLR tr.t 5f ft 1:013 H ●Aug 17 SLR tr.t 6f ft 1:122 H Aug 11 SLR tr.t 1 ft 1:42 H

Nordic's Girl
DAVENPORT C L **113**
Own.—Simpson H
B. m. 7, by Nordic Prince—Ivy League Girl, by Solo Landing
Br.—Miller L R (Ky) 1990 14 1 3 2 $43,550
Tr.—Palen Robert D 1989 13 1 1 0 $14,886
Lifetime 67 10 10 4 $132,627 Turf 20 2 2 1 $30,104

23Aug90-7Dmr 1 :463 1:104 1:354ft 14 LB 1115 1hd 31 54 610½ Belvoir V 4 Ⓕ 32000 76-16 SmrtDeception,OurOlLdy,StrPstr 7
5Aug90-3Dmr 1 :464 1:11 1:354ft 33 L 1085 1½ 2hd 3½ 34 Belvoir V 1 Ⓕ 35000 83-14 SssySlew,YnkHostss,Nordic'sGirl 9
7Jly90-7Hol 1 :454 1:11 1:364ft 14 L 116 1hd 31½ 65 610 Black C A 4 Ⓕ 32000 70-19 GoRmmyJdy,SssySlw,PlyngThrgh 8
22Jun90-9Hol 1 1/16 :473 1:114 1:44 ft 11 116 3½ 2hd 3nk 33¼ Lopez A D 3 Ⓕ 40000 77-18 MnznitII,YnkeHostss,Nordic'sGirl 6
7Jun90-9Hol 1 1/16 :463 1:11 1:433ft 3½ 116 2hd 1hd 2½ 23 Lopez A D 5 Ⓕ 32000 79-18 YnkHostss,Nordic'sGirl,NoRomnc 6
25May90-9Hol 1 :443 1:101 1:352ft 9½ 115 3nk 1½ 1½ 45½ Black C A 3 Ⓕ 25000 81-16 Sumba'sSong,Bea'sLuck,Lcrosse 10
17May90-9Hol 1 1/16 :462 1:104 1:44 ft 6½ 116 2hd 1hd 2½ 49 Meza R Q 1 Ⓕ 32000 71-20 MnznitII,MoonlitDesrt,NoRomnc 7
20Apr90-8SA a6½f Ⓣ:21 :4311:124fm 76 114 44 78 811 711½ GarciJ 7 ⒻⒷMt Wlsn 85-03 PprPrncss,WrnngZon,TrpclStphn 8
20Apr90—Wide into stretch
6Apr90-3SA a6½f Ⓣ:212 :4341:133fm 65 114 75½ 75¾ 76½ 54 Cedeno EA 3 Ⓕ 85000 89-07 SrvN'Volly,TropclStphn,CoxClssc 8
22Mar90-7SA 1 :462 1:11 1:371ft 4¾ 116 31½ 22 24 26½ VlenzuelPA 4 Ⓕ 35000 74-23 SumthingRre,Nordic'sGirl,SuitUp 7
22Mar90—Rank 6 1/2 to 3/4
Speed Index: Last Race: –8.0 3–Race Avg.: –7.3 8–Race Avg.: –5.6 Overall Avg.: –6.1
●Sep 4 Hol 5f ft :594 H Aug 16 Hol 4f ft :48 H ●Jly 29 Hol 5f ft :592 H Jly 23 Hol 4f ft :481 H

Radiant Colors
STEVENS G L **111**
Own.—Field S M
B. f. 3(Feb), by His Majesty—Radiant Glow, by Northern Dancer
Br.—Wygod M J (Cal) 1990 9 3 0 0 $33,550
Tr.—Fanning Brett C 1989 1 M 0 0
Lifetime 10 3 0 0 $33,550 Turf 5 2 0 0 $22,475

26Aug90-10BM 1 1/16 Ⓣ:46 1:1121:443fm *7-5 LB 116 46½ 33 1hd 12 Schacht R 6 Ⓕ 32000 82-14 RdntColors,MorTorqu,Goyv'sPrd 7
17Aug90-7Dmr 6½f :22 :45 1:16 ft 28 LB 115 72¾ 74½ 64 57 Davis R G 4 Ⓕ 32000 81-11 Showmnshp,RttnSpd,Shrly'sSvn 11
18Jly90-7Hol 1 Ⓣ:4621:0941:351fm 7½ L 115 54 54 54½ 65½ Garcia J A 6 Ⓕ 70000 82-12 Horsche, Intercivet, Glassware 8
18Jly90—Bumped at break
6Jly90-7Hol 1 1/16 Ⓣ:4811:1221:423fm 53 L 112 11½ 3½ 85¼ 87 DavisRG 1 ⒻⓈMnglw 75-10 Nijinsky's Lover,BimboII,Cat'sAir 8
16Jun90-4GG 1 1/16 Ⓣ:4831:1241:45 fm 7¾ 117 33 32 31 11½ StvnsGL 1 ⒻAw21000 87-10 RdntColors,TrqosDwn,VrtyPrncss 8
9May90-9GG 1 Ⓣ:481 1:14 1:392fm 8½ 116 77½ 65 54½ 44 SchmidtCP 5 Ⓕ 32000 71-25 Shannon, Catlina,Knight'sReward 8
27Apr90-7Hol 7f :213 :44 1:224ft 45 113 78 813 813 815¼ Meza R Q 1 Ⓕ 35000 76-11 FinlFrontier,RottionSpeed,HtPrd 8
27Apr90—Steadied 5 1/2
13Apr90-4SA 6f :214 :453 1:121ft 10 117 42 54½ 32½ 1hd StnsGL 4 ⒻⓈM32000 75-25 RdintColors,PlyfulTims,Wyntrco 12
21Mar90-4SA 6f :22 :46 1:131ft 7½ 117 41¼ 44¼ 55 66½ StevnsGL 5 ⒻⓈM32000 63-21 MesquiteMiss,Saski,ArchdleRod 12
30Aug89-6Dmr 6f :221 :453 1:104ft 31 1125 1011 910 913 925¼ JureguiLH 3 ⒻⓈMdn 59-10 SrosTresure,LtstRcr,FlyingKndr 10
30Aug89—Rough start
Speed Index: Last Race: (—) 3–Race Avg.: (—) 12–Race Avg.: (—) Overall Avg.: –9.2
Aug 3 Dmr 5f ft 1:001 H Jly 28 Dmr 5f ft 1:012 H

No Romance
NAKATANI C S **113**
Own.—Longden E J
B. m. 6, by Kennedy Road—Jungle Tabu, by Jungle Road
Br.—Longden E J (Cal) 1990 7 0 1 3 $20,800
Tr.—Longden Eric J. 1989 12 2 1 2 $54,925
Lifetime 41 4 6 8 $123,525 Turf 6 0 0 1 $6,750

30Aug90-7Dmr 1 1/16 :463 1:11 1:432ft 6¼ LB 116 75¼ 32½ 3½ 21¼ Baze R A 1 Ⓕ 25000 83-11 Manzanita II,NoRomance,Seaside 7
30Aug90—Veered in start
23Aug90-7Dmr 1 :463 1:104 1:354ft 13 LB 116 2hd 21 43½ 58½ Baze R A 5 Ⓕ 32000 70-16 SmrtDeception,OurOlLdy,StrPstr 7
23Aug90—Wide into drive
4Aug90-1Dmr 6½f :221 :451 1:161ft 9 L 115 86¾ 74 53 33 Baze R A 6 Ⓕ 32000 84-09 ShowtimeLdy,CookiBr,NoRomnc 8
4Aug90—5 Wide stretch

7Jun90-9Hol 1 1/16 :46³ 1:11 1:43³ft 2¾ 116 65¾ 44¼ 44¼ 36 NakatniCS 4 Ⓕ 32000 76-18 YnkHostss,Nordic'sGirl,NoRomnc 6
17May90-9Hol 1 1/16 :46² 1:10⁴ 1:44 ft 2¾ 116 75¼ 53¾ 43¼ 35 NakatniCS 7 Ⓕ 32000 75-20 MnznitII,MoonlitDesrt,NoRomnc 7
17May90—Wide into stretch
10May90-7Hol 6½f :22³ :45³ 1:15³ft 5 117 63½ 63¼ 65¼ 57¼ NakatniCS 5 Ⓕ 40000 80-08 FeelingTipsy,RunwyBlues,Lcrosse 7
28Feb90-5SA 1 Ⓣ:46³1:10⁴1:36 fm 17 1105 53½ 42½ 31½ 42 NakatniCS 9 Ⓕ 75000 81-17 CsPetron,BllPoitrin,Dot'sL'Nturl 10
28Feb90—Wide 3/8 turn
31Dec89-2SA 1 :46 1:10⁴ 1:37 ft 13 1115 77½ 41¾ 11½ 15 NakatniCS 5 Ⓕ 40000 84-12 NoRomnce,DerMorgn,LttrsOfLov 8
31Dec89—Broke in a tangle
11Nov89-3SA 1 :46³ 1:10⁴ 1:35⁴ft 8¾ 1115 22 2⁴ 35 58¾ CastnonJL 4 Ⓕ 50000 81-11 Codex'sBride,Besey,FillAFirPockt 6
9Oct89-9SA 1 1/16 :46³ 1:12 1:44³ft 24 1115 87½ 63½ 1½ 13 NakatniCS 9 Ⓕ 32000 78-19 NoRomnc,Prt'sHorh,CmpltAccrd 9
9Oct89—Wide 3/8 turn
Speed Index: Last Race: -6.0 3–Race Avg.: -6.0 7–Race Avg.: -5.4 Overall Avg.: -5.0
Sep 7 Dmr 3f ft :36¹ H Aug 11 Dmr 5f ft 1:00¹ H Jly 27 Dmr 6f ft 1:14³ H Jly 21 Dmr 5f ft 1:01⁴ H

Keep On Top B. m. 5, by Obraztsovy—To the Top, by Bold Hour
VALENZUELA P A 117 Br.—Martin Mr-Mrs C A (Ky) 1990 7 1 1 0 $25,265
Own.—McKee Mr-Mrs R H Tr.—Grissom O Dwain 1989 10 2 2 2 $72,085
Lifetime 29 7 4 3 $140,311 Turf 8 2 0 0 $35,101
22Aug90-3Dmr 1 Ⓣ:47⁴1:12¹1:37 fm 6½ LB120 2hd 21 53 59¾ PincyLJr6 ⒻAw55000 79-13 WeddingBouquet,Bldomero,Felidi 6
22Aug90—Wide 3/8 turn
8Aug90-9Dmr 6½f :21³ :44 1:15⁴ft 4½ L 116 31½ 32 2hd 12 VlenzuelPA1 Ⓕ 50000 89-12 KeepOnTop,VlidAllure,Heln'sLov 7
8Aug90—Broke slowly
8Jly90-9AP 1 Ⓣ:47³1:12¹1:37 fm 17 L 116 42 42½ 44½ 44½ Meier R3 ⒻAw28000 87-10 SwtRun,HostofAnglsII,Epmthus 10
30Jun90-10Aks 1 1/16 :46² 1:11² 1:45 ft 3 116 49 47 47 411½ LestrRN2 ⒻAw14000 77-15 StiffQuestion,BoldCost,AWildPst 7
8Jun90-8Aks 1 70 :46⁴ 1:13¹ 1:44³gd *6-5 116 37½ 34 68½ 49 WllsRD6 ⒻAw13000 71-20 AncintRivr,StffQuston,WltzngFrn 7
27May90-9Aks 6f :22⁴ :46¹ 1:11³ft 7¾ 120 42½ 43½ 34 23½ WllsRD5 ⒻAw13000 77-28 StiffQuestion,KpOnTop,AWildPst 6
13May90-8Aks 6f :22³ :46⁴ 1:13²ft 3 116 107½ 107½ 78½ 57¼ Lively J8 ⒻAw13000 64-31 Sh'sDBlck,ClcktyClck,StffQston 11
9Sep89-8Dmr 1 1/16 Ⓣ:47¹1:11¹1:42⁴fm 16 113 43 54 86½ 88¾ NtnCS8 ⒻⓈOsnts H 77-14 Nikishk,DringDoon,GoldFircrckr 11
11Aug89-11LA 1 1/16 :45³ 1:10³ 1:41¹ft 2½ 117 2nk 11 13 16½ NtnCS7 ⒻLs Palmas 99-01 KpOnTop,TropclStphn,HllownBby 7
2Aug89-5Dmr 1 1/16 Ⓣ:47²1:12¹1:42³fm 6¾ 1095 14 16 16 15 NakatniCS9 Ⓕ 75000 87-13 KeepOnTop,Bragor,CherDuphine 10
Speed Index: Last Race: -8.0 3–Race Avg.: -5.6 3–Race Avg.: -5.6 Overall Avg.: -3.6
●Sep 2 Dmr 4f ft :46 H

Fraulein Maria B. f. 4, by Darby Creek Road—Washoe Zephyr, by Windy Sea
DELAHOUSSAYE E 119 Br.—Lerille A J (Cal) 1990 13 2 4 3 $81,700
Own.—Milch & Young Tr.—Young Steven W 1989 14 3 2 2 $39,910
Lifetime 27 5 6 5 $121,610 Turf 11 2 4 2 $77,800
15Aug90-5Dmr 1 1/16 Ⓣ:48³1:12³1:43¹fm 8¾ LB116 98¾ 97¾ 42½ 21¾ DelhoussyE1 Ⓕ 55000 89-09 BoldCosta,FrauleinMri,Softscpe 10
15Aug90—Checked in chute
19Jly90-9Hol 1 1/16 Ⓣ:46⁴1:10³1:41³fm *9-5 L 119 31½ 31½ 21½ 22¾ Stevens GL2 Ⓕ 50000 84-16 MjsticSound,FrulinMri,RdThCrds 9
19Jly90—Bumped early
28Jun90-5Hol 1 1/16 Ⓣ:47 1:11 1:41 fm 6½ 119 65½ 64 73½ 63½ VlenzuelPA2 Ⓕ 62500 86-08 Sonilla,MjesticSound,CsPetrone 10
28Jun90—Boxed far turn
17Jun90-10GG 1 1/16 Ⓣ:47¹1:12 1:44⁴fm *8-5 118 63 52½ 11 13½ HnsnRD1 ⒻAw23000 88-15 FruleinMri,Vulcress,WoodingRits 9
17Jun90—Lugged in
1Jun90-8GG 1 1/16 Ⓣ:47³1:12³1:44²fm *6-5 121 43 3¹ 1hd 22½ Black K6 ⒻAw23000 87-10 BeautifulRedhed,FruleinMri,Brs 7
9May90-3Hol 1 Ⓣ:47¹1:11¹1:35¹fm 3 116 32 22 22½ 33½ DlhssyE6 ⒻAw34000 84-12 RegIFwn,SpectcuirFce,FruleinM 7
11Apr90-5SA 1⅛ Ⓣ:47 1:10⁴1:46³fm 4½ 118 21 31½ 23½ 36½ DlhssyE8 ⒻAw42000 85-10 BeutifulMelody,Softscp,FrulinMr 8
28Mar90-5SA 1 Ⓣ:46³1:12¹1:36¹fm 9¾ 119 98¾ 96½ 73¾ 42¾ DlhssyE10 ⒻAw42000 79-18 RnTJnny,ElgncInDsgn,SpcictrFc 10
17Mar90-5SA a6½f Ⓣ:21³ :43³1:13⁴fm 6 119 52½ 33 34 44¾ DlhssyE4 ⒻAw38000 87-08 HckrCrst,ElgncInDsgn,DrmngB 10
28Feb90-7SA 1 Ⓣ:47⁴1:11⁴1:36¹fm 4 118 42 43 31½ 2no Stevens GL8 Ⓕ 80000 82-17 VelvetBlue,FrauleinMri,RegIFwn 10
Speed Index: Last Race: (—) 3–Race Avg.: (—) 12–Race Avg.: (—) Overall Avg.: -2.6
Sep 7 Dmr 4f ft :49² H Sep 2 Dmr 6f ft 1:14¹ H Aug 23 Dmr 4f ft :51 B Aug 12 Dmr 3f ft :37³ H

La Tropicana Ch. f. 4, by Bold Tropic—Raise Mas Ninas, by Raise a Native
SOLIS A 115 Br.—Valpredo D (Cal) 1990 2 0 0 1 $5,700
Own.—Flint B S Tr.—Flint Bernard S 1989 16 3 2 2 $69,630
Lifetime 18 3 2 3 $75,330 Turf 8 0 0 2 $15,300
27Aug90-5Dmr 1 Ⓣ:47³1:12 1:36⁴fm 6½ LB116 21½ 21½ 31½ 32¾ Solis A 8 Ⓕ 62500 87-12 BoldCosta,Grandiflora,LaTropicn 8
27Aug90—Rank early
8Aug90-9Dmr 6½f :21³ :44 1:15⁴ft *2 L 115 2hd 2hd 3nk 65½ Garcia JA 3 Ⓕ c50000 83-12 KeepOnTop,VlidAllure,Heln'sLv 7
8Aug90—Broke slowly
31Dec89-5SA a6½f Ⓣ:21¹ :43²1:13⁴fm 17 1095 2½ 2hd 43 95½ NakatniCS 4 Ⓕ 85000 93-01 LdyBrunicrdi,Dremt,ScremingSu 11
31Dec89—Erratic in drive
7Dec89-9Hol 1 Ⓣ:46³1:10³1:34⁴fm 20 115 41¼ 31 41½ 79 Cedeno A 10 Ⓕ 62500 81-10 Codex'sBride,ProfitIsland,Besey 10
7Dec89—Wide throughout
11Nov89-5SA a6½f Ⓣ:21 :43¹1:13¹fm 8 1115 54¾ 34½ 43 73¾ CstnnJL 1 ⒻAw34000 98 — Excellent Lady, Bif, Dancitus 10
21Oct89-7SA a6½f Ⓣ:21¹ :43 1:13¹fm 30 114 41¾ 1½ 12½ 3¾ FlorsDR 2 ⒻAw34000 101 — Kiwi, Dancitus, La Tropicana 11
1Oct89-10Fpx 1 1/16 :46 1:11¹ 1:42³ft 2 114 2½ 21 25 214 FlrsDR 4 ⒻⓈAmndaS 84-11 TppingTudor,LTropicn,YnkHostss 5
22Sep89-12Fpx 1 1/16 :45² 1:10³ 1:45²ft 9-5 114 2½ 2hd 1hd 3¾ FlrsDR 4 ⒻⓈCTBAM 83-15 Teach You,Conclaire,LaTropicana 7
11Sep89-7Dmr 1 Ⓣ:47³1:12¹1:36⁴fm 14 1115 42 43½ 25 42¼ CstnnJL 2 ⒻAw40000 85-11 CollectiveJoy,Seside,HthrAndRos 7
11Sep89—Bumped hard late

25Aug89-5Dmr 1 Ⓣ:4731:12 1:371fm 2¼ 117 21½ 53¾ 69 814 Pincay LJr 6 Ⓕ 80000 71-14 CllctvJy,SplnddTrsr,RchCrm'sBst 8
25Aug89—Rank 1st turn
Speed Index: Last Race: -1.0 3-Race Avg.: -4.6 4-Race Avg.: -7.2 Overall Avg.: -4.8
Sep 5 Dmr 4f ft :494 H Aug 18 Dmr 4f ft :49 H ●Aug 5 Dmr 3f ft :343 H Jly 29 Dmr 5f ft :592 Hg

Motel Swing

PATTON D B **114**
Own.—Dizney D R
B. f. 4, by Bates Motel—Garden Swing, by Stage Door Johnny
Br.—Dizney Donald R (Fla)
Tr.—Zucker Howard L
Lifetime 38 5 6 7 $96,906
1990 13 1 1 3 $25,045
1989 16 2 3 2 $51,230
Turf 13 1 2 2 $39,535

25Jly90-8Crc 6½f :222 :452 1:183ft 12 L 116 54½ 51¼ 23 35½ Elliott S 4 Ⓕ 50000 86-17 SerchforTmmy,Srbelli,MotlSwing 8
5Jly90-9Crc 6f :221 :46 1:113sy 12 1155 22 46½ 37½ 510¾ VallesES 7 ⒻAw17200 81-08 OhMJsscP,SrchfrTmm,Mjst'sMss 7
21Jun90-9Crc 6½f :221 :453 1:19 ft 5¾ 1137 42½ 43½ 44½ 53½ VallesES 6 ⒻAw17000 86-16 SrchfrTmm,SChrmng,EllsOncAgn 7
1Jun90-9Crc 6½f :221 :453 1:19 ft 10 1077 21½ 21½ 1½ 1½ VallesES 2 ⒻAw16000 90-16 MotlSwng,Mjsty'sMssy,SChrmng 6
9May90-7Crc 6f :22 :454 1:131ft 7¾ 1085 [illegible] VallesES 5 ⒻAw17500 75-17 [illegible],SChrmng,SrchfrTmmy 5
27Apr90-7GP 6f :223 :462 1:123ft 4¾ 1107 61¾ 53¼ 32½ 22½ Valles E S 2 Ⓕ 50000 79-25 SrchforTmmy,MotlSwng,MdmJoy 8
13Apr90-3GP 6f :222 :461 1:12 ft 6½ 117 45½ 46½ 45½ 45¼ Fires E 1 Ⓕ 60000 80-23 AviJn,SunnyStunnr,SrchforTmmy 6
25Mar90-9GP a1 Ⓣ 1:38 hd 46 119 42½ 611 716 719 VlienteD 9 ⒻAw20000 70-15 LttlBrnn,BngkkLdy,HstfAnglsII 10
27Feb90-10GP a1 Ⓣ 1:401fm 11 117 95¾ 65 66¼ 44 CrugutJ 2 ⒻAw20000 74-21 VnTrns,SmmrScrtry,ChorsAtDwn 9
17Feb90-6GP 1 Ⓣ:48 1:12 1:352fm 2½ 119 52 21 34½ 37½ CrugutJ 6 ⒻAw24000 89-03 LghndBMrry,Contmlos,MtlSwng 11
Speed Index: Last Race: -15.0 3-Race Avg.: -9.3 3-Race Avg.: -9.3 Overall Avg.: -2.5
Sep 4 Dmr 5f ft :59 H Aug 27 Dmr 4f ft :473 H

Majestic Sound

MEZA R Q **117**
Own.—Power M S
B. f. 4, by Majestic Light—Decision, by Resound
Br.—Post Time Inc (Ky)
Tr.—Haynes Jack B
Lifetime 26 3 4 0 $70,350
1990 13 2 2 0 $54,850
1989 11 1 2 0 $15,500
Turf 18 2 3 0 $65,850

30Aug90-3Dmr 1 1/16 Ⓣ:47 1:12 1:434fm 7¼ LB116 21½ 21½ 68½ 618¾ DsormuxKJ6 Ⓕ 75000 69-12 Softscpe,Dncingintheprk,Quyfeor 6
30Aug90—Wide down chute
15Aug90-5Dmr 1 1/16 Ⓣ:4831:1231:431fm 4 LB118 21½ 1hd 2½ 55 Meza R Q3 Ⓕ 55000 86-09 BoldCosta,FrauleinMri,Softscpe 10
19Jly90-9Hol 1 1/16 Ⓣ:4641:1031:413fm 4 L 115 11½ 11 11½ 12¾ Meza R Q9 Ⓕ 45000 87-16 MjsticSound,FrulinMri,RdThCrds 9
28Jun90-5Hol 1 1/16 Ⓣ:47 1:11 1:41 fm 6½ 116 12½ 11½ 11½ 21¼ Meza R Q5 Ⓕ 55000 89-08 Sonilla,MjesticSound,CsPetrone 10
7Jun90-8Hol 1 1/16 Ⓣ:4631:1041:413fm 10 116 11½ 11½ 11½ 11¼ Meza RQ6 ⒻAw35000 87-13 MjsticSound,C'sSong,T.V.Listing 9
25May90-8Hol 1 Ⓣ:4621:1031:352fm 7¾ 116 22½ 2hd 2hd 53½ Meza RQ9 ⒻAw35000 83-11 Camisverde,Cee'sSong,CshInNow 9
12May90-9Hol 1⅛ Ⓣ:4731:1121:481fm 12 116 11½ 11 2hd 22½ Meza RQ1 ⒻAw32000 84-10 TafftShwl,MjesticSound,StrPster 7
28Apr90-9Hol 1 1/16 Ⓣ:47 1:1111:42 fm 58 1085 2hd 2½ 42½ 87¾ DvnportCL2 Ⓕ 70000 77-15 Nimes, Belle Poitrine, Seaside 12
12Apr90-5SA a6½f Ⓣ:211 :4341:133fm 105 118 64½ 64¼ 64¼ 63¼ Solis A2 ⒻAw34000 90-07 PlumePoppy,RadintStr,TfftShwl 12
22Mar90-5SA 1⅛ Ⓣ:4541:1041:483fm 44 1115 2½ 32 511 417 DnprtCL8 ⒻAw37000 65-18 ButifulMlody,CllOfGold,MyGidgt 8
Speed Index: Last Race: (—) 3-Race Avg.: (—) 12-Race Avg.: (—) Overall Avg.: -6.4
Aug 27 Dmr 4f ft :47 H Aug 6 Dmr 6f ft 1:132 H

*Grandiflora

CASTILLO P R **115**
Own.—Lowery & Payne
B. f. 4, by Gorytus—Summer Bloom, by Silly Season
Br.—Samar Ltd & Potomac Ltd (Ire)
Tr.—Sanders W Allen
Lifetime 13 3 2 1 $38,352
1990 3 0 2 0 $11,800
1989 3 1 0 0 $18,761
Turf 11 3 1 1 $34,952

27Aug90-5Dmr 1 Ⓣ:4731:12 1:364fm 21 B 113 11½ 11½ 2hd 22¾ Castillo PR7 Ⓕ 55000 87-12 BoldCosta,Grandiflora,LaTropicn 8
1Aug90-10LA 6½f :214 :45 1:153ft 7½ 116 21 2½ 22 26 Bazan J2 Ⓕ 20000 89-03 MuchoDnrd,Grndflor,ChoxMmson 6
18Apr90-7SA 6f :213 :444 1:104ft 43 116 89 810 815 818½ Sibille R2 Ⓕ 40000 63-17 LnrBty,TmlyWllw,PppngChmpgn 8
1Jly89-9CD 1 1/16 Ⓣ:4821:14 1:461yl 14 122 51¾ 52¼ 87¼ 913 McDwllM 9 ⒻRegret 72-15 JstcWHCm,LthrsLnch,MtnnLmn 10
29May89-10RD 1 Ⓣ:4621:11 1:364fm*2-3 124 45 33 27 48½ McDllM8 ⒻS Bonnet 82-09 Demonry,TiaJuanita,LunrPrincess 8
18May89-8CD 1 Ⓣ:4631:13 1:381fm 6 116 34 31½ 3nk 11 Day P2 ⒻAw33720 98-02 Grndiflor,MotlSwing,LunrPrincss 9
7Oct88◆4Ascot(Eng) 7f 1:353gd 12 122 Ⓣ 13 CrsonW TnkrvlleNrsryH FlyByKnife,LaristonGale,Hwwm 15
22Sep88◆6Ascot(Eng) 6f 1:162gd 12 123 Ⓣ 1114 Reid J Gldn Gtes Nrsy H Musinc,KnghtofMrcy,BMyRunnr 14
10Sep88◆1Goodwood(Eng) 7f 1:292fm 8 135 Ⓣ 64¼ RousB RpdRclnNrsryH Nightstlkr,LdySpdStck,Gzttlong 11
25Aug88◆6Salisbury(Eng) 7f 1:30 gd 10 126 Ⓣ 12½ Reid J HrstbrnNrsryH Grandiflora,Hawwam,ErlyBreeze 10
Speed Index: Last Race: (—) 3-Race Avg.: (—) 12-Race Avg.: (—) Overall Avg.: -8.5
Sep 6 Fpx 5f ft :594 H Aug 23 Fpx 7f ft 1:254 H ●Aug 16 Fpx 4f ft :47 H Aug 10 Fpx 1 ft 1:391 H

Runaway Blues *

GARCIA J A **113**
Own.—Friendly Natalie B
Gr. m. 5, by Runaway Groom—Trumpet Blues, by Personality
Br.—Madden Mrs Linda L (Cal)
Tr.—Fallon Jacque
Lifetime 32 3 11 5 $120,000
1990 8 0 3 2 $34,750
1989 9 1 1 1 $27,775
Turf 4 0 1 0 $13,025

20Aug90-7Dmr 6½f :22 :45 1:161ft 2½ LB116 68¾ 66 54½ 33¾ DelhoussyE 3 Ⓕ 40000 83-09 SelctASong,FrostyFrz,RunwyBlus 6
20Aug90—4 Wide stretch
14Jly90-3Hol 6½f :222 :45 1:162ft 3 L 117 66½ 67½ 55½ 44¼ DelhoussyE 1 Ⓕ 50000 89-09 Frosty Freeze, Rack, Valid Allure 7
27Jun90-7Hol 6½f :222 :444 1:152ft *2½ 116 55 44 42½ 22½ DelhoussyE 6 Ⓕ 57500 95-05 Jo'sJoy,RunwyBlues,FrostyFreez 6
27Jun90—Wide early
31May90-7Hol 1 :461 1:11 1:364ft 4¼ 116 52½ 63½ 52½ 22 DelhoussyE 1 Ⓕ 40000 78-20 SssySlew,RunwyBlus,MoonlitDsrt 7
31May90—Off slowly
10May90-7Hol 6½f :223 :453 1:153ft 2¾ 117 42 2hd 2½ 21¾ DelhoussyE 1 Ⓕ 40000 95-08 FeelingTipsy,RunwyBlues,Lcrosse 7
10Mar90-5SA a6½f Ⓣ:211 :4341:134fm 11 116 1112 117¾ 85¾ 44¼ DelhoussyE 7 Ⓕ 80000 88-08 Dot'sL'Nturl,CoxClssic,ImprilStr 12
10Mar90—Wide into stretch
25Feb90-4SA 6½f :213 :45 1:171ft *9-5e 116 915 912 55½ 34¼ DelhoussyE 8 Ⓕ 62500 80-17 Kryos,FrostyFreeze,RunawyBlues 9
25Feb90—Very wide late

11Jan90-7SA 6¼f :22 :444 1:16²ft 3½ 117 78½ 610 49½ 45½ StvnsGL 2⊕Aw38000 82-16 InvrnssLdy,HckoryCrst,CrneyCrt 1
  11Jan90—Wide into stretch
29Dec89-7SA 6f :21³ :442 1:00⁴ft 15 117 812 86½ 67 36½ StvnsGL 8⊕Aw38000 80-13 HiddenGrden,Unpintd,RunwyBlus 8
15Nov89-7Hol 6f :22² :451 1:10²ft 12 116 811 77½ 54 1ⁿᵒ Stevens GL 8⊕ 40000 83-10 RunwyBlues,Toulng,ShowtimLdy 8
  15Nov89—Wide throughout
  Speed Index: Last Race: –2.0   1–Race Avg.: –2.0   1–Race Avg.: –2.0   Overall Avg.: –1.8
Sep 3 Dmr ⑦ 6f fm :49⁴ H (d) Aug 13 Dmr 5f ft 1:01³ H Jly 30 Dmr 5f ft 1:00 H

With a 10-point advantage on the figures (five lengths) and no reservations about relative class, Fraulein Maria has a fifty-fifty chance to win here, which translates to even money as a fair-value bet. With concessions to racing's error factor, I will accept 8–5, but not less, in these situations.

I wagered a prime amount on Fraulein Maria, and under Eddie Delahoussaye, she won for fun.

I also bought a $20 exacta ticket with Panic Stricken on the underside. The second-high figure, that filly regularly had finished second, and lit the board at 19–1. When Jockey P. Mercado did not catch Grandiflora from mid-stretch to the wire, Panic Stricken missed second by a short head, costing me roughly fifteen hundred.

Another case of mixed emotions, conflicted reactions. So, what's new at the races, anyhow?

Del Mar / Turf Figures

1	Racing Rascal	Won	10–1	22.00	
2	Mehmetori	Won	3.7–1	9.40	
3	Kept His Cool	Out	3.1–1	(2.00)	
4	Short Timer	2nd	4.9–1	(2.00)	
5	Olanoya	Won	8.3–1	18.60	No Play
6	Softscape	Won	4.7–1	11.40	
7	Royal Touch	Out	2.2–1	(2.00)	No Play
8	Dream of Fame	3rd	4.1–1	(2.00)	
9	Aksar	2nd	1.5–1	(2.00)	No Play
10	Cowell	Out	1.4–1	(2.00)	No Play
11	Rosie Potts	3rd	2.7–1	(2.00)	
12	Sonilla	Won	8–1	18.00	
13	Maison Maestro	2nd	4–1	(2.00)	
14	Novelty	Won	2.5–1	7.00	
15	Rogue's Realm	3rd	3.5–1	(2.00)	
16	Treig	Won	9.5–1	21.00	
17	Itsallgreektome	2nd	1.8–1	(2.00)	No Play
18	Girl of France	Out	3.5–1	(2.00)	

7/18/39% Win	1	740	3.7
36/107.40/300% ROI	2	940	4.7
	3	1600	8.0
	4	1900	9.5
	5	(200)	4/25.9
	T	$4980	Ave. 6.325

Turf Figure Charts

28 Racetracks

Aqueduct

	Pace	1M	1 1/16M	1 1/8 M	Adj's
Classified Alw Pars	112^3	137^4	144^2	151	6^3 - 7^3
Par Zone/Late Speed Pars	112^3 - 113^3	25^1	31^4	38^2	6^3 - 6^3

Unusually Slow Pace	113^4 and Slower
Faster Than Par Pace	112^2 and Faster

1/4 M		5/16 M		3/8 M		1/8
3	121	4	120	36	129	
4	119	30	118	1	126	
23	118	1	116	2	124	
1	116	2	114	3	122	
2	114	3	112	4	119	
3	113	4	110	37	117	
4	111	31	108	1	114	
24	110	1	106	2	112	
1	108	2	104	3	110	
2	106	3	102	4	107	
3	105	4	100	38	105	
4	103			1	102	
25	102	32	98	2	100	
1	100	1	96			
		2	94	3	98	
2	98	3	92	4	95	
3	97	4	90	39	93	
4	95	33	88	1	90	
26	94	1	86	2	88	
1	92	2	84	3	86	
2	90	3	82	4	83	
3	89	4	80	40	81	
4	87	34	78	1	78	
27	86	1	76	2	76	
1	84	2	74	3	74	
2	82	3	72	4	71	
3	81	4	70	41	69	
4	79	35	68	1	66	
28	78	1	66	2	64	

Arlington Park (Main)

Classified Alw Pars	113[1]	137	143[4]	150[3]
Par Zone/Late Speed Pars	113[1] - 114[1]	23[4]	30[3]	37[2]

Unusually Slow Pace	114[2] and Slower	Adj. 6[4]
Faster Than Par Pace	113 and Faster	

1/4 M		5/16 M		3/8 M	
1	122	4	128	2	139
2	120	28	126	3	137
3	118	1	124	4	134
4	116	2	122	35	131
22	114	3	120	1	129
1	113	4	118	2	126
2	111	29	116	3	123
3	110	1	114	4	121
4	108	2	112	36	118
23	106	3	110	1	116
1	105	4	108	2	113
2	103	30	106	3	110
3	102	1	104	4	108
4	100	2	102	37	105
		3	100	1	103
24	98			2	100
1	97	4	98		
2	95	31	96	3	97
3	94	1	94	4	95
4	92	2	92	38	92
25	90	3	90	1	90
		4	88	2	87
		32	86	3	84
		1	84	4	82
				39	79

Atlantic City

		1M	1 1/16M	1 1/8 M
Classified Alw Pars	Pace	112^3	137	143^3	150
	(a) Pace	113^1	139	145^3	152
Par Zone/Late Speed	$111^3 - 112^3$	25^2	32	38^2
	(a) $113^1 - 114^1$	25^4	32^2	38^4

1/4 M		5/16 M		3/8 M		a1/4 M		a5/16 M		a3/8 M	
23	119	3	124	3	134	3	118	4	126	3	138
1	118	4	122	4	131	4	116	30	124	4	136
2	116	30	120	36	129	24	114	1	122	36	134
3	114	1	118	1	126	1	113	2	120	1	131
4	113	2	116	2	124	2	111	3	118	2	129
24	111	3	114	3	122	3	110	4	116	3	126
1	110	4	112	4	119	4	108	31	114	4	124
2	108	31	110	37	117	25	106	1	112	37	122
3	106	1	108	1	114	1	105	2	110	1	117
4	105	2	106	2	112	2	103	3	108	2	117
25	103	3	104	3	110	3	102	4	106	3	114
1	102	4	102	4	107	4	100	32	104	4	112
2	100	32	100	38	105	26	98	1	102	38	110
				1	102	1	97	2	100	1	107
3	98	1	98	2	100	2	95			2	105
4	97	2	96			3	94	3	98	3	102
26	95	3	94	3	98	4	92	4	96	4	100
1	94	4	92	4	95	27	90	33	94		
2	92	33	90	39	93	1	89	1	92	39	98
3	90	1	88	1	90	2	87	2	90	1	95
4	89	2	86	2	88	3	86	3	88	2	93
27	87	3	84	3	86	4	84	4	86	3	90
1	86	4	82	4	83	28	82	34	84	4	88
2	84	34	80	40	81	1	81	1	82	40	86
		1	78	1	78	2	79	2	80	1	83
		2	76	2	76			3	78	2	81
				3	74			4	76	3	78
				4	71			35	74	4	76
				41	69			1	72	41	74
								2	70	1	71
								3	68		

Bay Meadows

	Pace	1M	1 1/16M	1 1/8 M	al 1/8M
Classified Alw Pars	111^2	136^3	143	159^2	147^3
Par Zone/Late Speed Pars	$111^2 - 112^2$	25^1	31^3	38	36^1

Unusually Slow Pace 112^3 and Slower
Faster Than Par Pace 111^1 and Faster

1/4 M		5/16 M		3/8 M		a3/8 M	
3	121	3	120	3	129	34	126
4	119	4	118	4	126	1	124
23	118	30	116	36	124	2	122
1	116	1	114	1	122	3	119
2	114	2	112	2	119	4	117
3	113	3	110	3	117	35	114
4	111	4	108	4	114	1	112
24	110	31	106	37	112	2	110
1	108	1	104	1	110	3	107
2	106	2	102	2	107	4	105
3	105	3	100	3	105	36	102
4	103			4	102	1	100
25	102	4	98	38	100		
1	100	32	96			2	98
		1	94	1	98	3	95
2	98	2	92	2	95	4	93
3	97	3	90	3	93	37	90
4	95	4	88	4	90	1	88
26	94	33	86	39	88	2	86
1	92	1	84	1	86	3	83
2	90	2	82	2	83	4	81
3	89	3	80	3	81	38	78
4	87	4	78	4	78	1	76
27	86	34	76	40	76	2	74
1	84	1	74	1	74	3	71
2	82	2	72	2	71	4	69
3	81	3	70	3	69	39	66
4	79	4	68	4	66		
28	78	35	66				

Belmont Park

	Widener Course			Inner Course	
Clf Alw Pars	110^2	135	141^3	111^2	142^1
Par Zones/Late Speed	$110^2 - 111^2$	24^3	31^1	$111^2 - 112^2$	30^4
Unusually Slow Pace	111^3 and Slower			112^3 and Slower	
Faster Than Par Pace	110^1 and Faster			111^1 and Faster	

1/4 M		5/16 M		5/16 M	
22	120	29	122	29	118
1	118	1	120	1	116
2	116	2	118	2	114
3	114	3	116	3	112
4	113	4	114	4	110
23	111	30	112	30	108
1	110	1	110	1	106
2	108	2	108	2	104
3	106	3	106	3	102
4	105	4	104	4	100
24	103	31	102		
1	102	1	100	31	98
2	100			1	96
		2	98	2	94
3	98	3	96	3	92
4	97	4	94	4	90
255	95	32	92	32	88
1	94	1	90	1	86
2	92	2	88	2	84
3	90	3	86	3	82
4	89	4	84	4	80
26	87	33	82	33	78
1	86	1	80	1	76
2	84				
3	82				

Calder

	Pace	1M	1 1/16M	a1M	al 1/16M	al 1/8M
Classified Alw Pars	110^4	135^1	141^3	137	143^1	146
Par Zone/Late Speed Pars	110^4 - 111^4	25^2	30^4	26^1	32^2	35^1

Unusually Slow Pace   112 and Slower
Faster Than Par Pace   110^3 and Faster

1/4 M		5/16 M		a1/4 M		a5/16 M		a3/8 M	
2	118	4	120	24	119	30	124	4	129
3	116	28	118	1	118	1	122	33	126
4	114	1	116	2	116	2	120	1	124
24	111	2	114	3	114	3	118	2	122
1	110	3	112	4	111	4	116	3	119
2	108	4	110	25	110	31	114	4	117
3	106	30	108	1	108	1	112	34	114
4	105	1	106	2	106	2	110	1	112
25	103	2	104	3	105	3	108	2	110
1	102	3	102	4	103	4	106	3	107
2	100	4	100	26	102	32	104	4	105
				1	100	1	102	35	102
3	98	31	98			2	100	1	100
4	97	1	96	2	98				
26	95	2	94	3	97	3	98	2	98
1	94	3	92	4	95	4	96	3	95
2	92	4	90	27	94	33	94	4	93
3	90	32	88	1	92	1	92	36	90
4	89	1	86	2	90	2	90	1	88
27	87	2	84	3	89	3	88	2	86
1	86	3	82	4	87	4	86	3	83
2	84	4	80	28	86	34	84	4	81
		33	78	1	84	1	82	37	78
				2	82	2	80	1	76
						3	78		

Canterbury Downs

Classified Alw Pars	111^3	135^4	140	142^2
Par Zone/Late Speed	111^3 - 112^3	24^1	28^2	30^4

Unusually Slow	112^4 and Slower
Faster Than Par	111^2 and Faster

1/4 M		1-70 M		1 1/16 M	
1	116	1	120	4	120
2	114	2	118	29	118
3	113	3	116	1	116
4	111	4	114	2	114
23	110	27	113	3	112
1	108	1	111	4	110
2	106	2	109	30	108
3	105	3	107	1	106
4	103	4	105	2	104
24	102	28	104	3	102
1	100	1	102	4	100
		2	100		
2	98			31	98
3	97	3	98	1	96
4	95	4	96	2	94
25	94	29	95	3	92
1	92	1	93	4	90
2	90	2	91	32	88
3	89	3	89	1	86
4	87	4	87	2	84
26	86	30	86	3	82
		1	84	4	80
		2	82	33	78

Churchill Downs

Classified Alw Pars	112^4	138^4	145^2	151
Par Zone/Late Speed Pars	112^4-113^4	26	32^3	38^1

Unusually Slow   114 and Slower
Faster Than Par 112^3 and Faster

1/4 M		5/16 M		3/8 M	
24	116	2	122	4	129
1	114	3	120	36	126
2	113	4	118	1	124
3	111	31	116	2	122
4	110	1	114	3	119
25	108	2	112	4	117
1	106	3	110	37	114
2	105	4	108	1	112
3	103	32	106	2	110
4	102	1	104	3	107
26	100	2	102	4	105
		3	100	38	102
1	98			1	100
2	97	4	98		
3	95	33	96	2	98
4	94	1	94	3	95
27	92	2	92	4	93
1	90	3	90	39	90
2	89	4	88	1	88
3	87	34	86	2	86
4	86	1	84	3	83
28	84	2	82	4	81
				40	78

Del Mar

Classified Alw Pars	111^4	136^1	142^4	149^2
Par Zone/Late Speed Pars	$111^4 - 112^4$	24^2	31	37^3

Unusually Slow Pace   113 and Slower   <u>Adj</u>. $6^3 - 6^3$
Faster Than Par Pace 111^3 and Faster

1/4 M		5/16 M		3/8 M	
1	118	3	124	2	126
2	116	4	122	3	124
3	114	29	120	4	122
4	113	1	118	36	119
23	111	2	116	1	117
1	110	3	114	2	114
2	108	4	112	3	112
3	106	30	110	4	110
4	105	1	108	37	107
24	103	2	106	1	105
1	102	3	104	2	102
2	100	4	102	3	100
		31	100		
3	98			4	98
4	97	1	98	38	95
25	95	2	96	1	93
1	94	3	94	2	90
2	92	4	92	3	88
3	90	32	90	4	86
4	89	1	88	39	83
26	87	2	86	1	81
1	86	3	84	2	78
2	84	4	82	3	76
3	82	33	80	4	74

Unusually Slow Pace (race):	Add 100 to basic figure and divide by 2.
Faster Than Par Pace (race):	For each 1/5-second frontrunners and pressers have exceeded par at the pace call, add 2 points to their basic figures. Does not apply to off-pace types and closers.

Delaware Park

Classified Alw Pars	111^4	136^1	143	149^4
Par Zone/Late Speed Pars	111^4 - 112^4	24^2	31^1	38

Unusually Slow Pace   113 and Slower   <u>Adj.</u> 6^4 - 6^4
Faster Than Par Pace   111^3 and Faster

1/4 M		5/16 M		3/8 M	
2	116	29	122	3	129
3	114	1	120	4	126
4	113	2	118	36	124
23	111	3	116	1	122
1	110	4	114	2	119
2	108	30	112	3	117
3	106	1	110	4	114
4	105	2	108	37	112
24	103	3	106	1	110
1	102	4	104	2	107
2	100	31	102	3	105
		1	100	4	102
3	98			38	100
4	97	2	98		
25	95	3	96	1	98
1	94	4	94	2	95
2	92	32	92	3	93
3	90	1	90	4	90
4	89	2	88	39	88
26	87	3	86	1	86
1	86	4	84	2	83
		33	82	3	81
				4	78
				40	76

Note- At Delaware Park, the "About" (a) distances on grass are
normally run 2/5 slower than the regular distances. Late-
speed figures will be the same as above, but these changes
are recommended:

Par Zone   112^1 - 113^1
Unusually Slow Pace 113^2 and Slower
Faster Than Par Pace 112 and Faster

Fairgrounds

	Pace	al M	al-70 M	al 1/16 M	al 1/8 M	Adj's
Classified Alw Pars	114^3	133^1	139^3	146^2	153^1	
Par Zone/Late Speed Pars	114^3 - 115^3	18^3	25	31^4	38^3	6^4 - 6^4

Unusually Slow Pace	115^4 and Slower
Faster Than Par Pace	114^2 and Faster

a3/16 M		a1/4 M		a5/16 M		a3/8 M	
4	112	23	116	29	128	2	139
17	111	1	114	1	126	3	137
1	109	2	113	2	124	4	134
2	108	3	111	3	122	36	132
3	107	4	110	4	120	1	129
4	105	24	108	30	118	2	126
18	104	1	106	1	116	3	124
1	102	2	105	2	114	4	122
2	101	3	103	3	112	37	119
3	100	4	102	4	110	1	117
		25	100	31	108	2	114
				1	106	3	112
4	99			2	104	4	110
19	98	1	98	3	102	38	107
1	96	2	97	4	100	1	105
2	95	3	95			2	102
3	93	4	94			3	100
4	92	26	92	32	98		
20	91	1	90	1	96		
1	89	2	89	2	94	4	98
2	88	3	87	3	92	39	95
3	86	4	86	4	90	1	93
4	85	27	84	33	88	2	90
21	84	1	82	1	86	3	88
1	82	2	81	2	84	4	86
		3	79	3	82	40	83
		4	78	4	80	1	81
		28	76	34	78	2	78
						3	76
						4	74
						41	71

Garden State

Classified Alw Pars	111^3	136	140^1		142^3	149^1	Adj's
Par Zone/Late Speed Pars	111^3- 112^3	24^2	28^3 (1-70M)		31	37^3	4^1 - 2^2 - 6^3 - 6^3

Unusually Slow	112^4 and Slower
Faster Than Par	111^2 and Faster
Adjustment	6^3
1M to 1-70M	4^1
1-70M to 1 1/16M	2^2

1/4 M		5/16 M		1-70 M		3/8 M	
2	116	29	120	3	118	3	124
3	114	1	118	4	116	4	122
4	113	2	116	27	114	36	119
23	111	3	114	1	113	1	117
1	110	4	112	2	111	2	114
2	108	30	110	3	109	3	112
3	106	1	108	4	107	4	110
4	105	2	106	28	105	37	107
24	103	3	104	1	104	1	105
1	102	4	102	2	102	2	102
2	100	31	100	3	100	3	100
3	98	1	98	4	98	4	98
4	97	2	96	29	96	38	95
25	95	3	94	1	95	1	93
1	94	4	92	2	93	2	90
2	92	32	90	3	91	3	88
3	90	1	88	4	89	4	86
4	89	2	86	30	87	39	83
26	87	3	84	1	86	1	81
1	86	4	82	2	84	2	78
2	84	33	80	3	82	3	76
3	82	1	78	4	80	4	74
4	81	2	76	31	78	40	71
27	79	3	74	1	77	1	69

Golden Gate

Classified Alw Pars	111^3	137	143^3	__Adj.__ 148^4	__Adj.__
Par Zone/Late Speed Pars	111^3 - 112^3	25^2	32	5^2 37^1	6^3

Unusually Slow Pace 112^4 and Slower
Faster Than Par Pace 111^2 and Faster

1/4 M		5/16 M		3/8 M	
3	122	3	124	35	126
4	121	4	122	1	124
23	119	30	120	2	122
1	118	1	118	3	119
2	116	2	116	4	117
3	114	3	114	36	114
4	113	4	112	1	112
24	111	31	110	2	110
1	110	1	108	3	107
2	108	2	106	4	105
3	106	3	104	37	102
4	105	4	102	1	100
25	103	32	100		
1	102			2	98
2	100	1	98	3	95
		2	96	4	93
3	98	3	94	38	90
4	97	4	92	1	88
26	95	33	90	2	86
1	94	1	88	3	83
2	92	2	86	4	81
3	90	3	84	39	78
4	89	4	82	1	76
27	87	34	80	2	74
1	86	1	78	3	71
2	84	2	76	4	69
3	82				

Gulfstream Park

				al M	al 1/16 M
Classified Alw Pars	110^4	135^1	141^3	136^2	142^4
Par Zone/Late Speed Pars	$110^4 - 111^4$	24^2	30^4	25^3	32
Unusually Slow Pace	112 and Slower		Adj's	6^2	
Faster Than Par Pace	110^3 and Faster		(a) 6^2		

1/4 M		5/16 M		al/4 M		a5/16 M	
3	114	29	118	2	116	30	120
4	113	1	116	3	114	1	118
23	111	2	114	24	114	2	116
1	110	3	112	1	111	3	114
2	108	4	110	2	110	4	112
3	106	30	108	3	108	31	110
4	105	1	106	4	106	1	108
24	103	2	104	25	105	2	106
1	102	3	102	1	103	3	104
2	100	4	100	2	102	4	102
				3	100	32	100
3	98	31	98				
4	97	1	96	4	98	1	98
25	95	2	94	26	97	2	96
1	94	3	92	1	95	3	94
2	92	4	90	2	94	4	92
3	90	32	88	3	92	33	90
4	89	1	86	4	90	1	88
26	87	2	84	27	89	2	86
1	86	3	82	1	87	3	84
2	84	4	80	2	86	4	82
3	82	33	78	3	84	34	80
4	81	1	76	4	82	1	78
27	79	2	74	28	81	2	76
1	78	3	72	1	79	3	74

Hawthorne

	Pace	7 1/2 F	1 M	1 1/16 M	1 1/8 M
Classified Alw Pars	111^3	129^4	136^1	142^3	149^1
Par Zone/Late Speed Pars	111^3 - 112^3	18^1	24^3	31	37^3

Unusually Slow Pace 112^4 and Slower   Adj's 6^2 - 6^2 - 6^3
Faster Than Par Pace 111^2 and Faster

3/16 M		1/4 M		5/16 M		3/8 M	
4	108	2	118	29	120	1	129
17	107	3	116	1	118	2	126
1	106	4	114	2	116	3	124
2	105	23	113	3	114	4	122
3	104	1	111	4	112	36	119
4	102	2	110	30	110	1	117
18	101	3	108	1	108	2	114
1	100	4	106	2	106	3	112
		24	105	3	104	4	110
2	99	1	103	4	102	37	107
3	98	2	102	31	100	1	105
4	96	3	100			2	102
19	95			1	98	3	100
1	94	4	98	2	96		
2	93	25	97	3	94	4	98
3	92	1	95	4	92	38	95
4	90	2	94	32	90	1	93
		3	92	1	88	2	90
		4	90	2	86	3	88
		26	89	3	84	4	86
		1	87	4	82	39	83
		2	86	33	80	1	81
		3	84			2	78
						3	76
						4	74

Hollywood Park

	$\underline{1\,M}$		$\underline{1\,1/16\,M}$		$\underline{1\,1/8\,M}$			
Classified Alw Pars	110^1	135^2	110^2	141^2	111	148^1		
Par Zone/Late Speed Pars	$110^1 - 111^1$	25^1	$110^2 - 111^2$	31	$111 - 112$	37^1		
Unusually Slow Pace	111^2 and Slower		113^3 and Slower		112^1 and Slower		Adj's	6 - 6
Faster Than Par Pace	110 and Faster		110^1 and Faster		110^4 and Faster			

$\underline{1/4\,M}$		$\underline{5/16\,M}$		$\underline{3/8\,M}$	
3	121	29	120	35	126
4	119	1	118	1	124
23	118	2	116	2	122
1	116	3	114	3	119
2	114	4	112	4	117
3	113	30	110	36	114
4	111	1	108	1	112
24	110	2	106	2	110
1	108	3	104	3	107
2	106	4	102	4	105
3	105	31	100	37	102
4	103			1	100
25	102	1	98		
1	100	2	96	2	98
		3	94	3	95
2	98	4	92	4	93
3	97	32	90	38	90
4	95	1	88	1	88
26	94	2	86	2	86
1	92	3	84	3	83
2	90	4	82	4	81
3	89	33	80	39	78
4	87	1	78	1	76
27	86	2	76	2	74
1	84	3	74	3	71
2	82	4	72	4	69
3	81	34	70		
4	79				
28	78				

Unusually Slow Pace (race):   Add 100 (Par) to Late Speed Figure and divide by 2.

Faster Than Par Pace (race):   For each 1/5-second frontrunners and pace pressers have exceeded par at the pace call, add 2 points to their late-speed figures. Does not apply to off-pace horses and closers.

Keeneland

| Classified Alw Pars | 112^3 | | 144^1 | 149^4 |
| Par Zone/Late Speed Pars | 112^3 - 113^3 | | 31^3 | 37^1 |

| Unusually Slow Pace | 113^4 and Slower | Adj's 5^3 |
| Faster Than Par Pace | 112^2 and Faster | |

5/16 M			3/8 M	
3	120		35	126
4	118		1	124
30	116		2	122
1	114		3	119
2	112		4	117
3	110		36	114
4	108		1	112
31	106		2	110
1	104		3	107
2	102		4	105
3	100		37	102
			1	100
4	98			
32	96		2	98
1	94		3	95
2	92		4	93
3	90		38	90
4	88		1	88
33	86		2	86
1	84		3	83
2	82		4	81
			39	78

Laurel

Classified Alw Pars	111^4	136^3	143 149^3
Par Zone/Late Speed Pars	111^4 - 112^4	24^4	31^1 37^4

Unusually Slow Pace   113 and Slower   <u>Adj.</u> 6^4 - 6^4
Faster Than Par Pace 111^3 and Faster

<u>1/4 M</u>		<u>5/16 M</u>		<u>3/8 M</u>	
3	118	1	120	3	125
4	116	2	118	4	123
23	114	3	116	36	122
1	113	4	114	1	119
2	111	30	112	2	117
3	110	1	110	3	114
4	108	2	108	4	112
24	106	3	106	37	110
1	105	4	104	1	107
2	103	31	102	2	105
3	102	1	100	3	102
4	100			4	100
		2	98		
25	98	3	96	38	98
1	97	4	94	1	95
2	95	32	92	2	93
3	94	1	90	3	90
4	92	2	88	4	88
26	90	3	86	39	86
1	89	4	84	1	83
2	87	33	82	2	81
3	86	1	80	3	78
4	84	2	78	4	76
27	82	3	76	40	74
1	81	4	74	1	71

Louisiana Downs

	Pace	1M	1 1/16M	a1 M	a1 1/16 M
Classified Alw Pars	111^1	136	142^2	135^4	141^2
Par Zone/Late Speed Pars	111^1 - 112^1	24^4	31^1	24^3	30^1

Unusually Slow Pace	112^2 and Slower
Faster Than Par Pace	111 and Faster

1/4 M		5/16 M		a1/4 M		a5/16 M	
23	114	3	116	4	114	1	114
1	113	4	114	23	113	29	112
2	111	31	112	1	111	1	110
3	110	1	110	2	110	2	108
4	108	2	108	3	108	3	106
24	106	3	106	4	106	4	104
1	105	4	104	24	105	30	102
2	103	31	102	1	103	1	100
3	102	1	100	2	102		
4	100			3	100	2	98
		2	98			3	96
25	98	3	96	4	98	4	94
1	97	4	94	25	97	31	92
2	95	32	92	1	95	1	90
3	94	1	90	2	94	2	88
4	92	2	88	3	92	3	86
26	90	3	86	4	90	4	84
1	89	4	84	26	89	32	82
2	87	33	82	1	87	1	80
3	86	1	80	2	86	2	78
4	84	2	78	3	84	3	76
27	82	3	76	4	82	4	74
				27	81	33	72
				1	79	1	70
						2	68

The Meadowlands

	Main Course			Inner Course		
	Pace	1M	1 1/16M	Pace	1 M	1 1/16 M
Clf Alw Pars	110^3	134^1	140^4	110^4	134^4	141^2
Par Zone/Late Speed	$110^3 - 111^3$	23^3	30^1	$110^4 - 111^4$	24	30^3

Unusually Slow Pace	111^4 and Slower	112 and Slower
Faster Than Par Pace	110^2 and Faster	110^3 and Faster

1/4 M		5/16 M		1/4 M		5/16 M	
4	114	28	122	22	116	3	120
22	113	1	120	1	114	4	118
1	111	2	118	2	113	29	116
2	110	3	116	3	111	1	114
3	108	4	114	4	110	2	112
4	106	29	112	23	108	3	110
23	105	1	110	1	106	4	108
1	103	2	108	2	105	30	106
2	102	3	106	3	103	1	104
3	100	4	104	4	102	2	102
		30	102	24	100	3	100
4	98	1	100				
24	97			1	98	4	98
1	95	2	98	2	97	31	96
2	94	3	96	3	95	1	94
3	92	4	94	4	94	2	92
4	90	31	92	25	92	3	90
25	89	1	90	1	90	4	88
1	87	2	88	2	89	32	86
2	86	3	86	3	87	1	84
		4	84	4	86	2	82
		32	82	26	84		

Note- Convert 1-70M final times to 1 1/16M by adding 2^2 seconds. Applies to both courses

Monmouth Park

	Pace	1M	1 1/16M	1 1/8 M	cl 1/16 M	cl 1/8 M
Classified Alw Pars	111^3	136^2	142^4	149^1	142^1	148^3
Par Zone/Late Speed Pars	111^3 - 112^3	24^4	31^1	37^3	30^3	37

Unusually Slow Pace   112^4 and Slower   Adj's   6^2 - 6^2 - 6^2

Faster Than Par Pace   111^2 and Faster

1/4 M		5/16 M		3/8 M		c5/16 M		c3/8 M	
3	119	29	122	1	129	1	121	3	129
4	118	1	120	2	126	2	119	4	126
23	116	2	118	3	124	3	118	35	124
1	114	3	116	4	122	4	116	1	122
2	113	4	114	36	119	29	114	2	119
3	110	30	112	1	117	1	113	3	117
4	108	1	110	2	114	2	110	4	114
24	106	2	108	3	112	3	108	36	112
1	105	3	106	4	110	4	106	1	110
2	103	4	104	37	107	30	105	2	107
3	102	31	102	1	105	1	103	3	105
4	100	1	100	2	102	2	102	4	102
				3	100	3	100	37	100
25	98	2	98						
1	97	3	96	4	98	4	98	1	98
2	95	4	94	38	95	31	97	2	95
3	94	32	92	1	93	1	95	3	93
4	92	1	90	2	90	2	94	4	90
26	90	2	88	3	88	3	92	38	88
1	89	3	86	4	86	4	90	1	86
2	87	4	84	39	83	32	89	2	83
3	86	33	82	1	81	1	87	3	81
4	84	1	80	2	78	2	86	4	78
								39	76

Note- Chute or Straitaway, Monmouth Turf has same Pace Pars.

Philadelphia Park

	Pace	1M	1 1/16M	1 1/8 M
Classified Alw Pars	111^3	136^1	142^4	149^2
Par Zone/Late Speed Pars	111^3 - 112^3	24^3	31^1	37^4

Unusually Slow Pace 112^4 and Slower   Adj's 6^3 - 6^3

Faster Than Par Pace 111^2 and Faster

1/4 M		5/16 M		3/8 M	
2	118	4	124	35	134
3	116	29	122	1	132
4	114	1	120	2	129
23	113	2	118	3	126
1	111	3	116	4	124
2	110	4	114	36	122
3	108	30	112	1	119
4	106	1	110	2	117
24	105	2	108	3	114
1	103	3	106	4	112
2	102	4	104	37	110
3	100	31	102	1	107
		1	100	2	105
				3	102
4	98			4	100
25	97	2	98		
1	95	3	96		
2	94	4	94	38	98
3	92	32	92	1	95
4	90	1	90	2	93
26	89	2	88	3	90
1	87	3	86	4	88
2	86	4	84	39	86
3	84	33	82	1	83
				2	81
				3	78

Note- Convert 1-70M Final times to 1 1/16M Final times by adding 2^2 seconds.

     (a) +4/5 seconds

Pimlico

Classified Alw Pars	111	135⁴	142²

Classified Alw Pars   111 135^4 142^2

Par Zone/Late Speed   111 - 112 24^4 31^2

Unusually Slow Pace 112^1 and Slower

Faster Than Par Pace 110^4 and Faster

1/4 M		5/16 M	
23	114	2	120
1	113	3	118
2	111	4	116
3	110	30	114
4	108	1	112
24	106	2	110
1	105	3	108
2	103	4	106
3	102	31	104
4	100	1	102
		2	100
25	98		
1	97	3	98
2	95	4	96
3	94	32	94
4	92	1	92
26	90	2	90
1	89	3	88
2	87	4	86
3	86	33	84
4	84	1	82
27	82	2	80
1	81	3	78
2	79	4	76
3	78	34	74

Rockingham Park

	Pace	1M	1 1/16M	1 1/8 M
Classified Alw Pars	113^1	138^4	145^3	149^3
Par Zone/Late Speed Pars	113^1 - 114^1	25^3	32^2	36^2
Unusually Slow Pace	114^2 and Slower		Adj's 6^4- 4	
Faster Than Par Pace	113 and Faster			

1/4 M		5/16 M		3/8 M	
3	116	1	122	1	126
4	114	2	120	2	124
24	113	3	118	3	122
1	111	4	116	4	119
2	110	31	114	35	117
3	108	1	112	1	114
4	106	3	108	2	112
25	105	4	106	3	110
1	103	32	104	4	107
2	102	1	102	36	105
3	100	2	100	1	102
				2	100
4	98	3	98		
26	97	4	96	3	98
1	95	33	94	4	95
2	94	1	92	37	93
3	92	2	90	1	90
4	90	3	88	2	88
27	89	4	86	3	86
1	87	34	84	4	83
2	86	1	82	38	81
3	84	2	80	1	78
				2	76

Santa Anita

	1 M		1 1/8 M			
Classified Alw Pars	109^3	133^3	109^4	146^4		
Par Zone/Late Speed Pars	$109^3 - 110^3$	24	$109^4 - 110^4$	37		
Unusually Slow Pace	110^4 and Slower		111 and Slower		Adj's	$13^1 - 13$
Faster Than Par Pace	109^2 and Faster		109^3 and Faster			

1/4 M		3/8 M	
22	116	35	124
1	114	1	122
2	113	2	119
3	111	3	117
4	110	4	114
23	108	36	112
1	106	1	110
2	105	2	107
3	103	3	105
4	102	4	102
24	100	37	100
1	98	1	98
2	97	2	95
3	95	3	93
4	94	4	90
25	92	38	88
1	90	1	86
2	89	2	83
3	87	3	81
4	86	4	78
26	84	39	76
1	82	1	74
2	81	2	71
3	79	3	69
4	78	4	66
27	76	40	64

Unusually Slow Pace (race): Add 100 (Par) to Late Speed Figure and divide by 2.

Faster Than Par Pace (race): For each 1/5-second frontrunners and pace-pressers have exceeded par at the pace call, add 2 points to their late-speed figures. Does not apply to off-pace horses and closers.

Saratoga

	Main Course				Inner Course			
	Pace	1 1/16 M	1 1/8 M		Pace	1 M	1 1/16 M	1 1/8 M
Clf Alw Pars	111	141	147^3		111^2	135^2	142	148^3
Par Zone/Late Speed	111 - 112	30	36^3		111^2 - 112^2	24	30^3	37^1
Unusually Slow Pace	112^1 and Slower				112^3 and Slower			
Faster Than Par Pace	110^4 and Faster	Adj. 6^3			111^1 and Faster	Adj. 6^3 - 6^3		

5/16 M		3/8 M		1/4 M		5/16 M		3/8 M	
2	116	2	126	22	116	3	120	35	126
3	114	3	124	1	114	4	118	1	124
4	112	4	122	2	113	29	116	2	122
29	110	35	119	3	111	1	114	3	119
1	108	1	117	4	110	2	112	4	117
2	106	2	114	23	108	3	110	36	114
3	104	3	112	1	106	4	108	1	112
4	102	4	110	2	105	30	106	2	110
30	100	36	107	3	103	1	104	3	107
		1	105	4	102	2	102	4	105
1	98	2	102	24	100	3	100	37	102
2	97	3	100					1	100
3	95			1	98	4	98		
4	94	4	98	2	97	31	96	2	98
31	92	37	95	3	95	1	94	3	95
1	90	1	93	4	94	2	92	4	93
2	89	2	90	25	92	3	90	38	90
3	87	3	88	1	90	4	88	1	88
4	86	4	86	2	89	32	86	2	86
32	84	38	83	3	87	1	84	3	83
		1	81	4	86	2	82	4	81
				26	84	3	80	39	78

Turf Paradise

	Pace	7 1/2 F	1 M	1 1/16 M	1 1/8 M
Classified Alw Pars	112^1	130^1	137^1	143^4	150^2
Par Zone/Late Speed Pars	$112^1 - 113^1$	18	25	31^3	38^1

Unusually Slow Pace 113^2 and Slower   Adj's $7 - 6^3 - 6^3$
Faster Than Par Pace   112 and Faster

3/16 M		1/4 M		5/16 M		3/8 M	
17	106	23	116	2	122	4	129
1	105	1	114	3	120	36	126
2	104	2	113	4	118	1	124
3	102	3	111	30	116	2	122
4	101	4	110	1	114	3	119
18	100	24	108	2	112	4	117
		1	106	3	110	37	114
1	99	2	105	4	108	1	112
2	98	3	103	31	106	2	110
3	96	4	102	1	104	3	107
4	95	25	100	2	102	4	105
19	94			3	100	38	102
		1	98			1	100
		2	97	4	98		
		3	95	32	96	2	98
		4	94	1	94	3	95
		26	92	2	92	4	93
		1	90	3	90	39	90
		2	89	4	88	1	88
		3	87	33	86	2	86
		4	86	1	84	3	83
		27	84			4	81
						40	78

Woodbine

	Marshall Course				Inner Course			
	Pace	1 M	1 1/16 M	1 1/8 M	Pace	1 M	1 1/16 M	1 1/8 M
Clf Alw Pars	109⁴	134	141	147⁴	111²	136²	143¹	148²
Par Zone/Late Speed	109⁴ - 110⁴ 24¹	31¹	38		111² - 112²	25	31⁴	37

Unusually Slow Pace	111 and Slower	112³ and Slower	Adj. 7 - 6⁴
Faster Than Par Pace	109³ and Faster	111¹ and Faster	Adj. 6⁴ - 5¹

1/4 M		5/16 M		3/8 M		1/4 M		5/16 M		3/8 M	
3	113	1	118	4	126	4	118	2	124	4	126
4	111	2	116	36	124	23	116	3	122	35	124
23	110	3	114	1	122	1	114	4	120	1	122
1	108	4	112	2	119	2	113	30	118	2	119
2	106	30	110	3	117	3	111	1	116	3	117
3	105	1	108	4	114	4	110	2	114	4	114
4	103	2	106	37	112	24	108	3	112	36	112
24	102	3	106	1	110	1	106	4	110	1	110
1	100	4	104	2	107	2	105	31	108	2	107
		31	102	3	105	3	103	1	106	3	106
		1	100	4	102	4	102	2	104	4	102
2	98			38	100	25	100	3	102	37	100
3	97	2	98	1	98			4	100		
4	95	3	96	2	95	1	98			1	98
25	94	4	94	3	93	2	97	32	98	2	95
1	92	32	92	4	90	3	95	1	96	3	93
2	90	1	90	39	88	4	94	2	94	4	90
3	89	2	88	1	86	26	92	3	92	38	88
4	87	3	86	2	83	1	90	4	90	1	86
26	86	4	84	3	81	2	89	33	88	2	83
		33	82	4	78	3	87	1	86	3	81
				40	76	4	86	2	84	4	78
						27	84